Youth Up in Arms

A Political & Social World Survey 1955-1970

George Paloczi-Horvath

ALSO BY GEORGE PALOCZI-HORVATH

In Darkest Hungary
The Undefeated
Kruschev – The Road to Power
The Writer and the Commissar
Mao Tse-Tung
The Facts Rebel
Youth Takes Over the World
Stalin

YOUTH UP IN ARMS

A political and social world survey
1955–1970

GEORGE PALOCZI-HORVATH

DAVID McKAY COMPANY, INC.

NEW YORK

Sponsored by the Center for the Study of
Democratic Institutions, Santa Barbara, California

First printed in Great Britain, 1971
First American edition, 1971

Library of Congress Catalog Number: 75–154284

Printed in the United States of America

For my wife

GEORGE PALOCZI-HORVATH is Hungarian by birth. After student years in Austria and America, he worked for the liberal daily, *Pesti Naplo,* as European roving correspondent and later as foreign editor. As a leading anti-Nazi he had to escape from Hungary in 1941 and was until the end of the war in British Special Operations, mainly in the Middle East. Demobilized in London, he returned to Hungary in 1947. The Security Police arrested him there in 1949, and he was sentenced to fifteen years at hard labor on rigged-up charges. After five years and a week in jail he was released and rehabilitated. Being blacklisted as a writer, he worked in the Institute of History of the Hungarian Academy of Sciences. He took part in the 1956 Hungarian Revolution and escaped to Britain after its defeat.

Since that time he has published ten books, of which *The Undefeated* and his *Khrushchev* and *Mao* biographies have been published in more than ten countries.

Jacket design by Joseph del Gaudio

CONTENTS

ACKNOWLEDGEMENTS 9

INTRODUCTION 11

I The revolution of revolution 24

II Youth: new class or new species? 36

III Defrauded revolutions 53

IV The 'youth of today' – Western version 77

V Youth and adults in the Soviet orbit before the Hungarian Revolution 100

VI The Hungarian Revolution of 1956 123

VII From teen gangs to students rebels 153

VIII 'Their' students and 'ours' 182

IX Students versus society 205

X From the Berkeley explosion to the Ohnesorg murder 226

XI 'To each according to his imagination': Paris–Prague 1968 265

XII 'A man looketh upon his son as an enemy' 294

XIII The champions of the impossible 324

SOURCE NOTES 341

$6.95

The rebellion of today's youth is a wholly *new* social pressure, a political, economic, and spiritual force that must be understood if civilization is to avoid its own destruction through civil war in the near future.

Financed in part by a California foundation, George Paloczi-Horvath, who took part in the Hungarian Revolution, has traveled thousands of miles interviewing young activists throughout the world. Dissatisfied with the "official" interpretation of student convulsions in Budapest, Berkeley, Paris, and Berlin, the author painstakingly retraces events to present us with a picture that is as disturbing as it is undeniable. He examines the fibers of universality that bind one movement to another, rejecting the concept that regional issues alone are responsible for the destructive forces.

This is a lively and controversial report. It is optimistic and pleads for understanding. In a world where over half the population is under 21, *Youth Up in Arms* is a timely and important record of the emergence of youth in the past decade as the idealistic and critical conscience of our time.

ACKNOWLEDGEMENTS

I am greatly indebted to The Center for the Study of Democratic Institutions in Santa Barbara, California, for sponsoring my work with the help of a most generous grant given by Mr Laurance S. Rockefeller.

When my book was at the half-way stage, the members of the Center discussed it with me for several days, challenging me with their comments, questions and criticism to think anew and try to find new questions where there were no old answers. I am indebted to all of them, especially to Robert M. Hutchins, Harry S. Ashmore, W. H. Ferry, Stringfellow Barr, Elisabeth Mann Borghese, Scott Buchanan, John R. Seeley, Harvey Wheeler and John Wilkinson.

Professor Dennis Gabor, FRS, gave me the first encouragement to undertake this work and used his prestige and world-wide connections to help me in every way. I am particularly grateful to him and to Martha Gellhorn, Anthony Godwin and Richard Dunsmore for reading and rereading the MS and for their constructive criticism. I am also most grateful to Professor J. A. G. Griffith, London School of Economics, Dr Szabolcs de Vajai, UNESCO (Paris), Dr Louis Henry, Inst. Nat. d'Etudes Demographiques (Paris), Adrian Cristobal (Manila), Charlotte Fiedler (Hamburg), Shintaro Ishihara (Tokyo), Michael Rossman (Berkeley), K. Sinha (Calcutta), Simon Vinkenoog (Amsterdam), Dr D. W. von Essen-Zeeman, International School of Philosophy (Ammersfoort) and to Drs Carmen and Gary Yuen-Kong (Hongkong).

Lastly I wish to express my respect and gratitude to a great many young people who gave me courageous help but who do not want to be named.

Photograph by Peter Fisher

GEORGE PALOCZI-HORVATH

INTRODUCTION

1

The war between generations will go on for a long time to come, despite temporary lulls. In this war the front lines cut across countries, families and age-groups. Young and old are found in both camps. The conformism of non-intellectual majorities is clashing with the critical conscience of intellectual minorities. Law and order seem to run amuck from time to time. In hundreds of cities of the world unarmed young people are being attacked by gas-masked police, by planes and tanks. Heavily armed bands of young fanatics turn some city districts into stone jungles for urban guerrillas.

The war is on. The battlefield is the globe. And in wars only the stars are neutral, the chroniclers of war and their readers are certainly not.

Although I was present at many of the upheavals described, in the book itself I have avoided subjectivity. I have not dealt with my personal experiences and on-the-spot impressions. Here, however, I feel duty bound to introduce myself. Readers belonging to this or that warring camp are entitled to form an impression of the degree and the quality of my non-neutrality; of my background and my motivations.

I was born in Hungary within the fortress of the ruling establishment. My family of great landowners were right-wing with strong feudal prejudices, so I became vaguely leftish, almost as a child. My political education was almost entirely a process of seeing for myself. I saw how abominably estate servants were treated, and when I learnt from history what my kind did to the serfs in the past, I began to hate some of the ancestors whose blood lurked in my veins. I did not hate all of them, since the geographical position of their part of Hungary drove some of them into rebellion. At times, that part of the country where my family lived was for years or even centuries under Austrian, Turkish or Russian occupation. Seven of my forefathers were executed as anti-Hapsburg rebels, many of them fought in the revolutionary wars of liberation that flared up every hundred years or so. But by the twentieth century, between the two wars, there were no rebels in the family, save my elder brother and myself. We both opted out of the family in our teens.

I worked my way through university in Austria and in the United States. I studied social anthropology with a vague idea of teaching it in America, instead of which I became a writer and journalist in Budapest. Besides writing novels and books on current affairs, I worked for the liberal daily, *Pesti Naplo*. As a roving foreign correspondent I reported the last prewar years of Western Europe, the occupation of Austria, the tragedy of Munich and Hitler's rape of Czechoslovakia.

In 1941, after *Pesti Naplo* had been banned for good, my choice seemed either to go to prison as an anti-Nazi publicist, or, at best, to serve in the Hungarian army that was to fight on Hitler's side. Instead I chose desertion and escaped to Yugoslavia, arriving in Belgrade the day Hitler's planes did their best to destroy it. Through Yugoslavia and Greece I escaped to Egypt, where I was allowed to join the 'Baker Street Irregulars' (the British Special Operations Executive). I served in several countries in the Middle East and Africa.

Ever since my university days I had read a great deal of Marxist literature. The last pre-war years, the Spanish non-intervention comedy, the Munich era, convinced me that the choice was between fascism or communism, and I was more and more inclined to choose communism. During the war, like so many people in the West, I became strongly pro-Russian. This did not clash then at all with my loyalty to SOE and Britain. Many of the young parachutist-intellectuals in whose ranks I served were just as enthusiastic admirers of the Red Army as I was.

The first book that I wrote in English was published at the end of 1944, in London. In 1945 I was demobbed and stayed on in London while preparing for my return to Hungary, though I did not feel like returning. I had spoken and read English since I was sixteen. By then I wrote and thought in English, having experienced the war mostly in English. The writer in me wanted to stay, my conscience sent me back to Hungary.

My conscience was at peace, and I was entirely happy when, in 1947, I was allowed to join the Hungarian Communist Party. In September 1949, I was suddenly arrested by the authorities of the communist state, in connection with the non-existent Rajk conspiracy. When I realized that the Party had had me arrested, I felt like someone who has been kicked in the stomach by his mother. During the next months, László Rójk, one of the heroes of the Spanish Civil War, and dozens of my friends and acquaintances were executed. I was only sentenced to fifteen years' hard labour for having 'spied for the United Nations'. (I happened to be Secretary General of the Hungarian United Nations Association in 1949.)

Although the Rajk trial and all similar show trials were like murderous Dadaist jokes, although I knew that the Communist Parties in Russia and East Europe tortured and executed tens of thousands of their most loyal adherents, I clung to my communist faith during the fourteen-months-long nightmare of the investigation period, and during much of the astonishingly inhuman prison existence. Many of us were doubly imprisoned. We were captive minds of an ideology that did not care for adherents of our type. My inner liberation was a slow and painful process. I was liberated by the process of seeing for myself.

One saw and learnt a great deal in jail as the purge went on, and our prison-wing was soon populated by former generals of the Spanish Civil War, by high-ranking policemen and even former members of the Political Bureau. My mind was finally liberated, however, with the help of twenty-three workers, with whom I happened to share a communal cell for a while. They were communists, the sons and grandsons of workers. They were all obviously innocent; they became convicts in order to illustrate a footnote to the latest purge-trials. The Party was purging itself from itself. It was intent on securing its existence as pure and simple bureaucratic despotism.

Though our minds were now liberated, we had good reason to feel that we should remain convicts for the rest of our lives. Unlike normal convicts, we political prisoners were completely isolated from the outside world. Our families were told that we had been executed.

Most of my prison-mates were nostalgic for their past. I longed to witness the future. I had been in more than fifty countries in my time, and in jail I yearned to revisit them in a decade or two, when those born then would be young men and women. I imagined all sorts of futures that I, as a camera or a chronicler, would record.

Then, in 1953, Stalin died. Next year Imre Nagy became Prime Minister and during his short-lived 'new course', I was released, together with some ninety thousand other 'spies and saboteurs'. I had spent exactly five years and one week in jail.

We were all declared innocent by the Supreme Court. The former Party members were offered Party rehabilitation. I preferred not to rejoin. For this reason the Party blacklisted me as a writer. I got a research fellowship at the Historical Institute of the Academy of Sciences.

I did not begin to publish until the pre-revolutionary ferment in 1956, when the communist writers rebelled against censorship. I took part in the 1956 revolution, and after its suppression I escaped with my young wife and one-year-old son to Britain. I am a Londoner now, and travel a great deal. I have written nine books and a great many essays and articles in English.

Five years in jail did not embitter me or change me into a professional anti-communist. It turned me against tyranny, mindless dogmatism and irresponsible bureaucracy. I came to believe that fanaticism is the original sin. During the Hungarian Revolution we fought for ordinary human rights; for a multi-party system; for the right to stay neutral; for the right to differ. We fought against the vast complex of lies that governed our lives and led to the murder of tens of thousands of innocent people. We felt that we were 'fighting for the truth'. Some of our critics remarked that our obsession with the concept 'truth' was naïve and unscientific. Nevertheless, we dreamt of a system of common-sense and common decency that had got rid of the Big Lie and all the lesser lies.

During the three days of our phoney victory in 1956 I did not join any of the freshly resurrected political parties. In time, I would probably have joined the democratic socialists, provided they had advocated participatory democracy. Politically, and in every other respect, my mind remains open to alteration, rethinking and revaluation.

My fourteen years in the West have not lessened the importance

I attach to the concept of truth. One of the basic ingredients of the communist syndrome is the Party leaders' insistence on their infallibility and on their right to manipulate the truth. But they are not alone in denying the existence of a single criterion of right and wrong. For the majority of Westerners, and for most of their governments, there is no such thing as 'the truth', according to which a rational being or a rational society knows how to act. I am sorry to see that the word 'truth' is also in disrepute among academics, that science is supposed to be morally neutral, and that there are no institutions devoted to establishing the truth about the history of the recent past.

2

Having been out of circulation for many years, when we settled in London my curiosity drove me to find out what had happened during those years. As a writer, journalist and lecturer I managed to revisit or visit for the first time many countries in four continents, and everywhere I was alarmed by the bias or outright hatred against the young, and the amount of misinformation about youth that a great many people in high positions carried round in their skulls.

I was afraid that something akin to *La Grande Peur* (The Great Fear) during the French Revolution would recur on a global scale. That 'Great Fear' was a ferocious wave of mass hysteria that swept through the French provinces in July–August 1789. It left in its wake destruction and death. At that time there were no means for the quick dissemination of 'the truth'. In the global-village situation of our age, the literate and illiterate alike can be reached instantly by radio and TV, yet 'the truth' is still not known. It is probable that only the universities of the future – as 'establishers of truth' – will be able to protect people from the devastating effects of *Grandes Peurs* and *Grandes Haines* (Great Hatreds) amplified by ignorance and fanaticism, multiplied by instant electronic infection, exploited by mutually hostile camps.

The cold war between the generations was constantly intensified by accidental or deliberate misinformation throughout the sixties. The layman's image of the 'youth of today' became increasingly distorted. This popular image – 'you only have to read the papers to know what youth is like today' – often played a larger role in developing the triggering-off outbursts than the real issues in a real conflict.

Having retained my obsession with truth, I decided early in 1966 to write a true chronicle of a decade in the generation war. I planned to do about two years of research and write the book in the third. At that time I anticipated that by the mid-nineteen-seventies the cold war between the generations would have led to civil wars or even international revolutionary wars between youth and the adult world. I feared then that by 1970 or so, people would stop talking to each other across the generation divide, and discussion and the weapons of logic would be replaced by the logic of weapons.

Few authorities agreed then with this assessment of the future. For instance, at a youth seminar I held at the International School of Philosophy at Amersfoort, in Holland, some of the academics present maintained that my assessment of the present and future was entirely mistaken. With the exception of a few Provo intellectuals, the majority agreed with them. In fact the rate of change proved to be far greater and speedier than even I had expected. Scenes that I imagined might occur in 1975 or later were already happening in 1968–9. I had to change the plan and the scope of this book. My study of youth and revolution during the decade 1955–65 was disrupted and enlarged by youth explosions during the period 1966–70.

I had to test the conceptual techniques and hypotheses that I had tentatively established for the study of youth and revolt in the midst of battles between the generations in Macao, West Berlin, Berkeley, New York, Paris, Tokyo and in many other places.

In the intervals between trips to catch the making of history red-handed, I worked in my London study trying to keep calm amidst a population explosion among my files; amidst the alarming growth of the infant mortality rate of my tentative hypotheses; while ordering purges among the favourite findings of the last few weeks. I enjoyed the anti-academic thaws that led to the speedy rehabilitation of my unjustly purged intuitions, my emotional jumping-to-conclusions, irreverent passions and other ordinary decent folk.

Thanks to the non-conformist intellectuals who were my sponsors in this work, I could afford to go almost anywhere, at a moment's notice, and to hire research associates; that is, to pay some local sociology or anthropology students to help me for a few days or weeks with my local research, interviews or observations. On several occasions my student friends and I participated in mass demonstrations and/or watched youth *v.* police confrontations from various vantage points high above the *mêlée*. I usually reserved for myself the privilege of being down in the crowd, instead of watching them and the police from above, with stopwatch, note-book and camera. This entailed some risk. The police do not scrupulously examine why someone is present in a street battle. And, on occasions, even my conspicuously white hair was not sufficient protection from police batons.

In many cases it required a great deal of subsequent work to find out what had really happened from second to second during an important event, and what had been the underlying and momentary causes of various actions and reactions.

On the night of 2 June 1967, for instance, a West Berlin policeman killed with a single revolver shot a student called Benno Ohnesorg. It took me and two young friends two weeks of full-time work to establish what really happened during the few hours preceding the killing and how and in what circumstances the shot was fired (see Chapter x). Our work was aided by all the relevant cuttings from West German newspapers; by the text of broadcasts and TV discussions; by a number of documentary books and pamphlets on the subject; and lastly by the minutes of the court proceedings against the policeman in question.

The world at large, however, knows only the newspaper reports and TV sequences about this event, published or broadcast the next day. Journalists reporting that night had no reason to doubt the factual statements of the West Berlin Chief of Police, though he was forced to admit days later that he had lied and, as a consequence, resigned.

In theory, the West German reading public had a chance during the twelve months after this event to learn the true facts. But foreign sociologists and psychologists interested in youth remained totally misinformed, unless they made special efforts to find out the true facts. Their information regarding current events derives from quality newspapers, and this material, despite the striving of their editors and correspondents to avoid this, is apt to contain some bias-screened, bias-amplified or even entirely mistaken information.

The quality newspapers cannot be blamed for this situation.

17

Facts accumulate at a much faster rate today than the understanding of them does. The great mass of daily events is so complex, they happen in such swift succession, that it is totally impossible to check the details of news reports in a few hours after the event.

It would, of course, have been impossible to check in as painstaking a manner as in the Ohnesorg case all the hundreds of important youth-events that took place between 1955 and 1970. Instead, my aim has been to examine the most important revolutionary upheavals in which youth has played a principal role. In addition, I have tried to deal with various types of youth movements from the Campaign for Nuclear Disarmament to the Dutch Provos, from the situationists to the APO or some of the Zengakuren factions. In Hongkong and Macao, besides interviewing escaped Red Guards with the help of three Chinese co-workers, I studied the ways in which the mass-media throughout the world processed news about youth in Red China.

My early years as a roving foreign correspondent taught me the advantages of on-the-spot impressions and personal encounters. Though I did not want to write an impressionistic, subjective chronicle, I tried to be on the spot and meet as many young people as possible. In striving for personal encounters and first-hand experience, I did not hope to change basically the picture I had gained from my research into primary and secondary sources, from my reading and from the documentary evidence offered by the film archives of TV and cinema newsreel companies. During these meetings I simply tried to guard myself against going off at a tangent in my work, prompted by facile generalizations or by attractive 'creative suspicions'. And they helped me to visualize young individuals behind the statistics and within the crowds, gangs, demonstrations and disturbances.

Having stayed at students' digs in Berkeley, Amsterdam and Frankfurt, having spent days at hippie pads in Haight-Ashbury and in East Village, having sat through many marathon teach-ins and meetings at scores of campuses, I just got 'the feel' of things. Nothing more. All this did not turn me into an expert, I am not even an expert on myself. But it helped me to get certain perspectives. A Danish social-anthropology student, a girl of nineteen, for instance, opened my eyes to the age-centrism of the over-thirties. It is difficult for us to envisage things from the viewpoint of younger generations. She showed me a collection of quotes from the writings of people between forty and sixty, who all assume that the future does not exist or, if it does exist, that it is unimportant or inscrutable or both. This girl, who hoped to be healthy and active in the year 2010 or 2020, demonstrated to me that despite the fact that my work was concerned with futurology and cybernetics I, too, made some age-centric mistakes.

Japanese students demonstrated something else: they showed me curious scars on their feet. Since in old Japan (which still exists side by side with new Japan) disobedience is considered a grave sickness in a child, the traditional cure is to burn some dried mugworth (vermouth) on the upper part of the base of the big toe. To one of them, a sparrow-boned girl from a 'good family', this was first done when she was not yet seven. The child is not supposed to scream, or even whimper. Watching the screaming snake of a Zengakuren demonstration, I wondered how many of those students had curious scars on their feet.

Or another instance of these revealing meetings: on a summer evening in a Munich beer-garden I sat in a quiet corner with two extremely mature men: a nineteen-year-old American mathematics student and a twenty-year-old German, studying electron-physics. Their general attitude can be fathomed from this question of mine: 'Why do you think it utterly pointless and childish to think or talk about the political situation in the world?'

The American mathematician: 'Why pay any attention to a senseless clash of badly constructed, badly operated, obsolete systems of communication and control?'

The young German expressed his contempt for political interests in ruder terms. About three years later I met this young man again in Munich as one of the militants demonstrating against the *Notstandgesetz* or Emergency Law. Afterwards, when he was relaxed in his digs, we had a long talk. He was *engagé* all right. His American friend, now a graduate student, was an SDS organizer.

Some writers, sociologists or psychologists complain that studying a certain type of the young, one cannot avoid smoking hashish, or at least being present while it is smoked, and this entails the risk of arrest and imprisonment. The possibility of a sojourn in jail does not worry me unduly and I have no complexes about hash. I smoked it through *narghile* in the Middle East before this had been made illegal. I often watched healthy and tough-looking but very old Arabs smoking these water-pipes without it ever occurring to me that they represented a danger to themselves or to their communities. I may be mistaken, of course, but I see greater dangers in alcoholism and gun-owning, than in marijuana or hashish. I mention this only to stress that I did not have to make sacrifices for the sake of this work.

Some of the student militants and the more talkative drop-outs taught me to pay more attention to the deeper moral and emotional dimensions of their personality. This was a great help. The conformists, who disregard this and persist in thinking of activists as exclusively rational political animals, do not quite understand the activists' attitude. The conformists expect a person in the midst of a convulsive catharsis to have a ready-made blue-print of the personality which will be born in him after the collapse of his old personality. They insist, furthermore, that all revolutionaries should have exact plans of the institutes and organizations with which 'they intend to replace the existing ones'. The idea that some institutions and organizations should not be replaced at all is far too unfamiliar. It is no good reminding the upholders of the *status quo* that when Hercules was given the task of cleaning out the Augean stables, he was not expected to furnish them anew.

3

The bias against the study of current history that still prevails in academic circles is responsible, among other things, for the fact that universities do not study the history of youth. Self-respecting historians are not supposed to deal with the young people of today and yesterday, only with those of thirty or fifty years ago.

For the establishments of the day, the artificially induced controversial state of the history of the last three or five decades was, at all times, most important. Most of the information on which the actions of governments are based is top secret. Their cabinet meetings and confidential discussions are protected from contemporary democratic scrutiny. Only their mistaken actions and missed opportunities are no secrets.

A systematic, non-controversial history of the immediate past could reveal even graver mistakes, and many more missed opportunities. Therefore in most countries the state archives are not made available for research before they are at least thirty or fifty years old. The authorities do their best to ensure that basic information should not flow in time to be of real use.

University authorities defend their ban on the history of the last three or five decades in the name of respectable scholarship. To laymen it seems idiotic that the potential sources available to us for delineating, say, French history in 1968 are much poorer than those which can be used for exploring the origins of the medieval guilds, or the foreign policy of Charlemagne. Yet many eminent academics deny the possibility of writing a scholarly history of the last decades.

It seems obvious to me that if the recent past must always stay controversial, then human societies will never find out what condition they are in and in what direction they are going. Conversely, if diagnosis is possible, history as a discipline must be able to help. By admitting that I am strongly prejudiced in favour of history as a discipline, I risk not only the hostile contempt of retrograde academics, but also that of some young revolutionaries who deny the relevance of history in the struggles of today and tomorrow.

Although the present global human condition is entirely without precedent, although revolution itself is being revolutionized, only suicidal fanatics want to turn against the entire human past. Those young simplifiers who deny the relevance of the past with all its history, science and art are turning against humanity. Ultimately, these young revolutionaries are, in this respect, the allies of government and academic authorities who have much to fear from the historical approach.

The present academic bias against the study of current history leaves the examination of the contemporary scene to sociologists and psychologists. This examination, in turn, cannot be entirely satisfactory without the concepts and methods of historical research. Some psychologists and sociologists tend to disregard the passage of time. Laymen can be excused for forgetting that the young people who shocked and angered them a few years ago belong to a different age-group, and are a different collection of individuals, from the 'youth of today', who, in turn, are not identical with the youth of tomorrow. Social scientists, however, cannot be forgiven for an a-historical approach. Yet, in sociological writings in the nineteen-sixties, one frequently came across generalizations about youth based on 'post-war studies'. In fact, what these post-war studies indicated about, say, Britain in 1949, is quite different from the conclusions of studies conducted in 1953, 1961, or any other year.

There is, of course, no such thing as a psychology or sociology of youth, independent of a specific time and place. A United Nations report stated in 1958: 'One can no longer think of generations in traditional terms. Interests and activities are today changing so fast that sets of young people not more than seven or eight years apart in age may be as far apart in their thinking and behaviour as the generations once were.' This assessment underestimated the speed of change, and did not consider the factors causing sudden changes in the thinking and behaviour of young people only one or two years apart in age.

It is, of course, not at all unprecedented for the young, and for that matter the adults, to 'change out of all recognition' from one year to the next. The Europeans of 1846–7 were quite different in behaviour from their 1848–9 selves. A revolutionary wave swept through Europe in 1848, beginning in Paris (22–4 February), then Vienna (7–13 March), Budapest and Berlin (from 15 March), Milan (18–22 March) and so on to Turkey, Denmark and other countries. The millions of individuals in Europe did not 'change'. They reacted to each other in a greatly changed situation. The proper study of revolutions is human interaction.

The revolutions of 1848 in many European countries were not instigated by one or several organizations or individuals, and differed considerably in their objectives. But they had a common background in a revolutionary situation: unrest caused by an extremely bad harvest, famine in the countryside, unemployment in the towns; the repressive and sterile conservatism of the Matternich, Guizot and other regimes; romantic and intransigent nationalism, the rebellious mood of the middle-class intellectuals. It is for this reason that historians are wary of depending too much on psychological studies that ignore the historical background and the historical present.

Clarendon, discussing the arguments for and against the study of contemporary history, wrote that on the one hand, 'it may be a useful guide to present conduct; on the other, it may give offence to the living'. Any factual chronicle of the last ten years or so cannot help giving offence to many of the living by recording their deeds, statements and behaviour. The recent Algerian war is a good example for this type of so-called offence.

For the Arab world, the history of this war gives no offence. The Arabs are proud of the young heroes of the war for Algerian independence, who in France and some other countries were described as young terrorists. On the other hand, this very long war produced a crisis of conscience in France, mainly among the young who were awaiting their call-up. Some of the young *insoumis* or 'insubordinates' went into hiding or exile. A few hundred even offered to join the Algerian nationalists. The protests of young Frenchmen, who were unwilling to die in a war that they regarded as both immoral and hopeless, angered a considerable section of French adults. The government confiscated newspapers which discussed *insoumission* and the young 'peaceniks' were treated as cowardly scum or outright traitors. When, after many years of pointless bloodshed, France finally abandoned colonial rule over Algeria, the young French *insoumis* – many of whom died in Algeria after having been forced to fight there – were not rehabilitated. Any chronicle of this epoch rehabilitates them; and angers some French politicians by recording their evil and stupid deeds and utterances.

But it is by no means the authorities and the extreme conformists alone who are 'offended' by contemporary history. This chronicle offends – and means to offend – all closed minds and fanatics, whether young or old.

I

THE REVOLUTION
OF REVOLUTION

'If you wait to examine the entrails of an
era until after it's born, it's too late to
prophesy its birth.'

Walter M. Miller, Jr.[1]

1

This book is a study of youth and revolution based on the history
of the generation war during the period 1955–70. Its starting
point and one of its main hypotheses is that the present era is a
far greater historical watershed than was the transition from the
ancient world to the Middle Ages, or that from the Middle Ages
to the so-called Modern Age, now mostly a thing of the past.

The speed and scope of change in the global human condition
since the middle of the twentieth century has been much greater
than during the previous five thousand years. Since peoples and
their governments were unable to adapt to these colossal changes,
the obsolete structures of societies clashed with vast new forces.

Youth is one of these forces.

Societies everywhere seemed to be in a cataclysmic phase that
was similar in scope and effect to the great geological upheavals
in the history of the earth. During such cataclysmic changes, there
is not much sense in demanding that the emerging great earth-
masses account for their actions or give exact descriptions of the
mountains they will ultimately produce. If we continue with this
analogy, one of the main causes of the present upheavals is the
upsurge of great masses of youth. It seems reasonable to assume
that no matter what the young participants of a given revolutionary wave are consciously striving for, all the waves taken
together may have a discernible general direction. One of the aims
of this work is to find this general direction.

Taken one by one, the revolutions and upheavals between 1955
and 1970 cannot be chronicled in a single volume with the aim of

producing a definitive text. But it is possible to present a global view of the revolutionary waves sweeping across continents that will show the outlines of an emerging new pattern faintly super-imposed on – or half-hidden by – familiar old patterns.

Without constantly referring to such a global pattern, it is pointless to designate committees to study recent violence or revolt in this or that city or university in isolation. To study all uprisings and revolutions in a given year in one country – or, for that matter, in all countries – without a study of the human condition in that entire epoch, is also pointless.

The first step towards a diagnosis of the human condition in a given period is to form a hypothesis about its place in world history. It is assumed that the period of five thousand years, the beginnings of the end of which we have been witnessing since mid-century, is the political prehistory of mankind. During this era man was still politically at his 'Neanderthal' stage, as far as his communal and international affairs were concerned. In the spheres of politics and social ethics, man did not deserve the name *Homo sapiens*.

The early beginnings of the end of this extremely long political prehistory of mankind coincide with the end of a far shorter era: the 'modern epoch'.

The crumbling medieval world gave birth to modern man, whose civilization seems to be now in its death-throes. Several young generations are searching for a new, alternative civilization, for a new culture and a new morality. Our 'present' has come to represent the dying past that has become totally irrelevant for many of those who have a long future ahead of them.

As the cold war, and later the hot war, between generations went on, more and more observers felt that the short-term tactical or even strategical student campaigns and youth revolts – from Budapest to Paris and Prague, from the Berkeley Free Speech Movement to the desperate struggle to stop the Vietnam war, to the West German youth offensive against the *Notstandgesetz* – were part of a great Youth Revolt spanning several generations. This was a revolt against a civilization and a culture that the moral and intellectual yeast within the world of youth regard as totally bankrupt. Convinced that the adults had failed in every-thing from their political institutions to their economic organiza-tion, from their use of the arts and sciences to their private lives, an ever-growing proportion of young people contracted out of the adult scene. It was not only hippies, flower children, Provos and their like who dropped out of the prevailing culture and civilization. There were a great many hidden drop-outs, who lived as camouflaged internal exiles within the adult world. For every activist aggressively demonstrating his refusal to accept the 'great leaders' of the adults, who condoned the napalm bomb but urged vicious punishments for the marijuana-smoker, there were hundreds or thousands of sympathizers in whose minds and hearts the *status quo* had been defeated long ago.

Confronted with the closed minds of those in authority, these young men and women looked for inspiration, for guidance and leadership among their own ranks, or among the ranks of non-conformist intellectuals and rebels, who all had a common characteristic: though mature in years, they remained 'rational-altruistic'* individuals.

The majority of young rebels believe that the decay of our present civilization is not caused by its failures but by its great achievements. The arid materialist Utopia of communism and capitalism alike – 'to each according to his needs' – is in sight, and this sight seems to be abhorrent to the 'inheritors of the earth' from Moscow to Los Angeles and from Paris to Tokyo.

Beginning with the post-medieval era, the European type of scientific-technological civilization spread all over the world. 'Modern man' became the model that people tried to imitate almost everywhere. This model successfully survived many man-made revolutions. The type of human being who was at home in the civilization produced by post-medieval Europe was not in fact changed by the Russian revolution of 1917. The Bolshevik revolution did not destroy this civilization, nor did it rejuvenate it. The medium of the bourgeois educational system remained unchanged in the USSR; and in this case, the educational medium was truly the educational message. This is why the USSR, the communist-governed countries of Eastern Europe and all the other developed countries in Europe, America and elsewhere are part of the same civilization.

Modern man, the model that has been the energy-source of Western thoughts and emotions since the Renaissance, is being drained of all his dynamism by his great successes. The post-modern man is just now emerging. He will be the product of a

* This term denotes the highest stage in character development (see Chapter XIII).

26

'man-making revolution'. Man-made revolutions are over in a few months or years. Then they become as extinct as extinct volcanoes. Man-making revolutions last several generations because it takes a great many decades to destroy the beliefs and dogmas of the past, which are what guide the majority of ordinary people. By destroying them, man-making revolutions change the whole inner world of peoples.

The last man-making revolution culminated in the great peasant uprisings in the summer of 1524, when castles were ablaze from Austria to the Black Forest. One of the revolutionary leaders of that era, Thomas Müntzer, the Anabaptist, asked his followers to have the 'courage and strength to realize the impossible'. Social revolutionaries were swept off their feet by the outburst of ecstatic energies. As in the Paris of 1968, imagination took over. The revolutionary 'government of saints' in Münster invented a new way of life, aspects of which earned the hatred of the rest of the world: they established a kind of polygamy and a romantic sort of communism. Some historians date the origins of socialism from the time of the Anabaptists, not so much because of their revolutionary actions or their revolutionary ideology, as because they changed people's moral-emotional inner world.

Before the era of the Anabaptists, Hussites and other rebels, the oppressed multitudes were convinced that their miseries, their place in society, their entire fate were part of the divine order of things. Their revolutionary experience, however, liberated their minds from the fatalistic acceptance of the inhuman *status quo*. A ferment began within individuals and within society that, in a few generations, produced the revolutionary demand that individuals should be masters of their own fate.

This was then a colossally audacious and shatteringly new idea: the common people should be masters of their own fate!

The present man-making revolution is harder to identify, not only because it is probably in its initial stages, but also because it is taking place in a far more complex situation. The earlier revolution was against the oppressive structure of European feudalism, that is, against a single politico-religious system. The present one is a global rebellion against the dogmas and obsolete structures of almost all regimes in the world. It strives to liberate people's minds from the fatalistic acceptance of the delusion that human societies must be completely at the mercy of the 'blind forces of history'. According to this delusion, individuals and societies

cannot influence the future course of history. The present revolutionaries struggle for and dream of a situation in which societies,
the whole of mankind, will make their own history. They want
Homo sapiens to act as the creator and inventor of his own future.

The current audacious and shatteringly new idea is that people
should wake up from the nightmare of history and should be
masters of and responsible for the future of all mankind.

The young rebels, who belong to the whole world, who are
members of no pattern – religious, national or ethnic – known to
their parents, fight against all dogmas and forces that endanger
mankind's survival. The important revolutionary change, as in
the time of the Anabaptists, is within individuals. Again, the
aspiration is directed towards the entire human being, the total
individual. In this situation, the old revolutionary patterns are
becoming irrelevant. Revolution itself is being revolutionized.

2

Most of our established knowledge of revolutions, rebellious mass
movements and political upheavals is based on generalizations
derived from situations and events in the nineteenth and early
twentieth century.

All those revolutions took place in a world situation which had
very little in common with the present one. If by change we
mean new developments which inevitably influence, condition and
alter the daily life and future possibilities of individuals, nations
and the whole of mankind, then never before in history has the
rate of change been as gigantic as during the past two decades.
The sociological studies of revolutions written before these changes
took place offer few adequate intellectual tools for the study of
upheavals since 1955.

As for the psychology and sociology of 'youth', our established
knowledge in these fields is even more obsolete. Since 1945, the
social role, the economic position and the biological characteristics
of 'youth' have undergone extraordinarily large changes. Since
biological and mental maturity come much earlier than in even the
recent past, wider age-groups must be included in the term
'youth' than ever before. It is only since 31 December 1964 that
over half of the world population is under twenty years of age.
Never before in history has the proportion of youth in general
and of students in particular been as high as it is today. Moreover,

during the decade 1955–65, the thirteen to twenty-three age-group showed a larger growth and growth-rate than anticipated by demographic forecasts. The sheer pressure of numbers – not to mention a great many other factors – transforms some age-groups into a 'critical mass' in its pre-explosion stage.

The present generation change is different both in scope and nature from the slow and continuous change of generations to which people were accustomed until the middle of the twentieth century. The complaint that it is difficult to generalize about the young because 'youth' changes all the time has a far stronger basis today. When this complaint was most often being made, sociological and psychological studies of youth were usually concerned with middle-class male youth. At that time, not more than 3 per cent of the eighteen to twenty-two age-group was at university. By 1970, 15 to 45 per cent of this age-group was at university in the highly industrialized countries, and in several disciplines about half the students were girls.

As an introduction to an analytical history of the generation war between 1955 and 1970, the next two chapters deal with youth and revolution in general. Chapter II begins with a historical résumé of the categorization of the ages of man. This shows how greatly the definitions of 'youth' and 'child' varied in the past. People believed in each era that their almost accidentally conceived concept of youth represented both immutable human nature and the eternal structure of God's universe. The historical account deals at some length with the eighteenth-century invention of 'adolescent status'. With this invention mankind took a wrong turning, as far as youth and maturity are concerned. Adolescent status was forced on young males, as a straitjacket is forced on violent lunatics.

Touching on the social, legal, moral, educational, biological, sexual and demographic aspects of the youth phase in the present situation, this chapter describes how and to what extent youth is taking over the world. Here it is assumed that by the nineteen-seventies, youth has come to represent the most influential pressure group for human survival.

Chapter III first deals briefly with revolutionary theories and practices past and present. It then gives a documentary analysis of present-day counter-revolutionary policy in the USA and the Soviet Union that rests on the very same 'ideology-free' theory of 'insurgency'. According to this American–Soviet theory, the *status quo* always represents health, and rebellion is always an illness, or a sign of an illness, not of the system but of the rebels.

In maintaining that defeated revolutions, as opposed to victorious ones, are always active volcanoes, as long as they are capable of inspiring revolutionary movements and actions, Chaper III identifies the common source of uprisings and revolutions in the Soviet orbit. In 1919–20 Lenin, Trotsky and their associates turned the terror machine against the working class and the peasantry. This was done for the 'ultimate good of the people', but the Red Terror during these two years effectively liquidated democratic socialism by making the 'soviets' (councils) at all levels mere instruments for carrying out central orders. In 1921, in Kronstadt, the original stronghold of the 1917 revolution, and in Petrograd, Red sailors and workers staged an uprising against the dictatorship of the Leninist party and demanded 'Soviets without Communists'. The first two Russian Revolutions were in 1905 and 1917. The third one in Kronstadt in 1921 was bloodily suppressed by Trotsky's Red Army. Ever since that time, since the unsuccessful Kronstadt rebellion, the 'third revolution' remained an active volcano. Chapter III maintains, and the rest of the chronicle tries to illustrate and document the thesis, that the third revolution of democratic socialism against bureaucratic despotism, of soviets against monopoly communism, is going on in the Soviet-dominated world. The uprisings in East German and Czechoslovak cities in 1953; the rebellious *coup d'état* within the Party in Poland in 1956; the Hungarian Revolution of the same year; all the other lesser upheavals and stirrings in East Europe and the USSR; and, finally, the Czechoslovak 'bloodless revolution' of 1968 – all these are periodic eruptions of that active volcano, the 'third revolution'.

3

Chapters IV to VIII chronicle the first phase of the generation war which in Europe and America lasted from 1955 until about 1962–3. During wars the normal peacetime tensions within societies are usually weakened or forcibly suppressed. This, naturally, applies first and foremost to the biologically and sociologically normal tensions between generations. The Second World War was no exception. During and after this war there were comparatively few complaints against youth. Since in peacetime the

hroughout the five continents, Chapter IX places the
n of the university in its historical and global perspective.
uments the relevant aspects of the origins of the university
cusses the question why, all through history, the university
has never been fully accepted as a member of society.

4

ears after American sociologists of the calibre of David
n or Kenneth Keniston gave documented analyses of 'the
in political involvement among university students', the
y explosion' of 1964 opened a new era of university
als in the United States. There is no need to stress that
iologist's diagnosis of the US students of 1959–62 was
They were, on the whole, conformists and careerists. The
us students of the later period were the sons and daughters
er vintage of parents and were moulded by a changed
nd political climate. These rebels – unlike the passively
nt sheep of 1959–62 – were drawn into the political
by the grave moral and physical dangers that the Civil
issue and the Vietnam war meant for them.
last part of the book – the chronicle of the generation war
period 1964–70 – deals with the emergence of minorities
the young who are not inhibited by ignorance, or conven-
habit from taking a bold and independent view of how
cieties should be run. These young people, who feel com-
act as the critical conscience of their world, represent an
nt minority in the student generations of the period. It
at the members of this minority are passive when they are
ked by what they regard as suicidal policies. In revolu-
situations they have a considerable influence on the student
a whole. In calmer periods they are not eager to com-
te because they see no point in shocking their environment
ir ideas. They lead outwardly conventional lives, or live
dent bohemians or hippies – and emerge as the active
nts in pre-outbreak ferments, if and when reality pro-
em. This seems to be one of the reasons for the strange
a student mass behaviour in our age.
three years that elapsed between the Berkeley explosion
and the Ohnesorg murder in Berlin in 1967, everything
ted to the intensification of the generation war. Chapter

'youth of today' is usually blamed for the real or alleged behaviour
of those age-groups who went through their youth-phase during
the previous decade, youth was not in the dock of public
opinion in the immediate postwar years.

During the first phase (1955–62/3) the objects of adult anxiety
and hatred were the teenage gangs, the Teddy Boys and their
equivalents elsewhere, and the middle- and upper-class 'rebels
without a cause', who had committed pointless crimes just for
kicks. Violence and delinquency in this era had little or no
political, or even rational, motivation. In these years, the general
public had little reason to pay attention to the universities.
American and European university authorities, sociologists and
psychologists were firmly convinced that students were politically
disinterested and tended to turn towards a 'world of private and
personal satisfaction'. The students of the Western world were
described as members of an 'ego-centric', 'enervated', 'sceptic' or
'passive' generation. American and Russian educators were
equally worried by the decline in political involvement among
university youth. In Hungary, the Communist authorities complained about the political passivity of students a few months
before the 1956 revolution, which was sparked off by the students.

Since the various obsolete concepts of, or myths concerning,
'revolution', 'youth' and 'adults' are just as important in shaping
society as the actual facts – or, at times, even more important –
they deserve just as much earnest attention as serious theories.
When any psychological or physical disturbance of peaceful everyday existence causes people to take sides, these myths, and what
they believe is happening, become supremely important. Often
the knowledge of what is actually happening is far less effective.
For this reason, all the historical chapters deal with these ever-
changing myths whenever relevant. These chapters give evidence
that politicians, magistrates, policemen and others were, in many
cases, not seeing the real flesh-and-blood youth with whom they
momentarily had their dealings, but a curious composite Franken-
stein's monster – the layman's image of the 'youth of today': his
hands were taken from a murderous teenager of the New York of
1959; his voice from Mick Jagger; his head from Rudi Dutschke;
parts of his body from the Californian Hell's Angels or the hated
French or American 'peaceniks'; and his sex-organs from a
detested 'delirium-inspiring coast-to-coast male sex-symbol'.

Chapter IV traces the origins of the cold war between the

generations back to the immediate postwar era when a war-shocked and peace-shocked generation of timid neurotics and cautious conformists was bringing up families and shaping the future. The Teddy Boy and similar teenage movements originated in these families. This chapter describes the eruption of gang violence and of rock-'n'-roll riots all over the world. It demonstrates that some marginal youth groups play a considerable role in the generation war because their very existence breeds anti-youth prejudices. The importance of Teddy Boys, *Raggaren*, Mods, Rockers, *Blousons Noirs*, *Gammler* and their like, and of juvenile delinquents, is greatly increased by the fact that they are the main sources of the social infection that afflicts the adult world.

In the nineteen-fifties, the Western version of the 'youth of today' differed very greatly from its counterpart in the Soviet world. Chapter V describes at some length the situation, the attitudes, the prejudices and the fears of adults and young people in the Soviet orbit. As the Second World War and the Nuremberg trials were the grave moral shocks that motivated Western intellectual youth for a time, so the mass-murders of innocent people during the Stalin era were the gigantic moral shocks that moved virtually everyone in the Soviet Union and her satellites.

Chapter VI gives a short history of the Hungarian Revolution of 1956. At that time, the cold war between the generations was still in its initial stages in the Western world and its mental and emotional climate had not yet penetrated the Soviet orbit. There was an almost abnormal lack of tension between the generations. The people as a whole shared the convictions, sentiments and aspirations of the young *avant garde* of the revolution. For this, and some other reasons, the Hungarian Revolution can serve as a control case, since most other youth disturbances and revolts occurred in countries where there were normal tensions between youth and adults (Red China, Indonesia during the anti-Sukarno demonstrations), or in the abnormal atmosphere of cold war between the generations in the Western world. The history of this revolution was still not cleared up by 1970. It had to remain controversial because the boys and girl who had died for their cause demonstrated a number of 'truths' that were equally repugnant to liberals and communists; to conservatives and black nationalists; to the adherents of Orwell or to those of Sartre; to governments almost everywhere from Moscow and Washington

to Bonn, Paris, Tokyo and Cairo. The
establish the non-controversial facts of t
it in the context of the 'third revolution' i

Nineteen hundred and fifty-seven wa
and convictions. Suez and Hungary ex
the Old Right and the Old Left. Starting
VII and VIII bring the chronicle up to

Between 1957 and 1964 the youth sce
– went through an overall transformati
the world. These were the years when th
hipsters and all sorts of displaced persons
lect was spread by the media all over tl
years of CND and the Aldermaston ma
sex 'explosion' that spawned sexual jea
While there was a great deal of gang wa
until the end of the fifties, after 1962 lo
how found a cure for their addiction to
recounts how, in 1962–3, on Merseyside
rooming of pop groups led to a steep
The pop groups, however, with their lon
and fabulous earnings, only increased the
parts of the adult world.

By this time, the youth-of-today image,
image, led to occurrences in which the bi
duced the very disturbances they wish
demonstrated during the 1964 Whitsun
The last section of Chapter VII establish
pened during these widely misrepresentec

While Western students were still mostl
contests in piano-wrecking, goldfish-swall
phone booths, students led protest move
revolutions in Venezuela, Turkey, Soutl
Indonesia and Japan. Since these upheav
tion to the great outbreak of student revol
America, they are not discussed in this boc
place, but in Chapter VIII, which summa
phase of the generation war. These revolu
Latin America, South Korea, Turkey an
scope for studying the army's role in youth

As an introduction to the second phase
when there were student rebellions in ove

sities
proble
It doc
and d
stude

Two
Riesm
declin
'Berke
uphea
the s
corre
rebell
of a
social
comp
strug
Righ

Tł
for tl
amoi
tion,
their
pelle
impo
seem
unpr
tion
bod
mur
with
like
ingr
vok
cycl

I
in 1
con

X deals with these events, and discusses the significant stages in the escalation of the generation war. The emergence of the Amsterdam Provos and of the Chinese Red Guards in 1966–7 contributed disturbing features to the layman's image of the youth-of-today. Therefore, two sub-chapters describe the Provo and the Red Guard movements.

The French Revolution of May–June 1968; the Czechoslovak attempt to establish 'communism with a human face'; the youth crusade for the presidential candidacy of Senator McCarthy; the police riots from Chicago to Zurich; the brutal over-reaction of the authorities in Mexico, Brazil, Argentine and in many other countries; the hot war of 1969 between students and police from Japan to the United States – all these take up most of the rest of this book.

The final chapter examines the place of dissent and conformism in the evolution of *Homo sapiens* and concludes that the student revolt and the violent clashes between conformism and critical intelligence do not constitute a global epidemic that will be over as soon as some effective anti-toxins have been found. Whatever their forms, this revolution and this generation war are parts of a fight to ensure that human reason and human freedom will determine history.

II

YOUTH: NEW CLASS
OR NEW SPECIES?

1

The definition of youth and the concepts people have of the stages
in the life of the individual have varied throughout history. In
each era, most people believed that their ideas concerning the
three, four or seven ages of man were based on unchangeable
human nature. It is, however, enlightening that through most of
history the ideas, customs and regulations relating to childhood,
youth and 'senectitude' were more in harmony with contemporary
reality than ours have been since the middle of the eighteenth
century.

Throughout most of history, everyday practice recognized only
three ages: childhood, youth and old age. The word 'young' or
'youth' referred to healthy and active mature individuals. The
age-groups of Neolithic times, the Greek *paideia*, presupposed
a difference and a transition between the world of children and
that of adults, a transition made by means of an initiation
ceremony, usually preceded by some education. The initiation
turned the child overnight into a young adult, just as in most
of the known primitive cultures of the distant and recent past.

For Aristotle, and for all Antiquity, there were only three ages
of man: childhood, youth and old age. In Aristotle's usage 'young'
included any age from about seven to forty or even forty-five (that
would be the equivalent of about sixty to sixty-five today). According to Aristotle, and according to everyday usage in Antiquity, one
was young as long as one was strong and healthy enough to function as an adult. Below this stage were the children, beyond it
the decrepit old. When the Ionian philosophers of the sixth

century BC decided that the ages of man must correspond to the number of the then known planets – seven – the fourth age was called youth 'because of the strength of the person to help himself and others'. The text makes it clear that for these early philosophers the word 'young' meant a healthy adult. The next category was 'senectitude', which is 'half-way between youth and old age'.

Aristotle, the other philosophers, and most of Antiquity did not identify adolescence in any shape or form. There was no age between childhood and youth (i.e. adulthood) in their categorization.

The ancient Romans did not differentiate clearly between infancy, childhood and young adulthood. One was an *infans* till one's seventh years. *Puerilis* and *adolescens* were often used synonymously and applied to young males without reference to age. 'Octavianus at nineteen was called *puer* and Julius Caesar, at about thirty-eight, *adolescentuluss*'.[1]

It was Constantine the Great who, in his division of human life into seven ages, called the third age 'adolescence', the period during which 'the person grows to the size allotted to him by Nature'. In his usage, then, adolescence was another name for late childhood.

The 'ages of life' were frequently discussed in medieval treatises, too. They were: childhood, puerility, adolescence, youth, senility, and finally old age. But this categorization had very little to do with everyday usage or with legal practice.

Until the end of the Middle Ages, the child moved into the adult world between his fifth and seventh year, and then stayed 'young' so long as he or she was able to do 'a good day's work'. This pattern remained on the whole valid for the lower classes until well into the twentieth century.

The next section of this chapter will report on our present knowledge of sexual maturation. It should be stressed here that the onset of puberty has not been steadily declining over the last two thousand years. In the sixth century, in most of Europe the age of legal majority, considered then to occur when a person became capable of reproduction, was fixed at fourteen for boys and twelve for girls. A thousand years later, the Council of Trent in the fifteen-fifties set the earliest time for marriage at the same ages. In the fourteenth century, one of Chaucer's women says: 'Since the age of twelve, thanks to God whose life is eternal, I have taken a husband five times at the church porch.'

So for a thousand years, from the sixth to the sixteenth century, a child passed into adult status between twelve and fourteen. The actual status of age-groups and of sexes did not always correspond to their legal status. Women among the early Greeks and Romans never came of age, but by the time of Justinian they were permitted, along with men, to reach their majority at the age of twenty-five. In later medieval common law a knight came of age at twenty-one, while the son of a burgher was of full age when he was able to count money, measure cloth or make a table; in other words, when he could conduct his father's business. It was not exceptional for a person to continue to be legally a minor for six, seven or even ten years after his or her marriage.

During most of the Middle Ages, the idea of childhood was bound up with the idea of dependence and this was, of course, based on socio-economic reality. The words 'sons', 'varlets', 'boys', 'knights', *'Knechte'* were also words in the terminology of feudal subordination. From early feudal times until the middle of the seventeenth century, people left childhood only by achieving a superior economic or social status. 'A lowly person was called a "child" regardless of age . . . Dependency – physical, economic, social or legal – played and still plays a large role in the definitions of "developmental status".'[2]

Verbal usage was just as vague throughout the Middle Ages as in the times of Julius Caesar. The word *enfant* (child, in modern usage) was used in medieval France as a synonym for *valeton, garçon* or *fils*. At the end of the Middle Ages, a certain *enfant* was chided for 'starting brawls in brothels', and 'he never came across a woman without raping her'.[3]

Lily's Latin grammar in English, which was used from the sixteenth to the nineteenth century, was intended for 'all lytell babes, all lytell children'. According to some sixteenth-century calendars, 'at the age of twenty-four a child is strong and brave'. Since at that time boys were permitted to marry at fourteen – and there were fourteen-year-old lieutenants in the French army – a 'child' of twenty-four probably looked like a man in his early forties today.

Birching and other kinds of corporal punishment were until the twelfth century confined to children below the age of seven or ten. Later, all persons who went to school began to be treated as under-tens. At the beginning of the fourteenth century, undergraduates who did not belong to a college were free gentlemen, while by the end of the fifteenth century they became mere school-boys not only in Oxford but also in Paris. The development of the colleges transformed the free citizen of the university into a disciplined schoolboy. From the fifteenth century onwards, corporal punishment became the fashion. Adult members of the lower classes and children of all classes were beaten. Students were beaten even after their twenty-first birthday.

At the beginning of the modern era and until the seventeenth century, in many languages there were only three words for the ages of man in general usage: childhood, youth and old age, just as in the ancient world. Though we find many descriptions of the seven ages of man in novels and plays, it was only childhood that continued to represent a socio-economic status. This was an extremely low status, and it was further worsened between the sixteenth and nineteenth centuries.

The Reformation raised the issue of original sin. Calvin declared that the whole nature of children was 'a seed of sin' and that only by whipping could their inherent wickedness be eliminated and their salvation ensured. Bunyan described children as 'cursed creatures'.

For the ruling age-groups the idea and practice of pushing up the upper age-limit of childhood to fifteen, later to eighteen and even twenty-one, was not at all obnoxious. In the eighteenth century, public opinion ceased to admire child prodigies – manifestations of their extraordinary talents were to be suppressed later – and the age of starting school was raised because of 'the imbecility or incapacity of little children'. Childhood was artificially extended to well after full sexual maturity.

But even after all these precedents, the worst mistake in the categorization of man was committed in the eighteenth century. It was then that mankind took one of its historical wrong turnings as far as 'youth' and 'maturity' were concerned. The 1967–70 youth explosions (and the far greater ones to come) originate partly in the unhealthy social convention concerning youth that was evolved in the eighteenth century and has been kept up by the conventional wisdom of both communist and capitalist societies to this very day.

In his *Youth and Social Order*, Dr Musgrove dedicates an entire chapter to *The Invention of the Adolescent* and says: 'Adolescence was invented at the same time as the steam-engine.

The principal architect of the latter was Watts in 1765, of the former Rousseau in 1762.'[4]

It was a bad invention. For the bourgeois male it inserted a long transformation period of dependence and immaturity between childhood and adulthood. Soon after the great French Revolution had established the political supremacy of the middle classes in the towns, the bourgeois took it for granted that this mis-categorization of a stage in human life was deeply rooted in social and biological reality.

In most of the countries that went through the bourgeois revolution or came to be moulded under its impact, adolescent status was forced on a minority of young males with quite brutal measures. Family, school and the whole of society co-operated in forcing the young males of the middle and upper classes to live in a biologically unnatural, psychologically unhealthy state of immaturity and dependence. It was soon implied by most civilized languages that this pedagogically induced immaturity and economically enforced dependence were inherent in human nature. In the primitive languages that are outside the scope of academic history and are specially dealt with by anthropologists, the term 'adolescence' did not exist. After a short initiation period, the child became a man or a woman. And he or she was mature from then on.

In most tribal societies, as in ancient Greece, China or Chaldea, the institutions, customs and morals of the tribe were in harmony with the fact that the freshly initiated young adults (or 'adolescents') were mentally and physically mature enough to play their special role in society. This role was usually that of the hunter-warrior.

This tribal way of life took care that the young 'boiling heads' of both sexes should be able to be 'wildly young' without causing distress to themselves or to society. It appears that most primitive societies found a wiser and more satisfactory way of dealing with young adults than the civilized societies of modern times.

In the eighteenth and nineteenth centuries, inside the schools adolescents were confused with children, with whom they had to share the humiliation of corporal punishment, the chastisement meted out to villains and army recruits. (Birching went on in the Continental and British armies till well into the nineteenth century.) But in the eighteenth century and the early nineteenth, a young adult could not escape inferior status even if he avoided going to school or university. Rousseau was an enemy of schools. He urged fathers to educate their sons at home : 'Exercise his body ... but keep his mind idle as long as you can.'* Privately educated adolescents were, in most homes, flogged as often as those who were sent to Eton or Winchester, or to schools of similar standing in Europe.

At the beginning of this century, and even in the thirties, the overwhelming majority of the over-fourteens or over-fifteens were not identified as 'adolescents' or 'youth' in North America and Europe. A male wearing a cloth-cap was a worker, whether fifteen or fifty-five. Appearance, clothing (the sign of class), physical maturity and strength were what counted in categorizing the lower classes, not chronological age.

It is only since the middle of the twentieth century that in most post-industrial societies the majority of the twelve- to twenty-one-year-olds have been identified in everyday practice as adolescents or youth. The overwhelming majority of works on the psychology and sociology of youth, however, ignores the massive facts of life of the last two decades, and still deals only with middle-class, male youth.

The class and sex bias is quite manifest in certain works, in others it is only latent. Writing in the *Journal of the American Academy of Sciences*, Bruno Bettelheim stated that in psychological and sociological literature on adolescence and youth, the majority of studies deals with the male. These works give the impression that 'female adolescence, if it exists at all, does not create problems equally worthy of the sociologist's or psychologist's interest ... There must be a reason why the male adolescent and his problems dominate public attention and that of the scholarly expert.'[5]

Many sociologists and psychologists use the term 'adolescent' because society has succeeded and still succeeds in keeping a large number of young people in an artificially created state of immaturity. It is, however, not emphasized often enough that by this term a great many academics refer not only to the male of the species, but to the middle-class male of the temperate zone. Many otherwise very objective and open-minded European and American scholars still write about Western temperate-zone societies as if the rest of the world were of no account; as if the

* See Chapter IX, section 2.

majority of mankind were only on the 'exotic fringes'; as if the 'problems of our times' were the problems of their white, Western civilization.

Most dictionaries and encyclopedias currently in use must, of necessity, accept those definitions concerning youth that are in accord with present social convention, legal practice and conformist bias. According to *Webster's Third New International Dictionary* (1961), adolescence is 'the state or process of growing up; the period of life from puberty to maturity terminating legally at the age of majority'. Youth is 'the period between childhood and maturity'. The 'age of maturity' and that of legal 'majority' at twenty-one, when a person becomes 'of age', had medieval origins. In the Middle Ages knighthood was conferred at twenty-one. Yet, legislation and general social practice from the Soviet Union to Red China, from the United States to Britain and many European countries still assumed in 1968 that people under twenty-one or even twenty-four to twenty-five were 'immature' in many respects.

The *Concise Oxford Dictionary* gives the following definitions:

Childhood: time from birth to puberty.

Puberty: being functionally capable of procreation, the age at which puberty begins.

Adolescent: person growing up, between childhood and manhood (fourteen to twenty-three) or womanhood (twelve to twenty-one).

Youth: the period between childhood and full manhood or womanhood.

Communist countries are even more rigid than capitalist ones in enforcing dependent-immature status on those above sixteen, particularly so if they are students. As far as sex relations are concerned, these allegedly Marxist governments are even more rigid in ignoring biological reality than non-Marxist establishments. Soviet and Chinese legislation and governing practice assumes that people become sexually mature only between twenty-one and twenty-five years of age.

Yet, according to the Soviet Russian Criminal Code of 1961, persons above sixteen are fully responsible for their crimes but cannot be executed before they reach their eighteenth year. (Article 10.) Persons between fourteen and sixteen years of age can be sentenced to prison for murder and manslaughter

(Articles 102–112), for rape (Article 117), burglary (91 and 146), theft (89 and 144), sabotage (86, 98 and 149). Other Soviet legislation and general practice assumes that they are sexually mature only between twenty-one and twenty-four years of age.[1]

In Red China, the criminal responsibilities of teenagers are similar to those in the USSR. But while in the USSR a very high proportion of teenagers is kept in school until fifteen or sixteen, and even after that in part-time schools, in China the overwhelming majority of the unfortunate twelve-year-olds are treated as adult labourers. Yet, both young men and women are constantly admonished by the Chinese Communist Party and the government not to get married before they are twenty-five years old.

In Western societies ignorance of the facts coloured the reaction of the adult world at least up to the middle of the present century. 'Adolescent' sexual activity was discouraged, forbidden or denounced not only because it was regarded as sinful but also because, allegedly, it was premature. The entire social, moral and legal system was based on the assumption that young girls were not ripe for a sex life before they were seventeen to nineteen and boys before they were twenty-one or more. Havelock Ellis, Magnus Hirschfeld and many other sexologists pointed out many decades ago that at that time sexual maturity and potency reached its peak in the late teens, and continued on this peak for decades. They also referred to the fact that this observation was valid only for their own time and place; the first decades of the twentieth century in Europe, the United States and Canada.

By the nineteen-sixties children reached sexual maturity three to five years earlier than at the turn of the century.

Criticizing pre-sixties practices, Walker and Fletcher wrote:

There is a considerable time-lag between the speed of physical growth and the speed of education for social responsibility as a result of which our young people remain emotionally unweaned and dependent for *long after they have become physically adult human beings.* . . . The emotional and spiritual development of our children is being *actively retarded from without.* . . . Something is alarmingly wrong with our methods of family training and formal education. . . . It is as cowardly as it is immoral to require our young people to assume responsibilities for the consequences of inaptitude, and unjust to blame them if the burden proves too heavy for them to bear.[6]

The adult world seems to insist that it is up to the authorities to decide when 'adolescence' ends. The myth of sexual immaturity is, of course, badly shaken by the fact that in the Western world alone each year many millions of girls and boys between fifteen and nineteen marry and bring up children. The myth of the mental and moral immaturity of those between sixteen and twenty-one has even less foundation in fact than the one concerning sexual immaturity. Yet in most countries those age-groups are still excluded from the adult world.

Persons who pay taxes when they start work at fourteen or fifteen; who can and do marry between fourteen and seventeen; who are permitted to drive cars or be in sole control of aeroplanes at seventeen; who are conscripted or drafted into armies at eighteen; who are held criminally responsible from ten, fourteen or sixteen, and in some countries can be executed for their crimes at sixteen or eighteen – these very same persons are not considered responsible enough to vote in most countries, and are treated as immature until twenty-four or twenty-five if they happen to be university students.*

In adolescence the young attain physical maturity, the height of their sexual powers, the peak of intellectual capacity . . . [yet] a small minority must be prepared to accept a position of dependence and tutelage while they remain in educational institutions until their twenties.[7]

The 1964 Geneva Conference on Auxology (the science of growth) approved Professor Ettore de Toni's report that the human stature, which had remained virtually unchanged for thousands of years, had recently started to sprout. 'Men of the ancient world were shrimps compared to those of today. The ancient Romans were between 160 and 163 cm tall. The average rate of growth during this century has been between five and seven centimeters, making' – as the professor said – 'beds inherited from grandfather much too short. Julius Caesar's legionaries, who conquered

* In Britain the voting age was lowered to eighteen in 1970. In Brazil, Israel and Uruguay the voting age is also eighteen. But in most countries of the world, with the US and the USSR in the lead, the voting age is twenty-one. In the US, with the exception of Georgia and Kentucky (where the voting age is eighteen), Alaska (nineteen) and Hawaii (twenty), the twelve million Americans who were between eighteen and twenty-one in 1969 did not have the right to vote. The constitutional amendment to lower the voting age requires a two-thirds majority in Congress and has to be ratified by the legislatures of three-quarters of the different states.

half of Europe, would be declared unfit for today's Italian army.'
People are not only taller and stronger than they were for many
centuries, but they reach their full height years earlier than they
did even at the beginning of this century.

In 1968 Dr J. M. Tanner summarized in the *Scientific
American* the findings of studies concerning the earlier physical
maturation of children conducted in countries in the five continents. During the past five or six decades, children in North
America, Europe (including Russia), Japan and even parts of
China have come to puberty progressively earlier. Now they reach
sexual maturity three to five years sooner than at the turn of
the century.

Eleven-year-old boys and girls of similar economic circumstances in North America, Europe, Japan and some other countries were, on the average, four inches taller in 1965 than their
counterparts in 1905. The average age at which growth stops is
also much lower, indicating that people reach full physical
maturity much earlier.

The gain in weight and in other bodily dimensions is approximately proportional to the gain in height. . . . The upward trend in
size has been slowed from time to time by the famines of economic
crisis and, to a greater extent, the famines of war. In Moscow,
during the 1940s the height of the 12-year-old boys declined as much
as an inch as an effect of the war.

Records are available on menarcheal age for Britain, many other
European countries and parts of America. The main conclusion is
perfectly clear: girls have experienced menarche progressively earlier
during the last 100 years, between three and four months per decade.
On this basis puberty is attained 2½ to 3½ years earlier than it was a
century ago.[8]

Dr Tanner added that 'when the environment is good, the onset
of puberty is controlled by genetic factors'. We do not know yet
exactly what environment is 'good'; all we know is that even in
the most prosperous parts of the United States boys and girls do
not mature as early as genetic factors would permit them to do.

An investigation of past records indicates that the earlier
maturation is mainly – but not exclusively – caused by better diet,
hygiene and general economic and social factors. Records kept
or periodical recordings compiled since 1820 in London, Manchester, Warsaw and elsewhere show that peasant and working-

45

class women mature more than a year later than middle- or upper-class women.*

Any serious study of youth and maturation should attempt to explore the causes of much earlier puberty in cities than in the countryside. In Northern Scandinavia, among the Lapps for example, who have maintained their nomadic way of life, the age of menarche remained steady at sixteen and a half years, while that of their Norweigian neighbours fell by two years over the same fifty-year period. Surveys in India and Ceylon indicate that girls living in towns begin to menstruate about eighteen months earlier than those in rural areas. There are strong indications that genetic influences are overridden by environmental factors: Japanese girls growing up in California menstruate eighteen months earlier than those in Japan.[9]

The onset of puberty in boys shows similar trends and characteristics to that in girls. The measurements of army recruits in countries as far apart as Russia, Italy and the United States show similar increases in average height.[10]

According to the US Surgeon General's office, army recruits in 1968 were on average 1.2 inches taller and 18 pounds heavier than those of the First World War. Between 1965 and 1967, Vassar and Smith freshmen were 2 inches taller and 10 pounds heavier than they were at the turn of the century. The average age of marriage for US women has declined from 21.2 years in 1920 to 20.5 in 1968. But 40 per cent of all new brides were between fifteen and eighteen years of age. According to the Washington Population Reference Bureau, the most frequent marrying age in the US for women with only elementary school education was between fourteen and sixteen in the mid-nineteen-sixties. Their husbands were between seventeen and twenty-one.

In an article on the earlier physical maturity of US boys and girls in *Newsweek*, in 1968, the author, wrote : 'More surprisingly, there is new evidence that emotional and intellectual maturity parallel physical growth.'[11]

It has been known for quite a long time that in persons of average ability 'mental maturation' is completed by seventeen or

* In 1820 the menarcheal age for girls who completed their education, i.e. the middle and upper class, was 14.6; for the working-class girls 15.8. The Warsaw women, with a per-decade decline of only 2.8 months, the country women, who had a poorer, more unhealthy existence, had a very late menarche until the eighteen-nineties, and with the improvement of their condition, their menarche came 5.4 months earlier per decade.

eighteen, given reasonable educational chances. The more gifted boys and girls are mentally mature by fifteen or sixteen, or even earlier. 'Mentally mature' refers to a person with a fully developed brain, the basic ability to handle abstractions, to solve problems, to form hypotheses and make deductions. This, however, is not full human maturity without the habit of rational or rather 'rational-altruistic' behaviour.

3

'It takes considerable time to see the simple and central fact about anything,' wrote G. K. Chesterton many decades ago, when historical change was extremely slow in a world peopled by less than half of the present global population. There are today a few simple and central and, one might add, colossal facts waiting to be seen, not to speak of hundreds of rather complicated facts. First among the simple facts is that youth is taking over the world, with a speed and to a degree for which there has been no parallel in recorded history.

Many generations of adults, refusing to contemplate the long-range consequences of their actions (and their inaction), contributed to the creation of today's situation, in which so many people are worried by youth power and student power.

Never before in history has youth been in the majority in the global population.

For the first time in the history of Asia and Africa, youth represents as much political power today as old age did in the past. The traditional oriental or primitive tribal socities of Asia and Africa were ruled by old men according to the old ways – now suddenly these societies have to be modernized by young men, according to new ways.

In the short history of the industrialized nations youth has never had as much economic power as it has today. The under-twenty-ones constitute the single richest consumer group in these countries. Their tastes in all sorts of goods and in mass-entertainment have an unparalleled influence on developments.

Young people are more important and influential in all fields of science than ever before. Of all the scientists who have ever lived and worked throughout human history, 90 per cent live today. And more than half of these are under twenty-eight.

Never before has there been a global situation in which 'old knowledge' became as swiftly obsolete as it does today.

Professor Musgrove wrote in 1964: 'The hatred with which the mature of Western society regard the young is a testimony to the latter's importance, to their power, both potential and actual.'[12]

The students' power, both potential and actual, is even greater. The students of today are targets of hatred because, besides being 'youth', they represent the feared minority of non-conformist intellectuals; that is they represent brain power.

The 'student of today' was seen as the enemy of authority and established order in Spain, France, America, the USSR and Britain, not to speak of Czechoslovakia and of the West German consumer's paradise. In 1968, Messrs Kiesinger and Ulbricht had little in common save their hostility to the students' extra-parliamentary or extra-communist-apparatus opposition. In February 1968, Karl Schutz, Chief Burgomaster of Berlin declared: 'There are no longer classes, there are no longer political parties, there are only the citizens who are against the students.'

In March of the same year, shortly before he was deposed, President Novotny, Czechoslovakia's Stalinist dictator, told a Prague audience: 'The working class is actually not at war with capitalism, but with the students and writers who demand reform.'

While the global population has doubled since the turn of the century, the number of under-twenty-ones has more than trebled, and in the post-industrial countries the proportion of students is four to ten times what it was fifty years ago. In California, over 72 per cent of the university age-group was actually at university or college in 1968.

Since the Second World War, it has been a truism to say that the people of all five continents can study their own near or distant future in the United States of America. Within the US, in turn, California indicates the near future of the rest of the country.

The California of the nineteen-sixties was regarded as the most successful region in the world. It was the richest, fastest-growing youngest and presumably happiest state in the US. This California paradise, towards which the Western world seemed to have been striving throughout the last centuries, offered a better life to its young people and a greater slice of its success than any young people anywhere could dream about. Yet, California produced the 'rebels without a cause' in the nineteen-fifties (who, of course, had massive reasons for their rebellion). Later, sizeable minorities of the young people refused to accept their slice of the great Californian success. It was not the underprivileged but the overprivileged youth, the children produced by 'the most successful generation of Americans', who dropped out or contracted out of the continuing saturnalia of affluence.

No student generation of the past was assured as well-paid a future as the undergraduates and post-graduates at California's universities and multiversities. Yet it was the pampered children of the success generation who initiated the American era of university rebellion in 1964. Hundreds, and soon thousands, of university students were willing to undergo hardship, to risk being brutally beaten up by the police, to go to prison, to ruin their prospects, on behalf of principles and causes that were none of their personal business. They risked everything, in order to behave as rational-altruistic beings.

Robert Poulet, the Belgian writer, likened youth to the performers of a play who descend from the stage into the audience after the final curtain, to become adult spectators of the play, which now starts anew. This analogy is, however, more relevant to the past than to the present. The actors, as we have seen, are far more numerous today than in the past, and they also stay longer on the stage. Some stay there for good.

One can study the process which altered the generation change by considering the history of the 1956–70 period. An astonishing thing occurred during these years, best observable in California. To remain within Poulet's analogy: more and more actors refused to turn into spectators. The stage of youth grew out of all 'normal' proportion and the audience began to dwindle, not only because it was not replenished from the stage, but also because many spectators turned traitor and joined the actors. In plain language, more and more young people refused to be like their conformist parents. A minority of those between thirty and ninety joined the youth camp, since the students came to represent the most influential pressure group for human survival.

The cold war between the generations contributed very much to the growth of the youth camp. Young people who leave school at fifteen and would in time have become very similar to their conformist parents are held back from joining the sheep because in their free time they look and behave like the 'new youth'. Long

49

hair and hippy-ish clothes put the part-time flower children in the same camp as the student rebels and the non-conformist intellectuals. Various types of haircut or clothing represented the uniform of the youth army or the yellow star of the youth outcasts. A Munich *Gammler* told me in quite matter-of-fact language in 1966 that because of his appearance many adults treat him as if he were wearing a yellow star. In the same year, a motion was put forward in the Brighton Town Council that certain types of young people ought to be put into concentration camps.

The commerce and industry of the adult world, and the mass media operated by adult entrepreneurs, recognized youth as one of the two most important consumer groups. A great many aspects of 'youth culture' in such matters as behaviour, fashion and entertainment were the invention of the media merchandizers, but they had to base their inventions on the likes and dislikes of actual flesh-and-blood girls and boys.

Youth culture is one aspect of the false consciousness of the age. But it is also responsible for the fact that a great many people between thirty and fifty became the enthusiastic fellow-travellers of youth. Lastly, youth culture strengthens in many direct and indirect ways the camps of revolutionary youth.

During the nineteen-sixties, some observers of the current scene came to feel that youth was the unidentified and unnoticed new class. This class is made more integrated or united all the time by adult attacks and indiscriminate adult hostility to all youth. There are cities and regions where youth comprises eighteen different year-groups, covering those between twelve and twenty-nine. Slim, young-looking, young-dressed people; those who feel solidarity with youth, post-graduates and young academics, young married middle- or working-class men who, with their wives, prefer to remain in the youth camp – ever-larger groups are wearing the yellow star of youth, as far as the police, conventional adults and the conformity-ensuring authorities are concerned.

Whether or not one agrees with those who believe that the Western working classes (plus those of the USSR and East Europe) have ceased to be revolutionary masses, it is a fact that with automation the proportion of industrial workers is decreasing. In California and in many other regions of the United States, the workers are no longer the largest class. Their place has been taken by the workers of the knowledge-producing and related industries, by students, teachers, scientists, professional people and intellectuals. The workers of the knowledge-producing industries represent a larger class or segment of the adult population than the industrial workers and farmers taken together. Since consumer societies cannot exist without the mental production of former students, the proportion and the absolute number of students and others in the knowledge-producing industries will go on growing.

According to the same observers, the best-trained, most mature, most gifted and most progressive class, that of the students, is at present also the most oppressed. It is deprived not only of human rights, but even of adult status.

The students represent the majority of the thinking class, the non-conformist intellectuals of all ages and all professions.

Two American writers, J. and M. Rowntree, believe that the 'new proletariat' in the world of today consists of the masses of the backward countries and the young of the United States: 'The American economy is increasingly dominated by two industries that are large, public and rapidly growing – defence and education . . . The essential exploited class for the perpetuation of the existing economic system is now the young. The youth occupy the critical workplaces: they man the war-machine and the idea-factories.'[13]

Those observers who see only the political side and analyse it in the terminology of the past miss large areas of what is new among youth. By using a sufficiently vague language, one comes nearer to understanding the essence of the intellectual-revolutionary aspects of the new developments. A. Touraine, Professor of Sociology at Nanterre University, belongs to this category. Two months before the great May Revolt in France he wrote:

Today it is impossible to avoid any longer posing this question: are the student movements, from Berlin to Nanterre, from Prague to Trent, the avant-garde signs of a new confrontation of society in both theory and practice, revealing new forms of domination and new social conflicts . . .? Does not the university now occupy the same place in society as the great capitalist businesses once did, and does not the student movement have the same significance as the workers' movement of the previous era?[14]

Whatever the student movement's significance, Professor Touraine was right: French students did reveal new forms of social conflict – and much more. The unknown student who on 13 May wrote the Sorbonne poster, 'We are inventing a new and original world', should perhaps have written : 'We are about to become a new and original world'.

It is not a question of a new 'class' taking over from another one. It is, of course, true that after the great *embourgeoisement* of the workers, they ceased to be a dynamic revolutionary class. The students in many countries were already, and no doubt will be in the future, the *avant-garde* of the revolution, and at the same time constitute most of the revolutionary army.

But these young people, whether revolutionaries or not, are already very different. One can see and feel that many of them live in a different kind of moral-emotional world. The new youth, whether it takes an active part in the great contracting-out or not, whether it is personally aware or not, is already in the process of transformation.

III

DEFRAUDED REVOLUTIONS

1 *Counter-revolutionary practice*

During the past decade, governments and their official and unofficial opponents were surprisingly uninformed about the contradictions between revolutionary theory and revolutionary practice. Centralized monopolistic bureaucracies operating their military-industrial complexes paid fervent lip service to their respective ideological façades, but in their actual practice they stuck to 'ideology-free' counter-insurgency.

The Special Operations Research Office of the Pentagon launched a sociological research project to help the army 'discharge its responsibilities in the overall counter-insurgency programme of the US government'.* 'Indigenous governments' of Latin-America, before being given help in their 'counter-insurgency operations', were to be thoroughly investigated by US scholars. One of the questions to be answered about indigenous governments was this: 'Was the Government guilty of excessive toleration of alienated, insurgent, or potentially insurgent groups?'

In the very same period, the Soviet government, the Red Army and the KGB carried out their overall counter-insurgency programme in Czechoslovakia. The country was occupied because the government of the USSR fround the Dubcek regime excessively tolerant towards 'alienated' or 'potentially insurgent groups'.

US and Soviet counter-revolutionary practice has its roots in all systems of centralized authoritarian rule. The adherents of the idea and the necessity of centralized authoritarian leadership have

* See section 4 of this chapter.

always insisted on falsifying the history of revolutions. These people, when faced with the spontaneous eruption of collective energies in a revolution, look for the leaders who lead these 'seemingly' unharnessed forces, and for the national and regional headquarters from which the typhoon of the masses is directed. The leaders and national and regional offices are always found, since the establishments and police chiefs of the old regimes are firmly convinced that the wild multitude is essentially loyal to the old regimes and that only a tiny minority of evil conspirators and agitators is leading them astray. On their side, the various groups of professional revolutionaries and would-be leaders pretend that they are or were in charge of the typhoon, that it was they who unleashed the revolution.

Professional politicians whose *métier* is to provide centralized, authoritarian leadership are, without exception, against true revolution. Whether they camouflage their strong anti-revolutionary stand by the mumbo-jumbo of parliamentary or presidential democracy, or by Lenin's dictatorship of the proletariat directed by 'democratic centralism', they regard revolution as an untoward or necessary incident within an otherwise ordered system of centralized rule. The daily or even hourly participation of the people in shaping history is regarded by politicians as an abnormal episode, when political action is taken from its proper place into the street. Centralized bureaucratic regimes cannot admit that revolutions are the living expressions of fundamental social forces, on which the existence, the preservation, and the development of human society depends.

Like volcanoes, the victorious revolutions of the past had an active period during which the destruction of the old order went on and the new revolutionary *status quo* had not yet been established. The first phase was always a spontaneous eruption of a considerable part of the population. Power is in the hands of the revolutionary multitude, this multitude 'votes' all the time with spontaneous mass action. The eruption might or might not produce momentary leaders or mouthpieces, but the sum total of the people in revolt is not a mass which has no will and no initiative without a leader. The temporary mouthpieces or momentary leaders are replaced if and when they cannot keep up with the goals and the speed of the eruption. In this most vital phase, revolution is the boiling over of the masses.

In many languages from English and French to Russian and

Spanish the word 'revolution' is based on the astronomical term used for a revolving movement to some pre-established point and, by implication, swinging back into the pre-ordained position. In England, the Glorious Revolution of 1688 referred to the restoration of the monarchy. In Hungarian, revolution is *forradalom,* which means, literally, a 'boiling over' of the masses.

Only when this first and main phase of the revolution is over do the professional politicians emerge and take over power from the masses. In the second phase, the revolution is usually defrauded by a few simple tricks. The masses are conned into handing over power to the self-appointed leaders who have almost always convinced them that, in order to consolidate the achievement of the revolution, the multitude must be disciplined and must help in the creation of the revolutionary state ('your state', 'the state machine of the people'). When this new state apparatus – the guardian of the new *status quo* – is complete, the state has only one enemy: the continuation of the revolutionary process. By this time the revolution is just like an extinct volcano. Revolution is replaced by counter-revolution.

The true history of the Russian Revolution demonstrates this process excellently.

In the recent past, conformist, law-abiding citizens approved only of those extinct revolutions that were part of the historical heritage of their own political system. These revolutions were defined as 'great upheavals in the cause of freedom' or as 'major political and social upheavals of mankind which can be looked upon as turning points in human progress'.

In this sense, the gradual change of the political system is not regarded by conformists as inimical to the cause of freedom or to human progress. In principle, no one is opposed to reforms which are gradual, legal, within-the-system changes. Only radical reforms or basic reforms are feared, because they come too near to changing the entire system. The two other main types of within-the-system change, *coups d'état* and rebellions, though they, too, aim only to improve the system or to restore it to its original ideal state, are suspect because of their extra-legal or unconstitutional methods. In current usage, the 'organizers' of *coups* or rebellions are not enemies of the existing system: they want only to replace a corrupt government with a just one, a usurper with a legitimate ruler, a tyrant with a constitutional government, a Stalinist first secretary with an anti-Stalinist party leader.

The chronicle of the period 1955–70 will show that all the revolutions of the past, whether extinct or active, still serve as models for some groups, movement or organizations. Theories of revolution, whether right or wrong, can and do inspire and guide individuals and groups. In Budapest in 1956, boys and girls faced tanks guided by the ideology and emotions of 1848. The Soviet and American theory of revolution, though entirely obsolete, is still a potent force for provoking revolts.

2 *Monopoly communism*

During the last fifteen years, it occurred several times that the USSR and the USA governments created revolutionary situations in a place and at a time when their politico-social systems were in no real danger, and people did not want to secede from their camp. Up to the first part of 1970, there were no signs that the government and Establishment of the USA and USSR were able to liberate themselves from the obsolete theory that guided their actions. These actions turn reformers and rebels, who want to improve the established order, into revolutionaries, who want to destroy it.

The theory of revolution on which the governments of the USA and the Soviet Union base their policies has been obsolete for the last two hundred years. The belief that a handful of conspirators or agitators can stir up great mass movements has never gone unchallenged, though there have always been people who likened it to the belief that the unruly movement of tree tops stirs up the wind.

The period 1955–70 constantly showed that the American, the Soviet, the Gaullist and other governments were guided by a superstition that was described by Karl Marx more than a century ago as obsolete:

The times of that superstition which attributed revolutions to the ill-will of a few agitators have long passed away. Every one knows nowadays that, wherever there is a revolutionary convulsion, there must be some social want in the background which is prevented by outworked institutions from satisfying itself... Every attempt at forcible repression will only bring it forth stronger and stronger until it bursts its fetters.[1]

According to the still prevalent myth, the Russian Revolution of

56

1917 was the outcome of decades of ideological-conspiratorial preparatory work, done by Lenin and his small group of professional revolutionaries. In fact, from February to October 1917 the great eruption of the Petrograd and other Russian multitudes was contrary in content and in aim to the entire theory and practice of revolution as evolved by Lenin between 1902 and 1917. Lenin was from the outset, as he said himself, a 'principled enemy' of rule by soviets, that is, by permanently sitting workers', peasants', soldiers' and other councils. During the Russian Revolution in 1905, which was just as spontaneous (and just as unforeseen by Lenin) as the 1917 one, the revolutionaries established soviets and demanded that the workers and peasants should have control. Lenin attacked these 'anarchistic tendencies' as symptoms of 'infantile disorder'.[2]

Lenin made it perfectly clear that the working class, and even members of the revolutionary vanguard, the party, were unable to recognize and to pursue their own, long-term interests. When left to their own devices and led by their own instincts, the workers are utterly incapable of developing 'true socialist consciousness' or any conception of their historic mission as revealed by Marx and Engels. All this 'can only be brought to the workers from the *outside* . . . The teachings of socialism have grown out of the philosophical, historical, economic theories which were worked out by the educated representatives of the possessing classes.'[3]

According to Lenin, these representatives, recognizing the universal validity of the teachings of Marxist scientific socialism, renounce their own classes and embrace the cause of the working class. The theory of scientific socialism brought into the revolutionary proletarian movement from the outside, is the pre-condition of its success. Otherwise, the movement must certainly fail, because 'alone, by their own forces, the working class is capable of developing' only 'a pure and simple trade-union consciousness'. This '*spontaneous* development of the workers leads precisely to . . . the ideological enslavement of the workers to the bourgeoisie'. To avoid this, the working class and its party must be led by the élite of professional revolutionary intellectuals, these self-appointed (or rather, Lenin-appointed) guardians of the movement. This classless élite must 'dictate to all classes', they must 'dictate a positive programme of action'.[4]

In his two important programmatic works of 1902 – *What To Do* and *Where To Begin?* – Lenin developed the pattern of his authoritarian power machine. He split the revolutionary movement in 1903 in order to have his very own power apparatus. He made it quite clear that the trade unions must be subordinate parts of his machine. This pattern was vehemently denounced by such figures as Trotsky, Rosa Luxemburg and Lenin's former mentor, C. V. Plekhanov. They all denounced Lenin's striving to become the sole dictator of the revolutionary movement, because this theory of the dictatorship of his party leadership over the party and over the working class meant just that. Plekhanov wrote in 1904: 'In the view of Lenin we see *not Marxism* but·... a new edition of the *theory of the hero and the crowd* ... Since he declares himself to be the only active element in history, he considers the masses as only ... strong but obedient tools.'[5]

Lenin was against the idea of the soviets because these were set up by the spontaneous action of the masses. Spontaneous revolution and the masses of people as active elements in history were repugnant to him. During the 1917 revolution he was often furious that the multitude was not obeying the commands of his party, the 'vanguard of the revolution'. His party machine was not an organ of revolution, but an organ for the direction and suppression of revolution.

When Lenin worked out his party system at the beginning of the twentieth century, he cloaked it under the name of 'democratic centralism'. His proposed party constitution was attacked by many of his leading comrades. Commenting in 1904 on the 'pitiless centralism' proposed by Lenin, Rosa Luxemburg attacked:

. . . the blind subordination, in the smallest detail, of all party organs to the party centre, which *alone thinks, guides and decides for all.* . . . Nothing will more surely enslave a young labour movement to an intellectual élite hungry for power than this bureaucratic straitjacket, which will immobilise the movement and turn it *into an automaton manipulated by a Central Committee.*[6]

From 1917 Lenin himself (and from 1924 Stalin) was guided by the following theses formulated by Lenin:

The scientific concept, dictatorship, means neither more nor less than unlimited power resting directly on force, not limited by anything, not restrained by any laws or any absolute rules. *Nothing else but that.* . . . Soviet Socialist democratism does not in any way contradict one-man management *and dictatorship.* . . . *The will of the class is sometimes given effect by a dictator,* who sometimes does more alone and is often more necessary.[7]

Democracy is a state which recognises the subordination of the minority to the majority, i.e. *an organization for the systematic use of violence* by one class against the other, by one section of the population against the other.[8]

Leninism was in this respect the systematic use of violence by the dictator against the whole population, the party members and leadership included. The party apparatus was to become an automaton manipulated by the dictator.

From February until October 1917 the revolutionary movement of the Russian masses refused to be manipulated by Lenin and his Central Committee. The revolution did not follow Lenin's revolutionary programme; its ideology was permeated by the ideas and demands of Mensheviks, Essers, Left-Essers, Anarcho-Syndicalists and others. The establishment of soviets was an anarchist goal. Lenin himself astonished his party when, for tactical reasons, in order to suborn the revolutionary masses, he paid temporary lip service to the demand: 'All Power to the Soviets'.

During the summer of 1917 Lenin and the Bolshevik party were repulsed and alarmed by the militancy of the masses, and they often felt compromised by the violence of the revolution. Writing in 1918, Rosa Luxemburg saw in the virulent period of the 1917 revolution the 'expression of the real will of the popular masses. Then the leadership of the Russian revolution *leapt up to balance on their shoulders,* and once more appointed itself the all-powerful director of history, this time in the person of His Highness the Central Committee. . . .'[9]

After the victory of the October Revolution, Lenin consolidated the revolutionary achievements by taking away all power from the soviets and by transforming them so that they had merely ceremonial camouflage functions in the state–municipal apparatus, directed by the party centre. The masses, as usual, realized too late that they were being defrauded of the achievements of *their* revolution.

According to Lenin, revolutions are, as a rule, impossible without a revolutionary situation. This situation is based on three main factors: (a) A crisis inside the ruling class and its political apparatus; the rulers are tired of power and of struggle; they are decadent and convinced of the inevitability of their downfall;

59

(b) An economic crisis, a war or a famine make the people desperate; (c) People are no longer resigned to their misery; they are ready to fight. Given these objective pre-conditions, the outbreak of the revolution is impossible without the 'subjective revolutionary situation', that is, the revolutionary activity of individuals, groups or political parties. According to Lenin, in an objective revolutionary situation a small group of activists can spark off a revolution with their proclamations or rebellious actions.

Quite apart from the fact that Lenin demonstrably overestimated the role of the revolutionary vanguard, he erroneously claimed that there cannot be a revolutionary movement without a precise revolutionary theory. Lenin regarded the 1917 October Revolution as very much of his own making, yet it was not his theory that inspired the revolutionary movement, but the Russian past, the idea of the village *mir* (or soviets), the preachings and ideas of Narodnyiks, Essers, anarchists and many others. The true ideology of a revolution is evolved only during the revolution itself.

Lenin, Trotsky and their entourage could not understand the essence of the revolution they witnessed and pretended to lead because they were unable to admit that it was spontaneous, as are all true revolutions. Contrary to Lenin's thesis that the masses cannot develop a true revolutionary consciousness by themselves, in fact most revolutions show that the leaders (the later usurpers of revolutionary power) were unable to rise to the level of the revolutionary consciousness of the masses.

Both the professional revolutionaries and the authorities opposed to them overestimate the role of the 'organizers' and 'agitators' in the real, virulent phases of revolutions. Conspirators and agitators cannot create revolutionary situations, nor can they determine the timing of the actual outbreak. The people who are most often surprised by the outbreak of a revolution are the professional revolutionaries on the one hand, and the authorities on the other. The authorities and their police agents try to prevent revolutions by catching conspirators and agitators – preferably sinister foreigners – instead of opening their eyes to revolutionary situations. Given these situations, anything can detonate a revolutionary explosion. Revolutions have been sparked off by the performance of an opera (by Daniel Auber in Brussels in 1830); a student dropping his cane into the orchestra pit from the balcony (in Munich in 1948); the punishment of a group of merchants by bastinado (in Tehran in 1905); or a campus brawl about a rule forbidding boys and girls to visit each other's bedrooms (in Nanterre in 1968).

Lenin, the professional revolutionary *par excellence,* was surprised by the outbreak of the 1905 revolution and the February and October revolutions in 1917. He and the other Bolshevik leaders struggled to keep up with the boiling-over of the masses and, instead of directing the revolutionary waves, they were swept along by them.

The Leninist theory of the revolutionary vanguard as the force leading the popular movement during the revolution is nothing but wishful thinking. After the virulent mass upheaval had destroyed the power apparatus of the old order, after the consolidation of the new *status quo* had begun, only then did the 'vanguard' take over power and start to rule.

3   *The Third Revolution*

'At Kronstadt the foundation stone has been laid of the Third Revolution. This will break the final chains which still bind the working masses and will open up new paths of socialist creation.'[10]

Kronstadt Izvestiya, 1921

The Red Terror officially launched by Lenin in 1918 was originally directed only against class enemies. At first, the Cheka had left workers, peasants and ordinary party members alone. Barely a year passed, and the iron fist of the party smote down all 'enemies of the revolution', that is, all enemies of the Leninist dictatorship. Lenin annihilated all political parties, the Communist Party included, and transformed the latter into the instrument of dictatorship.

The proletariat turned against the Bolshevik rulers. The village councils and most other soviets at all levels were highly critical of the government or openly hostile to it. For the 'ultimate good of the people', Lenin and his associates turned the terror machine against the people. Democratic socialism and rule by council was liquidated by making the soviets at all levels simply instruments for carrying out central orders. Critical or recalcitrant members of the soviets were liquidated by the Cheka.

By 1920 it became painfully obvious to everyone that the

'dictatorship of the prolateriat' was the dictatorship of Lenin's party centre over the proletariat. The Russian masses realized that they were again subjects of a centralized state, that instead of being masters of their own destiny in the democratic socialist order of the soviets, they were under the iron rule of monopoly communism.

Lenin claimed for the small Political Bureau of his party eternal monopoly of representing the cause of historical progress; absolute monopoly of representing the true interests of the working class, and, ultimately, of representing all humanity.

The Leninist creed placed the possessor (or possessors) of dictatorial power beyond any kind of democratic control or criticism. From the tactical slogan of 'all power to the soviets', Lenin passed over to the original aim: all power to the Politbureau. The dictatorial party–state machine controlled by the Politbureau had no built-in self-regulatory or self-correcting devices. Even the 'vanguard of the working-class', the Communist Party, was not to be trusted with the right to elect its officers and superior organs freely. Democracy and freedom of speech were effectively banned from the party as a whole, from its Central Committee, and at times even from the Politbureau.

In principle the Marxist–Leninist tenets were beyond and outside the realm of reason. The party chief or chiefs had an absolute monopoly in interpreting Marxism–Leninism, this 'science of all sciences'. The masses were supposed to take it for granted that progress from prehistoric primitive communism to slave-owning societies, then to feudalism, capitalism, socialism, to the lower and then the higher forms of communism at the end was not merely a hypothesis but the discovery of the 'objective historical process'. Instead of an open society in a democratic socialist regime, a closed society under dictatorship can serve as the only progressive force in history. History itself is closed and entirely determined by the inevitable progress to the inevitable future.

Based on the inevitable victory of communism as the highest stage of all social forms possible for mankind, this Leninist creed had a truly three-dimensional quality. For the true believer, not only the past and present were concretely given, but also all the inevitably approaching stages of the future.

The task of the leaders of all progressive forces is simple: they have to find the best day-to-day tactics and the long-term strategy for bringing about the next stage of the inevitable future as fast

revolutions. In the twentieth century, the American establishment began to turn not only against wars of independence and liberal revolutions but even against liberal reforms. By the early nineteen-sixties, one of the Supreme Court Judges of the United States, William O. Douglas, had occasion to write:

One reading American history and the stirring sentences of our Declaration of Independence would suppose that we would be on the side of the people and against the colonial rulers. The contrary has been true. The Dean Achesons who staffed our State Department stood firmly against Indonesian independence for five long years. The Henry Cabot Lodges who manned the United Nations stood resolutely against independence for Morocco or Algeria or Vietnam....

When Guatemala showed signs of revolt, we helped to install a Fascist regime. When Mossadegh in Persia started basic reforms we became alarmed. That man, whom I am proud to call my friend, was a democrat in the La Follette-Norris sense of the term. We united with the British to destroy him; we succeeded; and ever since our name has not been an honoured one on the Middle East.[15]

Hannah Arendt wrote in 1963: 'Fear of revolution has been the hidden *leitmotiv* of postwar American foreign policy in its desperate attempts at stabilisation of the *status quo,* with the result that American power and prestige were used and misused to support obsolete and corrupt political regimes that long since had become objects of hatred and contempt.'[16]

The extreme anti-revolutionary bias of the Washington policymakers, and, indeed, of the entire American establishment, has been pointed out and analysed by a great many American and foreign observers. How extreme and primitive this bias is was revealed in the greatest documentary detail by the Project Camelot scandal in 1965. In the second half of 1964, the United States army and the Department of Defense decided to launch the greatest ever 'strategic social science' research project to find out how to prevent revolutions. They decided to spend if necessary about fifty million dollars on this 'great interdisciplinary venture'. As a first step, in December 1964, the American University and its parent body, the US Army's Special Operations Research Office (SORO),* invited a large number of American and foreign scientists to take part in Project Camelot, a three- to

* On the stationery 'SORO' was set in larger type than 'American University'.

67

four-year 'feasibility study', mainly concerned with 'counter-insurgency prophylaxis'.

According to project descriptions mailed to American and foreign scholars, the initial feasibility study was

... conceived as a three- to four-year effort to be funded at around one and one-half million dollars annually. It is supported by the Army and the Department of Defense, and will be conducted with the cooperation of other agencies of the government. Camelot is an unclassified, open project the results of which will be made available through normal scholarly channels.

The project description emphasized that a major reason for launching Project Camelot

... is the recognition at the highest levels of the defense establishment of the fact that relatively little is known, with a high degree of surety, about the social processes which must be understood in order to *deal effectively with problems of insurgency*. Within the Army there is especially ready acceptance of the need to improve the general understanding of the processes of social change if the Army is to discharge its responsibilities *in the over-all counter-insurgency program of the US Government*.[17]

Next day, SORO sent out a working paper containing details of the project:

If the U.S. Army is to perform effectively its part in the U.S. mission of counterinsurgency it must be recognised that *insurgency represents a breakdown of social order* and that the social processes involved must be understood. Conversely, the processes which produce a stable society must be also understood.

... Responsibility for conducting counterinsurgency operations must rest with the indigenous government. Carefully applied assistance and advice by U.S. governmental agencies can, however, materially influence the outcome.... The programs recommended to the indigenous government may include advice on

(1) the use of military force,
(2) police activities,
(3) educational programs,
(4) social improvement programs, etc.

The U.S. military must be prepared to participate in developing these plans and programs.

... It is by no means essential that all countries studied be among those listed as critical by the special precedence groups for counter-insurgency. However, early and highly probable utility of the findings of our project would require choice of countries of current and lasting concern for U.S. interests.

Countries recommended:

A. For Comparative Historical Studies:

In Latin America: Argentine, Bolivia, Brazil, Colombia, Cuba, Dominican Republic, El Salvador, Guatemala, Mexico, Paraguay, Peru, Venezuela.

In Middle East: Egypt, Iran, Turkey.

In Far East: Korea, Indonesia, Malaysia, Thailand.

Other countries: France, Greece, Nigeria.

B. For Survey Research and Other Field Studies:

Bolivia, Colombia, Ecuador, Paraguay, Peru, Venezuela, Iran, Thailand.[18]

The 'indigenous governments' of the countries listed above, before being given help in their 'counterinsurgency operations', were to be thoroughly investigated by Camelot scholars. The programme for comparative historical studies, issued by SORO on 1 April 1965, asked the investigators to probe the strength of 'insurgent parties', to give approximate numbers of 'forces available for counterinsurgency'; to say whether the regime fomented foreign wars or 'black *coups*' to suppress internal unrest, and so on. And to answer the already quoted question about indigenous governments: 'Was the Government guilty of excessive toleration of alienated, insurgent, or potentially insurgent groups?'

Although Chile was not singled out, several Chilean members of the Latin American Faculty of Social Science, and Dr Johan Galtung, a Norwegian professor at that time associated with the University of Chile, received invitations to take part in this project. Dr Galtung and his Chilean colleagues exposed the project as 'scientific colonialism'. Soon the Chilean Senate and the left-wing Chilean press denounced it as 'spying under the auspices of sociological research', and as 'barely camouflaged imperialist intervention'. In May 1965, United States troops fulfilled their counter-insurgency task by occupying Santo Domingo in the Dominican Republic. By that time, the Camelot documents were quite well known in Latin America and the unity between the newly revealed US anti-revolutionary ideology and actual practice helped to create a unique scandal. The US Ambassador to Chile, Ralph A. Dungan, who was not informed about Project Camelot, sent a protest to Washington and asked for an unconditional cancellation of Project Camelot's Chilean activities. In

Chile, meanwhile, all newspapers agreed that Project Camelot was 'intended to investigate the military and political situation in Chile and to determine the possibility of an anti-democratic *coup*.'

The Senate Foreign Affairs Committee under Senator Fulbright conducted private hearings to ascertain the damage done by 'sociological snoopers'. In the end, President Johnson cancelled the whole project, not because of its obsolete, immoral and dangerous ideological basis, but because of the scandal it caused, President Johnson's decision emphasized that 'no Government sponsorship of foreign area research should be undertaken which in the judgement of the Secretary of State would adversely affect United States foreign relations'. Similar research projects* were not cancelled by the President.

Writing in the *St Louis Post-Dispatch,* Senator Fulbright outlined the American establishment's behaviour and attitudes in 'An Age of Revolution':

University campuses are inhabited by proliferating institutes and centers with awe-inspiring names that use vast government contract funds to produce ponderous studies of 'insurgency' and 'counter-insurgency' — studies which, behind their opaque language, look very much like efforts to develop *scientific techniques for the anticipation and prevention of revolutions, without regard for the possibility that some revolutions may be justified or even desirable.*

Observers of the American sociological scene were not particularly surprised by the Camelot revelations. It is not only the US army's Camelot documents that describe movements for radical change as a disease, and a society 'so infected' as 'sick'. Adherents of 'value-free' sociology and psychology in the US were and still are strangely addicted to the established order and its stability. They regarded and regard agitation for within-the-system change and protest marches organized by reform movements as signs of abnormality, or symptoms of a social illness. In the Camelot document, studies of Paraguay are recommended 'because trends in this situation [General Stroessner's murderous and most stable dictatorship] may also render it unique when analysed in terms

* *Project Revolt* (French Canada) and *Project Simpatico* (rural politics in Colombia), sponsored by the Defense Department; *Project Michelson* (China, USSR), sponsored by the Navy Department; *Socio-political precursors to insurgency* (study of insurgency and causes related to it to determine the role the Navy plays). Research conducted by Pennsylvania State College, etc.

of the transition from dictatorship to political stability'. Adherents of value-free sociology outside the Department of Defense wrote in similar vein.

The American Anthropological Association discussed Project Camelot at its November 1965 meeting at Denver, Colorado. Professor Marshall Sahlins of the University of Michigan pointed out that:

... revolutionary movements are described in Camelot documents as 'antisystem activities', indications of 'severe disintegration', varieties of 'destabilising processes', threats to 'legitimate controls of means of coercion within the society', facilitated by 'administrative errors'.... Here was a program for diagnosing social illness, a study of *'epidemiology'*, called just that by a senior researcher. Another consistently refers to revolutionary movements as 'social pathology'. ... *A third conceives the growth of demands for change as 'contagion'*.... Did the government couple limited and managed reforms with repressive measures to prevent contagion and spread of social unrest? Of course, waiting on call is the doctor, the U.S. Army.... The indicated treatment is *insurgency prophylaxis*.... If Camelot had been given a more appropriate title, it might have been: 'The Established Order: Do Not Fold, Spindle or Mutilate.'[19]

In his introductory essay to *The Rise and Fall of Project Camelot,* Professor I. L. Horovitz wrote in 1967:

... the end of Project Camelot does not entail the end of the Special Operations Research Office nor does it imply an end to research designs that are similar in character to Project Camelot. In fact, the termination of the contract does not even imply an intellectual change of heart on the part of the originating sponsors or key figures of the project.[20]

It should be unnecessary to emphasize that their identical attitude to revolutions and radical changes does not make the US and Soviet establishments equivalent. Despite its great many short-comings, America is still an open society and, therefore, infinitely preferable to the total bureaucratic despotism of Soviet-type closed societies.

The techniques for the preservation of a structure of freedom that have been evolved since the American and French revolutions of the eighteenth century – separation of powers, free elections in a multi-party system, human rights, particularly freedom of the press and public opinion, judiciary independence and a constitutional state – show many signs of breaking down. Free elections and the multi-party system do not guarantee people real influence in shaping their destiny. Even the theoretical right of electing representatives once in four or five years was and is being eroded. But as far as the rest of these techniques are concerned, their importance cannot be overestimated. Freedom of thought, of the press, public opinion, the other basic human rights, together with national independence, are rights in defence of which or for the attainment of which rebellions and revolutions occurred and still occur. The revolutionary ferment in the Soviet world does not aim at a restoration of capitalism or for joining the imperialist camp. The struggle is for these basic human rights in an open society. The struggle is on for the victory of the Third Revolution.

4   Catastrophe or radical change

'We have the physical means of destroying civilisation and the human race, but we lack the moral fibre to oppose such destruction. Nations continue to brandish their intercontinental missiles, and it may be that, from escalation to escalation, they choose to wipe out humanity rather than lose face. *One of the hardest – almost impossible – tasks facing your generation is to put an end to these stupid and childish games.... Your victory over rhetoric will determine the survival or death of the human race.'*

André Maurois, at the age of eighty-two[21]

The identification of revolution and radical change with social pathology was and still is one of the principles on which US and Soviet internal and international policies are based.

In the USA and the West in general, this identification is given sociological respectability by the functionalist creed of 'order, stability and pattern-maintenance'; that is, the unchanged preservation of the structure, the system and the ideology of a given regime. In the Soviet orbit, this identification gained renewed Marxist-Leninist backing due to developments in Czechoslovakia. In September 1968, Soviet ideologists discovered a new 'phenomenon of history', which they identified as 'peaceful counter-revolution'. Its proponents 'disguise their aims by claiming that their aim is merely to improve socialism, not to oppose it'. On 11 September 1968, *Pravda* tried to explain why Czechoslovakia continued to resent the uninvited presence of the Warsaw Pact forces and why pro-Soviet Communist Parties throughout the world failed to understand the need for such interference in another communist country's internal affairs.

According to *Pravda,* the 'anti-socialist forces' in Czechoslovakia pretended to be for 'good' socialism and against 'bad' socialism. This tactic lulled the vigilance of the working people who did not realize that criticism of conservative bureaucrats ('bureaucratic despotism') in the state and party apparatus, together with calls for 'healthier' economy and the 'normalization of relations with socialist countries' really 'cloaked the desire to dismember the Communist Party and remove it from the leadership of society'.

Only in its first stages, when demands are made for democratizing and improving the system, is this 'new form of counterrevolution' peaceful, *Pravda* asserted. It would inevitably be followed by a more violent one, involving the smashing of the communist state apparatus. *Pravda* has, in fact, served notice that the Kremlin leaders alone have the right to act as arbiters of what constitutes 'true' communism and to step in when they think fit to prevent the development of any prototype other than their own.

The principle of different roads to socialism endorsed with such jubilation at the Soviet Party Congress in 1956 had been abandoned, not only in practice, but also in theory. Leninist monopoly communism was resurrected in its full rigidity. The *Pravda* article did not conceal from Soviet readers that the overwhelming majority of the more important Communist Parties throughout the world condemned the Soviet action in Czechoslovakia.

According to some students of the Soviet scene, the Russians would not have publicized this theory and that of the limited sovereignty of communist countries had they been able to sustain their original excuse for intervention in Czechoslovakia – that they were invited by certain Czechoslovak leaders. Only when this widely disseminated lie was fully exposed by subsequent events did *Pravda* assert the principle of limited sovereignty.

This is not a return to Stalinism but scrupulous adherence to the Lenin line. Lenin said in February 1918: 'No Marxist, without renouncing the principles of Marxism and socialism generally, can deny that *the interests of Socialism are higher than the interests of the right of nations to self-determination. . . .*'[22]

'The 'interests of socialism' are higher than the interests of the human rights of individuals or the rights of nations to self-determination. And by this definition, the momentary rulers of the Kremlin have the monopoly to determine what the interests of socialism happen to be. Change, improvement, adaptation to new conditions – any sort of development – can originate only in their decisions. Any type of within-the-system change that is not approved by them is 'peaceful counter-revolution' and must be severely suppressed.

As the Soviet Union's leaders would not permit different roads to socialism, despite the advice and demand of much of the socialist camp, so the American establishment tends to view with hostility all different roads to 'Americanism'. Harvey Wheeler wrote in 1961: 'America must realize that there may be "more than one revolutionary path" to Americanism. And she must realize that in the twentieth century her traditional form of revolution is not one of them.'[23]

The credo that sees in demands for radical reform and revolutionary movements dangerous social diseases, however outdated and ill-informed, is very powerful whenever it guides the overt and clandestine actions of the two main powers of the world.

Change, even revolutionary change, radical reform to adapt societies and the entire international community to changed conditions, are obviously necessary for the simple physical survival of mankind and for the complex survival of truly human qualities.

The materialist values of the capitalist and communist consumer societies do not create a moral climate in which the pressing questions of human survival can be adequately discussed, let alone solved. Living in the shadow of a possible nuclear explosion, approaching the almost inevitable population explosion, facing all those material and spiritual developments that dehumanize the life of human beings, those who have the longest future demand change. Since the middle of this century, the world has been shaken by a long series of risings and revolutions, in which the desperate energies of mass demands, mass hopes, mass fears and hatred have erupted. Much of these eruptions are prompted by the conviction that only by inventing a new world with new customs and new institutions can the human race secure its survival.* The two super-powers, however, are guided by a creed that abhors change, even within-the-system change. As long as this creed prevails radical change can only be the outcome of catastrophe.

The basic attitude behind various functionalist or 'value-free' schools of sociology and social-psychology is as old as humanity. This attitude is determined by a diffuse fear of change and the belief that anyone who wants change must be abnormal. Referring to the people of ancient Rome in the sixth century BC, F. R. Corwell wrote:

> In their deep attachment to the way of their ancestors, which they venerated as the *mos maiorum,* the custom of the great majority, *that is of the dead of the previous generations,* the Romans had a deep suspicion of anyone wanting to introduce change. 'New things', *res novae,* was indeed their expression for 'revolution' in politics; the inference being clear that new things were bad and alarming.[24]

Because of this attitude, and this creed of order, stability and pattern-maintenance, throughout most of human history radical change has been the child of catastrophe. The 'faceless revolution' of the young is directed against this creed. In a sense, their revolution aims to awaken humanity from this nightmare of history. The nightmare will go on as long as radical change can only be the outcome of catastrophe.

The rigidity of the super-powers and the rigidity of the authorities, together with the increasing hatred of the adult world manifested towards the young, have produced in the youth camp various extremist trends, one of which has come to regard all human history as a catastrophic 'wrong turning'. It is a symptom of the apocalyptic tensions of the age that some mentally alert and deeply committed young men and women despise any preoccupation with the inhuman past (according to them, it has been inhuman until today!). All human history – they feel – can offer only corruption to the young. People with a knowledge of history are ready to compromise with vast amounts of dishonesty and self-destructing stupidity, whereas the young who know only the present refuse to accept treachery, dishonesty and self-

* Some sociological schools describe these as 'value-oriented movements' directed towards a 'basic reconstruction of society'. According to this terminology, early Christianity was such a value-oriented movement!

destructive stupidity just because there are historical precedents for all of them.

In 1968, Professor Chomsky had reasons for begging some Columbia students not to be the kind of people who thought that Marx should have burned down the British Museum rather than sit in it to write *Das Kapital*. In an age when many of the old revolutionary movements still act as active or potentially active volcanoes, while there are the many new, still faceless, revolutions, the extremization goes on.

The history of the recent past is basically and ultimately the history of a great many revolutionary waves directed towards the survival of mankind together with all truly human values.

IV

THE 'YOUTH OF TODAY' – WESTERN VERSION

1 *The peace-shocked generation*

During 1955 and 1956, the 'youth-of-today' caused a great deal of exasperation, disgust and even despair in the adult world of the West. According to widely conflicting press reports, speeches by politicians and clergymen, this was a nauseating, or wild, or too quiet, or apathetic generation. Murderous teenage gangs endangered the cities; well-to-do 'rebels without a cause' indulged in pointless violence. Teddy Boys (or *blousons noirs, halbstarke, skinkenknutter* and their girls offended public morality, or took part in frightening rock-'n'-roll mass riots.

The majority of university students were rather quiet in most countries. Sociologists and publicists saw the 1955 student as 'enervated', 'apathetic' and 'a-political'. In West Germany, the youth-of-today was described as the 'sceptical generation', *die skeptische Generation*, with a prevailing 'without me', *ohne mich,* attitude. In France, papers wrote about the *je m'en foutisme* attitude of the passive students. On the whole, university disturbances were exceptional; the word 'student' was not yet associated with political protest or violence, and had no pejorative undertone.

According to the 1955 usage of the word, 'youth' comprised those between fifteen and twenty-one, that is, the seven year-groups born between 1934 and 1940. These year-groups went through the Second World War and its immediate aftermath as children or teenagers. In many countries in Europe and Asia, this meant various traumatic experiences, ranging from sudden separation from parents to air raids, from the spectacle of death to existence in battle areas, and/or under enemy occupation. Millions of children and teenagers found out with horror that they belonged to a 'guilty' people.

As mentioned earlier, the youth-of-today is usually blamed for the behaviour of those year-groups who lived through their youth phase during the previous three or four years, or for the youth of the previous decade or two. The 1955 youth-of-today were fortunate because their 'history of crimes' was not too long. It simply couldn't be.

During wars the normal peacetime tensions within societies are usually weakened, or forcibly suppressed. For obvious reasons, this applies first and foremost to the biologically and sociologically normal tension between the generations. As far as public opinion was concerned, during the last two years of the Second World War youth as a social role or as an identifiable segment of society virtually disappeared.

This was not a psychological fact, but an objective one: in many countries during the war, male and female young people became workers at the age of fifteen or sixteen. The majority of the males over eighteen and a minority of females of the same age were conscripted into the army. During the Second World War there were almost no 'adolescents'. Children, and young people as workers, lived in bombed cities, often sheltering in cellars for long periods. The over-eighteens fought in a war they had not declared.

In the occupied parts of Europe, children and teenagers fought and died in the resistance, or played the role of Jews in the concentration and extermination camps.

The war-time press in Germany, Japan and Italy on the one hand, and that in America, Britain or the Soviet Union on the other, contained almost no complaints about youth. In Britain, the United States and in a few other countries such as Germany, a minority of female children and teenagers disgusted and angered the authorities because they provocatively offered themselves to men in uniform in the cities and in the vicinity of military camps. In London and the other bombed cities of Britain, teenage girls from the industrial suburbs swarmed to pick up men in uniform, preferably Americans. In the United States: '... mere children were found soliciting in the streets; and in 1942 it was proposed that the New York parks be closed to children in the evening, since girls were to be found in them at 4 and 5 a.m. It had already proved necessary to impose a curfew on Boston Common, where remarkable scenes had been reported.'[1]

According to the press reports of those days, these extremely promiscuous teenage girls – some of them between thirteen and fifteen – were responsible for a steep rise in cases of venereal disease in the USA. They were also responsible for helping to keep up the age-old myth that it is always the present generation of young people who, spontaneously, produce a great deal of shocking 'immorality'. These 'immoral girls' in wartime America were in their early or late forties in 1969.

With a few exceptions, the European countries went through the catastrophe of defeat, invasion and occupation by foreign troops. Straight after the war, vast numbers of uprooted children, millions of orphans and young fugitives roamed the countrysides. Between 1945 and 1949 there were about fifteen million people in flight in Germany alone – families fleeing from bombed-out homes, and refugees and deportees from the East, among them more than five million children and adolescents. France, Italy, Austria all had their millions of displaced persons, or unaccompanied or vagrant children and teenagers.

In the great postwar chaos, in half-ruined Europe, gangs of these vagrant children and adolescents mushroomed everywhere. Many of them were in a condition of hopeless illegality, having no personal documents and therefore unable to obtain ration cards for food or permission to settle anywhere. It took years to sort them out. The last postwar International Conference on Child Vagrancy was held in October 1949 in Charleroi. Convened by UNESCO, this conference worked out proposals for normalizing the situation 'during the years to come'.

The children who robbed supply dumps, the expert thieves who stole from moving lorries, the little swindlers and retailers of the black markets, the thirteen-to-sixteen-year-old girls who were exploited by vicious adults as prostitutes were, of course, in the minority during these years of chaos. But the majority, indeed an entire European generation, lost its childhood and adolescence during these troubled times. And those who belong to this generation – who were between twelve and twenty in 1943-7 – are among the parents of the European teenagers of today and tomorrow. They can hardly be blamed by their offspring for having forgotten that they, too, were children once.

79

As soon as everyday life started to become normal and orderly again during the years of reconstruction, the majority of war-shocked children turned into surprisingly well-behaved, law-abiding teenagers. Juvenile delinquency declined. Europe in this period had many troubles, but there were very few problem adolescents. If anything, some adults were worried by their benumbed passivity, by their lack of adolescent frolics and quest for adventure.

For those who were over ten in 1945, the shock of war was followed by a long series of peace shocks. The explosions over Hiroshima and Nagasaki – the beginning of the nuclear age – changed everything. No one knew what the future would bring. Would there be a future at all? There certainly seemed to be very little hope for devastated, half-starved, paralysed Europe. Some fathers returned from prisoner-of-war camps, others did not. Millions were dead. Other fathers and mothers were suspect in the period of war-crime trials, when from Norway to France the victorious countries were arresting and trying the collaborators. Some mothers and elder sisters had their heads shaved as punishment for their affairs with enemy soldiers. Defeat was sheer horror. Victory was a sad shock of disappointment. A French poet wrote in this age the line: 'The icy fingers of victory are knocking on the window-pane.' The world was in a mess. The adults were in a mess. There was little to eat, life was drab and hard. Adolescents looked at adults with unasked questions in their eyes.

In Germany children were informed by the world that theirs was a guilty nation. 'Sentenced to eternal shame for our fathers' crimes,' said a bitter young man later. How can you have hopes, ambitions, beautiful thoughts in a country of criminals and suspects? In a country where so many people committed or suffered outrages? Stories of rape by occupying troops. Stories about half-starved women, who sold themselves for a bar of chocolate. Stories about the women of a country with five million men missing. How true were these? Stories about concentration camps and gas chambers.

The philosopher Theodore Adorno warned German poets: to go on writing lyrical poetry after Auschwitz is barbaric. But then, what is not barbaric? Is it all right to smile, to sleep well, to live, to think about tomorrow?

The first peace year was called in Germany *Nullpunkt,* the zero point. It was the Zero Year. One should start from scratch. A complete break with the past and start anew. But how can you break with the past, if the past is all around you? Any grown-up might be the past.

If in Germany there was an invisible barbed wire of anger and suspicion between many adults and many adolescents, a feeling of unease, a lack of trust separated youth from adults in many other countries. In Italy, after twenty years of Fascist dictatorship and imperial megalomania, the adult world was insecure. All authority was suspect. Teachers, professors, fathers had to account for their behaviour during Mussolini's rule. As Mario Bertone was to sum it up later, youth was sceptical, agnostic, reluctant to take the adult world seriously: 'We have come to distrust many of our teachers and elders whose failures, betrayals, and even cowardice we have seen with shame. We were starved for good examples, but all too often we did not get them.'

In France that part of youth which had hoped to contribute to a new start began to fear in 1946 that their war-weary country would again be dominated by tired old men as before. In the prewar years France was becoming an old nation. The population was decreasing and youth was becoming the smallest age-group. And the tradition-blinkered 'oldsters' seemed to think that this would continue in the future, too. In 1946, liberated France produced 200,000 more babies than in war-time 1945, but the government appeared to believe that this was an exceptional post-war phenomenon and that soon the population would decrease again. That 'grown-up France' really thought so became crystal-clear later. Nothing was done to provide elementary schools until 1946 babies were six years old. Though there were fine speeches about doing everything for future generations, young people knew that they were being neglected in the postwar confusion.

Jean Paulhac's beautiful novel *Nous n'avons pas demandé à vivre* was published several years after these 'peace shocks'. It is the tragic story of a Parisian boy, an 'orphan with parents', a victim of moral squalor. When his prisoner-of-war father, the hero of his childish dreams, returns he brings only bitter disappointment.

The adult world underestimated and still underestimates the effect of the Nuremberg trials and of the message of Nuremberg on children and teenagers. For twenty years, the war-crime trials went on teaching their simple lessons:

Nothing is beyond and above the realm of reason and of common decency, nothing at all.

The individual, with his own conscience, is responsible for being an ardent patriot in a country led by criminals; for being a law-abiding citizen, who upholds the wrong law and the wrong order.

Authorities, laws, supreme commanders must not be blindly obeyed.

Carrying out the orders of higher authorities is no excuse.

The individual, with his own conscience, must decide whether a war is just or unjust, whether a command is criminal or not.

The 'My country right or wrong' slogan is evil and it can lead you to the gallows.

Year after year, these lessons were driven home to those who passed through their late childhood or adolescence between 1946 and 1968.

The Nuremberg trials, with the authority of America, Britain, France and the USSR behind them, with the approval of the United Nations, promulgated the law concerning the responsibility of the individual for his country's policies. Each year, millions of children and teenagers heard or read about death sentences or long prison sentences passed on people who were guilty according to this law.

The Nuremberg message warned against blind conformism and obedience. And exceptional young people, who tried to live up to this message, were imprisoned and persecuted in many countries from Russia to America and France. As a student remarked once: 'The oldies did not even have the guts to say outright: they made a mistake in Nuremberg, or that its law was only relevant to the Second World War.'

Last, but not least, one of the new crimes defined in Nuremberg was genocide, the killing of a whole people. Killing six million Jews was partial genocide. People were convicted for their role in this crime, while the nations that provided the judges were the nuclear powers. They competed with each other in the production of bigger and better A bombs, later H bombs and cobalt bombs, each of which could exterminate ten, twenty or more million people.

'Mature' Americans, Britons, Frenchmen and Russians succeeded in pretending to themselves that the race in nuclear armament was neither criminal nor insane. But some young people were unable to imitate this suicidal mass self-delusion.

Peace, victory, liberation, the promise that never, never again would there be senseless carnage – beneath all the big words lurked disappointment for those young people who cared to think, or yearned for the truth. Others, the majority, perhaps instinctively, tried not to pay any attention to the mess the grown-ups were making.

The political parties fought. The cold war was on. And those who did not ask to be born went on living.

They grew up into a 'silent', 'sceptical', 'sour' or simply 'too careful' generation. In 1954, Gerhard Sanden analysed numerous self-portraits written by young Germans, then aged between twenty and thirty. He found that they were a 'well-hidden' generation of silent individualists:

They distrust every mass-movement. They obviously hate and despise brute force but they won't counter it in open battles, they prefer to deal with it, so to speak, in partisan fighting. They are all individual fighters, not an army. They try to hide from any possible sort of authority. They see compulsion in things that we older people would excuse as 'order'. They will seemingly submit to any compulsion and yet, just because they do not show their faces, they are more dangerous opponents of any compulsory order than those who are today between forty and fifty....[2]

In France, Italy and the rest of Europe, as in Germany, a minority of cause addicts, intellectuals and politically active partisans clamoured for the attention of public opinion and in this way helped to hide the majority of this silent generation who went on working and living quietly, trying to be as inconspicuous as possible. Their only ambition was to be left alone, to live as they pleased. In this, there was no great difference between victors and vanquished. The majority was anxious to return to a normal life of obedient conformism, with everyone minding his own business.

While the minority hit the headlines with their political parties and movements, with manifestos and protests, the majority of this war-shocked and peace-shocked generation were bringing up families. They were shaping the future.

This generation of timid neurotics, cautious conformists or

enervated patriots had lost all illusions. They were unable to have faith in anything but material success and immediate gratification of the senses. Their all-pervading insecurity had to be repressed all the time. They had to pretend that the long series of great and small fears was not there. Prudent businessmen and cowardly office workers had to get used to the feeling of the nuclear risk. They feared lung cancer, obesity, depression, *et al.* Most of them lived as *hasardeurs contre-coeur* (unwilling gamblers). There was nothing left to believe, only the message of 'I consume, therefore I am'. It was this generation that voted for the welfare state or worked hard and produced consumer societies with their economic miracles.

There were no human miracles. Their obsession with consumer goods did not produce stable adolescents, whose nervous systems were bursting with health.

2   The birth of the Teddy Boy movement

Britain has the distinction of having given birth to one of the first conspicuously uniformed, and therefore easily identifiable dissident youth movements, that of the Teddy Boys, which originated in the suburbs of London.

These Teddy Boys were dressed in tightly tapered stove-pipe trousers and coat-jackets reaching almost to their knees, with enormous padded shoulders and velvet lapels. The waistcoats were flowery and vividly coloured. As if all this, together with their loud socks and very thick crêpe-soled shoes, were not enough, the teddies wore enormous side-burns and conspicuously bushy hairdos. Dressed thus, these Teddies would have attracted attention anywhere, but they were astonishingly incongruous in the grey and dismal streets of London's working-class suburbs.

Most of this style was not their creation, but that of Saville Row, the 'fashion centre for gentlemen', which wanted to revive the conspicuous elegance of the Edwardian age after the long years of wartime drabness and postwar austerity. The Teddy style, designed for the dandies of upper-class Mayfair and Belgravia, had a very short sway there. Instead, it spread to the working-class suburbs, first of all to the 'wrong side of the river', to the slums and semi-slums south of the Thames. It was first adopted there by young 'spivs' and 'drones' (idlers, black marketeers and other shady but prosperous underworld characters). They were soon imitated by the socially and economically lowest group of unskilled or semi-skilled youth. From 1952 onwards, a growing number of these young people could afford to pay £20 or more for a complete Teddy outfit. Soon there were many Teddy Boy gangs in and around London, and even more young school-leavers who bought themselves the Teddy outfit and hoped to join one of the gangs. To outsiders each group of boys dressed as Teddies gave the impression of being a gang. In fact, many of the groups were only imitating the real gangs, which contained a fair proportion of hooligans and even of professional criminals.

From the outset they were ridiculed and disliked in their own districts. To counter the contempt of their surroundings they sneered at everyone. They were also feared because wherever they went fights were likely to start. They became rough when other teenagers or adults made remarks about their masquerade.

By 1953-4, 'Teddy Boy' became almost synonym for juvenile delinquent. The criminal or semi-criminal gangs figured in the news with their thefts, burglaries and violent robberies. In addition to this, they, and the groups that imitated them, fought each other, attacked non-Teddy Boys and adults who crossed their path. Both types of gang grew addicted to various very nasty sorts of pointless violence. In many poor districts this kind of group violence became a part of ordinary street life after dark. Cafés and youth hostels were attacked, furniture broken up, windows smashed. Whole neighbourhoods were terrorized. There were cases of rape and even of murder. Gangs fought each other with bicycle chains, broken-necked bottles and flick knives.

It seemed that the age-old rebellion of adolescence had some-how merged with the tradition of criminal gangs. It soon became obvious, however, that the criminal origins of Teddy Boy-ism had a lesser effect on the movement than the entirely new type of adolescent rebellion. These rebels had more freedom and more money than the preceding generations of teenagers, yet they felt more insecure and seemed to have more and deeper grievances.

They were called the 'rebellious youth of the welfare state'. In fact, they were mostly the products of squalor amidst growing affluence. They lived in squalid homes, in squalid districts and attended squalid schools. Many of them were typical 'orphans with parents' or came from broken families. The father's author-ity was diminished in the family since the mother and children were also earning good money (and for many other reasons); in the over-crowded schools of the rough districts, most of the original non-criminal Teddies were failures at the secondary schools, which they left as early as possible.

Being barely able to read and write in a society where the educational competition was becoming intense, they rightly felt that they had lost this race at the outset. As unskilled labourers (apprentice road workers, market porters, van boys, for instance), they had no pride in their work and no feeling of security. There was no career ahead of them. Their future seemed to be hopeless. They could not expect respect and they could not assert themselves in society as a whole, so they sought means and areas where they could assert themselves and where they could feel secure. Having a grudge against society, they chose the safety of gangs, where they 'belonged' and found approval. Later, as the Teddy Boy movement spread and changed, the majority of the gangs no longer consisted of semi-literate failures. But this streak persisted, both in this movement and in its successor.

The relationship between Teddies and girls in general also changed with the times. At the beginning, Teddies did not accept girls as members or even as camp followers with equal status. As in slums and semi-slums almost everywhere, the gangs regarded them as objects to be used, or as prey. Many gangs had their own territory and looked upon the girls living there as potentially theirs. At times they invaded other territories to get girls. And although there were many 'easy girls', who went on nightly prowls for boys in districts where they were most likely to be picked up, there was in the boys a general hostility towards girls. Some of them said quite openly: 'Why should the girls get all the attention? Yes, I have my hair permanently waved, and I have nice clothes. I want to look good, too.' The dress and the beauty of the girls was envied and scorned at the same time. Although these boys turned against adult society and contracted out of the world of ordinary citizens, they shared with much of the rest of British society its unhealthy attitude to sex. Still strongly influenced by the remnants of puritanism, these Teddies, like most conformist adults in Britain, were suspicious of beauty and sex. Girls were suspected, despised, hated and desired because of their sexual attraction.

The early Teddies had their young female camp followers, usually girls coming from the submerged tenth of the social pyramid. These girls were also fugitives from dismal homes and families. They, like their kind of boys, were school drop-outs, rather dumb and ignorant. Unlike their male counterparts, however, they did not feel wholly inadequate and insecure. Being conscious of their extreme youth and their power over all males, they did nothing but play their part in the sex chase. To say that they – or the boys – enjoyed this game and its object would be somewhat misleading. Their promiscuity was the saturnalia of the joyless. These girls escaped from hopelessly drab lives into hopelessly squalid sex adventures. In addition, their emotional climate was that of the cynics. Teddies and their girls were not only uniformly dressed, they also had a uniform facial expression. The fashion was to go about with a morose, bored, cynical expression.

Margareta Berger-Hamerschlag taught art in a youth centre in one of the worst London districts during the first years of the original Teddy cult. After class, her students would go on their nightly quest for sex. The girls went out in twos or threes for 'a bit of fun'. Both boys and girls talked about their promiscuity in factual, non-pornographic terms. As a matter of fact, these semi-literate or illiterate teenagers between thirteen and seventeen hated everything faintly smacking of pornography. They shared the hates and prejudices of their most puritanical proletarian elders. Their lady instructor brought to their class one day a small plaster copy of the Venus de Milo. The promiscuous ones became furious with indignation: 'Take away that filth.' They thought of the nude human body, however beautiful, as 'dirt', as revoltingly obscene:

It is plain to see that the main difficulty of these adolescents is their attitude to sex. They regard it as something sinister and shameful, yet irresistible. An attitude like this, pregnant with fear and self-accusation, can in its extremes lead to assault and murder. If you have given way to natural desires and your shame is overpowering, you may try to remove the object of temptation. Take away the fear and disgust and you have people who can enjoy life which they dreaded before....

...Remnants of puritanism linger...a puritanism utterly deprived of religious content. Thus these young people regard soul and flesh as belonging to hostile camps, and do not know the unity of both, and the warmth and beauty of a relationship with the opposite sex.[3]

Adult society was slow to understand these thoroughly

immoral moralists, these utterly inexperienced disillusioned young people who lived in a state of constant fear, hatred and insecurity. Even Margareta Berger-Hamerschlag misjudged these barely articulate semi-humans. Their main difficulty was not their attitude to sex, but to life and society in general. They were the totally innocent victims of society. In the educational slums of the primary schools, they had lost almost every chance in life before they were ten.

Apart from the professional criminals and semi-criminals among them, the *lumpenproletariat* Teddies of 1953-5 were imprisoned in a dimness, a half-aliveness from which they sometimes flared up into violence. Detesting their surroundings, their entire situation, they could not be bothered to think how they could get out of it. Shakespeare called adolescents 'boiled brains'. These early Teddies were singularly 'unboiled' brains. Their brains were not boiling with the impatience, restlessness and dissatisfaction of youth.

Their general ignorance and lethargy dimmed their whole world and all their emotions. They had a minimal interest in the outside world. They were unambitious and scorned the idea of ambition, or indeed any kind of effort. The boys did not learn the skills which any man-about-the-house of previous generations knew. The girls never learnt cooking, sewing or how to run a household on a budget. Having left school early to earn money and so escape from the authority of parents and teachers, they used the full-employment situation to drift in and out of unskilled jobs. If at their place of work someone reprimanded them for their carelessness, they left at once. Being very touchy, they saw insults everywhere. Their general mood was that of an immense yet vague grudge against the world. They disliked everyone who seemed to be happy or smugly satisfied in this world. When in groups, their general apathy gave way to sudden anger and, pointlessly, they would attack ordinary, decently dressed middle-aged passers-by, precisely because they looked so normal and smug.

It was much later that the adult world came to suspect that these 'dim ones' were not the products of the Teddy Boy cult, but of present-day society, which was unable to equip them culturally, emotionally and morally for life in the normal world. In the Teddy gangs (and later in other gangs), these dim boys and girls were only the rank and file. They doubtless figured in many scenes of pointless violence and even in senseless murders, but the greatest danger they represented was not and is not that of juvenile delinquency, but of general inadequacy.

As the Teddy Boy cult spread all over the country, as the 'dim ones' everywhere bought themselves Teddy outfits, even the impact of the original criminal influence disappeared, together with gang loyalty and the professional criminals' code of behaviour. Many gangs became more pointlessly vicious.

The Teddy fashion spread both vertically and horizontally. There were Teddies all over the country and in working-class, lower-middle-class and even in many purely middle-class districts. Instead of drab suburban street corners, the centres of the new groups were cafés, espresso bars and snack bars with juke boxes. By 1955, the original or true Teddy Boys were heavily outnumbered by all sorts of boys and girls dressed in a far less distinct Teddy fashion. Much of the general public regarded every boy and girl as a Teddy if he or she wore clothes in the Italian, French or American style of the day, had an unusual hairdo, or was even sloppily dressed. In addition, every rock-'n'-roll addict was classified as a Teddy.

The American film in which Bill Haley and his Comets exhorted youngsters to 'rock around the clock' was first shown in Britain in 1955. For several months there were teenage riots in cinemas all over the country whenever this film was shown. Screaming deliriously, boys and girls went wild, tore up and threw cinema seats about, attacked attendants, then spilled out into the street in dancing mobs. This film and Bill Haley's concerts had a similar effect everywhere in America and Europe. A large number of young people became rock-'n'-roll addicts instantly.

In two years, there were violent rock-'n'-roll riots in over five hundred cities and towns in three continents. According to some researchers, these were mainly 'consequential' riots. Young people were infected by newspaper and TV reports of similar riots. But the wave of riots had some other, equally important, causes and it was a symptom of an instinctive rebellion against order in the welfare state or in the consumer paradise.

Helmuth Schelsky pointed out 'the sociologically most important root' of this rebellion, when he suggested that the title of a book by Curt Bondy and others, *Juveniles Disturb Order*, should be changed to *Order Disturbs Juveniles*.[4]

According to Schelsky, these 1955-6 riots were explosive

emotional protests against the manipulated 'enjoyments' and the vague general 'conformity-pressure of modern life'.[5]

In America, as in Europe, many authorities declared war on this 'worm wiggle. We will stamp out this dancing with its vile gyrations and boys shoving girls around'. In Britain, a clergyman preached against it : 'Rock-'n'-roll is a revival of devil-dancing, the same sort of thing that is done in black magic rituals. The effect will be to turn young people into devil-worshippers, to stimulate self-expression through sex, to provoke lawlessness and impair nervous stability.*

3   Juvenile delinquency

Beliefs about 'the alarming growth of juvenile criminality' are among the many sources of social infection that afflict the adult world with a pathological hatred of youth. This is why the present chronicle deals briefly with this subject, but also because several forms of juvenile delinquency are types and sub-types of sub-conscious or deliberate revolt.

'Crime today,' as Glanville Williams and others keep on reminding us, 'covers everything from the housewife who shakes her doormat in the street after 8 a.m. . . . to the robber who hits an old woman with a length of iron pipe.' In police and court statistics, 'a criminal is a person convicted for an indictable offence'. Often it is up to the police or the magistrate to decide what is indictable. A young man who held a rolled-up *Times* in his hand was sentenced in Britain to three months in jail (see Chapter VII). In the statistics of crime this young man was numerically just as important a symptom of the depravity of youth as the girl who killed her grandmother to get her money.

In the nineteen-fifties 'juvenile delinquency' grew because of Teddy-type disturbances, because of the increase of violent teenage gangs and because of new ways of categorizing those indicted for an offence. Some offences, which had previously not been categorized according to age, now suddenly were. It was an innovation, for instance, when in some countries offences committed by prostitutes under twenty-one were treated as part of the

* In 1926, the Vicar of St Aidan's in Bristol said from the pulpit: 'Any lover of the beautiful will die rather than be associated with the Charleston! It is neurotic! It is rotten! It stinks! Phew, open the windows!' (Quoted in *The Age of Illusion*, by Ronald Blythe.)

juvenile delinquency statistics. In countries where compulsory military service was abolished, the juvenile delinquency statistics were not adjusted, though army personnel had not previously been treated as 'youth'.

In the atmosphere of the cold war between the generations, youth as a whole was in the dock.

By 1955, most of Western Europe had been rebuilt. Class differences were diminishing and masses of people had more prosperity and security than ever before. But unexpectedly for most people, the adolescents of this period started to go wild. They were the children of the generation moulded by war shocks and peace shocks. Countries which thought themselves immune from the American type of gang violence were shocked to see it in their midst.

The influence of the past alone was no explanation. Some of the adolescent-troubled countries were victorious in the war, others suffered defeat. Again, others like Sweden and Turkey were neutral – yet adolescents there were infected by the very same 'world malaise'. In 1958-60 the Committee of Crime Problems of the Council of Europe conducted a survey into postwar juvenile delinquency in twelve European countries.[*6] With some local variations, the situation was similar in all of them. Most countries reported that the age of onset of puberty and with it the crisis of adolescence occurred earlier than in the past. An increase in violence and/or sex offences was reported in many countries.

A small proportion of young people in many European countries joined juvenile gangs which behaved wildly when under the influence of infectious mass hysteria. The Swedish report, for instance, discussed many cases of spontaneous mass hysteria:

The most flagrant episode took place on New Year's Eve, 1957, when approximately 3,000 individuals, *about two thirds of them under 21 years,* collected in the centre of Stockholm. Policemen, many of them mounted, were bombarded with empty tin cans and other objects. The rioters attempted to frighten horses with firecrackers. They wrenched off car doors, which they forced to stop. . . . The antagonism of the crowd was thus directed at the police, but the underlying cause is difficult to explain.

* Austria, Britain, Belgium, Denmark, France, Germany, Greece, Italy, Netherlands, Norway, Sweden and Turkey.

The *Halbstarken* riots in Hamburg, West Berlin, Düsseldorf, Munich and many other West German cities in 1956-8; the 1959-60 gang fights and *blousons noirs* disturbances all over France from the Riviera to Paris and other cities; 'hooliganism' in Austria, Italy, the Netherlands and elsewhere, had only one thing in common: the young people who figured in these riots, in the vicious gang fights and other disturbances, comprised less than one per cent of all its young people. In spontaneous or 'consequential' riots, the sudden flare-up of mass hysteria infected all sorts of young people who happened to be present. In 'dead-end kid' crimes, and in the vicious gangs, the leadership consisted only rarely of real criminal elements. More often than not the leaders and the rank and file came from the ranks of the 'dim ones', or from the quite talented semi-literate school failures.

Surveys like that conducted by the Council of Europe found that the factors that produced juvenile delinquents and problem teenagers in America and Great Britain had the same effect in Europe:

A relatively high standard of living, together with full employment . . . seems to have an unforeseen effect, particularly on adolescence . . . which is aptly characterised by the French reply as *'une phase de fragilisation'* (a phase of susceptibility).

It is precisely at this stage that youngsters find themselves abruptly translated from the shelter and dependence of school to the very considerable independence which their first wages may bring them. . . . Many youngsters may not be quite ready for so much freedom. Their financial situation puts them on a level with adults, but in many ways they are child-like and erratic. . . .

The situation is difficult and may be exasperating for parents who may react *by abdicating their responsibilities completely or by seeking to impose their will by any means.* In the ensuing atmosphere of hurtful quarrels those who are predisposed to delinquent behaviour may drift into defiant crime.[7]

As in the United States and in Britain, it was found in Europe, too, that in areas where poverty lingers there are social problem groups which are reservoirs of juvenile crime. These areas were and are the regular breeding grounds of gangs. Many reports about gang fights in Paris, Turin, Milan or Hamburg were barely distinguishable from those about New York or San Francisco gangs. Most European countries were shocked by senseless murders, like the one in St-Germain-des-Près in Paris in 1958.

A French businessman was closing the door of his car while his wife and a lady friend went a few steps ahead to look in a shop window. Two *blousons noirs* stepped up to the ladies. The husband went to join them. One of the youths instantly stabbed him to death. The murderer, questioned later by the police, could give no explanation as to why he killed a perfect stranger.

The greatest shock for public opinion in France, Sweden and many other countries was the realization that middle-class adolescents were also susceptible to infectious juvenile delinquency. In the period 1955-68 the European press, like American and British newspapers, discussed often and at great length the problem of 'how to save our morally endangered youth'.

Not all quarters agreed. The often-quoted Council of Europe report of 1960 pointed out that: 'on the whole, youth does well in these difficult times. When the gap between generations is becoming so pronounced and there are so many complaints against youth and so much sharp condemnation of young people, it is well to remember from time to time how many work hard, *behave sensibly* – and fail to make headlines in newspapers'. For some observers this was the most frightening part of the whole report: the majority of young Europeans were allegedly growing up to become as 'sensible as their parents' and grandparents' generation'.

4   *The cold war between the generations begins*

> *Doc:* You kids are making this a lousy world.
> *Kids:* But that's the way we found it!
> *West Side Story*

By 1956-7 the Teddy fashion was gradually disappearing in Britain. This cult left its mark on British society, however, by helping to create a climate of mutual suspicion and hostility between the adult world and a whole generation of young people. Dr Josephine Macalister Brew gave her 'early warning' to Britain in 1957:

Young people have never been under more heavy fire; their manners, spending habits, their love of modern dancing and modern music, have all been the subject of abuse, and *for the first time in the history of this country a section of the community has not been able to dress as it pleases without virulent attacks and suspicion . . .* The relatively few cases of unquestionably violent gang behaviour have been magnified out of all proportion to their incidence.[8]

Suddenly there seemed to be too many and too strange adolescents. The authorities of the fifties ignored population growth to an even greater extent than in the sixties. In the suburbs and city slums there was no physical space for the economically emancipated working youth. The police of the big cities kept on reporting an 'alarming growth of juvenile delinquency', though the proportion of young criminals was still usually under one per cent of all young people. Nevertheless, these alarms played their role in increasing various *Grandes Peurs* and *Grandes Haines*.

Although the existence of adult criminals did not lead to generalizations about the entire world of adults, the criminal fringe of the Teddy Boy sects, teenage gangs, 'zoot suiters', *blousons noirs*, 'bodgies' and their like was discussed as typical in literature, theatre, press, films and on TV and radio.

Popular adult fantasy was titillated by fragmentary reports about the 'dangerous new youth'. There were learned conferences about the spread of juvenile delinquency and about the psychological background of youthful rebels without a cause. The *Halbstarke* in West Germany protested at a national convention against slanders from adult public opinion.

In Stalin's Russia of the period 1945-53, the *Stilyagi* (the Soviet Teddies and other 'anti-state youngsters') were entrusted to the tender care of the MVD. In Persia, during my visit there in 1957, the Ministry of Education and the Tehran Chief of Police launched a 'Hate Elvis' campaign and banned rock-'n'-roll because 'this new canker can very easily destroy the roots of our six-thousand-year-old civilization'.

In the nineteen-fifties many authorities from France to Brazil and from Poland to the Philippines regarded youth as 'villains infesting our times of confusion', to borrow a phrase from Shintaro Ishihara, the then very youthful author of a Japanese best-seller about teenagers.

In fact, the adult world was confused enough in its attitude to the youth-of-today. All young people were somehow blamed for juvenile delinquency, whose widely differing types were, and still are, misunderstood and mistakenly treated by most educational, police and legal authorities. Adult public opinion keeps on being puzzled by the mysterious causes of certain types of delinquency, although we know very well what the causes are and how this type of delinquency can be avoided. It is, for instance, a very well-known fact that large-scale slum clearance and new housing projects in the cities for freshly-arrived low-income families inevitably produce vicious teenage gangs, if certain prophylactic measures are not taken.

Writing about New York, Douglas M. Allen complained in *Newsweek*: 'Sizeable areas of the world's foremost metropolis are splintered into feudal enclaves, run in effect by gangs of ruthless, amoral teenagers. ... They reign by terror, and strangers enter their demesne after nightfall at their own peril.[9]

A few weeks earlier in the same year, Virginia Held wrote an article in the *Reporter* entitled 'What can we do about J.D.?'

There has probably never been a moment in history when adults were not shocked by what they regarded as an unprecedented wave of bad behaviour among children and adolescents. But in our time reports of gang warfare in the streets, teenage muggings, and senseless killings have *turned shock to cold fear*. Juvenile delinquency, particularly in the United States, has come to be considered one of the most urgent social problems of the day, and the epidemic of arrogance and crime seems to be spreading so fast that it obliterates the best efforts society can make to control it — *or even to understand it*.[10]

The Governor of New York State and the Mayor of New York City usually called conferences after some particularly vicious flare-up of gang violence and promised a 'teen gang clean-up'. Senatorial sub-committees, national conferences of educators, criminologists, social scientists and others were discussing this problem all the time. In 1959, for instance, special emergency measures to eradicate juvenile delinquency were announced in Baltimore, Los Angeles, New York, Philadelphia and San Francisco, following the sudden flare-up of teenage crime. There was plenty of juvenile delinquency in other cities, where no special measures were announced in 1959, for the simple reason that this had been done in 1957-8.

In the very same slum or slum-clearance areas, generation after generation of violent 'teen gangsters' kept on terrorizing their neighbourhoods. As with everything else, the United States is oversaturated by books, articles, lectures, conferences and seminars on the teen gangs of the slums. A study of this vast literature, much of it heavily documented, shows the constant characteristics of these gangs:

1. The gang's existence depends on a certain well-defined small area in a slum : a segment of one or two streets, a few courtyards, maybe part of a park or a playground. Within this territory, members of the gang feel safe and secure. Beyond the gang's very own 'turf' lies not the rest of their home town, but a viciously hostile jungle teeming with dangerous packs of young beasts, ever ready to attack them.

2. All members are obsessed with safety and security. The integrity of their territory and the loyalty of all gang members to each other is the guarantee of this security. Treason is punishable, in principle, by death.

3. For the members, the gang is the only authority in the world. They leave, physically or in spirit, their homes, their families, if they have any homes and families at all. They contract out of the adult world. The only conformism they accept is that of the gang.

4. The supreme virtue is extreme, even senseless, courage (heart). New recruits are trained to fight. In these training fights and mock battles knives, flick guns, bicycle chains and broken-necked bottles are not used; they are nevertheless pretty frightening affairs.

5. In the overwhelming majority of gangs the conscious aim of boys and girls is not any criminal activity, only the defence of their territory and their own selves. Most of the rest of anti-social or criminal behaviour among gang members is marginal, incidental.

6. Most students of gang behaviour agree that these boys and girls have many anxieties and difficulties, but sex is usually no problem for them. The 'debs', 'chicks', 'outlawettes' or whatever name the girl members are known by, are just as disciplined soldiers of the gang as the boys. In the new or old slums, these boys and girls have sexual experience early and go on being promiscuous or having longer or shorter affairs with each other. Their pointless violence or sadistic rage is certainly not caused by sexual repression. One long-time student of New York gang life remarked in this context that 'real tigers behave like tigers for many reasons, but certainly not because of sexual complexes.'

But why were these boys and girls behaving like jungle beasts? Harrison Salisbury in his classic on New York gangs – *The Shook-Up Generation* – wrote this about a New York housing project, built on the site of a former slum area: 'Fort Green and projects like it are forcing centres of juvenile delinquency. They spawn teenage gangs. They incubate crime. They are fiendishly contrived institutions for the debasing of family and community life to the lowest common mean. They are worse than anything George Orwell ever conceived."[11]

The refugees from the American South or from Puerto Rico soon discover that knowledge about how to live and work in a rural society is meaningless in a strange metropolis. Father no longer towers high above his children as a bastion of security. Together with them, he has to learn the new way of the great city. The children learn faster. The wives are soon influenced by the position of women in American cities. More often than not, the women are earning more as needle women, or in other jobs, than their unskilled labourer husbands. Teenage girls find it easy to get work. The family lives in congested slum quarters. Mother is out working, often until late evening. When all the members of the family are at home, there is no room for the children to play, so they have to face the streets that are part of the juvenile jungle. At school they are at the bottom of their class, because in their worried state, among contemptuous class mates, they cannot progress in their studies. In their slum dwellings it would take great effort to learn their lessons properly. So they do badly from the outset, many of them developing mental blocks to reading.

Put into the lowest stream, among slow learners, or subnormals in their class, they deteriorate speedily. These early failures, full of bewilderment and disillusionment, feel deeply insecure.

The entire adult world has abandoned them. Father dethroned, mother mostly a nagging room-mate. The school: a scene of constant humiliation and wounded pride – where to turn, how to find a safe place in this bitter, obnoxious world?

Walking to and from school, running on an errand for mother, indeed every time they emerge from the room, there is intolerable danger unless they join the local gang. Most newcomers are eager to join. Some who are reluctant are beaten up once or twice, and then they, too, join. It takes exceptional luck and courage to remain a 'coolie', a non-gang boy or girl, whose neutrality is respected by the gangs. For most teenager newcomers, the question seems to be simply this: join the gang, or perish.

Once in the gang, they find authority, safety, law and order. At school, young 'Hatchet' might be a slow learner, at home his desperate father might treat him as a good-for-nothing, in the gang he belongs, his comrades respect him for his courage.

For the gang, he is an important person in his own right: one of them. So the 'orphan with parents' finds his family.

It is a curious, hectic, vicious, at times murderous, and often artificial family. Much of the folklore of the gangs is second-hand, taken over from horror comics or TV thrillers. Some youngsters enact crimes invented by some hack writer of comics, or ape the manners of a popular film gangster. Often everything is phoney about them; only the killings and maimings are terribly real.

The fear and hatred they provoke is also real, though these much-publicized New York teenage gangs represent a minute proportion of the entire adolescent population of the city. In New York City during the decade 1953-63, serious estimates of the number of 'vicious teens' (in 120 to 150 gangs) varied between six and nine thousand, less than one per cent of all teenagers.* These include all members of violent gangs, many of whom were never convicted for criminal behaviour. In the United States as a whole, these violent teenagers represented less than one third of one per cent of all American teenagers.

In the late nineteen-fifties Robert F. Wagner, then Mayor of New York, ordered a special committee to study delinquency. This committee investigated the so-called 'multi-problem families' of the city slums. One of the results of the investigation showed that some twenty thousand New York families were the source of seventy-five per cent of all delinquency in police records in the city.

So in these twenty thousand families, less than one per cent of the New York population, originated three-quarters of all New York juvenile delinquency.

Subsequent investigations by various agencies showed that this proportion is fairly constant: the number of 'multi-problem families' varies slightly, as does their share in all delinquency. But the families themselves are not constant. Just because they are plagued by what are politely called 'multiple problems', they are always broken up, their members disappear into prisons, various asylums or graveyards, or manage to be absorbed into the 'normal world'. But their place is regularly filled by new multi-problem

* I have taken the medium figures of police estimates, those of youth workers and other authorities. During the period 1953-63, there were some maximum estimates putting the figure at 12,000, or more. But even if these highest estimates were correct, they would not change the scope of the problem.

98

families, usually in the same housing projects, with much the same previous history of rootless drifting.

These housing projects do, in fact, 'spawn teenage gangs'. They do 'incubate crime'. Since the population explosion will be overwhelmingly urban in character – according to a UN demographic forecast, eighty per cent of the world's population will be living in cities by 1980 – it is highly relevant that parts of New York are turned into dangerous jungles by an exceedingly small minority of teenagers, and that the principal cause was found to lie in equally identifiable small localities.

All the babies who will have turned into juvenile delinquents by 1977-82 have already been born. Most of the mistakes and omissions have already been committed and many of the processes started which will ensure a growing production of juvenile delinquents and outcasts everywhere from New York to Calcutta, from Glasgow to Munich.* This, in turn, will intensify the cold war and the violence of the clashes between adults and the young.

* I have met criminologists and police officials who can not only predict a rise of juvenile delinquency in their countries or cities quite accurately—their past predictions have proved to be correct—but can pinpoint the suburbs or city districts which will have the highest rise. It is known, for instance, that in West Germany the steepest rise of juvenile delinquency in the nineteen-seventies will take place in the large cities of four of the *Bundesländer:* Bavaria, Baden-Württenberg, Hessen and Schleswig-Holstein. Frau Charlotte Fiedler, Chief of the Hamburg *Weibliche Krimpo,* told me in 1966 that she expects the largest rise of juvenile delinquency during the next decade to be in the Rahlsted and Neugraben districts of Hamburg.

V

YOUTH AND ADULTS IN THE SOVIET ORBIT BEFORE THE HUNGARIAN REVOLUTION

1

The terror and misery of the Stalin era in the USSR and in the European satellite countries are too well-known today to necessitate documentation here or even to require anything other than a brief reminder. Since Stalin's death it has been exposed by Soviet and other communist leaders as an era of murderous bureaucratic despotism. The senseless mass murders, the sufferings of millions of totally innocent people in prisons and concentration camps have been described by Russian, Polish and Hungarian writers of memoirs, historians, novelists and poets in great and moving detail.

In the USSR and in the Sovietized countries of Eastern Europe the narrow-minded, dogma-bound, over-bureaucratized system led to near economic bankruptcy in the industrial and agricultural sectors. The standard of living of the overwhelming majority of the population sank scandalously low.*

In order to show what kind of individuals the young and the adults were during this era, it is necessary to indicate briefly some specific healthy effects of the Leninist system of party dictatorship as exercised during Stalin's rule. This system had well-defined priorities for the transformation of the people and the country. In transforming the people, the first priority was given to communist political education, and the second to universal education. Technological and specialist education came third. Since

---

* It has to be stressed again that this work on youth and revolution cannot give detailed documentation for every statement made about the political and economic history of the epoch.

much of the funds of the party–state apparatus was diverted to cover these priorities and since everything was compulsory, the elementary political education of the entire people really was accomplished. This does not mean that everyone was indoctrinated successfully, only that everybody knew about the communist doctrines.

Communists and non-communists alike had to attend seminary courses on Marxist-Leninist political education. From peasants and unskilled labourers to office workers, from acrobats to doctors of medicine, from canteen cooks to washerwomen, everyone under sixty-five had to attend 'elementary' Marxist seminars. They had to learn about the development of social forms according to 'main types of relationships of production' from 'primitive communal, to slave-owning, feudal, capitalist and, finally to the socialist form'. These elementary, or basic, seminars were often repeated. Middle-aged peasants and workers who had had only a few years of schooling had to learn something about the abstractions of dialectical materialism and of political economy. They were given booklets on these subjects to study at home. Many people had to progress to seminars at the secondary level. This political education never ceased, and there were many simple people who sat through the primary seminar course almost every year for two decades. These seminars were conducted separately for party members (about seven million in 1953) and for the non-party majority and were conducted weekly at everyone's place of work. Everyone was expected to participate in the discussions.

In addition to the compulsory seminars, communists had to attend the meetings of their party cell, non-communists those arranged by the local trade-union cell. It was a very exceptional person in the Soviet orbit who did not attend at least one short discussion meeting per week (lasting only a couple of hours after work), and at least one long meeting monthly, lasting between five to eight hours. Not to participate in the discussion was dangerous, so everyone made the effort. Furthermore, people had to show up a little earlier in the morning at their place of work, so that they could participate in groups of ten to twenty in a fifteen-minute discussion of the news and views contained in that morning's party daily ('the *Pravda* quarter of an hour'). At these meetings people got accustomed to discussing home and international developments in the spirit of the party line of the day.

Ignorance of the often-changing party line on these matters was instantly reprimanded by the group leader, and it could have unpleasant repercussions.

Familiarizing oneself with the rudiments of turgid Marxist terminology, with some of the abstractions of Marxist philosophy and political economy; being informed about home and world affairs and being able to talk about them in *Pravda* language in the seminars and innumerable meetings, became a way of life for everyone under sixty-five. Everyone had homework. However tired, people sat up to read at least the underlined parts of a brochure or pamphlet about the latest doings of the imperialist warmongers.

The Soviet and satellite regimes were most successful in their programme for universal education. Illiteracy was wiped out and the Leninist pattern forced a kind of cultural existence on everyone. Lack of entertainment, the drabness and poverty of life in general, made great readers of masses of people who in normal situations would have read very little. The many compulsory readings gave them practice in reading. As the officially sponsored contemporary literature was mostly infuriating and boring, they turned to their classics. Tens of millions of Russians read the wonderful classics of their literature. The situation was the same in the satellite countries, where the national classics were read together with Russian and Western classics. In short, the terrific pressure and the education-oriented policies of the governments improved the qualities and the latent potentialities of the adults by keeping them in life-long student situation.

All this strengthened the other, greater forces that keep adult populations in an exceptionally mature mental–emotional state. It is a truism that dangerous challenges tend to bring out some of the good qualities inherent in people. The total terror of the Stalinist police state is, of course, the ultimate in dangerous challenge.

Chapter xiii stresses the fact that in open societies the overwhelming majority of the population is not mature in the sense of being in a rational-altruistic (that is, truly human) frame of mind. They are politically disinterested, they are not alert or attentive. They insist on reducing themselves to being purely private persons. All this is changed if and when the public sector becomes the source of deadly dangers. Terror transforms politically neutral private persons into alert political animals. There is no longer the possibility of retiring into a private shell. Like an animal of the jungle, the average person has to be ever alert to the slightest signs of danger. When even a momentary disregard of the constantly changing political scene entails for everybody the danger of demotion, imprisonment or execution, then even washerwomen become political analysts, if not quite in the sense in which Lenin hoped for this to happen. The tremendous never-ceasing pressure forced people to do a great deal of purposeful thinking, an activity not very general in an open society.

Living under murderous bureaucratic despotism can improve the mental state of people, but not necessarily their moral character. Fear and suspicion isolate people from each other, even though they really belong to the same camp, that of the tormented, over-worked, threatened subjects of a police state. When in a collective farm, a factory or an office, one of these subjects was arrested by the security police (on some such entirely unfounded, ridiculous charge as being an 'imperialist saboteur' or a 'Trotsky-ite deviationist from the party-line'), everyone who knew him had to denounce him at the next meeting in the proper *Pravda* language. But these frequent public denunciations of one's friends and colleagues were known by everyone for what they were: ceremonial gestures necessary to save one's neck. When, however, it is not dangerous to stick together against the hated and despised authorities, people tend to do so.

The very long working hours, the endless meetings after work, the many so-called voluntary activities (enforced by the security police) and all the other difficulties of existence toughen people. Though in outward, observable behaviour they appear to be thoroughly enslaved and apathetic, in most of them there is a yearning for a situation in which they can do something against 'them'. This vast reservoir of potential resistance is forced at gun-point into passivity. But when terror halts or abates, the pressure of the mature, politically alert population starts to grow and is soon active in all walks of life.

2

The history of the western communist world during the post-Stalin era and the history of the Hungarian Revolution illustrate the relevance to the present era of De Tocqueville's well-known thesis:

It is not always by going from bad to worse that a nation is driven to revolution. It often happens that a nation which has suffered without complaint, almost as if were insensible to the most oppressive laws, will suddenly reject them with violence *at the first sign of alleviation. . . . Experience suggests that the most dangerous moment for an evil government is usually when it begins to reform itself.* Only great ingenuity can save a prince who undertakes to give relief to his subjects after long oppression. The sufferings that are endured patiently, as being inevitable, become intolerable the moment it appears that there might be an escape. Reform then only serves to reveal more clearly what still remains oppressive and now all the more unbearable; the suffering, it is true, has been reduced, but one's sensitivity has become more acute.[1]

After Stalin's death in March 1953, the wish to stay alive prompted his heirs to deny the right of the eventual next dictator to execute anyone in their ranks. This, and the wish to appease the population, led to the immediate curbing of the excesses committed by the security police. The post-Stalin leadership promptly granted a large-scale amnesty; they promised 'socialist legality'; they had the heads of the vast security police apparatus arrested for 'extorting false confessions' by torture, for executing and imprisoning masses of innocent people. They also began the process of rehabilitation of the millions of victims of the Stalin era who were still living. Some of these were declared innocent and set free after fifteen or even seventeen years in jail.

The ghost of popular revolt haunted Stalin's heirs, who with their collective leadership wanted to reassure the people that the era of the 'cult of personality' (their silly phrase for murderous tyranny) was over. This first period after Stalin's death received its name from Ilya Ehrenburg's novel *The Thaw*, published in 1954. It was not the first literary exposure of the entire climate of tyranny. Uspenskaya, Leonid Leonov and others had already published similar exposures in 1953.

In the USSR the gradual and very limited relaxation of terror prompted the unusually articulate and politically engaged population to press for further relaxations. At the inevitable meetings, instead of the compulsory *Pravda* language, some people were beginning to ask their own questions in their own style. Cautiously, astutely, some began to criticize and even express very prudent small demands. The party secretaries and other bosses up and down the hierarchy were unsure of themselves.

The growing pressure from below forced them to be on the defensive. As more and more people dared to believe that the terroristic 'ice age' really was being followed by a thaw, the questions and critical remarks became bolder. Within the Communist Party, the 'idealists' – those blinkered people who had persuaded themselves that the murder of innocent people, the dismal state of the economy and their unbearable lives were caused by isolated mistakes – were now intent on 'rejuvenating communism' through a kind of moral reformation. They joined the critics from below and were the loudest in demanding basic reforms that would make any 'violation of socialist legality' impossible in the future.

The great amnesties in the USSR and in some of the satellites brought hundreds of thousands of witnesses of security-police inhumanity out of prison and concentration camps. There were very few people in the Western communist world during this initial thaw period who did not hear some first-hand accounts of torture and of the horrible existence of the innocent prisoners, many of whom were ardent communists. The moral revulsion and the relaxation of censorship led to an astonishing literary renaissance in the communist world. After decades of organized public falsehood, a unanimous public opinion of resistance came into being. Thousands of poems were published about the victims of the terror era and about the poets' feeling of guilt for having believed the clumsy calumnies against these innocents.

From May 1953 onwards, disillusioned party members and people belonging to the non-party majority began speaking of 'the truth', and telling some of the truth about some aspects of terrorist bureaucracy that had made their existence needlessly poor and hard. Slowly and timidly some particles of anti-party 'truth' were spoken about and even discussed in the press. From the outset, there was a sprinkling of brave articles, brave at least for the Soviet public who learned to spot the hidden message in the text.

Russian newspapers and periodicals carried the infection of this 'truth' into the East European countries, where so many people were forced to learn Russian; first of all, of course, the young. In these satellites the terrorist police state was evolved in a third of the time it took in the Soviet Union. The onset of full Stalinism was short and brutal, and people were not as enervated as the Russians, who had had three and a half decades of it.

It is not surprising, therefore, that the communist leaders were offered their first lessons in the dangers of relaxation from East Germany and Czechoslovakia. The East German Communist Party and government officially admitted on 12 June 1953 that they had committed 'serious mistakes' with the 'consequence that many people have left the Republic'. The decision to socialize the East German economy at great speed was renounced, land confiscated from the peasants was restored to their owners, the enforcement of grain deliveries was eased and a limited amnesty was announced. Only the industrial workers' lot was not eased; on the contrary, the working norms were increased by ten per cent.

On 16 June 1953, a protest demonstration of workers and young people in East Berlin turned into a riot. Soviet troops and tanks were called out and crushed the revolt. Similar revolts by workers, students and other young people flared up in Magdeburg, Halle, Leipzig and other industrial districts. There was a simultaneous revolt in Pzen (Pilsen) in Czechoslovakia. For the first time Soviet tanks played the role that was later to be so familiar, fighting for weeks against workers and students. This event is mostly remembered in the West as the 'workers' rising in East Berlin'. But, as George Fletcher pointed out: 'the most surprising and significant aspect of the East German rising and of that in Pzen (Pilsen) was the fact that these were essentially the movements of *the young people* – the pampered, privileged, brainwashed favourites of the regime. These boys and girls have been regarded by their governments as the mainstay and future of communism.'*[2]

These risings were only potential lessons offered by history, as far as the communist bosses were concerned. They did not learn from these lessons. Reverting to the obsolete theory, so often ridiculed by Marx and Engels, that revolts and risings must necessarily be the outcome of conspiratorial plots and are instigated by sinister enemy agents, they convinced themselves that the East German and Czech risings were nothing more than unsuccessful anti-communist plots by 'imperialist warmongers' abroad and class-hostile elements at home. As usual the security-police truncheons obtained a few 'confessions', and the Soviet, East German and Czech party bosses carried on with their policy of very slow and gradual relaxations. They believed that without some sort of

---

* Section 3 of this chapter and the next chapter will try to show that they were neither pampered and privileged nor brainwashed.

'normalization' of their system, economic recovery would be impossible and they would not be able to 'overtake the capitalist world'.

The whole system of bureaucratic dictatorship was slightly loosened. The relaxations from above prompted renewed pressures from below. The thaw went on in administration, in the economic field and in most branches of science. The period from Stalin's death until the Twentieth Party Congress early in 1956 was an era of undeclared or half-declared de-Stalinization.

For Communist Party members and the *apparatchiki,* the gravest anti-Stalin step was the official rehabilitation of Marshal Tito of Yugoslavia in 1955. The denunciation of Tito in 1948 as an enemy of communism, a traitor to the working class of the world and an agent of imperialism was at the core of the communism of the day. The Warsaw Declaration of the Cominform published this denunciation in 1948 as a unanimous decision of the Communist Parties of the USSR and of all the satellites.

There was no communist leader in the Sino-Soviet orbit, or in the Communist Parties elsewhere, who did not call Tito a 'chained dog of the imperialists'.

During the anti-Tito purges many communist leaders with long and immaculate party records were executed in a series of rigged trials. In Bulgaria, Traitcho Kostov, who had spent eighteen years in various jails for his communist convictions and activities, was executed after a clumsy show trial which could not even produce his confession. In Hungary, László Rajk, of Spanish Civil War fame, was hanged with many other innocent members of the Communist Old Guard. In Czechoslovakia, Slansky, Clementis and scores of other old communists were executed. In Poland Wladislaw Gomulka was arrested and kept in jail as a Titoist, but was not brought to trial. Each main trial was followed by dozens, even scores, of 'connected trials', purporting to show the great scope of the conspiracy. In the satellite empire thousands upon thousands were executed and tens of thousands jailed because of their non-existent connections with Tito and the Yugoslav communists.

In May 1955, a Soviet delegation headed by Khrushchev visited Belgrade to apologize to Marshal Tito and to rehabilitate him officially, in the name of the Soviet Communist Party and that of most of the communist world. It had to be admitted that Tito and the Yugoslav communists were not treacherous enemies of the working class, that there was no Titoist conspiracy to over-throw the communist regimes.

Most important, the Soviet and other communist leaders had to expose as wrong and entirely pointless the execution of thousands of innocent communists.

Each of the various White and Blue Books about the trials of 'Titoist criminals' turned out to be a pack of stupid and murder-ous lies. The number of historical and theoretical works that had to be withdrawn from circulation in the communist orbit and by the Communist Parties elsewhere ran into millions. The position of the dictators of the satellite countries who had directed and boasted about the execution of thousands of 'Titoist conspirators' in their own countries became most precarious; if previously there had been some unrest and critical stirrings among communist officials, the admission of this murderous lie created internal pockets of opposition within all the Communist Parties of Eastern Europe.

The most far-reaching consequences of the rehabilitation of Tito and the 'Titoists' was its effect on communist students on the one hand, and on young intellectuals within the party apparatus on the other.

3

This section deals with the characteristics and situation of the twenty-to-thirty age-group as it was in the USSR on Stalin's death in 1953, and the same age-group in the satellites in 1956, on the eve of the Hungarian Revolution.

This age-group differed in the Soviet Union and in the satellites in some significant aspects. (Besides the obvious one, that the group in the satellites was of a three years later vintage.) But this difference is very small indeed, compared to the difference between children and youth in the Soviet orbit and those in the Western world in the fifties.

Many Western visitors recorded then their impression that 'these unfortunates had almost no childhood'. Earnestness was the key-word for anyone who attempted to generalize about Soviet and satellite youth in the fifties. The majority of boys and girls gave the impression that at thirteen they were greater realists, more prudent and cautious than many adults in the West. Their exceptional prudence and self-control, which so impressed foreign visitors, were the direct and indirect consequences of the Soviet system and Soviet conditions. They were forced by circumstances to acquire more self-discipline than youth anywhere else in the world, with the exception of Red China.

The Orwellian 'Big Brother is watching you' feeling was constant from childhood onwards. There were personal files drawn up about everyone from primary school onwards. These files, called 'cadre sheets', followed one from school to school and then to every place of work. The sheets contained facts about one's family circumstances, remarks about one's achievements and faults. First the teachers and the youth-organization secretaries, later the party secretaries and the personnel chiefs at one's place of work wrote on the sheets one's 'character sketch'.

Children learnt early that their future advancement, their hope for entering university or getting a good job also depended on the 'class descent' of their parents and grandparents (a 'class-hostile' grandfather, say a Tsarist post-office clerk, could stop one from getting accepted by a university). Millions went through their childhood and adolescence with a terrible black mark on their cadre sheet because some close, or even distant, relative had fallen victim to one of the purges. The young relatives of these 'political criminals' could do nothing to overcome this grave handicap.

But even those who were 'clean' in these respects had to learn early that any childish prank, any careless remark might get noted in the all-important personal files. It was not enough to study well and to refrain from being naughty at school – one had to take part cheerfully in the work of the organization of Young Pioneers, school clubs and in the many social activities organized by the school. Periodically, there were so-called criticism and self-criticism sessions, when the entire class examined one's past behaviour, when all one's school-mates were expected to criticize one and listen to one's self-criticism.

The school system itself was anything but permissive. Children had to learn just as hard as the pupils in the old-fashioned, too severe European or American schools of forty or fifty years previously. Professor A. S. Trace has written:

In Soviet primary schools first graders use a text-book with a vocabulary of 2,000 words (compared with the US first reader of 158 words). In the second grade the reading vocabulary is doubled to 4,000 words, and when a pupil finishes fourth grade, he or she is expected to have a (passive) reading vocabulary of 10,000 words, while the US fourth grader is still at work on a 'basal' reader with a vocabulary under 1,800 words.[3]

In the secondary schools the pupils took besides history, literature, mathematics, four years of chemistry, five of physics and six of biology. In the fifties, the average Russian secondary school student was taught five times the amount of natural science and mathematics that is necessary for entrance to the famous Massachusetts Institute of Technology.

These stiff standards naturally meant that Soviet primary- and secondary-school pupils had a great deal of homework. Their remaining free time was not entirely free either. The authorities expected them to devote at least part of it to 'constructive leisure activities', such as taking part in youth organizations, visiting youth centres or cultural club houses, learning crafts and hobbies and mastering extra subjects like painting or playing the piano or the violin.

On 13 August 1950, *Pravda* claimed that 'the USSR last year passed on to a universal compulsory seven-year education'. In some of the Soviet republics, however, there were many boys and girls who left school much earlier.

Marxist-Leninist political education, however, was a must. Western visitors were often amused when a fifteen-year-old peasant girl in Uzbekistan and a young factory worker in Leningrad used almost the same words to describe, say, the current African political situation and the achievements of Soviet economic planning. The visitors pointed out that the Soviet young repeated parrot-fashion the opinions they were supposed to hold. In fact, they learnt the compulsory Marxist-Leninist terminology early; they were informed about the Communist Party's current views on home and world affairs and were prudent enough to repeat them in proper *Pravda* language.

The brutal pressure of conformity was also there in their private life within the family. In the early nineteen-fifties, Soviet housing conditions were far worse than now. In the big cities, a single room for an entire family was not the exception but the rule. In a three-room flat three families would share the kitchen and the toilet. It was regarded as the most exceptional good fortune if a couple with three children had a two-room flat.

For children and adolescents, home life meant living in constant tension and bickering. They had to do their homework in a crowded room, sharing the only table with others, or lying on a bed. In the evening, furniture had to be pushed aside or stacked to create floor space for the mattresses. In the over-crowded co-tenancies it required an extraordinary effort of concentration to do homework well.

The 'Big Brother is watching you' feeling did not cease when one entered the room that was the family home. People had to take care not to make a critical remark about 'them' in front of a toddler, lest he blabber it next day at kindergarten. Hostile neigh-bours might overhear it and denounce them.

The private life of children and grown-ups was controlled or reported upon by the visiting 'people's educators', by the janitor, by the house warden and block warden. The USSR was then still in her 'Victorian' era of prudery. Since the great Lenin declared that laxity in sexual relations was a bourgeois sin, every-one had to give a most proper impression. At the same time, due to overcrowding, there was no sexual privacy. With adult couples, children and teenagers sharing the same room, children could not at times help getting acquainted with some audible aspects of sexual activities.

The general cultural climate also left its mark on children and teenagers. Press, radio, film, theatre and literature were controlled to teach, inform and politically influence the population, instead of entertaining it. In the absence of comics, crime novels and of any kinds of 'frivolous' book for adults or children, the average Russian secondary-school pupil grew to know and like the classics of Russian literature. For them, a Tolstoy or Gogol novel offered a wonderfully colourful, adventurous, humane, funny and enter-taining world. (The Soviet magazines for children and teen-agers were much more like readable textbooks than periodicals for entertainment.)

In the Soviet Union, those who were between thirteen and twenty-two when Stalin died had been through all or part of their childhood during the frightful years of the Second World War. They heard about the utmost horrors of the purge years, when millions perished, only from their parents. After the war, until the dictator's death, life became more frightening all the time. Children and adolescents felt it, were educated and steeled by it. At the same time they were brought up to worship and respect Stalin as the greatest, wisest man who ever lived. They watched the post-Stalin developments through the 'spectacles of youth'

111

that are proverbially supposed to see only two colours: the white of truth and the black of evil lies.

The more successful their teachers and party instructors were in installing in them the fanatical communist conviction that all truth and justice is embodied in their party, the greater was their shock when these illusions were shattered. They became overnight the most dangerous potential opposition to the Soviet or Sovietized regimes by insisting – as young people will – that truth and justice must prevail.

The satellites

For specific reasons, this shock was greater in the East European communist-governed countries than in the Soviet Union.

Boys and girls who were between thirteen and twenty-two in 1956 had lived as children or adolescents through the very fast and brutal Sovietization of their countries. They were between five and fourteen at the time of the establishment of the terrorist police state in 1948. From then onwards, children entering school were classified into categories, according to class descent. We describe here the system in Hungary, emphasizing that the categorization was identical or similar in the other satellites. In Hungary, the six categories were:

1. Worker
2. Small Peasant
3. Intelligentsia
4. Petty employee
5. Other
6. Class enemy – X

Categories 1 and 2 had no trouble ascending through middle school to university. Category 3 had much less chance of entering university or getting employment at executive level. Categories 4 and 5 received university education only in most exceptional cases. Those in category X were forbidden to go beyond primary school. The X children of 'class-enemy' descent were judged on a stricter basis than the Jews in Nazi Germany. A great-grandfather who was a factory owner or a landowner was enough to get a child into category X. While a category 5 child was only a fifth-rate person, an X-child was below humanity.

The majority of young people in this age-group had childhood memories of the nightmare years of 1944-5, when the last battles were fought in their countries between the Hitlerist army and the

112

Red Army. They remembered the nights spent in air-raid shelters, during bombing and during the days or weeks when their villages, towns or cities were under siege.

The surviving Jewish children (roughly two-thirds perished in the various gas chambers) were no longer in danger because they were born Jews. The time soon came however, when some of the Jewish as well as the non-Jewish children had to pay for the different kinds of 'sins' committed by their 'class-hostile' grandparents and great-grandparents.

From 1948 onwards, more and more of them became members of the Red Pioneers – the organization of communist children – or the Komsomol, the communist youth organization. Communist indoctrination was, if anything, more intensive than in the Soviet Union. This applied to the adults, too. In these countries, the 'capitalist past' was not something that had come to an end more than three decades previously. In 1956, the multi-party system, a more or less free press, virtual freedom from arbitrary arrest, were things that had ceased only nine years previously. Every adult and most adolescents remembered the more normal times of more freedom and less fear.

The security police was established in the satellites under communist chiefs straight after the war, two or three years before the communist take-over. The first wave of arrests hit the war criminals and the local Nazis and their collaborators. The second dealt with leading personalities of the old regimes, whether they had collaborated with the Nazis or not. Later waves filled the prisons and concentration camps with lesser, and therefore more numerous members of the former establishments, from army officers (down to captains) to branch managers of banks and minor officials in ministries and elsewhere. (Of course, not all members of these categories were arrested, in some cases only five to ten per cent, while the rest were free to live in fear.) The families of arrested people were usually evicted from their homes. Wives tried to earn their living as unskilled labourers.

In about 1948, it was the turn of the leaders and activists of the non-communist democratic parties – such as the peasant or small-holder party, the social-democrats or the liberals – to be arrested, convicted or simply sent to concentration camps. In elementary and secondary schools these waves of arrests meant that some children were denounced as sons or daughters of exposed enemies. Some pupils simply disappeared, since they were

113

deported together with the rest of their family.

In 1949, it was the turn of the 'idealist' communist leaders and activists. During the great anti-Titoist purges, hundreds of well-known communists were executed in the capital cities and thousands in the provinces. Tens of thousands were sentenced to long prison terms. Some children, who had up till then belonged to categories 1 or 2, suddenly became something worse than even category X.

Terror did not abate. Various waves of arrests and executions went on till Stalin's death. During the period 1950-3, in many satellites the innocuous members of the 'hostile classes' who had not yet been arrested were deported from the cities and towns to small villages in the distant provinces. Old-age pensioners, former factory owners and shopkeepers and their families were evicted from their homes at an hour's notice and had to try to earn their living as unskilled agricultural labourers. In each region, tens of thousands of people were thus deported, including, of course, children and adolescents.

All this was done, suffered and witnessed, so that under the guidance of the infallible party, the great Stalin and the great local Stalins, the most progressive and best of all possible systems, the communist system, should be established as quickly as posible.

Then came the shock of the denunciation of Stalin. In February 1956, at the Twentieth Congress of the Soviet Communist Party, N. S. Khrushchev denounced Stalin as a sadist, a mass murderer, a coward, an inept handler of economic questions, a military bungler and a falsifier of history. As a result, the already badly battered communist theoretical edifice was overthrown with a crash greater in resonance than the one when Hungarian steel-workers smote down the monumental statue of Stalin in Budapest a few months later.

The anti-Stalin tract, which was originally printed only in ten thousand copies for the party élite in Russia and in a few thousand copies in each of the satellites, was duplicated and roneoed everywhere in the Soviet orbit with such zeal that it soon reached everyone.

The Soviet press began to publish more daring criticisms of the era of the 'cult of personality'. No one in the Soviet orbit had any excuse from then on for not knowing about the terrible mass murders and mass imprisonment of the innocent. But the exposure of the near bankruptcy in the industrial and agricultural sectors was an equally grave shock. All during the years of terror and misery people had been told that by working very hard for a few years, they would build up their country and would create for themselves a better, richer and easier life. Instead, it turned out that thanks to a dogmatic bureaucracy all their sacrifices had been in vain. Their country was not only in moral and political bankruptcy, but also in economic chaos. People had given up their private lives for nothing. As the young saw it, the adults – both the oppressed and the oppressors – had arrived at a dead end. In some of the satellites, first of all in Poland and Hungary, the young demanded that the criminally stupid oppressors should be called to account. And they asked the oppressed: why did you permit this to happen?

There is space only for a few indications of the mood of the young. We single out Polish youth for two reasons: the behaviour of Polish youth was typical of the Soviet orbit; and the Polish 'bloodless revolution' was an important link in the causal chain that led to the Hungarian youth explosion.

4

. . . When the vultures of abstraction pick our brains.
when students are enclosed in text-books without windows,
when language is reduced to thirty incantations,
when the lamp of imagination is extinguished,
when good people from the moon deny us our taste,
then truly
oblivion is dangerously near.
· · · · · · · · ·
They ran to us, shouting:
Under socialism
a cut finger does not hurt.

They cut their finger, they felt pain.
They lost faith.
· · · · · · · · ·
We make demands on this earth
for which a million perished in battle :
for a clear truth,
for the bread of freedom,
for burning reason,
for burning reason.

We demand these every day.
We demand through the Party.

Adam Wazyk, 'Poem for Adults', in *Nowa Kultura*, Warsaw, 21 August 1955.

Adam Wazyk was one of the leading poets of Poland, a convinced communist, a party member formerly trusted by the regime's cultural commissars. Once, like so many other communist poets, he wrote an ode to Stalin. That a communist journal with the prestige of *Nowa Kultura* should publish his passionate and sweeping condemnation of all the crimes and failings of the regime (we have quoted only a tiny segment) had an explosive political effect. Though this poem could not have been written without the relaxations that already existed, the rehabilitation of the innocents and the consequent literary thaw in the Soviet Union, its importance cannot be emphasized enough. It mobilized the anti-Stalin opposition within the Polish Communist Party, it had a great affect on the students, and its echoes intensified the literary thaw in Russia, Hungary and in some other satellites.

Wazyk, like so many older communist writers, rebelled first of all against his own past and was fired by the hope of 'cleansing the party' and 'a moral rejuvenation of communism'. ('We demand through the Party.') The impact of the thaw writers and their role in the revolutionary causal chain will be discussed in detail in the next chapter. Here it is enough to stress that these communist writers expressed the feelings of the 'idealist' communists within the party, and those of the entire population.

The great disillusionment of Polish youth was a continuous process. The weekly paper for communist students and young writers, *Po Prostu*, began to publish daring criticisms of the oppressive regime even before Stalin's denunciation at the Twentieth Congress. In the issue of 22 January, for instance, there appeared 'Confessions of a converted cynic', by a young communist journalist called Jerzy Urban, who wrote:

Do you understand? In the name of higher aims ... the most normal human emotions were being scrupulously suppressed. For the good of socialism I was deprived of my most effective weapon — my sensitivity and the possibility of writing about these matters [social evils]. I lied doubly — by not writing about things that mattered and by varnishing the truth. And what is worse, I and others believed in the sense and the reason of these lies.

In April 1956 *Nowa Kultura* printed a letter from an eighteen-year-old student at the Warsaw Polytechnic, Michal Bruk, who described how his faith had repeatedly been shattered by the adult world. His brother had fought in the Polish Home Army of anti-Nazi resistance and was killed by the Nazis. This brother was his hero, but then the communists came and told him that the Home Army was made up of traitors. Then he sought solace in religion, but communist propaganda made him lose faith. In 1953, he became a communist and could not believe what his family and friends told him about secret-police terrorism, about Stalinist mass murders and about the falsification of history by the Communist Party. Now, in 1956, as Khrushchev and the other leaders admitted that all these accusations had been true, Bruk wrote: 'I am ashamed of all of you, and above all of myself because of my stupidity and credulity. I no longer know how to raise my head ... for I have no foundation for believing anything.'

He says to the adults: 'I have no reason to trust you ... please do not be surprised by us, young people.'[4]

Even the official party daily, *Trybuna Ludu,* published readers' letters like this one: 'What should we believe and whom should we believe? What is true and what is false? There is nothing strange in these questions. Today many people think on these lines: if in the past I could believe in lies and accept them as truth, who can guarantee that what I accept as truth today is not just another lie?'[5]

An ardent young Polish communist, Jan Stanislawski, wrote in *Po Prostu*: 'I can see one conclusion emerging from this chaos ... there are no authorities any more, and this applies from the district secretary to the First Secretary of the Central Committee. ... For me there are no more authorities. There are only people. They must be accountable to other people.'[6]

Thanks to the new and somewhat freer era, the Polish press started to describe everyday life in Poland truthfully, without embellishments. Polish writers of all ages wrote against despotism. Much of the press reported not only the senseless terrorism and the abuses of power of the recent past, but also the true facts of life of the present. In the great housing shortages, in the intoler-

117

able living conditions caused by poverty, millions of families were disintegrating. Tens of thousands of married couples had to live apart, because the authorities sent husbands and wives to different towns to work. The so-called workers' hostels, in other words barracks for male and female labourers, were described in some cities and towns as virtual brothels, where it required an exceptional moral and physical stamina to remain uncorrupted. In the drab drudgery that was everyday life, rootless men and women escaped into alcoholism and sex – taken 'neat', as vulgarly as the alcoholic who drinks neat spirit. There were tens of thousands of abandoned children, and many more illegitimate ones. There were far more legal and illegal abortions than births.

Tyranny, bureaucratic arrogance in moving millions of peasants and workers about all over the country, poverty and the deterioration of family life had produced by 1955-6 an entire underworld of young 'lost people', vagrant or semi-vagrant children, who started to drink at the age of ten, who formed gangs to rob and steal, who used fourteen- to fifteen-year-old prostitutes to entice men to the gangs' lairs to be robbed. The communist authorities, the schools and the police were unable to clear up the mental and moral slums that the unfortunate segment of youth lived in – because far more adults lived in similar slums.

The majority of the Polish people who had managed to retain their integrity, their moral and intellectual standards, read these revelations with horror. And these revelations were also read by students, by all sorts of articulate youngsters, who formed their own opinions.

The young communists and their organ, *Po Prostu,* demanded 'truth and justice'. Since the economy was in a terrible state, all through June 1956 *Po Prostu* urged that people should be told the truth about the economic situation. They promptly began to do this. Jerzy Urban (the 'converted cynic') wrote about the complete breakdown of economic planning, about the relentless exploitation of the workers, about the grave unemployment that was being officially denied, about the hundreds of ways in which the oppressive rule of dogma together with bureaucratic stupidity crippled industry and agriculture.

5

The 20,000 workers at ZISPO in Poznan, the fourth largest city in Poland, sent a delegation to Warsaw on 26 June 1956 to demand from the central authorities an easing of their miseries. The workers were dissatisfied with the meagre concessions their delegates obtained and on 28 June the night and day shifts decided to stage a demonstration. They formed a procession and started an orderly march towards the city centre, carrying improvised banners and posters: 'We Want Bread' and 'We want Lower Prices And Higher Wages'. They were joined by workers from other factories, by their wives and children and by students and other young people. They filled the large square in front of the town hall.

Several speakers addressed the demonstrators, including the propaganda secretary of the district committee of the party, who was frequently interrupted. As the morning passed, the demonstration developed a political and revolutionary character. More improvised banners and posters appeared: 'We Want Freedom!' 'Down With False Communism!' 'Down With The Soviet Occupation!'. The cumulative effect of the revelations during the thaw period inevitably manifested itself. As almost always, there was a *Grande Peur*. Acting on a false rumour that the ZISPO delegation had been arrested, the crowd attacked the city jail, freed the inmates and took away the arms of the prison guards. Not having found the delegation in the jail, the crowd attacked the UB (Security Police) building and the first shots were fired there.

That these actions were improvised on the spur of the moment is indicated by the fact that the crowd made a frontal attack against the UB building, instead of surrounding it or taking it from the rear.

The first shots wounded a woman and a child. Before it came to the first shots, two fire brigade cars using their hoses could have put an end to the demonstration. The authorities, however, very early on, before the first shots, called out the army. By the time two lorries of infantry and three tanks had arrived on the scene, the crowd was in an angry mood. They shouted 'Poles don't shoot Poles!' There were again a few shots, but within minutes Polish flags were hoisted on the lorries and the workers took over the tanks, which they did not know how to use. (This is another sign indicating that the flare-up was unplanned. It would have been easy for the 'plotters', had there been any, to find among the tens of thousands of workers former soldiers who would know how to handle tanks.)

119

Within the next hour more troops and tanks arrived. Many people believed that there was a nation-wide revolt and that the fighting in Poznan was a part of this; they also believed, mistakenly, that most of the fighting was done by Soviet troops. For these reasons, it took a considerable military force to bring the Poznan situation under control. There was some fighting during the night and the following day. By the time the revolt was suppressed, fifty-three people had been killed and over three hundred wounded.

As one writer has put it:

> From the point of view of the Party the events of the Black Thursday [in Poznan] were a disaster. They showed conclusively that the workers were bitter and ready to fight, that the population was solidly against the regime, the Party organisation was ineffective and bankrupt, the army at least partly and the uniformed civil police wholly unreliable.[7]

At first, the Polish Communist Party line was that 'imperialist agents and the reactionary underground' had exploited economic difficulties and the grievances of the population. But on 6 July the party daily, *Trybuna Ludu*, wrote: 'The strike action of Poznan workers – and this basic and painful truth must not be concealed or embellished – was to a considerable extent caused by bureaucratic distortions of the Proletarian State.'

The Soviet Central Committee resolution, however, asserted that 'the anti-popular riots in Poznan have been paid for from the funds of American monopoly capital' and that 'the working people of Poznan resisted the hostile actions and provocations'.[8]

The Poznan trials that began on 27 September very naturally offered no proof concerning 'imperialist agents' or 'reactionary *provocateurs*'. Of the 154 people awaiting trial only thirty-seven appeared in court. The majority of both groups were young people, students, other teenagers and young workers. All these youths were described by the prosecution as 'hooligans'. Their age was a good pretext for calling young workers hooligans, since it was taken for granted that hooligans are always young people.

The defence counsel, Hejmowski, told the court that these young men were no hooligans:

> The accused had been brought up during the war and the following period of the 'breaches of legality', when moral brakes had been removed. They had ceased to respect the authority of State, parents,

church or school, but whose fault was it? It was the fault of the older generation, which had lost the respect of the youth and created abnormal conditions of amorality.

Hejmowski said: 'When the workers of Poznan demonstrated in the streets, they were accompanied by young people, for youth is always the dynamic force of any demonstration against authority.'[9]

During the spring and summer of 1956, the communist opposition in Poland demanded that the 'reactionary' or 'Stalinist' communists in the leadership should be deposed and replaced by 'progressive' anti-Stalinist communists, such as Wladislaw Gomulka and his friends. Gomulka was the son of a worker, joined the Communist Party as a young man and served many prison terms for his beliefs. In 1936 he was luckily sentenced to seven years' imprisonment. He was safely in a capitalist jail in 1938, when Stalin liquidated the Polish Communist Party and killed most of its leaders. When war broke out in 1939 he was released, took part in the defence of Warsaw and later organized the communist underground. After the war he was First Secretary of the Party and Deputy Premier. At the beginning of the anti-Titoist purges, he was deposed as a right-wing nationalist and was arrested in 1951. Since he refused to confess, he was not executed and was released at Christmas 1954. His past makes it obvious why the rebellious communists and the young intellectuals fought for his elevation to power.

In the dangerous post-Poznan situation, the Polish Politbureau was shaken by a desperate struggle within the party. Much of the party and state apparatus was still in the hands of Stalinists, but the anti-Stalinist Gomulka wing also had its important power bases. The security police was taken over by General Komar, one of Gomulka's friends, and in the universities and factories students and workers organized anti-Stalinist resistance. There is no space here to describe the roles of the young communist intellectuals, of the students and the workers in the desperate struggle between the Polish Stalinist groups (backed with all the might of the Kremlin) and the adherents of Gomulka. Moscow's fury was strengthened by Gomulka's refusal to pay lip service to the ridiculous lie that the Poznan riots were organized by imperialist agents.

By 15 October the Polish Stalinist leadership was defeated and it was obvious that the Central Committee would elect Gomulka as First Secretary. Khrushchev and the Kremlin leaders tried to intimidate the Poles, without success. When it turned out that the Polish army was refusing orders to move against the 'rebels' led by Gomulka and, moreover, that it was ready to defend the country against Soviet troops, the Kremlin bosses retreated. The 'bloodless' Polish revolution apparently achieved all its aims.

On 20 October 1956 Gomulka, as the new First Secretary, made his report to the party and the nation. Since this speech is one of the most important documents for the Polish and Hungarian revolutions, some passages must be quoted here:

... The attempt to present the painful tragedy of Poznan as the work of imperialist agents and *provocateurs* was a great political *naïveté*. Agents and *provocateurs* can exist and be active everywhere and all the time, but never and nowhere can they determine the attitude of the working class. Comrades, the causes of the Poznan tragedy and of the deep dissatisfaction of the entire working class lie within us, the Party leadership and the Government.

... A reviving and healthy current stirred the Party members, the working class and the entire community. People started to straighten their shoulders. Silent, enslaved minds began to shake off the poisonous fumes of deceit, falsehood and duplicity. The creative and living word began to oust the cliché.... The criticism of the past came in a broad wave. It was the criticism of violence, of distortions and errors which affected every single sector of life. ... Above all the working people demanded that the whole truth should be told to them openly, and without any half-truths.

Gomulka proceeded to do so. He painted an all-round picture of the 'evil years', of the fake achievements of the industrial and agricultural plan; of Soviet exploitation; of the crimes against individuals. He then announced the 'Polish road to socialism', the essence of which seemed to realize what people all over the Soviet orbit were hoping for: that the stranglehold over their lives would be eased.

Three days later the Hungarian Revolution broke out.

VI

THE HUNGARIAN
REVOLUTION OF 1956

1 *The young protagonists*

The great 'youth explosion' in Hungary in 1956 was the first full-scale revolution in the 'global village' situation of the electronic age. Instant mass-media reportage modified and amplified the development of events from hour to hour and at times from minute to minute. The broadcasts from the numerous revolutionary radio stations were monitored and taped everywhere, thereby providing masses of historical documentation.

We also have the texts of the propaganda war of nerves addressed to the Hungarian population. The Hungarian-language broadcasts from the Soviet Union and other communist-governed countries, and Western broadcasts of all political shades from virulently and primitively anti-communist to relatively fair liberal reporting ('on the one hand' . . . 'on the other'), played on the nerves of all sections of the population.

Over ten thousand boys and girls between fifteen and twenty-three died in Budapest, fighting 'for something' or 'against something'. Some more can be found in the Central (*Kerepesi*) Cemetery of Budapest. While all other tombstones record only the year of birth and of death, in the case of the young revolutionaries, as a pathetic protest against the regime that suppressed the revolution, the parents had the month and the day carved on as well.* Thousands belonging to the same age-group died fighting in the rest of Hungary, wherever there was a need for fighting.

---

* Examples: 'Kovacs Janos 1934-1956, X. 24.'—'Szabo Ferenc 1937-1956 X.25'. Photos and films of this kind of tombstone in this and other cemeteries of Budapest and throughout Hungary are preserved in many photo and film archives.

There is a great deal of direct and circumstantial evidence that many boys and girls between thirteen and fifteen died as members of revolutionary fighting groups.

There were four or five times as many wounded. After the crushing of the revolt, the Russians deported thousands of young people. The Kadar government continued to execute child revolutionaries till the end of 1959: since, according to law, only over-sixteens can be hanged for political crimes, they were kept in prison until they were old enough to be executed.

Seven hundred journalists from the five continents witnessed this revolution for the world. TV and cinema teams recorded the battles in which the young rebels beat back or neutralized eight divisions of the Soviet occupationary forces. The great illustrated magazines were full of pictures of students, young workers and, indeed, boys and girls of fifteen or younger fighting against tanks.

Yet this first full-scale revolution in the era of instant electronic documentation was still at a controversial stage more than twelve years after the event. The reason for this is that by the time the Soviets reconquered Hungary from the Hungarians, the young rebels had destroyed too many of the myths and doctrines that still prevail in the communist world, the anti-Communist world and the so-called 'third world'.

In the vast literature on youth published in the world since 1957, there was till the end of 1970 not a single volume containing a systematic study of the role of youth in this revolt. Why? Why was the Hungarian Revolution still a controversial event in 1970?

The answer is quite clear. The many thousands of boys and girls who died for their cause inadvertently drove home lessons or demonstrated certain truths that were universally unpopular. For Soviet and satellite governments, and for most of the Communist Parties in the rest of the world, these lessons and truths were exceedingly dangerous. In other quarters they simply meant the need to give up pet prejudices or deep, though mistaken convictions. With all this, and the general repugnance felt by academics for the systematic study of recent history, world public opinion was shielded from these 'truths'.

Hungarian youth, while fighting and dying, confused and/or angered fanatics and extremists with a love of simplification everywhere. The cold-war era taught most people in the West that all communists are evil enemies. Yet in Hungary, thousands of young communists died as 'freedom fighters'. Western communists and their sympathizers knew that anyone who turns against a communist regime was a 'Fascist swine'. Yet in Hungary, workers, students and intellectuals, most of them adherents of democratic socialism, fought against the despotic communist regime. The Dulles doctrine, which still prevailed then, ruled out the possibility of a 'captive nation' liberating itself without outside help, by a mass movement of the left fighting for democratic freedoms. Yet it was precisely this 'impossibility' that came to be realized in Hungary.

Mussolini and Hitler were overthrown by the complete defeat of their armies, not by conspiracy or popular rising. Many people believed therefore that totalitarian dictatorships cannot be overthrown. Yet the Hungarian totalitarian dictatorship – aided by eight Soviet divisions – was overthrown by the people without outside help. Orwell's *1984* and US propaganda had convinced Westerners of the deadly efficiency of 'communist indoctrination'. Yet in Hungary this indoctrination was obviously a total failure.

Jean-Paul Sartre declared: *'C'est la déstalinisation qui déstalinisera les déstalinsateurs'* (It's de-Stalinization that will de-Stalinize the de-Stalinizers'). The hope expressed by this clumsy bit of verbal fireworks had, of course, no foundation in reality. But many people on the confused, 'homeless left' hoped that in time the 'de-Stalinizers' would in fact be 'de-Stalinized'. The youngsters of Hungary died because the exact opposite was true. Liberation movements in Africa and Asia, getting or hoping to get Soviet backing, disliked any reminder of Soviet colonialism. Academic psychiatrists in the East and the West wrote wisely about the inability of the young neurotic to adjust to his society. Yet communist youth, the 'efficiently indoctrinated' or 'pampered' children of the regime, together with most of non-communist youth, turned against the Communist Party and became extremely sane, most un-neurotic organizers and even political leaders of a movement for democratic socialism. And then fought and died by the thousands for their cause.

The young died under many labels. Two year-groups were serving in the army. Most of them took part in the revolution. Several year-groups had been 'workers' since they left school at fifteen or sixteen and fought together with the other, older workers.

By taking part in this revolution that aimed at national independence and democracy, the workers did not play their classical roles as fighters in the class war. The behaviour of these workers belied Lenin's thesis that the working class 'cannot rise above economic consciousness' without its 'valiant vanguard', the Communist Party. Young and old peasants did not behave as they should have either, according to various ideologies. But this was predominantly a youth revolution and, therefore, before discussing their politics, we should take a closer look at these year-groups.

None of the over three hundred books and thousands of articles and essays on this revolution mentioned the rather important fact that nowhere in the world was the proportion of young people in the total population as low as in Hungary in 1956. Compared to most civilized countries, Hungary also had the smallest proportion of university students. Since 1932 the absolute number of under-twenty-ones in the country had been steadily declining. The revolutionary generation of children and young people (between thirteen and twenty-four) were born between 1932 and 1943. During this period the average yearly percentage of live births was around 2.3 and the percentage of those who died before the age of one was between 11.1 and 14.5.

If we take the eighteen-year-olds in 1956 as an example, the figures below give an impression of this year-group:

Number of live births in 1938 . . .	over	182,000
Less: Died below the age of one . . .	over	23,000
Died because of illness, bombing, during the war, epidemics, at least an estimated . . .		8,000
Number of Jewish girls and boys who died in Nazi gas chambers, at least an estimated . . .		10,000*
Died as conscripts at the end of the war in the pro-Nazi Arrow Cross units . . .		1,200
Jewish children killed within Hungary by Arrow Cross units . . .		2,000
remains		138,000

Between 1944 and 1947 over 3,000 children of this year-group were taken to the West by their parents to escape from the communists. If we deduct also the ones who were studying in the

* Hungary had a Jewish minority of slightly over 825,000 people. Of these over 30,000 men died in the Jewish labour battalions on the Eastern front during the war. During the period of the German occupation of Hungary, from March 1944 to April 1945, a total of 501,500 Jews were killed as part of the Nazi plan for the 'final solution' of the Jewish problem.

Soviet Union or the satellites; who were in detention; who were deported together with their 'class-hostile' families to distant provinces and forbidden to live in towns and cities, then in the whole of Hungary there were less than 130,000 eighteen-year-olds at large as free agents. (Even the majority of those who had already begun their compulsory military service had a chance to escape their unit and join the revolutionaries.) The other year-groups, between the ages of seventeen and twenty-four, have a similar demographic and historical profile.

The number of university students and those studying at other institutes of higher education was very low. The various official Hungarian statistical publications and the information given by communist authorities to UNESCO are conflicting. For internal consumption, the authorities gave out higher figures by including those who trained as nursery- or primary-school teachers or enrolled in correspondence courses for adults. The number of students in the true sense of the word was less than 45,000 in the entire country, and of these over seventy per cent were of working-class or peasant origin. These were the students who led and fought the revolution, the historical background of which is described in the next section.

2 *The making of a revolution*

Only when all Soviet and Hungarian archives become available to researchers will it be possible to ascertain who was proportionally the greater mass murderer, Joseph Stalin or his loyal henchman, Mátyás Rákosi, 'the Stalin of Hungary'.

In 1949, when in every satellite 'Titoist conspirators' had to be unmasked on Stalin's orders, Rákosi was determined to execute and imprison every member of the vast party apparatus who was not blindly obedient to him. He also killed or imprisoned all his potential rivals. 'Non-Muscovite' communists and former Spanish Civil War fighters were his prime targets. László Rajk, – a tall, handsome man, Rákosi was short and very ugly – was a hero of Spain and a non-Muscovite to boot. He was chosen to head the non-existent conspiracy. In Budapest and the provinces over three thousand perfectly innocent communists were executed, and over ten thousand imprisoned. The uncouth sadism of the Rajk case, coming after the murder of tens of thousands of non-communist Hungarians, made Rákosi feared and hated not only among the majority of rank-and-file party members, but also among the communist 'priviligentsia'.

Therefore, shortly after the workers' risings in East Germany and Czechoslovakia, the Soviet leaders, fearing similar outbreaks in Hungary, decided to curtail Mátyás Rákosi's dictatorial powers. In June 1953 they deposed him as Prime Minister but left him in charge of the party. The new Premier, Imre Nagy, youth is always the dynamic force of any demonstration against authority.'[9] .

Premier Nagy's 'New Course', by easing slightly the plight of the workers and peasants, engendered hopes for a possible freeer life. Nagy released too swiftly and in too large batches over 80,000 completely innocent political prisoners. These measures, and Nagy's tolerant handling of writers and journalists, displeased the Soviet leaders, who permitted Rákosi to oust Imre Nagy, first from the premiership and later even from the Communist Party. After the brief Hungarian thaw, just when people were feeling that the terrorist stranglehold on their lives would be eased, Rákosi returned to full power in April 1955.

Hopes were raised once more the following month, when the Soviet leaders officially declared that there was no 'Titoist-imperialist conspiracy'. By this time, thanks to the tens of thousands released by Nagy, all Hungary had learned about the horrible tortures in the security-police cellars, by means of which the most ludicrous confessions were obtained. These revelations had, naturally, the greatest effect on children and young people. There remained very few people in the country who did not loathe the SP and its real chief, Rákosi, who liked to boast that he, personally, directed the 'extermination of the Titoist vermin'.

Yet the Soviet leaders, almost as if they wanted to drive the Hungarians insane, dashed their hopes again by publicly assuring Rákosi of their full backing.

After Stalin had been violently denounced at the Twentieth Soviet Party Congress in February 1956, communists and non-communists alike had new reasons for hoping that the Stalinist Rákosi would now be irrevocably ousted. At factory meetings workers publicly demanded his removal.

The growing anti-Rákosi feeling within the party apparatus itself made it possible for the university branch of the Communist Youth League (DISZ) to get permission to found a club for free discussions. It was named after Sándor Petöfi, a great poet and a Byronesque national idol who died fighting against Russian troops sent by the Tsar to suppress the Hungarian War of Liberty of 1848-9.

By using Petöfi's revered name, the communist university students demonstrated to the non-communist majority that they dreamt of a Marxism not opposed to national independence and to the 1848-9 ideal of liberty, equality, fraternity.

In a city where everyone was sick and tired of the many compulsory mass meetings, people waited by the thousand for hours round the large building of the Budapest Army Officers' Club in the hope of witnessing one of the famous Petöfi Club teach-ins. These usually ended with the unanimous demand that Rákosi should be replaced by Imre Nagy.

Irodalmi Ujság ('Literary Gazette'), the official weekly of the Writers' Union, was transformed into something unique in the Soviet orbit: a platform of free writing. In the spring and summer of 1956 the short stories, poems, essays and articles in *Irodalmi Ujság* exposed and attacked many aspects of the 'great lie' and of party dictatorship. In a few weeks its circulation trebled and quadrupled, and it would have grown twenty-fold if the party HQ had not drastically limited its quota of newsprint. The result was that some issues had a black market value of ten, twenty and even fifty times the original price. People delighted in reading the truth to a degree that is difficult to understand for anyone who has never lived under a terrorist dictatorship. Everyone knew perfectly well that Rákosi was a mass murderer. But to read careful hints (and later passionate statements) of this fact seemed wonderful. It gave courage to people. Courage for what? No one knew as yet.

Soon, quite a large proportion of the Hungarian press was in more or less open opposition to the Rákosi regime, which could have banned all the papers and arrested all the editors and writers at will. But writers and journalists in Poland and the USSR were in similarly rebellious mood. Rákosi could not risk doing anything at the moment.

On 27 June, a day before the Poznan rising, the Petöfi Club held a meeting lasting almost twelve hours, which turned into the greatest demonstration yet against Rákosi and for Imre Nagy. Rákosi replied on 30 June by issuing a party resolution strongly condemning the 'anti-party manifestations of the Petöfi Club', which were attributed to Imre Nagy and linked with the 'imperialist provocation of Poznan'. Rákosi planned the arrest of Nagy and four hundred other anti-Stalinists.

But the Soviet leaders would have none of this. They were preaching co-existence and wooing Yugoslavia. Rákosi became a ballast. Nevertheless, Kremlin-type shock treatment of alternating hope and despair went on. At the end of July 1956 the Soviet leaders decided to oust Rákosi and recall him to Moscow, but instead of replacing him with the popular Nagy, they appointed a certain Ernö Gerö, Rákosi's second-in-command. This life-long Comintern agent was despised and loathed by communists and non-communists alike.

All during August and September the revolutionary mood became stronger day by day, both in Poland and in Hungary. To conciliate all those communists who wanted to reestablish 'justice and truth' and, more important, to conciliate the thousands of communist survivors of Rákosi's anti-Tito purges, Gerö's Politbureau gave permission for the ceremonial reburial of László Rajk and the other innocent people executed with him. László Rajk's widow and orphaned son and over three hundred thousand other people gathered for this ceremony held on 6 October. This date had great significance for Hungarians. After their 1848-9 War of Liberty against the Hapsburgs, thirteen leaders of the defeated freedom revolt were hanged on 6 October. Gerö's henchmen (some of whom were stil in power in 1970) made fiery speeches about Rajk's heroism in the Spanish Civil War and solemnly pledged that never again would innocents be killed or imprisoned in a communist state. A few days later, Mihály Farkas, formerly Minister of Defence and immediate overlord of the security police, was arrested.

The revolutionary ferment changed in quality and became much more dynamic with the beginning of the university term. After the daring confidential memoranda of the communist priviligentsia; after the truly courageous inspiration given by many writers; after the revolutionary teach-ins in the Petöfi Club – the students realized that the time had come to attain for Hungary as much democratization and independence as was possible without provoking the Soviet leaders.

No doubt the communist priviligentsia, the Petöfi Club leaders, the very many followers of Imre Nagy and the rest of the ever-growing opposition within the Communist Party wanted the same. But they hoped to attain it within the system, within the 'party constitution'. They wanted the majority of the Central Committee to depose the then ruling Politbureau and replace the Stalinist Gerö with the anti-Stalinist Imre Nagy. These communist rebels were, so to speak, the parliamentary opposition of the Stalinist regime.

The communist and non-communist students and young workers firmly believed – they were, alas, soon proved right – that the then Central Committee would never turn against Stalinism, because they were Stalinists themselves. The students realized that they could not achieve their aims by 'Communist Party constitutionalism'. They knew that the efforts of the 'parliamentary opposition' to the Stalinist leaders were quite hopeless. They were the extra-system opposition, 'the extra-parliamentary opposition' as it were.

Hundreds of communist students spent their days visiting factories and the industrial suburbs. They met thousands of workers who had been imprisoned by Rákosi and released by Imre Nagy; they met young workers whose innocent fathers or brothers had been executed. They met discontented, nauseated, rebellious workers. It was thanks to these students that three hundred thousand people showed up at the Rajk funeral.

The news of the victory of the bloodless Polish Revolution gave everybody hope and courage. It showed that their dreams and plans were not too optimistic. When the Hungarian papers reported on 20 October that Gomulka (the Polish Imre Nagy, as he was then called) had announced the 'independent Polish road to socialism', a great many Hungarians became determined to attain similar independence.

The last act of the Polish Revolution was a vote in the Central Committee that elected Gomulka. The Hungarian Party priviligentsia still hoped that their Central Committee would do the same, and that there would be only a few days more to wait for the victory of the 'bloodless Hungarian Revolution'. The intellectuals and the rebellious young people were greater realists; they believed that the Hungarian Centcom could be forced to similar action only if they had unmistakable evidence that the majority of the people were in an angry, impatient mood, and that they wanted their 'Gomulka' and their 'independent road' now. They wanted to achieve everything by non-violent means, without provoking the Kremlin.

At the universities all over the country there were all-night student meetings, joined by most of the professors, planning details for the peaceful removal of the terrorist regime. At the high schools the sixteen-to-eighteen-year-olds formed committees to draft their messages to the nearest university, where one of the political manifestos of Hungarian youth was being written.

These boys and girls had been subjected to communist indoctrination since early childhood; most of them were the sons and daughters of workers and peasants, since, as we have seen, class origin was the regime's chief criterion for admission to university or even middle school; and finally, a great many of them belonged to the Communist Youth League. Yet it was this group of students which demanded 'a truly independent, democratic-socialist Hungary', 'the establishment of Hungarian-Soviet friendship on the basis of equality', 'workers' participation in factory management' – and 'the withdrawal of Soviet troops'.

And they were the ones who planned and organized the great Budapest demonstration that was, in fact, the prelude to the revolution.

3 *The explosion*

Since the Budapest demonstration of 23 October 1956 was one of the most important links in the chain of events in the development of the revolutionary situation, it is necessary to see when and by whom it was planned.

Students in all the university cities of the country were convinced that festive meetings or dignified processions should be organized as soon as possible to 'demonstrate sympathy for Poland', to 'protest against Stalinism in the spirit of Polish-Hungarian friendship', to demand 'an independent Hungarian road to socialism'. In Szeged, the second largest city in the country, the students founded their own independent organization outside the official communist one. The party leaders had to accept the *fait accompli*. There were meetings, sit-ins and teach-ins everywhere to decide on detailed demands.

In the universities and other institutes for higher education in Budapest there were various types of student meetings starting on 21 October. Some were legal as far as the university authorities were concerned, some illegal. Some meetings decided to organize a huge demonstration with speech choirs shouting carefully worked-out slogans, others voted for silent demonstrations. One of the latter type somehow became most effective as far as the people of Budapest were concerned. The Communist Youth Organization of the Building Industry Technological University in Budapest called a meeting for 3 p.m. on 22 October to discuss a series of student demands.* This meeting, which contrary to plans lasted eleven hours, until the early morning of 23 October, had a fluctuating attendance of between 4,000 and 5,000 people. During the evening a considerable number of workers joined it.

At first discussion was restricted to strictly student demands. Later, voices from all over the hall urged that the students should formulate and adopt a programme for the establishment of democracy in Hungary in the spirit of the 1848 revolution and submit it to the government. These and other demands (the withdrawal of Soviet troops, free elections, freedom of speech and religion) were written down in a draft resolution of ten points. During the evening and night, the original ten points became fourteen and later sixteen. Among the new ones was the removal of the statue of Stalin in Budapest and of the Soviet-style emblem from the Hungarian national flag.

The students also inserted in the resolution their decision to meet again on 24 October and to start a nation-wide debate on these questions. They demanded that the radio should give a live broadcast of this meeting, so that 'the working people will hear without distortion the true voice of Hungarian youth'. The plan to hold a demonstration next day was an almost accidental by-product of this meeting. A representative of the Writers' Union announced that the Union would celebrate Polish-Hungarian friendship at a small meeting, but the writers did not plan any kind of demonstration.

Again, voices from all parts of the hall urged a large, peaceful demonstration. It was soon decided that the Technological University should organize such a demonstration and call on all students and factory workers to participate. When professors advised the meeting to be cautious, students reassured them that they had thoroughly learned the need for caution. It was then emphasized: 'We want a silent demonstration because it is only

* In the technological universities the exclusion of students 'with class-hostile origin' was most strictly adhered to. This university approximated to the party ideal for the class origin of students: sixty per cent working-class, thirty per cent poor peasant and only ten per cent 'intelligentsia and others'. Moreover, the proportion of communist students (members of DISZ) was higher there than the national average in the universities.

by peaceful, orderly and silent demonstrations that we can gain our end.' (These engineering students did not know about the decision at other campuses to demonstrate with speech choirs.) When the meeting itself was closed, it was obvious that these engineering students attached far more significance to their 24 October meeting than to the hastily planned demonstration for the next day.

On 23 October the people of Budapest awoke in a buoyant mood. The various ten-point, twelve-point or sixteen-point demands were typed and roneoed by the thousand everywhere, and by morning they had been fastened to tree trunks on the boulevards, pasted on billboards, nailed to doors and stuck on the sides of tram cars. These manifestos – uncensored by the party – informed adults that the 'youth of October' was acting. All Hungarians knew at once that the form and style of the student demands aimed to remind everyone of Hungary's finest hour when the 'Youth of March', led by Petöfi, published their twelve demands that led to the instant victory of the 'bloodless Hungarian Revolution' of 1848. (It was only later that this was turned into a two-year war for liberty by the obstinacy of Hungary's Hapsburg oppressors.)

During the morning, preparations were made at all the universities and colleges and all the secondary schools of the capital for the long protest march through the main avenues and boulevards of Budapest. The route chosen was a manifesto in itself: the Hungarian War of Liberty of 1848-9, crushed by the Russians, had foreign heroes too; the greatest of them was the Polish general Joseph Bem, who became one of the most admired commanders of those nineteenth-century freedom fighters; the students announced that they would march from the statue of Petöfi on the left bank of the Danube to that of General Bem, some distance away on the other side.

On the same morning, the executive of the Communist Youth League and a majority of the Writers' Union decided to join the marchers. The rebellious writers formulated their own seven points since, as they wrote, 'the leaders of the Party and the State so far have failed to present a workable programme. . . The people responsible for this . . . are obstinately organizing themselves with the aim of restoring Stalin's and Rákosi's regime of terror in Hungary'. Tens of thousands of workers also decided to join the march.

The Stalinist leadership vacillated. The Minister of the Interior at first prohibited the demonstration then, when the march had already started, Budapest Radio announced at 14.23 that the government had withdrawn the ban on public meetings and demonstrations.

The demonstrators, joined by tens of thousands of passers-by, grew in number to nearly 300,000. The students, the other marchers, the onlookers, in fact the entire country felt that Hungary was marching towards the same sort of bloodless victory that promised some freedom to the Poles. They had many reasons for feeling this way. A great patriotic demonstration was taking place that had not been planned and ordered by the party; the terrorist regime which punished by torture, prison and death even a whisper of dissent had to order its organ of terrorism, the security police, to keep off the streets while the people were demonstrating specifically against them. The jubilant mood of the marchers was not entirely shared by the organizers. They were thinking of the possibility of provocation from the Stalinists and the SP so as to create a suitable pretext for the bloody suppression of the movement. The order of the day was: 'There mustn't be any violence!'

The march of the vast crowd lasted for hours. There was not a single incident. Some of the ordinary police in their blue uniforms joined the marchers. The brown-uniformed security police disappeared from the streets. The feeling of an approaching bloodless victory was strengthened by the sight of a great many soldiers among the marchers, including (as Radio Budapest stated at midnight) 800 cadets of the Military Officers' Academy, most of whom were the sons of leading party members.

The demonstrators sang the National Anthem and chanted slogans like 'Independence, Liberty'; 'Polish-Hungarian Friendship'; 'Down with Stalinism'; 'Imre Nagy for Premier!' But most of the time the crowd repeated two lines of the 1848 poem by Petöfi:

> This we swear, this we swear,
> Slaves we no more be!

The Hungarian communist emblem of hammer and wheatsheaf was torn out from the centre of the original Hungarian flag and these holed flags became the first banners of the revolution. The centre piece was replaced a little later by the old

135

Hungarian emblem of 1848. At about the same time another slogan was more and more often repeated by the crowd: 'Soldiers of each country are to return to their fatherland!'

After applauding several revolutionary speeches at the statue of Bem, the majority of the crowd surged on to the huge Parliament Square, to demand that Nagy should be re-instated as Premier. Meanwhile, a student deputation went to Budapest Radio to demand that their sixteen points be broadcast. Some workers, feeling that they had an important score to settle with the regime, hurried to Stalin Square to topple the twenty-five-foot bronze statue of the dead dictator. It was a very solid statue; the cable ropes fastened to its neck and pulled by heavy lorries could not move it an inch. The resistance of the dead metal had an even more inflammatory effect on the workers; it seemed to be symbolic. When someone called up the steelworkers of a suburb called Red Csepel they came by the thousands; their oxy-acetylene torches melted the enormous knees and, when the lorries pulled once more, the statue toppled forward and fell. The roaring crowd mounted the pedestal and built a bonfire on Stalin's boots, which were still standing; the flames were fed by their Communist Party membership booklets.

Meanwhile, the other huge crowd, growing in numbers all the time, waited in vain for the appearance of Imre Nagy on the balcony of the parliament building. Instead, at 8 p.m. Gerö, the Stalinist party boss, broadcast a speech in which he attacked the demonstration in the most vicious language as a 'counter-revolutionary attempt organized by the enemies of the working class'.

Everyone had been desperate to hear the news, good news, hoping that Gerö would announce the premiership of Imre Nagy and accept the victory of the bloodless revolution *à la Poland*. So thousands of radio sets were put in open windows and, as by now the streets were filled with people almost everywhere, the whole of Budapest heard Gerö's speech. They heard the virtual promulgation of a return to full terrorism. What people did not know was that by now Gerö and his Soviet advisers were preparing for the incident which they thought would help them back into full power but which, in fact, sparked off a total armed uprising. The security police opened fire on the as yet unarmed demonstrators before the Radio Building, killing many, and at the same time some army units arrived in lorries, called in by the SP. The first to die were some members of the student deputation. This

136

vicious murder changed the mood of the demonstrating crowd in seconds; they were 'their' children. The arriving Hungarian soldiers either handed over their weapons to the crowd or joined them in firing back at the security police.

The news of the unprovoked assault mobilized the youth of the capital, while the workers of the many industrial suburbs took the factory, warehouse and other lorries and hurried to 'help the kids against the security police'. In the armament factories workers raided the stores, and soon lorries full of small arms were being hurried to the city centre. In some of the military barracks where Stalinist commanders prevented the soldiers from leaving, the soldiers threw out their small arms to the rebels. Soon news of the battle of the Radio Building had spread to the provinces and, naturally, triggered off the pent-up fury of the people. From an uprising in a city it turned into a full-scale, nation-wide revolution.

Without planning or preparation, a people atomized and turned against each other by the ideology of hate, intolerance and suspicion became united in the belief in a better past (1848), so often observed in the emotional motivation of revolutions.

Before midnight on 23 October, there was sporadic fighting between SP troops and young people all over the capital. The mood was bitter and most imprudent. By dawn new slogans were scribbled on the walls: they were very different indeed from the peaceful ones of the previous day: 'Russki go home!'

But they were just coming.

Some medium-sized tanks and armoured riot cars of the Soviet MVD (security police) Brigade that were permanently stationed in Budapest were the first to fire at the rebels. By next morning, another MVD brigade stationed in nearby Székesfehérvár reached the capital. By 9 a.m. on 24 October, counting the MVD brigades and the Soviet troops guarding main airbases in Hungary, more than three Soviet divisions and thousands of Hungarian security-police troops had been fighting the 'handful of fascists' in and around Budapest for hours. At the same time the radio, still in Gerö's hands, announced that 'Hungarian government organs appealed to the Soviet forces stationed in Hungary, according to the Warsaw Pact, to help them restore order'. They also broadcast that the party's Central Committee, led by Gerö, had decided to 'recommend to the state authorities to appoint Imre Nagy as Prime Minister'.

The allegation that Nagy was willing to serve under Gerö was unfounded. Nagy was held a virtual prisoner at the party HQ during the first three days of his premiership, and was kept incommunicado. By then, most Hungarian regiments (young people in uniform) stationed in Budapest had joined the freedom fighters. All the ammunition in their barracks was, naturally, at their disposal. Several arsenals were taken over 'in the name of the revolution' by their own guards.

University campuses on both sides of the Danube were turned into guerrilla centres. The fourteen- to eighteen-year-olds formed their own fighting squads. Adult efforts to prevent the very young from fighting were absolutely useless. They put to good use their compulsory reading of Fadeyev's *Young Guard,* which gave detailed instructions on how to manufacture Molotov cocktails. This was swiftly and expertly done and soon the streets were littered with Russian tanks aflame.

As the fighting groups mushroomed everywhere in the city, the young rebels occupied the roofs and top floors of buildings at street crossings and machine-gunned the SP and the MVD tanks. In some of the industrial suburbs many of the guerrilla units were led by self-appointed commanders, while others were directed by the newly formed workers' councils. At first the fighting was completely unorganized and only some neighbouring groups were in touch with each other. A hastily improvised liaison network began to operate only after several groups had fired at each other under the mistaken impression that the others were SP men in civilian clothes. This is a most important point, as the Soviets, after the crushing of the revolt, alleged that 'the fascist counter-revolution' had been planned and organized previously and from abroad. When the Soviet propagandists spoke of a 'rucksackful of pistols' smuggled into the country, they were deceiving no one who was there, since Hungary had far more automatic pistols and tommy guns than men to use them.

Western journalists wrote with tolerant amusement about the 'irrational anger' of the young fighters when they heard about this. But for people brought up in the Soviet orbit, this 'obviously silly lie' was an official notification that in the event of defeat they would be executed as the 'paid agents of imperialism'.

The Stalinist leadership at that point made their first two most serious political miscalculations. They counted on the help of the Hungarian army, as their army. This was disproved within the first twenty-four hours and they came to realize then – and then only – that they could count on nothing and no one except the Russians.

The second mistake, just as serious, was to misjudge the importance and popular appeal of Imre Nagy. Rather than permit a Polish-style mild democratization, they temporarily compromised Nagy by lies and forgeries: yet he was the only person who sixteen hours earlier could have been accepted as the 'Hungarian Gomulka'. But the idea of a popular communist leader or of 'communism by consent' was loathed just as much by Khrushchev and John Foster Dulles in 1956 as it was by Brezhnev and Dean Rusk during the Czech crisis in 1968.

At noon on 24 October, Mikoyan and Suslov arrived by jet at a nearby Soviet airbase and a Soviet tank convoy delivered them to the Budapest party HQ. They decided to replace Gerö with Janos Kadar, one of Rákosi's former assistants in the anti-Titoist purges. The Soviet emissaries believed that Kadar would be accepted by the majority of the party, as Rákosi in his 'arrestomania' had sent him to prison in 1951, from which he was released only in 1953 by Imre Nagy. After arranging some other window-dressing changes in the Hungarian party leadership, Mikoyan and Suslov, accompanied by Gerö, flew back to Moscow next day, the decisive day of the revolution.

4   One day of a revolution: 25 October 1956

'History' moves with such astonishing speed during revolutions that there are some 'historical epochs' which last only a couple of hours, some only five minutes. In each epoch, the protagonists, the two or more mutually hostile camps and so on, are motivated by a slightly or greatly changed mental-emotional climate; they react to new facts-in-facts and facts-in-words; and even their false consciousness may have changed a bit.

Any day in any revolution resembles a most complex three-dimensional molecular structure that moves at great speed, while all its particles change their shape and direction all the time. An immense Panavision screen would give an impression of such a day by showing simultaneously what is going on in various rooms in which a few persons are tremendously busy arguing, deciding, telephoning and issuing orders in the belief that they are vitally influencing events, while by far the greatest area of the screen would show what the people as a whole are doing.

To remain within this wide-screen analogy, several film squares could show the various offices in the party HQ. In one of these Kadar, the new party boss, confers with his underlings, who are loyal to the Kremlin. Fiery debates go on about the methods to be used to force the captive Premier, Imre Nagy, to broadcast a text they have written for him.

Another film square: the stocky Nagy sits in the room which has been his prison since the night of 23 October. He says that he would rather die than read the Kadarist text. In the end there is a compromise, but Nagy's captors have to yield more.

Two other rooms. In the first, one high-ranking Stalinist intrigues against Kadar because he is too soft on the rebels. In the other, anti-Stalinist medium-rank functionaries plan to oust him because he still pretends to believe that this is a counter-revolution.

Still at party HQ, in a large office, Kadar's propagandists are writing the official communiqués from the non-existent Council of Ministers. Since one of the transmitters of Radio Budapest is guarded by Soviet tanks, these communiqués are broadcast to the people. On this decisive day, the first communiqué is broadcast at 5 a.m.:

'. . . The Army, the State Security Authority and the armed workers' guards, assisted by Soviet troops, have liquidated an attempted counter-revolutionary *coup d'état* during the night of 24-5 October.'
At 9 a.m.:
'The Army shall by midday finally liquidate the counter-revolutionary forces still to be found in Budapest.'
At 11 a.m.:
'Those who raise their arms against the State power of our People's Republic and fail to lay them down within the time limit fixed shall be annihilated without mercy.'
At 12.32 p.m.:
A communiqué informs the people that Gerö has been replaced by Janos Kadar as First Secretary of the party.
At 3.18 p.m.
Kadar broadcasts about 'the armed attack against the People's Democracy'.

140

Before midnight on 25 October:
There is a new ultimatum and the time limit to lay down arms is once more extended.

In the intervals between the ultimatums they play Viennese waltzes and operettas.

In the parliament, at the Writers' Union and elsewhere, Imre Nagy's friends and some members of his future cabinet are working all day long on preparations to free the Prime Minister. By the evening they succeed, and Nagy arrives at his Premier's offices.

In a huge city where everyone lives in blocks of flats, every flat is in the front line. The walls, which give a feeling of safety in normal times, are now pitifully, ridiculously weak. By this decisive day there were very few neutrals. One of the 'revolutionizing' factors was the incessant provocation by the SP and the MVD who, by firing from the roof tops on women and children queueing for bread, replenished the ranks of the city-guerrillas all the time. These provocations succeeded: more Soviet troops were called in while some people, although reluctant to get involved, turned into guerrillas after the murder of their next-of-kin. Deputations to party HQ were useless; one of them, an unarmed university deputation on 25 October, led by the Dean of the Faculty of History, Professor Toth, was machined-gunned by the security police. First to die was the old Dean.

For the Stalinists it was a most dangerous sign that many Russian soldiers were fraternizing with the Hungarians and that some of them had even joined the freedom fighters. The policy of making Russian a compulsory subject at all schools had now a very adverse effect. Too many Hungarians could talk to the Russians, hence many Russians had to be killed.

One important incident also happened on 25 October when a procession of workers, joined by their wives, marched unarmed to parliament. They carried Hungarian and black flags in honour of the dead. There, a handful of Soviet tanks and armoured cars were on guard and their commander, learning about the peaceful aims of the march, said that as long as no one fired at his tanks, he would not give orders to fire. The crowd cheered; some Hungarians even embraced the Russian soldiers. The security police, perched on a rooftop on the opposite side of the square, saw this and immediately fired at the Russians, thereby causing horrible confusion, and the death of some Russians and Hungarians.

By machine-gunning the square the SP got what they wanted. Everyone was now shooting at everyone else. This was the famous 'Parliament Square massacre' which was wrongly, but understandably, attributed to the Russians. The true facts were established a few days later by the freedom fighters themselves, but by that time the false rumour was widespread and had led to the death of further thousands of people.

By sheer accident, the Stalinist Minister of Defence presented the revolutionaries with a brilliant commander on this very day. The largest military complex in the city, Killian Barracks, situated in the centre of the capital, was in the hands of rebel officers and troops. On 25 October Colonel Paul Maléter was given orders to take the barracks with a tank battalion and disarm the 'counter-revolutionaries'. But Maléter, an anti-Stalinist communist, took the Killian in the name of the revolution. These barracks were at the crossing of Üllöi Avenue, the continuation of the important highway going through Budapest in an East-West direction, and the main boulevard. The importance of this crossing was realized not only at party HQ, but also by the people in the neighbouring working-class district. The six Pongracz brothers organized a regiment of young workers (most of them communists till the 23) and occupied the huge blocks called Corvin Mansions, opposite the Killian Barracks.

It was obvious to the Soviet command that Colonel Maléter's troops and the Corvin regiment were sealing off a very large section of Budapest. This crossing held out till the final victory. It was never on the defensive. Many offensives were launched against Soviet tank battalions trying to cross at other crossings in the vicinity.

Maléter, who was soon promoted Major General by Premier Nagy, sent young officers to various military barracks in the country, where Stalinists still had the upper hand, to get the men to chase away their commander and join the freedom fighters. Many of these emissaries were successful. Maléter, and former inmates of the SP prisons such as General Bela Kiraly, improvised a general staff for something that was turning into a war for national independence.

Some of the riskiest actions planned by this improvised high command were successful because of the unforeseen help of children and teenagers. By 25 October there were several hundred fighting groups in and around the capital, consisting mostly of children and teenagers. It was they who manufactured the Molotov cocktails. These were ordinary syphon bottles from the top of which hung two ribbons, 15 cm long. The syphon was filled with petrol, which saturated the ribbons. A match was lit, put to the ribbons and the bottle was thrown. In the next second a tank was aflame.

Some of the fighting groups of youngsters had older commanders. One group on the outskirts of Buda was commanded by a girl not yet fifteen.

The Soviet high command failed to realize till the very end that tanks are ineffective weapons against city guerrillas. They cannot manoeuvre well in narrow streets, and even in broad avenues they cannot fire at guerrillas crouching forward too near to them. The Molotov cocktails, the barrels of liquid soap poured out in great quantities all over the large squares, and many other improvizations made by the youngsters caused great havoc.

Although the four divisions permanently stationed in Hungary were joined by an additional four tank divisions, for this type of warfare the Soviet command needed infantry. Later, in Hungarian hospitals, wounded Soviet soldiers related that their infantry divisions started off for Hungary only on 26 October.

5 *Towards victory and defeat*

Imre Nagy, already a free man, appointed ministers and set up the nucleus of a cabinet apparatus in a country where most of the ministries, provincial government bureaux and municipalities had been taken over by revolutionary committees. These bodies refused to take orders from party or government.

Meanwhile, the official trade unions, as indeed all other existing institutions, were either replaced by new ones or taken over by revolutionary committees. The trade unions were replaced by workers' councils at all levels. Contrary to Lenin's thesis the workers, left to their own devices, led by their own instincts, were eminently capable of developing 'true socialist consciousness'. Having abolished the hated fake trade unions, the new workers' councils managed factories, municipal districts, entire towns.

Meanwhile, the former political parties stirred themselves to new life. In the safety of flats and air-raid shelters they planned how to get the largest possible portion of power for their group after the victory of the revolution.

Meanwhile, the children and the young were fighting and dying. To paraphrase Michelet: 'From the beginning to the end there was only one hero – youth.'

Something very rare in history had happened: the young of a whole nation had risen spontaneously and in the turmoil of fighting had taken momentary leadership. Tens of thousands of adults joined them. The uprising turned into a Hungarian War of Liberty.

Anna Kamienska, the Polish poetess, wrote that in the thaw period people were 'in a delirium of impossible possibilities'. In Hungary, young and old were equally affected. But the young were able to play the proper role of youth.

In 1956, the cold war between the generations was still in its initial stages in the Western world and its mental and emotional climate had not yet penetrated the Soviet orbit. It was almost abnormal how little tension there was between the generations. The people as a whole shared the convictions, sentiments and aspirations of the young *avant-garde* of the revolution.

For this and some other reasons the Hungarian Revolution can serve as a control case, since most other youth revolts occurred in countries where there were normal tensions between youth and grown-ups (Red China and Indonesia, for instance), or in the abnormal anti-youth and anti-student atmosphere in the Western world.

During the Rákosi era, the non-communist majority of adults regarded students and children as innocent victims of communist hypno-pedagogics, of indoctrination and intimidation. Like Western sociologists of the early nineteen-sixties, Hungarian party functionaries believed that undergraduates were becoming cautious old men at twenty, and turning their backs on involvement and social responsibility.

The behaviour of youth between 20 and 23 October, and the way they fought after that, showed that they had not been corrupted by indoctrination. For adult Hungarians with open minds, these students, young workers and children seemed less foolish, less recklessly brave, less delirious, than they seemed to the outside world. Subjected to the same sort of shock treatment of alternating hope and despair, and to the same sort of provocation, the young of any and every country would have behaved the same way, provided they felt that the majority of adults did not hate them!

Since state and party authority disintegrated almost at once, and since this revolution was entirely spontaneous, individual adults (such as policemen, army officers, hospital directors, telephone-exchange managers) were not directed by some central authority to hand over their arms or services and to join forces with the rebellious young. They did so because they agreed with the aims of the revolt and because, instead of having an anti-youth bias, they were pro-youth.

Hungarian youth and even many pre-teenagers proved themselves to be politically mature, though biologically they were in the puberty period, with chemical turmoil and a gonadic revolution going on in their bodies. No doubt they, too, had periods of hyper-excitability alternating with enervation or dejection, but the deadly political and later physical dangers round them made them shrewd and cautious verbal operators, efficient political animals and disicplined fighters in an unorganized revolution.

Young people and children played a decisive role in the first three days of the Budapest fighting. By 6 a.m. on 26 October the Budapest hospitals had taken in over 11,000 wounded. Nearly sixty-six per cent of all casualties were young men and women, and boys and girls between thirteen and twenty-one. Budapest had by that time over five thousand dead. Not all of them died while fighting. But among those killed in battle the majority were still under twenty-one, and of both sexes.*

After their escape from Hungary to the West, the young survivors of this period and of these battles were astonished to find how little attention was being paid by Western sociologists and psychologists to female youth. A detailed history of these battles would show many instances in which the initiative, the leadership, the inventiveness of a girl commander or girl fighter turned near defeat into victory.

* Since a great many books on the Hungarian Revolution maintain that writers had a principal role in it, I would like to emphasize that I do not want to belittle their role as mouthpieces of popular feeling and even as inspirers. I am not biased against the writers. I was one of the two representatives of the Writers' Union in the Killian Barracks when the Central Revolutionary Armed Forces Committee (*Központi Forradalmi Karhtalmi Bizottság*) was formed, and I wrote for the *Irodalmi Ujság*. But due to the various minor parts I played in the revolt, I was able to be an eye witness of events, when the great prudence or astonishing courage of the young people did more in a second than a great deal of most 'heroic writing'.

Budapest was once a city of light-hearted people, a city of jokes. By 26 October all sorts of grim and not-so-grim jokes circulated about the revolution; many of them were about children.

Here are two examples:

Two youngsters ring the bell of a fussy old lady living in a block of flats. 'Good morning, Mrs X,' they say. 'If we wipe our feet properly, may we come in and shoot out of your window?'

Young Peter comes home for a meal. Afterwards his mother wraps him up and says: 'I'll crown you if you catch cold.' 'I'll take care, Mummy,' says Peter, picks up his tommygun and goes back to the barricades.

Between 23 and 26 October eight Soviet divisions, the Hungarian SP troops under Russian commanders and the two Russian MVD brigades – especially trained and super-equipped to quell revolts – were unable to defeat the youth of Hungary. During the next three days, the freedom fighters beat the Soviet forces in most of Budapest and the provinces. The military successes would have been impossible without the thousandfold resistance of the whole country. As Dr Paul Kecskemeti has pointed out: 'To my knowledge, this was the first time in history that the syndicalist myth of the revolutionary general strike, as set forth by George Sorel, actually became the basis of sustained political action by the entire industrial population of a country.[1]

It should be added that the rest of the population participated fully in the general strike everywhere. Work went on only in those services that could materially assist resistance and keep the Hungarian population going. Many books and articles about this revolution belittle the role of the provinces and, especially, that of the peasantry. Only a picture of the overall developments can indicate how unjust this is. In some regions and towns there was heavy fighting. In the town of Magyaróvár the local SP massacred an unarmed procession led by women with babies in arms and little boys and girls, together with other people of all ages. They killed eighty people and wounded over three hundred. In other towns, the local SP commanders had disappeared by dawn on 24 October. In a few smaller cities and towns revolutionary councils seized power as early as 24 and 25 October.

The many freedom radios broadcast the victories in Budapest and the provinces. People believed them, since the Stalinist Radio stated several times a day that 'the handful of fascist counter-revolutionaries' had been annihilated during the last hour or so. The failure of the Soviets to crush the revolution in Budapest and elsewhere was demonstrated to the provinces by the long succession of violent ultimatums broadcast to the rebels, each one extending the time limit. The easy victories in many regions were greatly helped by these stupid propaganda tactics. Those provincial authorities that were still loyal to the Kremlin were thoroughly frightened by them.

The Hungarian peasantry did not remain aloof from the revolution. In most regions they were able to take over their villages and collective farms without firing a shot. Where there was resistance they killed the local party men and the SP. Then they proceeded to feed the cities. Tens of thousands of horse-drawn carts and collective farm lorries laden with food managed to reach Budapest and the other cities. Old and young peasants risked their lives by crossing Soviet or even MVD-held regions in the countryside. Many died. Most of the food was given away free.

On 28 October the Prime Minister announced that the Hungarian and Soviet governments had made an agreement according to which Soviet troops would immediately start to withdraw from Budapest. The government accepted the demands of the freedom fighters and intended to start negotiations with the USSR about the withdrawal of Soviet troops from Hungary. The security police would be immediately disbanded. On 30 October, the seventh day of the revolt, the Soviet government declared that it had given orders to the commander-in-chief in Hungary to withdraw his troops from Budapest 'as soon as the Hungarian government so desired'. The USSR was, furthermore, 'ready to open discussions on the general position of Soviet troops in Hungary'.

The revolutionaries felt that they had won. They had, in fact, defeated the oppressive regime and the Soviet occupying forces. Soviet troops withdrew from Budapest. General Maléter, the hero of Killian Barracks, became Deputy Defence Minister. Social democratic and other former parties were revived and many new ones formed. The country went on a spree of 'democratic pluralism'.

On 1 November Premier Nagy declared Hungary's withdrawal from the Warsaw Pact and proclaimed the country's neutrality. In a cable to its Secretary General he informed the United Nations of these steps and requested that UN observers should be sent to Budapest at once. This request was not granted. The Western powers did not guarantee Hungarian independence and neutrality; India and other recently liberated nations did not demonstrate that they stood for self-determination for all peoples, not simply for some African and Asian ones.

Hungary had three days of freedom. People enjoyed the luxury of debate and dialogue. After years of enforced fake unanimity in a one-party system, they were happy to disagree. But 'the truth' was still supremely important. Although most of the victorious revolutionaries fought for the freedom of the press, and certainly all of them were against any kind of censorship, newspapers were 'censored' by the crowds in the street. On 1 and 2 November many new journals appeared. If the crowds in the street found a real or alleged 'lie' in a paper, they took the entire bundle from the newsvendor or burnt it. One of the few papers that was not burnt in any part of the capital or the provinces was *Irodalmi Ujság*. So everything that was printed in its revolutionary issue of 2 November was considered to be the truth by eyewitnesses. Most of the paper was a homage to youth. László Németh, one of the outstanding novelists of the country, wrote:

Sitting here I am thinking of the young girl who was fighting on the Calvin Square roof. Her comrades, all men, had been killed at her side but she went on firing until her young body crumpled, too. . . . In my heart it is this little girl who speaks; it is she who has sent the message from the rooftop: 'Go on, old candidate of death. If I give my fine young life, what does it matter if you, poor human relic, do your own duty?'

Milán Füst, the poet, who was then sixty-eight years old, wrote in the flowery language of those hectic days:

Our beloved younger brothers and sisters, the youth of today, so often called frivolous and cynical—you have set an eternal example of not hesitating when the moment came to answer, when fate and time questioned us. Eternal gratitude to you for this lesson. You have grown into symbols for your fathers and for the youth of the future.

The leading article was about the 'double victory over tyranny'.

The first on the battlefields of the countryside and Budapest in recent days; the second during the long period of terror. . . . This terror wanted to ruin our people morally as well; reduce our back-bones to pulp: poison the souls of our youth. . . . In these days we proved to the whole world that they were unable to ruin us morally, to break our backbones, to debase our youth. The Age of Horror only toughened our children, turning them into good politicians and heroic fighters. The twelve- to fourteen-year-old boys and girls who attacked with their bare hands the troop-carriers of the SP hangmen and hurled petrol-filled bottles at the tanks had become fighters in these desolate times. We believe and avow that tyranny can lead only to similar effects in every country and in every people.

Most of the foreign observers, diplomats and journalists have stated repeatedly that the Hungarian uprising was one of the purest of all revolutions. All through the fighting there was no looting at all. Shop windows were shattered but the contents of the shops were left untouched. There were fewer house-breakings and thefts committed than during any average week in any big city in the world. A people engaged in a life-or-death struggle for liberty and independence does not loot.

But it is a fact that on 31 October and 1 November mobs of people lynched SP officers and men. The Writers' Union and the various revolutionary bodies of youth warned and protested against the lynchings. Radio broadcasts and newspaper articles begged everybody not to soil the revolution with the law of the mob. The new National Guard, formed from revolutionary youth, saved several hundred SP men. Some girls and boys even got wounded while defending SP men from the mob. Yet nearly seventy SP men were lynched in Budapest.

Those SP men who were saved by the young revolutionaries and taken to the safety of prisons were released by the Soviet army and were able to arrest those who had saved their necks.

On 3 November Nagy formed a new coalition government of Communists, Social-Democrats, Smallholders and National Peasants. All these parties had been licensed by the post-war Soviet authorities as proven anti-fascist.

On the same day the Soviet Embassy invited a Hungarian military delegation to the Soviet HQ near Budapest to 'negotiate further Soviet withdrawals'. The Hungarian plenipotentiaries, Generals Maléter and Kovach, were arrested. Thus the Russians deprived Hungary of its ablest leaders and completed their preparations for the next day.

At dawn on 4 November the people of Budapest were woken by the terrific roar of concentrated heavy artillery attack against the encircled city. In a 4.20 a.m. broadcast Imre Nagy informed the nation and the world of the Soviet attack against Hungary and its legal government.

Political preparations, too, had been made by the Russians at the same time. Janos Kadar, the new party boss, did history's fastest Quisling act. During the days of freedom, Kadar had broadcast his great admiration for 'this glorious uprising of our people' and had only praise for Imre Nagy. A few hours after Nagy had included him in his coalition government Kadar sneaked out from the parliament building to be spirited away by the Russians. Due to some hitch, he broadcast his 'government's' request for Soviet armed help several hours after the beginning of the Soviet offensive to reconquer Hungary from the Hungarians.

With their vast numerical superiority and with no need to have the slightest regard for world opinion (Eden and his associates chose these days for their Suez adventure), the Soviet commanders succeeded in suppressing almost all Hungarian resistance after eleven days of further fighting.

The facts of this revolution remain controversial, and they cannot be assessed at all without a brief review of the aftermath.

Hungary as a whole protested against the Soviet occupation and against the puppet regime with a nation-wide general strike that lasted from 5 November until 22 November. In those circumstances this total general strike involved great sacrifices and demonstrated the unanimity of the country.

The first news of mass deportations of young people came on 12 November, when Debrecen railwaymen found messages near the lines: messages from young men and women who were being taken eastwards in cattle trucks. They had scribbled their names and addresses on bits of paper and pushed the messages through the boards of the trucks. Next day Kadar and Co. were told by deputations of workers, miners, students and writers that the people would not stand for this. The miners threatened to flood the mines. The railwaymen refused to work. Kadar denied that he had any knowledge of deportations, but nevertheless promised that they would cease. General Grebennik, the Soviet Commander of Hungary, admitted that there had been a few deportations, which were the actions of 'individual units'. The UN was informed on 19 November that approximately 16,000 young

Hungarians had been deported to the USSR. Three authorities were arresting and deporting people: 1. The Soviet Army Command; 2. The Soviet MVD Command of Hungary; 3. The new security police of the Kadar clique.

On 23 November Imre Nagy and his associates, who had been given asylum in the Yugoslav Embassy, were tricked into leaving it by a guarantee of safety and were promptly arrested. On 5 December Soviet troops fired at 15,000 women in black demonstrating on behalf of the dead in Budapest. Deportations of arrested freedom fighters to Russia continued.

In the first three months of 1957 'counter-revolutionaries' were executed in batches; arrests continued; the Writers' Union and all Workers' Councils were disbanded. Russian became compulsory again in all primary schools. Striking was punishable by death.

During the winter of 1956-7 nearly 230,000 Hungarians escaped to the West through Austria and Yugoslavia, including over 50,000 industrial workers, 7,500 university students (over sixteen per cent of the total) and 4,000 miners out of a population of ten million.

The number of revolutionaries killed during the two Russian offensives is mostly put at between 50,000 and 60,000. There is a general consensus that the overwhelming majority of the dead (and of the 80,000 to 150,000 wounded) were between the ages of fifteen and twenty-eight.

The first 'counter-revolutionaries' to be executed – as published by Kadar's papers – were aged between eighteen and twenty-one. The total number of executed revolutionaries cannot be established without access to MVD and SP archives. But reports printed in Hungary and some circumstantial evidence make it likely that at the very least over 10,000 people were killed.

Imre Nagy (who, as we have seen, had once released Kadar from jail) and his colleagues spent nearly two years in MVD and SP prisons. Though he was old and sick, no amount of torture could bring Nagy to 'confess' that he had led a 'fascist counter-revolution'. General Maléter, and Geza Losonczy, a member of Nagy's cabinet, died during 'interrogations'.

On 18 June 1958 it was announced that Imre Nagy, Miklos Gimes and Geza Szilagyi had been executed. The Prime Minister of Hungary was Janos Kadar.

The executions of revolutionaries were not over yet. Since,

according to law, only over-sixteens can be executed for political crimes, some boys and girls were kept in prison for years in the knowledge that the day after their sixteenth birthday – sometime in 1957, 1958 or 1959 – they could be hanged. They were.

Under the impact of the television coverage of the Hungarian uprising and its aftermath, the resentment of and hostility against youth abated in the Western world for about three months. When thousands upon thousands of refugees arrived in the Austrian and Yugoslav frontier zones during the winter of 1956-7, this great and urgent drama inspired the people and governments of the five continents to help swiftly, wisely and cheerfully. Without this improvised rescue operation, which was without doubt the greatest in history, tens of thousands of refugees would have perished in the frontier zones from exhaustion, hunger and cold.

In the great flood of events this revolution was swiftly forgotten. Writing in 1970, it seemed ironical that the conformist establishments of the West and their greatest adversaries, the young activists, had one thing in common: neither of them studied, let alone profited from, the lessons of the Hungarian Revolution. These had and still have, however, a continuing effect on students, intellectuals and non-conformist politicians in the Soviet orbit. The various writers' and students' movements and revolts in Russia and her satellites over the last decade – not to speak of the wonderful behaviour of Dubcek and his country in 1968-9 – indicate that some people, at least, have profited a little from the 'lessons of Hungary'.

VII

FROM TEEN GANGS
TO STUDENT REBELS

'It is a difficult generation for the Old Left
to understand. It is the first in the history of
mankind to experience adolescence in a culture where the possibilty of human annihila-
tion has become an after-dinner platitude.'[1]

E. P. Thompson

'Woe, woe unto those who think that the
Beat Generation means crime, delinquency,
immorality, amorality.... Woe unto those
who don't realise that America must, will,
is, changing now.... Woe unto those who
believe in conflict and horror and violence
and fill our books and screens and living
rooms with all that crap....'[2]

Jack Kerouac

1

The main feature of the global youth scene between 1957 and
1964 was the change in the identity of 'problem youth'. Until
the early nineteen-sixties public opinion in the West was worried,
and at times terrified and enraged, by juvenile delinquency; by
the hooliganism of Teddy Boys, *Halbstarke, Raggaren, blousons
noirs* and their like, and by murderous teen gangs in the city
ghettos. By the mid-sixties these young people seemed to cause
far less trouble, while university youth unexpectedly turned into
a 'critical mass', threatening and actually staging explosions.

This chapter tries to give a bird's-eye view of this complex
period. In order to give a clear picture of the effect of the
American Beat Generation and of the hipsters on the rest of the
youth – to describe the British CND movement, or the emergence
of a new pop phenomenon on Merseyside – the various sections
start again and again from 1957 or 1959. Otherwise, only a multi-
screened cinema presentation could give the whole story simultaneously.

In 1959 the United States was thoroughly frightened by the extremely violent teen gangs and mildly worried by the passive obedience of the 'uncommitted generation' then at the universities.

From 1964 onwards the University of California became one of the world centres of student rebellion. Yet in 1959 Professor Clark Kerr, the then President of the University, said this about the students in his charge: 'The employers will love this generation. They aren't going to press many grievances. They are going to be easy to handle. There aren't going to be any riots.'

It is unnecessary to point out that Professor Kerr was right in his assessment of the California students of 1959.

Writing about student apathy in the April 1961 issue of the *Atlantic Monthly*, Dr David Riesman stated that during the previous years he had visited a number of US colleges of high quality where students had many complaints. They complained about the level of teaching, the high-handedness of the administration and the fact that they had no access to the faculty for other than merely routine matters. 'Yet when I ask such students what they have done about these things, they are surprised at the very thought that they could do anything. They think I am joking when I suggest that if things came to the worst, they could picket.'

The young Americans who were at universities between 1957 and 1961 were careerist conformists, they went meekly into the army if and when required, and were staunch supporters of the *status quo*. Americans were still worried by the violent teen gangs when Kenneth Keniston of Harvard University wrote in the 1962 winter issue of *Daedalus* about 'the decline in political involvement among college youths'.

In some countries the transition began and ended earlier, in others later. In the Soviet Union, Poland, Hungary and the other East European countries, communist functionaries had reason to complain in the 1948-53 period that students were politically disinterested and tended to turn towards 'a world of private and personal satisfaction', while the young hooligans who had left school early disturbed public order. In the Soviet orbit the changeover also came earlier. There the students became too violently interested in politics from 1955 onwards.

In countries as far apart as France and Japan the same change occurred somewhat earlier than in the United States, partly for specific local reasons, partly under the influence of the world-wide intellectual and emotional climate.

In Britain the changeover occurred somewhat later and was in certain respects less distinct than elsewhere because of the complexity of the youth scene. Michael Young, the eminent British sociologist, wrote in the *Observer* in 1963 that 'our modern undergraduates' were in danger of 'becoming cautious adults at twenty'. A year later Professor Musgrove wrote:

> The student population of our mid-twentieth century [British] university constitutes a negligible political force. Its *servility* ensures modest and comfortable ... social and economic rewards.
>
> There is no immediate prospect of any massive rebellion by the British young against their condition and the dominant customs, trends and institutions of our society.[3]

Outside the universities there were recurrent youth disturbances in Britain throughout the fifties. Outbreaks of organized gang warfare and brutality, of which the most sensational was the Notting Hill race riot in 1957, perplexed public opinion. Similar violent mass flare-ups occurred from time to time until the Middlesbrough one in 1961. What was especially disturbing was the element of callous, pointless cruelty – the frantic destruction of youth clubs and cafés, the beating-up of inoffensive coloured people or bystanders. The 'insecure offenders', who grew up 'absurd', seemed to be infected with a mysterious virus of criminal insanity. Governments, educational authorities, psychiatrists *et al.* did not know how to fight this malaise.

But by 1963 British lower-class youth had cured itself of teenage gangsterism without any help from the adult world.* This significant development went largely unnoticed. The layman's image of the 'British youth of today' still had the face of the 'long-haired, evil hooligan'. The anti-youth bias of the majority of adults produced artificially induced youth disturbances in 1964.† But there was as yet no hostility towards students.

During this period of transition, the cold war between the generations was also embittered by the behaviour of some segments of privileged youth. Sons and daughters of the middle- and upper-classes dropped out to become beatniks, nuclear disarmers, modes and other kinds of fashionable dissidents.

* See section 4 of this chapter.
† For the Whitsun seaside riots, see section 6 of this chapter.

That this overall transformation of youth was world-wide is, of course, beyond a shadow of doubt. The apparently inexplicable changes in the behaviour of youth were rooted in the immediate past.

2

The Western Communist Parties were decimated by the effects of the television and film coverage of the Hungarian Revolution. Tens of thousands of party members with not entirely closed minds could not resist being swayed by what they had seen of the battles between the masses of Hungarian youth and their Soviet oppressors. Only those whose initial fanaticism had petrified over the years into mindless bigotry were willing to repeat the Soviet fairy tales about an imperialist-fascist conspiracy behind the 'Hungarian events'. Former communists and former fellow-travellers everywhere became the first active ingredients in the political phenomenon that was soon labelled the 'New Left'.

Nineteen hundred and fifty-seven was a year of lost illusions, of lost convictions, of a new bitterness, of a new unorganized radicalism. Established political parties began to lose their young adherents. In the West, Suez and Hungary exposed the impotence of the 'Old Right' and the 'Old Left'. Elsewhere, monopoly communism began to lose both its sincere adherents and its opportunist time-servers. Organized liberalism – both in the American and the Continental senses – lost much of its waning attraction. Old and young intellectuals began to search for the possible new answers that long-forgotten syndicalist or anarchist ideologies might offer.

Neo-anarchists, neo-Marxists, together with the American and Continental versions of the New Left and the nuclear disarmers, prepared some of the ground from which the vague ideologies of the student movements of the sixties were to sprout. During the same transition period the message of the American 'Beat Generation' was communicated by the mass media to all the corners of the earth. From 1957 onwards there was large-scale cross-fertilization between the political and non-political groups of young outsiders.

The beat phenomenon – the word stands for 'beatific' and not for 'beaten' or 'jazz-beat' – had an exceedingly long incubation period. Jack Kerouac wrote his *On the Road* (the original title

156

was *The Beat Generation*) in 1941; it was rejected by publishers for the next sixteen years. Kerouac himself first saw 'hipsters creeping around Times Square' in 1944:

The hipsters, whose music was bop, looked like criminals but they kept talking about the same things I liked, long outlines of personal experience and vision ... rumbling of a new soul (that same old human soul). ...
... By 1948 the hipsters, or beatsters, were divided into cool and hot. ... The 'cool' [i.e. 1959] is your bearded laconic sage ... whose speech is low and unfriendly, whose girls say nothing and wear black; the 'hot' today is the crazy talkative shining-eyed (often innocent and open-hearted) but who runs from bar to bar, pad to pad looking for everybody, shouting, restless, lushy. ...[4]

In an article in 1952 the *New York Times Sunday Magazine*, headlined 'This is a Beat Generation', credited Kerouac with the recognition of this phenomenon. After this there was occasional talk about the Beat Generation, but not until *On The Road* was finally published in 1957 did the mass media take real notice: 'What horror I felt in 1957 and later in 1958 to suddenly see "Beat" being taken up by everybody, press and TV and the Hollywood Borscht circuit to include "juvenile delinquency" shot and the horrors of a mad teeming billy-club New York and L.A. and they began to call *that* Beat, *that* Beatific.[5] ...'

Whatever the mass media made of them, the message of the beatniks, the hipsters, of disaffiliated vagrants, of 'displaced persons of the world of the intellect' came through to young people in other countries. It was not even a message, it was a cloud of emotions with hypnotic qualities: an ecstatic feeling that something was happening; an innocent abandonment to the moment; an absence of hate and pride; a total disengagement from the world of non-drop-outs; a diffuse tenderness; a restless energy. It was a sub-culture with a great many sub-sub-cultures that drew their inspiration from hoboes, from the Negro underworld, from marijuana, from bums and junkies, from Walt Whitman, Thoreau, Genet, Kerouac, Mailer, Ginsberg, Rexroth, from Henry Miller's air-conditioned nightmare, from the entire human condition in the shadow of the obscene mushroom.

Not surprisingly, these sub-cultures were 'sick'. An analyst as perceptive as V. S. Pritchett saw this in these terms in 1958:

In Huck Finn's time the territory was open; now it is closed. ...

It is locked up and owned by the Squares, the good citizens with the dollars and the neutralising psychiatrists. . . . The only territory to light out into is the inside country of the 'beat', i.e. of the sick, the irresponsible, the delinquent, the psychopath. . . . In the coming anarchy, one will at least be equipped to survive in a world made for psychopaths.[6]

In a book published in 1959 Lawrence Lipton called them the 'Holy Barbarians'. He has been criticized for elevating the 'beatnik's indolence' to the dedication of a mendicant order and for attaching too much significance to a 'minor social phenomenon'. Significant or not, this phenomenon proved to be attractive or *simpatico* only to the young, and obnoxious to the over-thirties of those days.

The young adherents of the New Left, the neo-anarchists, the beatniks and the nuclear disarmers were worlds apart from each other in their ideologies, or their lack of ideology; they had mainly negative affinities; they turned away in disgust or boredom from the same kinds of people and things. And, of course, most of them were young and wore conspicuous, ultra-casual attire. The mass media, the authorities, the police, the adult world tended to look on them as belonging to the same camp of young outsiders. Their evolution and their experience during this period of transition contributed to the intensification of the cold war between the generations.

3

'Whether mankind will think itself worth
preserving remains a doubtful question.'
Bertrand Russell[7]

The British Emergency Committee for Direct Action against Nuclear War was founded in 1957, twelve years after Hiroshima, in the aftermath of Hungary and Suez. Though great men like Bertrand Russell and J. B. Priestley were among its distinguished founders, the press, radio and television ignored the committee. The mass-media boycott went on for months. When, in January 1958, the Campaign for Nuclear Disarmament was founded in Canon John Collins's study near St Paul's Cathedral, and the Ban the Bomb! movement was launched with an ambitious press conference, most of the British national newspapers did not bother

158

to send anybody, or, if they did, they did not print anything about the CND.

The Establishment, the adult world and the mass media made it abundantly clear that they had less interest in human survival than in a provincial contest for pretty lap-dogs. The CND nevertheless planned a large-scale public meeting in Central Hall, Westminster, for 17 February 1958. The prospects were not encouraging. Only a few minority weeklies wrote about the meeting in advance, yet it turned out to be extraordinarily successful. The huge Central Hall and three other halls were completely filled by masses of young people. A great many could not even get into the corridors and the halls where the subsidiary meetings were held.

From that day CND, its famous leaders and its young adherents were news. The Establishment, the majority of the press and consequently of adult public opinion reacted with a surprising amount of aggressiveness. The 'crackpot intellectuals' and their 'immature' followers were denounced as hysterical cranks. The message that humanity must be stopped from committing collective nuclear suicide was ridiculed. The leaders and followers of CND were also called defeatists, like those 'thoughtless pacifists' in the Britain of the nineteen-thirties who 'nearly let Hitler in'. The eighty-five-year-old Bertrand Russell, founder-President of the CND, was personally attacked as 'senile' because of his ambition to free humanity from the constant risk of universal death.

Those mentally and morally underprivileged politicians and publicists who took part in these smear campaigns helped the CND cause a great deal. Thanks to their attacks on the greatest intellect of the country, the number of young CND activitists grew week by week.

Canon Collins, Chairman of the CND, did not approve of civil disobedience, and consequently the CND did not officially take part in the first Aldermaston March, which was organized by Lord Russell's original Direct Action Committee. After the success of the first march, official CND took it over lock, stock and barrel.

The fourth of April 1958 was the day of the first Aldermaston March. Some 4,000 people marched the fifty-three miles from Aldermaston to Trafalgar Square. Years before the era of mass demonstrations by students, the large number of young marchers impressed non-hostile witnesses. Bayard Rustin, a middle-aged

American Negro (who was to organize the 1963 Civil Rights March on Washington) kept saying in a daze to his companion: 'All these young people, it's unbelievable!' As one writer said: 'Aldermaston had started something new and the sixteens to twenty-threes took to it like the children of Hamelin to the music of the Pied Piper.'[8]

Soon after the first Aldermaston March, Bertrand Russell forwarded an appeal from 618 British scientists to the powers-that-be that nuclear tests should be stopped by international agreement. The thousands of young CND activists regarded the agitation against nuclear tests as realistic political action. Yet at that time they were denounced as immature meddlers in politics.

By 1958 the Teddy fashion was almost totally over in Britain. This cult had, however, left its mark on British society by creating a climate of mutual suspicion and hostility between adults and a whole generation of youth. This rift was only widened by the thousands of young nuclear disarmers. They were decidedly unlike the violent Teddies, the gang kids or the lethargic, dim ones. These CND youngsters were not school drop-outs; there were many brilliant students among them. They were not dead-end kids, their ranks included boys from Eton, undergraduates from Oxford and Cambridge, LSE intellectuals, people bearing historic names and famous young people such as Vanessa Redgrave.

While most of Britain was in an 'I'm all right, Jack' mood of complacency, these young people and the elderly intellectuals who led them warned and protested against the possibility of a nuclear holocaust. This made them hated, with a greater and more irrational hatred than that encountered by the Teddies. From 1958 onwards the CND flags and emblems were associated with the sight of angry policemen hauling away limp bodies; of respectable elderly scientists, intellectuals, housewives and clergymen, together with hundreds of their young friends, sitting on wet pavements.

There were some thoughtful people in Britain who were somewhat dazed by the news that thirty-seven 'otherwise respectable' old and young citizens were spending Christmas 1958 in jail for being too enthusiastic about peace on earth. But there was still little sympathy for CND. The two large political parties were hostile to it. Even the communists, usually so quick to provide organization for any mass demonstration of the Left, opposed

CND in its first decisive years. This did not save the campaign from accusations that it had communist backing.

The leading members of the campaign were also conscious of the danger that some of the public would associate their cause with delinquent youth. The Aldermaston marchers were told in instructions printed in advance: 'Don't wear anything that will distract the attention of the public from our great issues!' The young marchers complied. But knowing that they would be marching in rain and wind for days on end; that they would sit for hours in the mud; would be forcibly carried away by policemen and thrown into police vans and then might spend days or weeks in jail, they dressed for the occasion in shabby raincoats, in jeans and boots. So as well as being suspected or detested for their demonstrations, part of the public transferred to them their general hostility to beatniks and 'unruly youth'.

The breakthrough for the CND, as far as the world of youth was concerned, came in 1959 with the second Aldermaston March. Over 16,000 people marched the fifty-three miles from Aldermaston to a Trafalgar Square that was filled with great masses of sympathizers. It was a breakthrough because from that time onwards the Ban the Bomb emblem and the Aldermaston-type march gradually became an integral part of the world-wide youth scene.

The treatment the 'system' gave to the nuclear disarmers was a continued object lesson in the political realities of the world. Until 1960, CND was an entirely legal movement. The agreed main object of the leadership was to convert the British Labour Party to a non-nuclear policy.* The failure of this endeavour split the leadership of the movement. Bertrand Russell and others formed the Committee of 100 with the support of a great many young members of the CND. The Committee of 100's policy of mass civil disobedience appealed to those young people who had become indifferent to all political parties.

The spectacular tactics and the newsworthiness of the Committee of 100 and the utter dedication of its old and young activists impressed young people in many countries. The Committee, and foremost among them Bertrand Russell and his secretary, Ralph Schoenman (together with Pat Arrowsmith,

*In October 1960 the Labour Party adopted a platform of unilateral nuclear disarmament in spite of the protests of party leaders Gaitskell and Brown. The platform was later reversed.

Peter Cadogan and others), planned a sit-down in Whitehall outside the Ministry of Defence on 18 February 1961. Though it was a cold, dark, drizzly day, over 20,000 people assembled at the pre-sit-down meeting in Trafalgar Square. Afterwards 5,000 people, including Bertrand Russell, sat or lay for two hours on the wet pavement surrounding the Ministry.

On 6 August, Hiroshima Day, the Committee of 100 arranged a mass meeting in Hyde Park. The police had forbidden the use of microphones there. Nevertheless, when a great crowd of young people assembled, Bertrand Russell spoke to them through a microphone. For this offence he and the other organizers were sentenced to two months in jail (this was later reduced to one week). When the sentence was passed on Russell, some spectators cried out : 'Shame, shame, an old man of eighty-eight !'* Russell served his week with the others.

It should be noted that by 1961 a new type of young anarchist had begun to be active in various movements and campaigns, among them the Committee of 100. They were described them as 'avowedly anarchists in the sense that they believe all politics are hopelessly corrupt or futile, and that in this apocalyptic age the only hope is to end what they regard as a pretence of democracy.'[9] In the sit-down demonstrations in 1961, young adherents of this belief took a prominent part. (During the two demonstrations the police arrested respectively 850 and 1,300 people.)

The anarchists and other believers in mass disobedience were not alone in offering political education to British and foreign youth. The British courts played their part as well. The generation which had been moulded by the era of the Nuremberg trials was brutally, if somewhat primitively, reminded that, according to the 'system', the Nuremberg principles were no longer valid. The young organizers of a large sit-down demonstration on the runways of the US Strategic Air Command's nuclear strike base at Witherfield, Essex, received stiff sentences. The judge told them: 'No one in this country, however strong and sincere are his convictions and however honourable he may be, has the right to arrogate himself to decide which laws are bad laws.'†

* Russell was greatly annoyed: 'What has age to do with this? I had deliberately incurred the punishment.'

† It was made perfectly clear that private or public morality has nothing to do with the law. One defendant was sentenced to two years in prison, the five others to eighteen months each.

In April 1962 the Aldermaston March was even more impressive, and the huge Easter Monday crowd – minimum (police) estimate 40,000, maximum (enthusiasts') 100,000 – showed that the nuclear disarmers could draw far larger crowds than any of the political parties. Even if one accepts the low police estimate, it is a fact that no such numbers of young people had ever before come together in Britain to support a political cause. And this cause was not represented by political parties or church organizations but by a half-legal movement of predominantly young people.

That Easter, 30,000 people marched in Copenhagen and there were marches in various parts of the US, Canada, West Germany, Holland, Italy, Norway and New Zealand. The movement also penetrated the Soviet Union; an article in the *Guardian* said: 'The CND provided the most direct challenge to official Soviet policies and ideas to have been presented to the Soviet man in the street since freedom of speech died under Stalin.'[10]

The idea and the spirit of the Aldermaston Marches and of the Committee of 100's sit-down demonstrations spread all over the world. The CND emblem was here to stay. From time to time British and foreign newspapers published obituaries of the 'pointless' Ban the Bomb movement, but it went on growing and spreading. There was a preliminary conference of an International CND in Oxford in 1963 and the following January the International Confederation for Disarmament and Peace was founded in Trynge, in Sweden. Member organizations were established in over thirty countries. Soon there were Aldermaston-type Easter Marches all over the world.

The conclusion of the test-ban treaty between America and the Soviet Union showed that the young CND activists were not entirely unrealistic when they designated this as their first aim.

At the universities in Britain and America the students were still more or less passive. But the idea of youth mass action independent of any existing political or other organization was no longer unfamiliar. Methods of protest were tested. Illegal passive resistance against what is inhuman and immoral was gradually taken for granted by some of the young as an inevitable ingredient of the contemporary scene.

In April 1963 J. B. Priestley, then sixty-eight, warned politicians that they should 'ask themselves why the more sensitive and articulate young English express so much contempt and disgust [in their plays and novels], appealing at once to a kind of un-focused rebelliousness among younger readers and playgoers'.

Even now . . . youth arrives among us with certain expectations, and some of these cannot be satisfied with money, food, clothes, sex, table tennis and records of pop-singers. They want to reach maturity integrated into a society that has a common purpose and noble aims and is not a slobbering mess of irresponsibility, mean devices and self-deception. . . . There is something in them, through what inheritance we do not know, that recoils from corruption. And this is the most corrupting society that England has known in my lifetime.[11]

And although in the Britain of 1963 it was still the lower-class teenage 'hooligans' who contributed most to the layman's image of the youth-of-today, some observers detected a new breed who might replace the apathetic and a-political university student: 'The duffle coat or the long black stockings which are the mid-winter garb of undergraduates have become, for the rest of us, signs of the emergence of a whole generation of people who will not be inhibited by ignorance, or convention, or habit, from taking a bold and independent view of how the world should be run.'[12]

The CND and the Committee of 100 had much to do with these developments. As Kingsley Martin put it: 'But for Aldermaston, a whole generation might have grown up with as little concern about foreign affairs as the adolescents of the Twenties, who awakened to the danger of war when it was too late. As it is, much of the younger generation today is profoundly concerned about the future of Britain and the world.[13]

4

Mr R. A. B. Butler, as Home Secretary, announced in January 1959, the largest ever prison-building project for 'young adult offenders'. He also declared that he was in favour of parents and schoolmasters using the cane. (After his retirement from politics, Mr Butler became Master of Trinity College, Cambridge.)

The offences of 'young adults' or 'juvenile delinquents' were of two sorts: ordinary criminal deeds on the one hand, and gang fights, mob violence, 'hooliganism' on the other. The adult world was unable to separate these two types of offender – whether they were in or out of prison. During the period 1959-63, the teenagers themselves succeeded in separating the two main types of offenders outside the prisons. Lower-class teenagers found an effective cure against gang warfare and even against gang criminality. They freed most of Britain from this social disease. While this collective self-cure went on, most of the adult world was violently opposed to the means of the therapy.

The young ones found their escape from the gang-ghettos in and through rock 'n' roll, 'beat', the pop bands. The wild animal rhythm of rock was on the exact wavelength of the gang kids. It acted in their case as an antidote to violence by offering vicarious violence. It dispelled the general atmosphere of boredom, vitalized many of the dimmer ones, gave many of them, for the first time in their life, an interest. And thousands upon thousands of dead-end kids listened to rock and danced, instead of going out on their dreary nightly search for pointless ugly violence.

The resistance of the authorities, dance-hall managers and youth-club leaders to rock 'n' roll led to disturbances. In 1956 and 1957 teenagers rioted at dance halls throughout Britain, because they were not allowed to rock. Rock, or 'beat' as it came to be called in Britain was suspect. Judging by newspaper reports, letters to newspapers and municipal council decisions, many adults were so alarmed by the spread of pop and its influence that they blamed it for encouraging most of the things that they detested in teenage behaviour.

The rock 'n' roll craze and all later pop music fashions contributed to the gradual break-up and disappearance of Teddyism. It was also a catalyst in the sense that it separated the new music and dance addicts from the criminal elements. Gangs broke up, new gangs and groups were formed which were really circles of boys and girls liking the same sort of music and going to the same sort of dance. Amateur or professional singing guitarists had already become quite popular in 1956. In many London pubs and cafés there were also loosely organized groups such as the Vipers in Soho, a temporary member of which was a young merchant seaman who a year later became known as Tommy Steele. When in 1957 and 1958 he and a few other young singers made their meteoric emergence as great names with fabulous incomes, amateur skiffle groups with washboards, guitars and tea-chest basses mushroomed everywhere. Dreaming of becoming new Tommy Steeles or Cliff Richards, many of them tried to become professionals and played for a modest fee at Saturday-night dances, in pubs, cafés or suburban dance halls.

Some of these semi-amateur groups were based on their gangs. On weekdays they practised by playing for their gangs and on their Saturday outings some gang members and their girls accompanied the groups in borrowed vans or cars. The criminal element, or those boys who enjoyed fighting more than dancing and accompanying the skiffle groups on their outings, resisted these developments. In consequence, most of these early skiffle groups broke up or got separated from their gangs.

The next development came in and around Liverpool, when the 'Merseyside beat' became popular. Boys and girls went to large beat clubs, like the Liverpool Cavern, to dance to the music provided by the various beat groups. These club premises were large, so they could not be monopolized by one or two gangs. Gang members and non-gang boys and girls got used to enjoying themselves in one another's company. Many gangs were completely taken over by would-be musicians or by ordinary pop addicts, boys and girls. These gangs were centred on their own group of beat musicians. Toughness, the ability to fight no longer seemed important; the gangs were proud of the popularity of their own beat group. In 1960 there were over 300 new amateur or semi-amateur beat groups on Merseyside alone. Gang boys and girls saved up money to buy or rent guitars and amplifiers for their group, as well as old vans and cars so that the whole gang would be able to accompany the group. The hard-working and therefore more prosperous new recruits were more welcome in these gangs than fight-crazy youngsters and ordinary young criminals. To fit out a beat group is costly: a guitar costs about £75, an amplifier £130.

The often criticized 'beat craze' gave the youngsters new interests, ambitions and concrete tasks. Many of the dimmer ones dropped out from the musical groups. Boys and girls in various dead-end districts, working in various dreary dead-end jobs, started to pay attention to the wider world around them and even to their own future, which was no longer unavoidably hopeless.

Nineteen-year-old Colin Fletcher, who was a member of two Merseyside gangs before he entered Liverpool University, wrote later:

All over the Merseyside gangs were giving birth to groups. Each gang had its musical element who had naturally become interested and then involved in the sound of rock.... The group inevitably came from the gang as there were very few boys on the Merseyside strong enough to resist joining one. . . .In June 1958, following the trend, the 'Park Gang' gave birth to the *Tremoloes*.[14]

This led in this period to a natural selection among the teenagers of the lowest social strata. The potential dim ones among the children who were now passing into their teenage phase came under the impact of this new climate of hope. The new teenage stars were loved, adored and worshipped not only because they belonged to the same generation, not even because their songs, their rhythms, their beat, their jerky movements were expressing the turbulence of adolescence, but mainly because they were living embodiments of hope. In their persons all teenagers could assert themselves and find a virtual security in the thought: 'I, too, can become like one of them; I, too, can be somebody; I, too, can be free of the adults.' Only the least gifted, most lethargic ones remained the modern dead-end kids. The rest became active and interested pop music fans, members of clubs or of gangs with their own pop groups.

The comparatively few gangs that resisted these developments were also changed. The leading criminal elements lost their rank and file, and the new recruits were usually very poor, very young and not very bright, the children of parents who had migrated from other parts of the country to live on new housing estates. This separation of the criminal gangs from the ordinary teenage groups was demonstrated by the fact that Merseyside, which produced proportionally the most pop groups, dropped well below the national average in juvenile delinquency. By 1963 the Liverpool figures for juvenile delinquency had dropped by more than two per cent, although the national figures rose by nearly ten per cent. Mr Herbert Balmer, Deputy Chief Constable of Liverpool, in 1963 said: 'At one time it was thought that the beat groups and crime went hand-in-hand, but that is certainly not so now.'

The beat groups were not everywhere as effective in separating city youth from its criminal fringe as in Liverpool, but the general trend was the same. With the exception of some city ghettos (like in Glasgow) where special local factors make it nearly impossible for resident teenagers to stay out of gangs, the spawning of pop groups put an end to, or greatly diminished, the proliferation of vicious teen gangs.

The pop scene as a whole did not get credit for this

extraordinary achievement. According to many of those who hated youth, the pop groups were lazy, overpaid, revoltingly long-haired, immoral, drug-taking good-for-nothings; their songs were not music: they were too noisy, the lyrics too sexy.

The layman's image of the youth-of-today was not affected by the positive achievements of pop. The faint memory of teenage gangsterism remained in that image, enriched by the features of the 'hairy brutes' who earned millions with their 'obnoxious screaming'.

5

The hostility of the majority of adults was not limited to juvenile delinquents, rowdies, beatniks, pop stars, peaceniks, nuclear disarmers and other minority groups of young dissidents; they were turning against the majority of young people of both sexes.

Betwen 1957 and 1964 most of the world was governed by people who were born between 1880 and 1900. Most of the presidents, prime ministers, leaders of industry, bishops, media executives, university vice-chancellors and all others in charge were moulded by the image of a strange past. And so were, of course, the great masses of people in the same age-groups. They went through their youth phase before the First World War, and were young adults or young middle-aged before the Second. These generations who were in power everywhere greatly influenced the mental climate of the majority of the over-forties, all of whom seemed to have prewar minds in an age of cosmonauts and computers.

After the Second World War the human condition changed out of all recognition and for this reason the generation gap – the communication gap between young and old – grew to be greater than at any other time in history. The older generations found themselves in an unfamiliar and for them frighteningly fast and overcrowded world – a too complex, abnormal world. For the young, it was the only world they knew. For them, the world of their grandparents' generation was abnormal, scary, even obnoxious. If and when they caught glimpses of that past, they were shocked by the general poverty; by the oppression of women and the young. They were surprised by the ugliness of people.

During the mid-sixties I asked groups of teenagers of both sexes in several countries to take a look at the world between 1900 and 1939; they were asked to view cinema newsreels, illustrated magazines and photo-albums of those years. Almost without exception, they reported the same general impression: they were surprised and shocked to see how ugly and unhealthy the majority looked on the streets, at mass meetings, in processions, in ballrooms or on the beaches. Only after reading about the recent past did they realize that they were the first generation of free young men and women. They learnt with a mixture of doubt and nausea that virtually until yesterday masses of men habitually bought love and masses of women sold their bodies, while millions were deprived of normal sex life altogether.

They had no idea how very widespread open prostitution and semi-prostitution were only a few decades ago. They were equally nauseated by the flesh-marts of the large brothels and by their impression that in the recent past most marriages were not based on love. For them it was strange to read in a book on love these lines: 'Owing to a misunderstanding as old as the universe, love has kept a foot in marriage. Society does its best to expel it. In order to succeed in this undertaking, it has invented the dowry.'*[15]

For these young people, Simone de Beauvoir's *Le Deuxième Sexe* refers to the horrid past when describing the fate of poor girls. This book was published in 1949, and the author evidently meant the situation that still existed then when she wrote in the present tense:

The existence of a privileged caste, which she can join by merely surrendering her body, is an *almost irresistible temptation to the young woman*; she is fated for 'gallantry' by the fact that her wages are minimal while the standard of living expected of her by society is very high. *If she is content to get along on her wages, she is only a pariah; ill-lodged, ill-dressed, she will be denied all amusement and even love.*[16]

By the time this was published, the liberation of young women was already on its way in France, too. The 'irresistible temptation' to sell herself was greatly reduced, if not quite obliterated,

* It should be mentioned in this context that in young French eyes, their country was also liberated between 1950 and 1965 from the conventionalized immorality of the eighteenth and nineteenth centuries, and the traditional conflict between love and marriage was breached.

by economic developments and by the emergence of the quite distinct and autonomous society of the young.

For the teenager of the mid-sixties it was quite natural that the majority of boys and girls were good-looking, that they could and did enjoy non-sordid sexual love. On the other hand, the adult camp was preoccupied by the sudden 'beauty explosion'. In the US and Canada, in Britain, France, Italy and Japan, magazines wrote about the sudden great increase of beautiful girls. The *Mädchenwunder* of West Germany was analysed to shreds. It turned out that by the mid-sixties the ideal female figure of the period was becoming the average figure of the young. As seen by older eyes, there were these great masses of young beauties protected by affluence, union wages and the pill, next to the great masses of overpaid overdressed and oversexed young men – and these two groups enjoyed all the good things in life, including each other, with reckless, immoral abandon. Reading some of the complaints about 'our immoral youth', one sensed a lurking sadness in the writers for having had a less adventurous and less sexy youth themselves.

Older generations were moulded by an age in which the cities were smaller, population growth slower, change almost imperceptible. They were used to far fewer people and a smaller proportion of youth. In 1900, the world population was 1,600 million and the elderly did not feel at home in a world with twice as many people; there were 3,000 million people in 1960, and 3,200 million by 1963. Older people now saw in the space of half an hour in any city centre more slim, pretty young women and handsome young men among passers-by than they had encountered in a month in their youth. This beauty explosion came at a time of an exaggerated beauty cult, evolved by the middle-aged sons and daughters of the young American sex-revolutionaries of the 'hectic twenties'.

The greatly commercialized treble cult of Youth, Beauty and Sex washed over the world from America in the nineteen-fifties. It was then an innovation that sex – in the form of half-nude glamour girls – became a super-commodity to advertise all commodities. By the time this cult became widespread a new crop of children had grown into taller, slimmer, more attractive teenagers, thanks to their newly-won independence, to general affluence, to sport, a healthier life and better diet.

For the older generations the treble cult of Youth, Beauty and

Sex was not very healthy. For many of them it mainly meant spectator beauty and spectator sex – from strip-tease to sexy films, novels and girlie magazines that did not satisfy their dreams and desires, but only made them feel even more frustated.

Older generations upheld laws, rules and institutional frameworks based on a façade of puritanism and a double morality (one for men, another for women). Traditional puritanism and Catholic asceticism were marked by a sense of horror and disgust at the form and functions of the human body. Spiritual emotions were of the soul, while the flesh was supposed to be at the mercy of the Devil. Tertullian described women as a 'temple built on a sewer'.

And all through the centuries during which the vast majority of men and women were poor, dirty, smelly, disease-ridden, their mouths full of decaying teeth, their bodies suffering from rickets, most of them becoming prematurely old because of a poor, unhealthy diet and dawn-to-dusk drudgery – the human bodies, these instruments of the Devil, were not greatly appealing. This period finally came to an end in America and Europe only in the second or third decade of the twentieth century. For those born between 1880 and 1900, it was a shock to see in the early sixties the emergence of a multitude of healthy young people who could not be persuaded that the human body is obscene and repulsive, and that sexual love has anything to do with sin.

In America and Europe, the post-Second-World-War liberation of youth as an oppressed age-group was the consequence of many social, economic and other developments, each of which had other aims than the emancipation of youth. Nevertheless, the new youth was here; the teenagers became a commercially powerful age-group with a special identity. In the United States, the same forces transformed 'the teens' into representatives of a tribal subculture. American adults were warned in 1962 against the 'teenage tyranny' which they themselves had evolved:

American civilisation tends to stand in such awe of its teen-segment that it is in danger of becoming a teen-society with permanently teen-age standards of thought, culture and goals. As a result, American society is growing down rather than growing up.... This is a creeping disease, not unlike the hardening of the arteries. It is a softening of adulthood.[17]

The authors, who give a documentary report of these US develop-

171

ments between 1956 and 1961, emphasize that: 'it is a tyranny that dominates most brutally the teenagers themselves. What starts with relatively innocent conforming to the ways of the crowd soon turns into manipulation of those crowd *mores* by a combination of inept adult leadership and plain commercial exploitation.'

The over-fifties with their built-in resistance to change and their slowness in noticing change were confronted with the (to them) sudden and inexplicable liberation of youth, a sudden invasion of the world of youth, beauty and sex. A great many adults felt subconsciously or even consciously sexually deprived, like a sort of 'sex-proletariat'. The anti-youth camp grew everywhere. Middle-aged men and women watched with growing resentment the upsurge of not-yet adult women who could earn good money, have few responsibilities but a great deal of free time, who could easily afford to look pretty and who were not forced to marry formless elderly men or sell their bodies to anyone. The new generation of free girls, however sexy they looked, were no longer sex objects but sexual equals, whether in affairs or in marriage. They were resented by older men, for whom such girls were hopelessly out of reach, and loathed or feared by older women. If marriage in mass societies leads to the transformation of people into domesticated animals,* young females are regarded by the 'tame' wives as dangerous wild animals, prowling around their marriage enclosures.

With the exception of those women who had kept their youthful figures, most of the rest resented the cult of the slim. They complained that most of the fashion industry seemed to cater exclusively for the young and slim. In the press and on TV there were many protests in this period against the underprivileged status of the non-young and of the corpulent. In West Germany this was at times discussed with brutal openness. Pastor Sommerauer, for instance, said on TV that the ever-present, slim, half-nude beauties on magazine covers and advertising billboards 'do not rest until husbands become aware what ugly things they have at home'.†

The age-groups which happened to be in the youth stage between 1957 and 1964 got most of the blame for the 'moral deca-

---

* '*Verhaustierung*' a process described by Dr Helmuth Schelsky, the eminent Hamburg sociologist.

† . . . auch der letzte Mann merkt, was für einen Mist er zu Hause hat'.

dence of our age', for the cult of 'sex-bombs', for the semi-porno-graphy market, and other products of earlier generations. The strip-tease clubs and the girlie magazines catered primarily, of course, for adult males. The curvaceous sex-bombs were their beauty ideal, and not that of the young. As far as public acclaim is concerned, the sex queens of screen and TV were dethroned by non-adult-looking pop singers.*

The male beauty ideal of the young world was the immature-looking, long-haired, carelessly dressed young man; his opposite number was the extremely slim, willowy, immature-looking girl.

The apartheid of the two camps was emphasized not only by the difference in physique but also in dress. The segregated camps of adults and of new youth evolved their own uniforms. The animal rhythm of beat or rock became the signature tune of youth. Pop touched an anti-adult hostility latent in most teen-agers and it became part of the universal youth scene. When the first long-haired beat groups finally succeeded in getting in front of the TV cameras, millions of parents turned off their sets lest these 'disgusting frenzied apes' corrupt their children. The resis-tance or loathing of most of the over-forties did not abate one bit, yet many of the pop groups rocketed to fame in a single year. The pop singers became the stars of the youth camp, and since this camp was more dynamic, these 'ugly apes' dethroned film stars oozing mature sex appeal. For the young, the 'ugly apes' had anti-adult appeal.

During the same period, the cold war between the female generations was intensified by the victory of teenage girls over the *couturiers* and over the rest of womanhood. At the beginning of the sixties, the Paris fashion world had to admit that the great ladies of society and the *couturiers* had stopped setting style once and for all. Skinny girls between sixteen and twenty-four produced their own fashions and led them to victory against the resistance of experts and that of mature womanhood. This led to the com-plaints already mentioned about the underprivileged status of the corpulent, and to the segregation of the female generations accord-ing to dress and physique. Fat, middle-aged women – or bulgy

* The most publicized super-sex-bombs were ignored at airports whenever they arrived in the same plane with, say, the Beatles, the Rolling Stones or some other long-haired, inelegant eccentrics. It was the latter who were mobbed by their hysterically enthusiastic young fans.

young sex-bombs – felt and looked awkward in a Courrèges suit, a Mary Quant dress or a mini.

By this time the civil war between the generations had affected the majority of young people and the majority of adults. The front lines were in every home, where teenagers and their parents co-existed. The conflicts were caused by the appearance of the young, by their habits, by their likes and dislikes. The authorities were in an anti-youth mood both in their official capacity and in their private capacity, as parents of sons who looked like 'ugly apes', or of daughters behaving too independently.

The mass media and the authorities were, most of the time, fully prepared to over-react to unruly youth. It was during this period that it became normal cataloguing practice in some libraries and newspapers to cross-reference the following: Hooliganism, see Youth. This includes the Index of *The Times*. In March 1963 a boy and a girl, both fourteen years old, attempted to kill themselves. This was indexed by *The Times* under Crime: juvenile. There were similar signs almost everywhere indicating the tremendious growth of an anti-youth bias.

The years between 1957 and 1964 were hard to take for people with prewar minds. They were becoming a change-shocked generation. From the first Sputnik in 1957 to the Luniks and Yuri Gagarin's space flight, from Castro's victory in Cuba to the erection of the Berlin Wall, from the birth of the Common Market to the almost total disappearance of colonial empires – the proliferation of momentous events made it necessary to readjust and to rethink.

During these years the number of young people between fifteen and twenty-five reached one thousand million; there were eighty-five million TV sets in the US, twelve million in Britain, three million in France, and two million in West Germany. In the person of John Kennedy, a young man moulded by the second half of this century became the US President. He caught the imagination of the young, and when the world witnessed and rewitnessed on TV his assassination, and that of his alleged assassin, there was a mass funeral of hopes. Overnight everything seemed to become bleaker. Anger was growing and there was a lot of violence in the air.

6

The 'horrible' Whitsun disturbances in some British seaside resorts in 1964 are still (in 1970) constituent parts of the youth image of many British, Continental and American adults in responsible positions. Although these disturbances were directly caused by adult hostility, magistrates went out of their way to give a wildly exaggerated picture of the violence which had in fact occurred. As a result, parts of the misinformed adult world were in an uproar of righteous indignation. The teenagers were called 'vermin', 'rats', 'thugs', 'wild morons' and 'dumb leather brutes', and it was suggested that they should be flogged, jailed, sentenced to forced labour and so on and so forth.

Time magazine's report on 29 May 1964 was typical of the information people outside Britain received about this event: 'For the three-day Whitsun weekend ... streaming out of London by scooter, motorbike and train, the kids streamed into two seaside resorts. ... There, in two days of juvenile violence without parallel in England, they left no stone unhurled to turn holiday into holocaust.'

This is what, in fact, happened.

During the 1964 Whitsun weekend less than 0.01 per cent of Britain's nine million teenagers disturbed (and also entertained) some adult holidaymakers in Margate, Brighton and other seaside resorts. They were cajoled, 'canalized' and even forced into these disturbances. They fought each other, attacked some twenty-odd adults (including policemen); they broke shop windows and burned more than fifty deckchairs. Nearly thirty people (adults and teenagers) were injured; nine of them had to be treated in hospital (nobody died). The total damage caused by the teenagers to property has not been calculated, but if the press reports were not exaggerated, the total cost seems to have been between two and four thousand pounds.

During the same Whitsun weekend, Britain's motor-car population killed ninety people and caused grievous and non-grievous bodily harm to more than four hundred others. As to the estimated damage to property, the cost, in totally destroyed or badly damaged cars, was certainly more than a hundred thousand pounds.

Yet the reaction of the press and public was incomparably greater to the adult-prompted teenage disturbances than to the mass-murder committed by motor-cars and their drivers. Public anger was equalled only by the burst of curiosity to find out why and how these 'horrible and detestable' disturbances had come about. Some papers wrote that 'youth experts are just as baffled as the rest of us'. Writing in the *Guardian,* Vincent Mulchrome summed up the momentary reaction of press and public: 'Everybody knows what happened. Nobody knows why.'

In fact, the majority did not know what happened, although there were hundreds of reporters and press photographers present, not to mention the TV cameras. The first reports told the story of how 'great hordes' of teenagers arrived at the seaside resorts in cars, trains, on motorcycles and in tourist coaches. During the pre-Whitsun Friday and Saturday these great hordes were, of course, dwarfed by the rest of the holidaymakers, tens of thousands of families with children of all ages, plus thousands of middle-aged and elderly couples. Soon the promenades and beaches, the terraces and amusement parks were filled with the protagonists of the day's events. By Saturday midday there were in Margate more than sixty thousand 'normals' (adults and children), about two thousand 'abnormals' (teenagers, the majority being more or less elegant boys and girls: the Mods; the minority wearing heavy jeans and butch leather jackets: the Rockers) and, lastly, for the defence of the overwhelming majority, large groups of white-helmeted policemen.

The protagonists were easily distinguished at first sight. The Mod girls, mostly in nylon anoraks and stretch slacks, the Mod boys with razor-cuts, short jackets and narrow trousers; the Rockers in their black leather jackets – they were vividly different from the crowds of 'normals'. Young and slim, they were a more pleasing sight on the whole than the adults among whom there was naturally a fair proportion of life-worn and rather shapeless individuals. This scene prompted some Sunday-supplement sociologists to write about the sexual jealousy the 'ugly adults' feel towards 'attractive youth'. *Time* magazine, however, reported for the world that 'the pallid, scruffy youths looked like a colony of sea slugs washed in by the tide'.

The beaches were not yet overcrowded, but the protagonists were already uncomfortably close to each other. The Friday arrival of teenagers led to an increase of both ordinary and mounted police. There were also police dogs with their handlers everywhere in sight. The white-helmeted police kept near the places where young people forgathered. There was an air of expectation, even of menace. The possibility did not occur to the authorities that this large-scale police mobilization and the sight of mounted police officers and police dogs might contribute to the tension and drive into hysterics the consistently persecuted young visitors.

The hostility of the adults of Brighton and Margate was demonstrated not only by the over-preparedness of the police, but by the active boycott of anyone under twenty-five. Although there were plenty of empty rooms, and many youngsters offered to sleep in corridors, lodgings were refused to them almost everywhere. Landladies did not bother to take in the 'rooms to let' signs. They were not for hire to youth. Most of the teenagers had to sleep 'rough', out in the open, or in sheltered spots, curled up in blankets. When they woke up, craving hot tea or coffee, they found that many cafés and restaurants refused to serve them. Tired as they were after an uncomfortable night, they had to make extra efforts to get some breakfast.

On Saturday, the invasion of 'normals' and teenagers continued, the crowds and the tension grew, yet there was no disturbance on Saturday either. The Sunday papers had nothing to report, save the fact that extra police had been alerted in the seaside towns to deal with possible disturbances. One of them, the mass-circulation *News of the World*, reported in front-page headlines that Margate was a likely scene for teenage disturbances.

On Sunday the influx of crowds continued. The adult-teenager ratio was still ten to one. There were over eighty thousand people in Margate. Many of the teenagers already had behind them one or two nights spent in the open. But on Sunday the crowds were already so dense, the beaches so overpopulated that the horse-play of the teenagers became uncomfortable for the adults nearby. They shouted, ran around, chased each other, played over-loud music on their transistor radios. In the morning there were already isolated cases of fights. The watching crowds, though still amused, were becoming a bit scared. The police waited uneasily, ready for action. The teenagers ran about the beaches in groups, jostling people, upsetting deckchairs. Mods and Rockers catcalled and threatened each other whenever they met and soon there were violent battles between them. In Brighton, according to reports in *The Times,* the *Guardian* and the *Daily Mail*:

> . . . deck chairs and rubbish were thrown as the gangs moved to the east end of the seafront. . . . The Rockers were chased along the terrace by pursuing Mods and escaped by scrambling over the wall and dropping to the road below. . . . Then Rockers on motor cycles

ran the gauntlet of litter-throwing Mods who lined the railings of the raised terraces....

... A Rocker who fled from the gang of Mods tripped and fell. He lay face downwards. Helpless.... There are no rules in the war between Mods and Rockers. And no mercy.... The Mod kicked the Rocker in the face. And when the Rocker was able to lift his head it was smeared with blood.

As soon as the Mods and the Rockers began to fight each other, the police leapt into action. According to their instructions, mounted police and dog handlers were to keep the teenagers moving 'to restore order'. This was reported by all papers. What actually happened was that on the overcrowded beaches there were groups of teenagers who had managed to keep out of the *mêlée*. When mounted police and police dogs forced them to 'keep moving', they were flung into the fights.

On Monday morning adolescents staged a fight at the station buffet in Margate. Two middle-aged women, the manageress of the buffet and a cleaner, were slightly hurt. Police horses and police dogs walked alongside the uniformed men as the teenagers attempted to stage a mass sit-down on the promenade.

After the disturbances came the court scenes. Dr George Simpson, Chairman of the Margate magistrates, was so preoccupied with his own image of youth that he did not seem to notice the appearance of the young culprits in front of him. He did not mince his words in sentencing 'these illiterate thugs':

It is not likely that the air of this town has ever been polluted by hordes of hooligans, male and female, such as we have seen this weekend, and of whom you are an example.

These long-haired, unkempt, mentally unstable petty little hoodlums, these are the sawdust Caesars who act like rats and hunt in packs.

In so far as this Court has been given power, we shall discourage you and other thugs of your kind who are infected with this vicious virus.

These words were addressed to a youth who pleaded guilty – not to sadistic murder but only to 'threatening behaviour'. He was jailed for three months. Being a Mod, he was modishly dressed, with well-kept short hair. The magistrate was venting his anger not on the real young man in the dock, but on his own image of the youth-of-today.

178

The impression given by Dr Simpson of the Margate events was corrected on Tuesday by the quality press, by radio and TV repots. It was mainfestly untrue that young 'hoodlums' . . . had turned or tried to turn 'holiday into holocaust'. Several newspapers and the BBC's Peter Steward reported that only four hundred yards of the Margate beach had been affected out of nine miles! The police could have offered living and playing space to the three thousand teenagers, instead of 'keeping them moving'. And, also according to the BBC, the *Guardian* and other papers, something like 80,000 Margate holiday-makers saw absolutely nothing of the 'terrible' Margate disturbances.

Yet, as it often is in the case of distortions of truth, those who read and listen to libel and slander do not necessarily listen to corrective statements. The following letter was written to *The Times* two days after the publication and broadcasting of the correct information: 'No one seems to know the cause of the recent terrible outbreak of hooliganism in our towns. Would it not be possible for some organization or society to discover it? If half a dozen of the ringleaders could be invited to reveal how they had spent the past few years of their life, something valuable might be revealed.'[18]

The magistrates of other resorts made many allusions to the fact that these 'hoodlums' were mentally and morally underprivileged. The public was given the impression that these teenagers were mostly semi-literate school drop-outs. Hundreds of them were arrested, sent to prison or given stiff fines. The fines exceeded the damage done many times over. Although youths under sixteen are normally sent to remand homes, the magistrates certified many of them as 'unruly' and sent them to adult prisons.

Four days after the disturbances, *The Times* shocked some of its readers by reporting that Arrested Boys Are From Respectable Homes:

Inquiries by *The Times* have shown that a great many of the youths arrested during the Whitsun holiday hysteria came from respectable backgrounds. . . .The investigation showed that it was an over-simplification to sort the youngsters into Mods and Rockers. A high proportion would appear to have gone for a day out with no preconceived idea of making trouble. Starting as onlookers they were caught up in the excitement. Some panicked, others ran with the crowd, making it impossible for the police to pick out the real culprits. Many ringleaders escaped while others involved are now in prison awaiting trial or sentence.

... From school records it would appear that an unexpectedly high proportion [of the arrested boys and girls] were of average or above average mentality.... On the walls of the room of a boy now serving three months' detention, four General Certificates of Education were displayed.[19]

Whether this boy was guilty of threatening behaviour or even of taking part in violent fights, or not, sentencing him and others to three months of jail was already seeming somewhat hasty or even unwise four days later. Public opinion was no longer unanimous in thinking of them as hooligans, and some people even thought of them as basically unspoilt young people, who might be harmed by three months' contact with adult criminals.

The teenagers themselves felt that judges, magistrates, Members of Parliament, the press, the entire adult world were prejudiced against them, that 'they hate youth – all youth', without taking the least bit of trouble to find out about this youth. Why, for instance, did the magistrate speak about Mods as 'long-haired, unkempt little hoodlums' when, in fact, Mods were not wearing long hair at that time?[20]

A nineteen-year-old participant told me after the seaside disturbances:

I am shocked by the orgy of adult prejudice. Some adolescents got carried away by crowd psychosis and behaved abominably. OK. This was then followed by unjust, savage sentences. Boys were sentenced for carrying offensive weapons. In one case it was a rolled-up newspaper, in another a boy was caught holding between his fingers two shilling coins. But this was enough for police and the judge to ruin their lives. Mods and Rockers suffered because of adult hostility towards some long-haired teenagers of the past and present. They associate long hair with the beatniks and with the nuclear-disarmers, whom they hate like anything.

By no means all youth disturbances of the period 1960-4 were associated with such an orgy of adult prejudice as the Whitsun riots in 1964. But Brighton and Margate were extreme cases of a typical phenomenon. In these resorts the authorities, the residents, the landladies, the café owners and segments of the mass media had such a great fear of youth that by their exceedingly harsh and inept preventive measures (withholding food and shelter from young visitors, mounted police, dogs, they willy nilly provoked the riots that they feared.

Over-reaction, unfortunately, was typical everywhere. In the period 1957-63, the bias against and fear of youth mainly affected teenagers, beatniks, 'young hooligans', but not yet the students. Although there were already numerous student disturbances during these years, these events were not yet receiving as biased a treatment from most of the mass media as the later ones.

VIII

'THEIR' STUDENTS AND 'OURS'

'We want to eradicate from university
organization the archaic and barbarous concept of authority which in the university is
a bulwark of absurd tyranny.'

The 1918 Cordoba Manifesto, University of
Cordoba, Argentina

1

At a time when, apparently, only 'their' students protested or
sparked off revolutions in Venezuela, Turkey, South Korea,
Eastern Europe or Japan, while 'ours' were mostly in the news
with their contests in piano-wrecking, goldfish-swallowing or
crowding into phone booths, we paid little attention to 'our'
students and not infrequently approved of 'theirs'. In the ranks
of 'their' students there seemed to be a far higher proportion of
courage, thoughtfulness and unselfishness than in the rest of the
respective populations. The political role of university youth was
most conspicuous in Central and South America. Our attitude
in the period before ours rebelled, was more or less similar to that
of Professor S. W. Washington, who reported to a UNESCO
Conference in Denver, Colorado in 1959:

> While some of us in the United States deplore the conformity of
> our students, no such charge can be brought against their counter-
> parts in Latin America. There the students have always been rebel-
> lious against what they considered to be the ineptness of the older
> generation and in most places they are still rebels. That wise
> Spaniard Dr Maranon is quoted in a Cuban student magazine as
> having said: The fundamental duty of youth is rebellion. A young
> conservative is an anachronism, as is an old rebel.'[1]

Had Latin American youth neglected their duty to rebel, the
continent would have been more dictator-ridden and, conse-

quently, much poorer, with more illiteracy and more corruption than otherwise.*

The so-called 'typical' Latin-American revolutions are, of course, only various types of *coup* in which only the president and his closest entourage are replaced, without any fundamental alterations in the social order, or even in government policies.† These are either *cuartelazo* (blows from the barracks) or proper *golpe* (*golpe de estado-coup d'état*) in which a new junta is formed by conspiracy, the blow being struck usually on a Sunday or holiday; the presidential palace, the radio and other key buildings in the capital are occupied, the president is arrested or exiled and the take-over is complete.

Latin American university youth played a leading part in the wars of independence at the beginning of the nineteenth century, and have gone on struggling against tyranny ever since. In Latin America the interests of the people as opposed to the dictators or

* Between 1935 and 1964 this was the Latin American record:

	Number of years of dictatorship	Number of revolutions
Chile	0	0
Mexico	0	0
Costa Rica	0	1
Panama	1	3
Uruguay	3	0
Colombia	8	2
Ecuador	8	6
Brazil	11	4
Peru	12	2
Bolivia	12	7
Honduras	16	2
Guatemala	16	3
Argentine	17	4
Cuba	21	2
Venezuela	21	3
Dominican Republic	26	1
Paraguay	26	5
El Salvador	27	4
Haiti	29	3

† This definition is used in *Government and Politics in Latin America*, edited by H. E. Davies (New York, 1958), and in many other contemporary works. These *coups* are facilitated by many general and local factors, one of the general ones being that (with the exception of Venezuela) the Latin American states adopted after their liberation not the parliamentary but the American presidential system of government. Since most of the important executive functions are vested in one man, the *coups* achieve their aim by replacing him. (Chile experimented with the parliamentary system from 1891 until 1925. In Uruguay, there have been periods of conciliar rule.)

183

despotic oligarchies were always advocated and defended by students, writers and intellectuals. By the twentieth century the cumulative experience of generations of fighting students had produced a very high level of political consciousness in Latin American university students. It was they who succeeded in reforming their universities from 1918 onwards to a level which was unsurpassed during the following fifty years in America, Britain, France or Germany.

In 1917-8 the students of the university of Cordoba, Argentine, staged a revolt against the existing political and university system. Ever since that time, university reform and student participation in national politics have been constant features of the Latin American scene. The *Cordoba Manifesto* demanded university autonomy and *cogobierno,* that is, a fair share for the students in the 'governance' of their universities. ('Youth . . . must elect its teachers and directors for itself!')

'In the old system there was no reform of curricula and no reform of rules, for fear that someone might lose his job because of the changes,' the *Manifesto* went on. The Cordoba students brought their new system to victory. All over the continent university autonomy became the issue of the day. National constitutions were rewritten and statutes passed placing university administration in the hands of authorities chosen by the universities themselves. The *Cordoba Manifesto* demanded a democratic system of university government; this was granted in many places (and revoked later by dictators).* Speaking about the situation in 1959, Professor Washington reported: 'The students' initiative in university reform also gave them a voice in the internal administrations of the various universities. Throughout Latin America they play roles in running universities that are almost inconceivable in United States institutions of learning.'

In this account there is space only for the description of one Latin American revolution in which students played a leading part. The Venezuelan Revolution of 1958 has been chosen because it displayed many features that figured in most of the similar revolutions or revolutionary attempts south of the Rio Grande.

Venezuela's first military dictator was Caracas-born Simon

---

* Cordoba-type demands were made in Peru (1919), Chile (1920), Colombia (1924), Paraguay (1927), Brazil, Bolivia and Venezuela (1926-8), Mexico (1929), Costa Rica (1930).

Bolivar ('the Liberator'), followed by a long line of despots. In 1908 Juan Vicente Gomez, the Tyrant of the Andes, began his twenty-seven-year reign of murderous terror and arrogantly open corruption. He called his system *Caesarismo Democratico*. In fact, Gomez ran Venezuela the way Chicago gangster chiefs ran their districts. All civil liberties were suppressed; the properties of the opponents of the regime were confiscated; police brutality was extreme; the secret police defended despotism with the aid of a network of informers, torture chambers and secret and open executions. The population was extremely poor and ignorant, seventy per cent of them being illiterate. Out of the oil revenues and landholdings, dictator Gomez amassed a personal fortune worth between 200 and 250 million dollars in 1930. His family his principal aides in the army and in the government all became extremely wealthy.

In February 1928 there occurred the first dangerous challenge to the rule of the Tyrant of the Andes, when students of the Central University in Caracas organized a week of student protest, hoping to spark off a popular revolt. Despite the rigid censorship, the 'boys of 1928' were informed about university reform in the Argentine; about Sandino's guerrillas battling against American Marines in Nicaragua; about the fight in Cuba against the dictator Machado and the fight against the Peruvian despot Augusto Leguia. They felt that the entire continent was in a ferment. Led by young men such as Romulo Betancourt, a twenty-year-old law student, Jovito Villalba, Gustavo Machado and others, the 'boys of 1928' at first attacked the dictator only in speeches. They were arrested and thrown into the cellars of the Gomez prisons, each clamped in leg irons weighing seven stones.

In April, soon after their release, they began an outright revolution. They seized Gomez's Miraflores Palace, they attacked the principal military barracks in Caracas and fought against the dictator's troops. Since most of the army and most of the people were too frightened to help, the revolution failed and its leaders went into exile.

In 1941 Gomez's successor permitted Betancourt and some other fellow exiles to return to Venezuela. In 1945 Betancourt and some military officers ousted the current dictator and installed a democratic regime. Betancourt became president, promised free elections and made a pledge not to perpetuate his presidency. He kept both promises and in 1947 the *Accion Democratica* Party's candidate, Gallegos, won the first free election in the nation's history. The next year General Perez Jimenez ended the democratic regime through a *golpe* and embarked on a rule of terror and corruption that surpassed even that of Gomez.* Betancourt and the other 'boys of 1928' were once more in exile.

The students at the Central University in Caracas never gave up the struggle against dictatorship. In 1952 Jimenez had to close the university for a while when student protests became too bold. At the end of 1955 a national University Front was secretly organized to overthrow the despot. In 1956 and 1957 the students, some of them the sons of the 'boys of 1928', embarked on a dual strategy to oust the dictatorial regime. While staging open demonstrations and circulating various leaflets of protest, they were also making clandestine preparations.

The exiled political organizations were also active. Betancourt's *Accion Democratica*, Villalba's URD (Republican Democratic Union) and others had their clandestine organizations within the country. When the dictator's security agents murdered one AD secretary in 1952, another took his place, and when in turn he, too, was assassinated, another secretary carried on. The AD's magazine *Resistencia*, though illegal, was one of Venezuela's most influential press organs.

Jimenez did his best to strengthen his stranglehold on the country from year to year. His secret police, the *Seguridad Nacional,* grew into an immense force of suppression. The armed forces were increased out of all proportion to the country's possible defence needs. The army leaders were paid over-generously and given many privileges. Foreign investment was encouraged by lenient tax policies and by the stern suppression of any attempt by the workers to raise their living standards. American investors owned three-fifths of the oil industry, and all the iron mines.

The miners, the industrial workers and the rural poor, that is the overwhelming majority of the population, detested the regime, which kept them in abject poverty while embezzling vast sums of public money and spending only on show projects in the capital. The urban middle classes were against the dictatorship because it treated them as second-class citizens, was causing acute

* Jimenez's fortune was estimated at 250 million dollars, that of all other members of his family another 100 million, while his chief aide, Colonel Pulido Barreto, had another 100 million. The number of arrests in Jimenez's ten-year rule were nearly as many as during Gomez's twenty-seven year reign.

inflation and, last but not least, was forcing everyone to live in an atmosphere of corruption, suspicion and fear.

The terrorism and corruption of the Jimenez regime grew to such dimensions that even the Catholic Church – which up till then had been the accomplice of the regime by its resounding silence – turned against the dictator. Archbishop Arias issued a pastoral letter in May 1957 denouncing the worst aspects of the dictatorship. From then on, articles in Church magazines exposed torture by the police, vice and corruption, growing unemployment and the utter neglect of education.

Also in May 1957, the similar dictatorship of General Rojas in neighbouring Colombia was smashed by a popular revolution sparked off by the demonstrations and riots of secondary-school pupils and university students in Bogota. During the nation-wide clashes with the dictator's police and army, several students died for their beliefs.

Since 1955, when Argentinian army garrisons, supported by university students and secondary-school pupils, rose in the province of Cordoba and unleashed a revolution that within three days had ousted the dictator Juan Peron, the Latin American dictatorships had had an uneasy period. This era was labelled by a well-known *New York Times* correspondent, Tad Szulc, in his 1959 book as *The Twilight of the Tyrants*. Although this trend was obvious to even the most superficial observers of the Central and South American scene, the US Government and big business went on supporting the tottering tyrants until the bitter end. In certain cases this support prolonged murderous dictatorships by a few months, or even years; but in the case of Venezuela, it was neither prompt nor brutal enough to save Jimenez. This dictator was one of the favourites of Washington; according to Tad Szulc:

The ... regime offered a sound guarantee that the strategic oil resources of Venezuela were safely protected against any Soviet inroads. The regime's assurances that it kept local Communists under severe control pleased Washington, which was not informed that *the dictatorship had a quiet deal with the Communists, using them as informers against the other political groups in return for a promise to leave them alone....* Both the Eisenhower Administration and the American business community held the regime in high esteem, *dismissing as relatively unimportant the stories of persecutions, murders, and denials of liberty*. Perez Jimenez was thus decorated with the

187

Legion of Merit and a United States Navy submariner's medal, and the successive American Ambassadors maintained the most cordial personal relations with the dictator and his top officials. As events were to show before very long, this blind complacent policy was fated to blow up into America's face.[2]

In December 1957 Jimenez organized a plebiscite to legitimize his 're-election' for a further five-year term. The plebiscite was organized and supervised by the dreaded *Seguridad Nacional* and by the Ministry of the Interior. The officials of the latter counted the votes and announced that eighty-five per cent of these were in the affirmative. This ugly farce, and the prospect of a further five years of Jimenez' rule, revitalized underground resistance and brought into being a new anti-Jimenez conspiracy. The suppressed political parties formed a secret Patriotic Junta and began close co-operation with the students' National University Front. Conspiratorial groups were also formed in all three branches of the armed forces. The latter, however, did not establish contact with civilian resistance, that is, with the majority of the revolutionary forces. The anti-Jimenez officers in the army made hasty preparations for a *cuartelazo*.

On the morning of 1 January 1958, Air Force jets from the Maracay airbase flew over Caracas, led by the dictator's personal pilot. They dive-bombed the palace as a signal to their fellow-conspirators in the army and the navy to start their attacks. In fact, only a tank regiment struck in time, and army units loyal to Jimenez easily suppressed the badly prepared and faultily co-ordinated *cuartelazo*.

The rebel pilots thought their dive-bombing attack on the dictator's palace would act as a *pronunciamiento,* mobilizing the forces of resistance throughout the country. After all, from the Church to the middle classes, from the students to the rural and urban workers, everyone was against the tyrant. Their failure seemed to indicate that a large-scale demonstration of students in the streets of the capital has a greater triggering-off and mobilizing effect than an attack by dive-bombers and a tank regiment.

An uneasy fortnight followed the failed *cuartelazo*. Jimenez was forced by the less power-blinded members of his entourage to make a few concessions. He dismissed two of his aides, who were the second and third most hated men in the country: the Minister of the Interior and the chief of the *Seguridad Nacional*. This, and a few other half-hearted concessions, did not placate the students.

Central University in Caracas became the dynamic centre of resistance and revolutionary preparations. On 14 January the students of Caracas began mass demonstrations and continuous riots against the regime. The men of the *Seguridad Nacional* and the army units loyal to Jimenez did their utmost to crush the revolt. The students fought on and were soon joined by hundreds of embittered young workers and by thousands of unemployed people living in the *ranchos,* the shanty towns outside the capital. The first day of these continuous street battles did have the effect of a *pronunciamiento.* The whole of Venezuela rebelled or was on the verge of revolt. In Caracas, the student-led masses erected barricades, burned lorries and buses and fought on.

The revolt in the capital was so vehement that almost the entire population was swept along. Liberal intellectuals and progressive businessmen demanded the dismissal of the dictator in outspoken manifestos. As new groups of resistance and of rebellion mushroomed everywhere, the underground Patriotic Front of the outlawed political parties gave the rebellion coherence and co-ordination. Betancourt, Villalba and Machado and other former 'boys of 1928' were able to give nation-wide political support to the students, the 'boys of 1958'.

During the days that followed, many of the citizens and the younger clergy joined the demonstrations. When five priests were arrested, the Vatican protested. Navy destroyers were ready and waiting, prepared to shell the capital if Jimenez did not give in. Army units started to march on the capital. Eight days after the university students launched their open attack against him, on the night of 22 January, Perez Jimenez was forced to escape from Venezuela. He flew to the safety of the Dominican Republic.

On the last day of the revolution the students, already joined by some of the troops, fought in central Caracas against *Seguridad Nacional* agents barricaded in their headquarters. After the revolutionaries had taken the building, they found among the personal papers of the security-police chief a letter from a former US Ambassador expressing hope that the regime would be able to suppress the rebellion.

Six months after Betancourt came to power, in July 1958, there was a political crisis caused by the threat of a military *coup* against the regime. Caracas Central University at once suspended the examinations that were then in progress, and both faculty and students decided to defend their country against the reintroduction of dictatorship. Knowing how to make Molotov cocktails, the students spread out in the capital, ransacked soft-drink stands and drained the petrol tanks of motor-cars; thus furnished with weapons, they occupied key points in the capital. Workers and slum dwellers rallied behind them, just as they had done in January. This show of force averted the *coup*. The provisional president went to University City and thanked the students for their help in preserving democracy.

In March 1964, Romulo Betancourt, the former 'boy of 1928' became Venezuela's first president in 134 years to complete his term.

2

Foreign Offices have no youth departments. The embassies, which are supposed to know about important trends in the countries in whose capitals they are situated, have military, naval and air attachés, cultural, press, commercial, labour and agricultural councillors – but whoever heard of a youth attaché or a youth councillor among diplomats?

A simple world survey of the protests, demands and demonstrations of university youth in the recent past indicates that student disturbance is usually a sign that political and social change is overdue. The great powers of the past and of the present could have pursued less irrational policies – and policies less directed against their own ultimate interests – had they regarded student protest as a political barometer of the national or even international scene. The thesis that student power can only be effective if it is backed by military power – and hence that it is enough to know the mood of the army in order to anticipate possible political storms – is not borne out by the history of the last decades. By 'the army' Establishment-minded people usually refer to the army high command, in practice to the top two to five per cent of the entire officer corps. But in fact, the army consists on the one hand of the professional soldiers, who should be divided into at least four interest-groups: (1) the high command; (2) the general officers in the medium command; (3) the younger officers; (4) the professional other ranks (from corporal to sergeant); and on the other hand, the troops are the people in uniform serving their

190

compulsory military training period; the reserve officers are some-what better-educated people in uniform.

In writing about Latin American *coups,* people usually use 'the army' to refer to one or two of the top three groups. But at times, when the military intervene in revolutionary action, 'the army' in fact means groups of dissatisfied younger officers or sergeants; at other times it simply means workers and peasants in uniform.

Student activism in Cuba has served as a political barometer ever since the nineteen-twenties. In 1923 a student revolt forced the authorities to grant Havana University some autonomy. The students went on to press for more reforms both at the university and in national politics. Still in the late twenties, Machado decided to stamp out 'once and for all' the centre of revolutionary agitation. His troops invaded the grounds of Havana University, the 'trouble-makers' were arrested and the university closed. In 1933 the student militants, in alliance with a group of rebellious army sergeants, smashed the Machado dictatorship.

This revolutionary *golpe* was usurped by one of the sergeants, Batista, who established his own dictatorship. Havana University once more became the centre of revolutionary activities. Batista closed the university in 1935, and it was reopened only two years later when its autonomy was recognized. During Batista's two dictatorships students were frequently in the vanguard of the urban and rural resistance movement. During Batista's last dicta-torship (1952-8) the Chief of Police saw the university as the main danger to the terror regime. Despite frequent protests by professors and students, the violation of university autonomy went on. Finally, in 1956, separate groups of students and professors decided on a total strike. Classes were not resumed until 1959, when Fidel Castro took over.

On 13 March 1957 Havana students organized and carried out an unsuccessful assassination attempt on Batista. During the attack against Batista's palace many students lost their lives. Afterwards, the survivors organized the *Directorio Estudiantil Revolucionaro* (Revolutionary Student Directorium) to launch their own urban movement against Batista, while Castro was conducting his guerrilla war. Many students joined Castro during the second phase of his operations.

The point is that student militancy against dictatorship served in Cuba, too, as a warning of an impending storm. In 1960 there

191

were several significant instances when university students changed the course of national or even international history.

In South Korea, an uprising of university and other students toppled the inefficient, wasteful and extremely corrupt dictatorship of Syngman Rhee. The old dictator, whose presidential palace was protected from the people by barbed wire and who drove around in a bullet-proof Cadillac, ruled by callously brutal police terror. Safe in the knowledge that he was protected by his own huge apparatus of repression and by the US troops stationed in the country, Rhee had only contempt for his democratic opponents and took hardly any notice of the 'howling of the young snot-noses'.

On 15 March 1960 elections were held. Syngman Rhee was elected President again and his most vicious henchman, Lee Ki Poong, became Vice-President. The Minister of the Interior revealed later that he had collected the written resignations of all Korea's mayors and police chiefs before the election, and told them that the resignations would be accepted unless they secured victory for Rhee and Lee Ki Poong. To make doubly sure the national police director filled the ballot boxes beforehand with forty per cent pro-Rhee votes. In a country where police terror reached down to village and city-block level, it was easy to secure an electoral 'victory' for Rhee's gang by these methods.

The answer offered by university and secondary-school students was several weeks of mass demonstrations against the regime. Rhee had to try to enforce martial law in Seoul and in the four other principal cities of the country. The police, and later the army, had many clashes with the rebellious students, who demanded that Rhee and his gang should be ousted at once and that the country should freely elect a democratic government. The clashes between Rhee's forces and the masses of students produced many casualties. Students died fighting against the police. Some student militants mysteriously disappeared – their bodies were found later. There was little doubt that they had been murdered by police-agents.

Despite martial law, the revolt flared up again and again during the weeks that followed the fake elections. By the middle of April it became evident that the only way the South Korean army could save Rhee's hated regime would be to shoot down students in droves. Despite this, Rhee and his US advisers played for time. Rhee went so far as to order his principal aide, Lee Ki

Poong, to 'apologize to the nation' for all those acts which he had carried out on Rhee's instructions.

The continuing student demonstrations against the universally hated and despised regime made the army an uncertain weapon of the government. Young officers sympathized with the revolutionaries. As for the troops, there were several signs that they were reluctant to attack the mass demonstrations of students. The army was virtually split. General Song Yo Chan, the Chief of Staff, and some other generals and colonels were ready to turn against Rhee.

Finally, the last massive onslaught against the regime succeeded. On 25 April 1960, university and secondary-school students staged a mass demonstration, while over three hundred professors of Seoul National University took part in an open-air protest meeting on the steps of the National Assembly building. All the demonstrators risked death. According to martial law, and to Rhee's instructions, the troops should have fired on them. The army tanks duly arrived everywhere on the scene, and drove on as if nothing untoward was happening.

Later during the day, well after the 7 p.m. curfew, some students clambered on to passing tanks, in the centre of Seoul, shouting 'Long live our soldiers!' The tanks stopped, the young officers and their troops took off their helmets and joined the crowd in tribute to the students killed in earlier demonstrations by singing a Korean war song:

> Sleep well comrades,
> We advance to victory
> Over your dead bodies.

In that second when soldiers and students sang a patriotic war song together the terror regime collapsed. The police disappeared from the streets. That night there were victory celebrations. Next day a delegation of five students, accompanied by Chief of Staff Song, went to Rhee's palace. After the students had delivered their ultimatum, Rhee replied: 'If the people wish it, I will resign.' The students rejoined the waiting crowd, shouting: 'We have won.' According to *Time*: 'Suddenly finding themselves the victors, Seoul's students showed extraordinary discipline. With virtually all the city's police in frightened hiding, students ran the police stations, directed traffic, even commandeered city trash trucks and laboriously cleaned up the riot debris.'[3]

The leadership of the young revolutionaries, in their turn, made sure that the National Assembly would formally depose Syngman Rhee. When the emergency session of the Assembly met – only 105 of South Korea's 231 Assembly members dared to show up – a sizeable number of university students was present. They watched the proceedings and cheered only when the resolution for Rhee's ousting, new elections and a new constitution was passed unanimously.

(Parliamentary democracy was destroyed the following year by a military junta, with the support of the US government and the US occupation troops.)

In May–June 1960 there was a further clinical demonstration of the limits of army power when faced with student power. In Turkey, the regime of repression was directed by Premier Adnan Menderes (head of the Democratic Party). In ten years of misrule the regime suppressed almost all civil rights, banned newspapers, jailed over two thousand political opponents and critics of the regime, among them two hundred journalists. When, at the end of April 1960, Menderes announced a further police drive against the opposition forces (a special commission to investigate the 'illegitimate, subversive' activities of the Republican opposition party), 1,500 Istanbul University students staged a protest meeting inside the campus. While the meeting was in progress, the Police Chief and a considerable police force arrived on the scene. The police entered the campus and tried to arrest some students. One of the girl students felled a particularly brutal policeman with a blow from her high-heeled shoe. The police responded by shooting. Three students fell. When the University President, Professor Onar, told the Police Chief that it was illegal for his forces to enter the campus, he was knocked down and carted off with a bleeding head to a police station.

The students – their number had swelled to five thousand by then – forced the police to bring back their president. Professor Onar pleaded with them in vain to disperse, and they left the campus for the adjoining Beyazit Square. While sympathetic soldiers looked on, they shouted 'Death to all dictators!', 'Menderes must resign!', 'Long live the students of Seoul!' The police threw tear-gas bombs, then mounted police were ordered to attack. The students jabbed lighted cigarettes under the horses, making them rear and throw their riders. The answer was concentrated .rifle fire that felled over twenty students. Although it was evident by then that further demonstrations meant risking lives, university students of all faculties* and of both sexes continued to demonstrate. By opening the Golden Horn drawbridge, the police prevented a large student column from crossing into the city centre.

However, there were demonstrations in many other parts of the city. Seeing the students in a determined mood, the tank crews just headed them off, but did not attack them as the police did. The government proclaimed martial law, and the university was shut down. The military governor prohibited any mention of the demonstrations in the press, and denied that anybody had been killed. (In the first few hours the hospitals reported seven dead and over thirty badly wounded. All of them were students.)

Next day, thousands of students demonstrated against dictatorship in Ankara, Istanbul and Izmir. In Istanbul the troops were able to break up demonstrations and to avoid bloodshed by deliberately marching and countermarching on squares and avenues.

The old General Izmet Inönü, leader of the Republican opposition, hero of two wars and president of Turkey from 1938 to 1950, told Menderes in Parliament:

Other regimes have ruled illegally and have justified their rule by arguments like yours. Syngman Rhee had an obedient police force, civil service and army in his hand, but you do not even command the loyalty of those forces. . . . Those who seek to establish a coercive regime must believe that the Turkish nation is imbued with less self-respect than Korea.

This 'insult against the nation' caused a general *mêlée* in parliament. Izmet Inönü was expelled from parliament for twelve sessions. Menderes, who never made a secret of the contempt he felt for the 'intellectuals of Istanbul', accused the Republicans of virtual treason in a broadcast to the nation, and asserted that : 'the students had become the tools of conspirators and fanatical party followers. Their demonstrations are plots against the country's security. They will soon learn what it means to stand against the state.' The students, however, refused to identify Menderes with the state. Their demonstrations went on. From their first

* In Venezuela, the law and arts faculties were reported to produce most student militants, the engineering faculty the least. In Istanbul and Ankara, as in Hungary, the engineering students were very active.

195

protest meeting at the end of April till the end of May. they did not ease their pressure against Menderes and his regime. All through May, mass protests went on. After a protest march by army cadets, all colleges and universities were closed.

In the end the army, or rather a part of the army, intervened. After a swift army *coup* on 27 May, in which young officers played a leading role, General Gursel, a former critic of the Menderes regime, formed a caretaker government. General Gursel insisted that the whole purpose of the *coup* was 'to secure just and free elections as soon as possible, and handing over the administration to whichever party wins the election. . . . I tried to reason with the politicians, but they were blinded by ambition. We had to act. They ignored my advice. They thought that the Turkish nation was a senseless herd.'

One of General Gursel's first acts was to recruit seven professors from Istanbul to help draft a provisional constitution for a democratic Turkey. One of them was Professor Onar, President of Istanbul University, who, as we have seen, had been badly beaten by Menderes' police while protesting against their violation of university autonomy.

(This *coup* did not end student grievances. University youth went on demonstrating against various policies during President Izmet Inönü's regime.)

3

Sit-in strikes were re-invented in the twentieth century by workers in the US car industry; certain forms of student boycott and strike were re-invented in Burma* (where the army felt compelled to dynamite the building of the Student Union); but several forms of mass demonstrations were innovations introduced by the students of Japan.

In September 1948 over 300,000 students from 145 universities† joined together in the All-Japan Federation of Student Self-Government Associations (*Zen Nihon Gakusei Jichikai Sorengo*), or Zengakuren. The great student federation, which by

* The earliest school occupations we happen to know about took place over 1,400 years ago. (See next chapter.)

† In 1940 there were 47 universities in Japan. During the American occupation and as a consequence of US educational policies there were by 1960 236 four-year universities and 274 other colleges. In Tokyo alone there were about 300,000 students.

1960 represented the majority of the country's 680,000 under-graduates and graduate students, failed to gain student representation or any kind of participation in the running of universities.

Many member associations of the federation were originally close to the Japanese Communist Party, but after the Hungarian Revolution of 1956 the majority of the federation turned against the party line. This majority came to be called the mainstream of Zengakuren, and since the official communists denounced the mainstream as Trotskyite, the rest of the press often used this label. The 'anti-mainstream' faction in the Zengakuren toed the official party line.

One of the spokesmen of the mainstream was Nobua Aruga, a fourth-year law student at Tokyo University, whom the press proclaimed in 1960 as a 'Zengakuren leader'. Aruga advocated co-operation with the socialists and the communists, but said that in time he hoped to fight them both. He frequently stated that in their view both capitalist and communist governments 'are enemies of peace, democracy and student freedom'. If it were not for the 'nuclear situation' he would not mind seeing an all-out war between the capitalists of the West and the communists because 'in that futile struggle between different types of bureaucrats the corrupt regimes of both would be annihilated. After that, the innate good sense of ordinary people would make it possible to have minimum control by government.'

In 1960 the mainstream Zengakuren rejected the lead of both the Russian and the Chinese brands of communism, and that of the American-led West. The 'anti-mainstream' faction regarded the United States as the principal enemy. The mainstream concentrated more on internal Japanese issues, on the overthrow of the existing system and on a policy of peace and nuclear disarmament in international affairs.

In 1958 the mainstream demonstrated against special police powers and in 1960 against the renewal of the Japan–USA Security Treaty. Prime Minister Kishi, who had been jailed for three years as a 'class A war crime suspect' and released without trial, pushed through the Diet (by a cynical parliamentary trick) the ratification of the Treaty. This move, on 19 May 1960, enraged much of public opinion, by no means only the Left. (When, four months earlier, Kishi had flown to Washington to discuss the renewal of this treaty, there were violent mass demonstrations in

Tokyo; students seized the airport building to prevent Kishi's take-off, which was made possible only after his car had reached the plane by various detours.)

During the weeks that followed liberal and other centrist students, together with the Zengakuren mainstream, demonstrated for new elections and against the impending finalization of the Japan–US Treaty on 19 June. The anti-mainstream wanted to prevent a visit by President Eisenhower to Tokyo, planned for the second part of June. Backed by the Japanese Communist Party, the anti-mainstream sent 10,000 demonstrators to Hanedo Airport on 10 June to protest against the arrival of James Hagerty, Eisenhower's press secretary. Hagerty could be saved from the wrath of the demonstrators only by a sudden helicopter rescue.

The main demonstrations were against the finalization of the ratification of the treaty. The Trade Union Council (*Sohyo*) backed the protest. Three hundred thousand trade unionists and over 40,000 Zengakuren militants approached the Diet building in the famous snake march. Although the majority of the TUC and Zengakuren leaders were not interested in preventing Eisenhower's visit, Kishi's government felt obliged to ask Eisenhower to cancel it. Eisenhower in reply expressed his 'full and sympathetic understanding of the decision taken by the Japanese government and his regrets that a small, organized minority, led by professional communist agitators . . . have been able by resort to force and violence to prevent the good-will visit.'

For once, the US authorities were right in blaming the communists for this. The non-communist Zengakuren mainstream wanted to prevent the ratification of the treaty. They regarded the all-out attack against Hagerty and against the Eisenhower visit as a diversion that weakened the struggle against ratification.

The subsequent history of Zengakuren and the Japanese student disturbances have no place in this chapter. It should, however, be mentioned that, like the French students of 1968, the Zengakuren was rejected by the workers at a crucial point in the political developments. Zengakuren offered financial aid to the striking miners of Miike. The miners refused to accept it.

The Zengakuren mainstream was the first large student movement to reject both capitalism and communism, and was denounced with equal vehemence by the pro-Moscow and pro-Chinese communists. The Zengakuren was the first independent mass movement of students to be punished for its independence by trade unions and various bodies of the working class.

A bird's eye view of student activities during the period 1957-64 shows that university youth produced everywhere untypical minorities of activitists, who, even in years when the overwhelming majority of students were a-political and non-committed, risked their lives for freedom and justice.

In 1960, the US Student Nonviolent Coordination Committee (SNCC) was founded at Raleigh, North Carolina, during an Easter week conference. The student Freedom Riders in the South, the sit-ins staged by Negro college students, the mass demonstrations against the hearings of the House of Un-American Activities Committee in May and June, indicated that not all US students were lethargic. In June 1960, the Students for a Democratic Society (SDS) was formed in New York City.

These minorities might have been untypical, but they were not exactly tiny. In May 1960, for instance, eight thousand students (the police estimate) in San Francisco picketed the House of Un-American Activities Committee's hearings. There were sixty-eight arrests after the police had managed to clear students from the City Hall steps by the use of water-hoses. This was followed by a nation-wide campaign, supported on many US campuses, for the abolishment of HUAC.

In France the UNEF – the student union – was the only major national organization that continued in its open opposition to the Algerian War, while the organized Left was silent. The student activists succeeded in October 1960 in sparking off mass demonstrations against the 'pointless and immoral' war. The war was ended two years later. By that time majority public opinion had come round to the view of the students.

4

In 1946 liberated France produced 200,000 more babies than in wartime 1945, and in fact this was a significantly higher percentage than during the last two peacetime years. Before the war France was worried by her 'galloping population decrease'. The government and most of public opinion assumed that the sudden and untypical increase in the proportion of babies was an exceptional postwar occurrence, 'nature's way of making up for the lost men'. As for the governments of the day, the fact that the

199

extra 200,000 babies would grow up was ignored. Though 1947 again produced an 'untypical' surplus of babies, the governments still seemed to assume that France was a country of endemic population decrease. Between 1946 and 1952 almost nothing was done to provide extra elementary-school places for the extra hundreds of thousands of boys and girls. The yearly vintages of children born in 1946-8 and later, became old enough to enter elementary and secondary schools – and there were not enough places for them.

French governments have always been late. They were late in providing secondary schools for these new waves of children; as far as university places were concerned, they were not late – they did nothing. Nor did these delinquent governments do anything to limit the number of boys and girls who could enter university. The French system, then and for years afterwards, was such that anyone who had passed the *baccalauréat* could enrol in a French university. There was no entrance examination for university faculties, and between 1955 and 1964 eighty-five to ninety per cent of the students in higher education did in fact go to university.

In 1955 no foresight was needed to know that the terrible overcrowding at the universities would lead to explosions. In 1950, 30,000 candidates passed the *baccalauréat*. The numbers grew each year. By 1955 all the babies had been born from whose ranks would emerge the university students up to 1972. In 1955 a conservative estimate would have shown this as an increase of over two hundred per cent. (It proved to be more by 1968.) The French government of the day announced in May 1955 that they were setting up a governmental committee on youth. This was done in the middle of September.

Despite committees, despite demographic evidence, nothing was done to ease the extreme physical discomforts to which students were exposed in the lecture rooms. The utter indifference of governments and the educational authorities to the miserable conditions in which the French students found themselves was hard to understand. In 1963 the Sorbonne had more than 32,000 students taught by 100 professors, one to every 320. The Sorbonne's one and only library, with a seating capacity of 500, could take in less than two per cent of the registered undergraduates!

The overcrowding in the five colleges of the University of Paris is hard to imagine. Less than half of the 100,000 students had any hope of fighting their way in to the lecture rooms and amphitheatres. I wrote in an earlier book about the situation at the Sorbonne in 1963:

The lecture rooms were impossibly overcrowded. Most of them looked like a scene from the Hitchcock film *The Birds*; students filled the benches, perched on balustrades, stood and squatted in the aisles, overfilled the remote stair wells, while hundreds crowded the halls and heard the professor through loudspeakers. Other thousands simply gave up the struggle and did without lectures. They studied in cafés, parks, at home, used mimeographed notes and saw their teachers only at exams.

The price of textbooks and lecture notes was very high. Student quarters were overcrowded and very expensive. Those thousands of students who simply could not squeeze into the lecture halls were often forced by the weather to study in left-bank cafés. But there they were allowed to remain only if they ordered something every hour. This made life even more difficult, since most of them were poor.[4]

For years these young people had the same demands: one student, one place in lecture rooms, libraries and canteens. The right to reprint lectures without paying the equivalent of two or three US dollars for each set. They asked for cheaper textbooks and cheaper living quarters. Those who had not asked to be born were asking for physical space to live and work in.

Finally, in 1962, the authorities acted. They forbade all public protests by university students. There were various minor protests against the protest ban and against their condition, until finally, in November 1963, came the first 'Sorbonne explosion'. About 10,000 students demonstrated for the improvement of their physical conditions. Since their demonstration was illegal, about 4,500 policemen battled against the students throughout the Quartier Latin from Saint-Michel to Montparnasse. Hundreds of boy and girl students were clubbed, kicked in the stomach, punched and hit by jets of water from fire hoses. Riot cars screamed and dozens of paddy wagons took away the arrested students. Banners on the Sorbonne told some of the story: 'The Sorbonne For The Students!'; 'Warning To The Government!'; 'National Strike!'

Next day, France's twenty-three universities were closed by a national strike of the country's 300,000 university students, and that of half of their professors. The strike was a protest against the fact that the lack of foresight and the passivity of a series of governments had turned the universities into cruelly overcrowded slums of learning. At that stage the students were demonstrating only for their minimum demands. There was not yet any great outcry against the unbelievably obsolete French university system itself.

In February 1964, the National Union of French Students called for renewed demonstrations to prompt the authorities into some action. The police, as usual, over-reacted. The students carried their banners and shouted their slogans. Near the Gare St Lazare the police dispersed them with repeated baton charges. One of them was later taken by the police to and from the Law Courts handcuffed, and led on a chain like a dog on a leash.

The NFS demanded his release and satisfaction for this treatment. The students' communiqué went on:

For two years the authorities have forbidden all demonstrations called by the students in a public place. These measures are all the more serious since it is only by demonstrations and meetings that the students can make public the inadequacies of the French universities, face to face with a government that refuses to listen or satisfy the students' grievances.

The young man who was handcuffed for daring to demand a place for each student raised the French juvenile delinquency figures by one. The outrageous adult delinquency of governments in ignoring the fact that babies do grow up went unpunished.

'Our' students in Europe and North America were mostly conformist, and there was among them a significant proportion of neurotic introverts. 'Their' students during this period were mostly non-conformist and ready to fight for their convictions, and there was also among them a significant proportion of neurotic introverts.

Professor Musgrove has dealt in some detail with the circumstances that cause universities and other institutes of higher education to prefer (and offer better chances to) neurotic introvert types:

Individuals who are stable and extrovert seem to do less well in the activities which are valued by grammar schools and universities, even though they are of similar intelligence. . . . It has been suggested that extraversion is not in itself a handicap in academic pursuits below the level of university education, but there is evidence that our present system is already penalising the (intelligent) extravert before this stage.[5]

Evidence of this was found by R. Lynn,[6] who discovered that present-day students obtain higher scores in introversion and neuroticism than equally intelligent people not attending universities.

It has been emphasized before that the Bolshevik revolution did not alter the essence of the outdated university system. This explains why Soviet and East European students score high proportions of introversion and neuroticism similar to university youth everywhere else. Though the situation in the universities could not display more different impressions than, say, in Moscow, Los Angeles, Tokyo, Caracas and London, one thing universities in these cities, and everywhere else in the world, had in common was that they caused a perceptible deterioration in the mental health of the student populations. This was not an exceptional circumstance, caused by some new factors produced in a particular short period. The university system as it existed and still exists endangers the mental health of its students.

Ferdynand Zweig dealt with this period in his amply documented and very alarming book *The Student in the Age of Anxiety*. In the era immediately preceding that of the great student explosions, Zweig found British students anxiety-ridden, conformist and lethargic: 'The students I interviewed did not strike me as young and carefree, on the contrary, they struck me as old, laden with responsibility, care and worry, with nightmares and horror dreams.'[7]

Although his findings were based on a survey of students at Oxford and Manchester, similar findings were reported from many countries in the five continents during the period 1946-63. In countries as far apart as the United States and Japan it was taken for granted that a significant proportion of the yearly intake of universities embarked upon a period of psychological deterioration.[8]

Compare the findings of American investigators at Vassar with those of W. D. Furneux[9] in the engineering department of a British University. At Vassar 'a consistent trend is for seniors to be higher than freshmen in the following scales: Hypochondriasis, Depression, Hysteria, Psychopathic Deviate, Schizophrenia and Mania.' Furneaux found that neurotic introversion seemed to be a precondition for university education and, in some degree, even for university admission.

In Britain, there was 'little doubt' in 1958 'that anxiety, in some sense of the word, contributes to rapid conditioning and to good academic achievement'.[10]

In the period 1957-64 there was some form of unrest at over two-thirds of the world's universities and other institutions of higher learning. Besides rebelling against repressive regimes, hopeless and immoral wars, against racial oppression and for civil rights and liberty, two or three student generations at the universities demanded with increasing intensity and frequency a radical reform of the university system itself. There were confrontations between university administrators (boards of governors, regents, or whatever they were called) and students in a great many countries of the world. In some confrontations a considerable proportion of teaching staff sided with the students. As long as these confrontations were not too vocal, were entirely non-violent and therefore not a threat to the prevalent torpor of the administrators, nothing was done to re-examine the ludicrously obsolete university systems.

IX

STUDENTS VERSUS SOCIETY

'Who wouldn't have pity on these homeless ones who, driven by their thirst for knowledge, expose their life to many dangers and are often manhandled without any reason by most inferior people.'

Emperor Frederic I (Barbarossa), in defence of university students in 1158*[1]

'Those who enter upon formal courses of higher education need not be so severely handicapped and penalised as they tend to be today. [They] need not be so dependent, humiliated, excluded from the life of their society, as commonly they are at present . . . Their sacrifices; their postponement of manhood, the stresses and conflicts to which they are subjected, should not be underrated.'

Frank Musgrove[2]

1

Never throughout his long history has the university student been fully accepted as a regular member of society. The first two universities in the world – Bologna and Paris – were founded at a time of great change in religion, philosophy, architecture, in the daily life of people, yet even this change-prone society found it impossible to accept these strange new and most irregular specimens existing on the outskirts of society. It was an age of intellectual and religious awakening, of the birth of Gothic architecture; of new mysticisms, of a new kind of rationalism. Huizinga wrote that 'the twelfth century was a creative and formative age without equal. There was actually much more of an awakening, an unfolding, in the eleven-hundreds than in the age to which we are wont to attach the name Renaissance.'[3]

* '*Wer sollte sich ihrer nicht erbarmen, wenn sie, heimatlost aus Wissendrang, ihr Leben vielen Gefahren aussetzen und von den minderwertigsten Menschen grundlos Tätlichkeiten ertragen müssen.*'

The great rationalist Abelard, the troubadour among the scholastics, was the most fabulously successful guru of his age. In the age of faith he was for doubt; he boldly quoted Aristotle: 'For by doubt we come to investigation and by investigation we ascertain the truth.' He was opposed by St Bernard of Clairvaux, the famous exponent of a new mysticism, who never ceased to express his ecstasy at the wonders of God's grace. In his wrath St Bernard did not shrink from name-calling. He called Abelard a *'goliard'*, which was at that time just as exotic as someone today calling Bertrand Russell a hippie, and rather similar in tone.

All through the tenth century the timid stirrings of a new thinking, a new world of feeling and a new poetry existed behind monastery walls and in various hidden nooks and crannies of the medieval world. Taking advantage of the changes in the eleventh century, thinkers and poets began to emerge. The European world grew more diverse and far more colourful. The past, the splendours of antiquity, began to fascinate and influence. The many new contacts with the East brought new ideas, new customs, new materials and new possibilities from strange foreign lands.

The world then was, indeed, in a fast spin. But even then the wandering scholar was too strange for ordinary people. He was an irregular, and therefore suspect, outsider by definition. He became a student by leaving or escaping from his inherited place in medieval society. He wore clothes similar to those of the clerics, but was not really one. In his place at the university he was protected by his corporation. But when he was on his way from one university to another, as he was wont to do, he was at everyone's mercy. He often became a member of the medieval underworld of outlaws, soothsayers, tightrope-walkers, sword-swallowers, whores, thiefs, beggars, street scribes. The wandering student–poets or student–singers, the vagrants or *goliards*, were the pop singers of their day. The authorities did not much care to find out who was a real vagabond, who a semi-vagabond, or who a poorly-dressed student–singer.

The popular image of the medieval student was richer and more sharply differentiated than the twentieth-century layman's image of the student-of-today. The students who invented, created and managed one of the first two universities of the world, that of Bologna, were by no means a uniform group. Some of them were young nobles who arrived with their own majordomo, cook, servants and stable boys. There were boys intent on escaping their inferior place in the feudal world, and also fairly prosperous mature clerics who hoped to advance in the church hierarchy by proofs of *studium*.

In an age in which books were rare, in which an ability to read and mastery over words was held in awe, much of the magic rubbed off on the student image. In popular superstition wizards were in the habit of disguising themselves as travelling students, and one never knew what powers of magic an unkempt, begging scholar possessed. The student was also the cheerful and too irreverent intinerant minstrel; a jester with unpleasantly sharp wit; a drunkard and a seducer of wenches.

It was not until the thirteenth century that the popular image of the student-of-today began to alternate between two extremes: the lazy and rowdy (frequently foreign) vagabond on the one hand, and the obstinately free intellect, without whose rebellious spirit the arts and the sciences would stagnate, on the other.

The authorities had their troubles with both extremes. Student–bandits were hanged in medieval Paris for their crimes, and non-conformist students were hanged for asserting that women have no more ribs than men, though Eve was created from one of Adam's ribs.

The two extremes of the student image did not necessarily coexist. The 'obstinately free spirit' version usually referred to the student of former times. The anecdote about the medieval student and the horse's mouth is revealing in this context: The learned professors of Paris were debating the number of teeth in the horse's mouth. All agreed that the number cannot be a multiple of three, since that would offend the Trinity. It cannot be a multiple of seven either, because God created the world in six days and rested on the seventh. Almost all possibilities were sacrilegious. The professors searched in vain for guidance in the works of St Thomas Aquinas and Aristotle. Then one of the students slipped out, opened a horse's mouth and counted its teeth. This scandalous behaviour in getting the answer 'right from the horse's mouth' shocked the good professors.

It is usually pointed out that this irreverent and undisciplined young man belonged to the untypical minority of students, yet his act marked the beginning of free enquiry and objective research at the universities.

In the background of the popular student image there was always the majority of obedient students who did their work without disturbing the peace or offending the conventional wisdom of the day. In discussions in the eighth-century Talmudic academies or in the thirteenth-century Sorbonne, or again in the twentieth-century American 'supermarkets of knowledge', people have frequently been guided by the assumption that 'majority' and 'typical' or 'characteristic' were synonyms.

The untypical minority and the typical majority were treated as a single hostile camp only during the periodic clashes between townsmen (or townswomen) and the students. At such times, laymen regarded the university as a breeding-ground for the 'enemies of citizens'. 'Town' and 'gown' have often been at loggerheads over the centuries. Town, whether it was Bologna, Paris, Oxford, Lisbon or Heidelberg, often felt that the gown was disloyal or not sufficiently loyal to society, to the momentarily ruling wisdom; that students were a rowdy (often foreign) rabble. The hostilities between citizens and students in Berlin and Oakland in 1968 were mild affairs compared to some of the medieval troubles or later battles between town and gown. In 1231 Henry III of England sent a series of letters to the sheriffs, commanding them to repress 'rebellious and incorrigible' students. There were large-scale town v. gown disturbances in Oxford in 1208 and in Cambridge in 1214.

G. M. Trevelyan describes in his *English Social History* how the rights of the university:

... were defended against all aggression by the hosts of turbulent undergraduates herding in the squalid lodging-houses of Oxford, who, when occasion called, poured forth to threaten the life of a Bishop's messenger, to hoot the King's officials, or to bludgeon and stab the mob that maintained the Mayor against the Chancellor.

Town and gown used daggers, swords, and even bows and arrows in their pitched battles in High Street. In 1355 the townsmen made a regular massacre of clerks and students: the survivors fled in terror from Oxford, and the University closed down until the King intervened to protect and avenge the scholars.[4]

Similar battles were fought from the eleventh to the fifteenth century in many university towns in several countries. The conflict between students and townsmen in the Middle Ages was solidly based on the nature of the towns on the one hand and that of the universities on the other. Their origin, their rights and their functions made it difficult for the universities to fit into the feudal order of things. Though in their internationalism they were the embodiment of the medieval ideal of a unified Christian world, this very fact made them suspect and unpopular in the eyes of ordinary people.

The two earliest universities, as we have seen, were those of Bologna and Paris. They differed in their systems but not in the characteristics mentioned above. All the later universities founded in the twelfth and thirteenth centuries were modelled on the Bologna or Paris originals, or were compromises between the two different systems.

The 'most ancient University of Bologna' was founded by a spontaneous gathering of mostly foreign students. They all spoke Latin, the international language of the educated. They all wanted to learn, so they formed corporations, hired and paid masters and managed their own affairs independently of the town authorities. The foreign students banded together in 'nations', which united in a single corporation (*universitas*) students from several countries. The word *universitas* did not refer to the totality and the unity of these free student corporations until later.

The Bologna type, invented and created by students who wanted to learn, was the *Universitas Scholarum*. The Paris model was invented and created by a spontaneous gathering of masters, who wanted to teach. This was the *Universitas Magistrorum*, the corporation of masters. Both students and masters were members of the same migratory élite, with the same cultural background, sharing Latin as their common language, broadly agreeing on the importance of the same *studium generale*. Scholars or masters, their home was everywhere in Europe where people wanted to learn and teach.

Naturally, these first universities had to have a legal place in the world. They were legally recognized by the pope, who backed and protected the freedom of the universities because the international community of scholars helped to unify the Christian world. The pope granted the *ius ubique docendi,* the right to teach and study everywhere. In principle, the local bishop was supposed to supervise the university in the pope's name; in fact, one of the bishop's officials, the 'chancellor', exercised this supervision. These supervisory powers were limited by the fact that the university's privilege was not localized; students and masters could move to the territory of another bishop. The chancellor's importance diminished in medieval times, and the elected head, the rector, became *primus inter pares* – the first among equals – at the university.

In Bologna, mature, financially independent law students were in the majority and they controlled their university through rectors, chosen from their own ranks. In 1200 there were about ten thousand students in Bologna, from many countries in Europe.

The corporation's privileges included jurisdiction in civil and, in certain cases, in criminal matters. The most important safeguard of university integrity was the right to strike, or to leave town in protest against some offence or insult to the university.[5]

Although under the Pope's protection, scholars and magisters did not regard themselves as servants of the Church, and most certainly not of the state. They were 'citizens of the university'. Even the secular clergy teaching or studying at the universities were academics first and churchmen only second.

It is easy to see why, in an age when even a short journey was an exceptional event for the overwhelming majority of the population, these free, irregular cosmopolitans were disliked by most authorities and particularly by the ordinary townsmen. And as the number of universities began to grow, all concerned had many reasons to hate and fear the students.

The medieval student, before the development of the college system had done its work, was riotous, lawless and licentious. He was miserably poor. . . . The authorities at the universities, imitating the folly of the authorities in Church and State elsewhere, forbade athletic exercises among the youth in their jurisdiction, but made no great effort to keep them out of the tavern and the brothel; some of them roamed the countryside in robber-bands.[6]

In many European countries students, and even schoolboys, were usually armed. These mostly foreign vagabonds and ruffians were at the same time somehow influential. Ordinary folk feared not only their daggers and foils but also all the mysterious knowledge in their heads. The students' image was made even more complex by the fact that he belonged to the powerful university.

The early universities were free and independent because they owned no buildings or any other property. The scholars and masters of Salerno University, which was acknowledged as the best medical school in the world, knew that any city or town would be glad to have them were they to decide to move. The townsmen and the authorities of the region knew this, too. In Bologna, when landladies began to charge exorbitant rents, the students decided to move their university out of town. They returned only when a deputation from Bologna guaranteed reasonable rents for masters and students alike.

The influence and power of the universities rested primarily on the fact that their students were to become high Church or state officials, lawyers, theologians, physicians, or stay on as masters. At times they fashioned the mind of an age and gave political guidance to the powerful. Once, in the fifteenth century, the University of Paris earned the description of a 'European power'. Doctors of law, medicine or theology were respected. In sixteenth-century Spain doctors of law were addressed as 'Knights' or 'Lords of the Law'. In their attitude to students, ordinary people were also influenced by their awareness that all these great ones had once been undergraduates themselves.

During the first flowering of the universities their place in the order of things and in the world was more firmly based than at any other time during their subsequent history. 'The medieval university was the organisatorial form embodying the public recognition of the corporate autonomy of specialized intellectuals who performed important functions.'[7]

The function of the original universities, as seen by their founders, was not to be of service to society, to the state, or to the community where they happened to be located:

Although the men produced by the medieval universities became leaders in the church and in the state, they did *not* advertise that their function was to produce such men. Such men were a byproduct of an enterprise in which they were engaged ... *the discussion of the most important questions.* They would have been startled if they had been asked to justify their existence in terms of the service they performed for society, for they would have had no doubt that the discussion they were carrying on was its own justification.[8]

Their aim and *raison d'être* was the disinterested pursuit of learning, and through this, according to Rashdall, they happened to create the possibility of placing 'the administration of human affairs ... in the hands of educated men'.

Those early universities that did not foster this spirit, or were firmly suborned by a king or prince, such as the University of Naples, distinguished themselves in medieval times by their

211

mediocrity and deteriorated in time to become 'almost unique specimens of pedantic imbecility'. (Walter Scott described thus the Neapolitan *Accademici* in his *Fragmenta Herculenacia*.)

It would, however, be a mistake to think that the university was originally conceived as a citadel of free enquiry, of constant examination and re-examination of currently accepted beliefs. The medieval university concentrated on the sum total of officially established knowledge of the age. In time, there were many magisters, particularly in Paris, or in the Paris-type universities, whose main aim was the transmission and refinement of a conformist culture, the self-perpetuation of orthodoxy.

On the other hand, there are in the history of the early universities plenty of instances of hot-headed students or heretical professors questioning some parts of the official *corpus* of knowledge or turning against intellectual traditions, thereby creating new academic traditions, and/or various new branches of science. The work of Vesalius in dissecting corpses, thereby establishing at last that women have no more ribs than men, signifies the beginning of modern medicine. And there were also at all times academics who, like Galileo's opponents at Padua, refused to look through a telescope at Jupiter's moons, since they knew for certain – no matter what they might see – that Galileo had been wrong when matched against Aristotle, 'the master of all who know'.

Even in such a brief sketch of the origins of the university student as a category, one cannot leave out a small, but eternally essential ingredient of the student world: the jester—goliard–bohemian–beatnik–hippie. The goliards, the impudent satirists, the drop-outs and the student-poets were there from the outset.

In the twelfth century, to quote Huizinga again, 'the spirit boiled over. In every direction, whether it was one indicated by its classical model or by its own passion, it went further than prudence and temperance would admit. . . . Antiquity had taken on a new meaning and a new tone for the youthful, vigorous spirit of the century.'

Peter Abelard, whose meteoric rise began in the turbulence of the early twelfth century, was the true forerunner and embodiment of his age. He spoke in a bold, new way; his logic was sharp, unfamiliar, abrasive. He was a new man and lived in a shockingly new way. He stimulated and provoked the age with the brilliance of his mind and with his passionate zest for life. In a strongly libellous and hostile open letter to Abelard, Roscellinus wrote that it was the unheard-of novelty of his way of life – *vitae tuae inaudita novitas* – that brought his contemporaries into revolt against him. One ought to add: not all of his contemporaries. The conformist majority certainly hated him as the philosopher-theologian who was the leader of all those striving for enlightenment in the medieval world. He liked to surprise, shock, irritate the conformists. His opponents in Paris warned against 'Magister Peter' as one 'who was not a debater but a quibbler and who preferred the role of the jester to that of the Doctor'. (And who remembers his opponents now?)

Even before his love for Héloïse became the best-known love story of the age, he had caused countless emotional storms. His passion without sentimentality, his logic without restraints, his emphasis on the importance of doubt, his great success as the guru of the disobedients, earned him many accusations of heresy. This guru, whose teaching was just as boldly new as his way of life, was admired and loved in the camp of the students, of the vagrantes and the goliards. If in the nineteen-sixties it was possible to 'draw a vector from the student–rebel to the hippie', Peter Abelard was the embodiment of such a vector eight hundred years earlier. At times in actual fact, always in spirit, he certainly was a goliard.

The vagrantes were simply the wandering student–minstrels singing goliard poetry. This name goes back to the Saturnalias and the Dionysus cult of Antiquity. Each year on 1 January in ninth-century Constantinople there was a great festive procession in the tradition of the Saturnalia. This procession was led by a 'Patriarch of all Lunatics' riding on a donkey, accompanied by twelve 'Lunatic-Metropolitans'. At first the image of Saturn, the lunatic–giant was carried in these processions; it was later to be replaced by that of the soldier–giant of the Bible, Goliath. This name was changed into 'golias', and later 'goliard', referring in the end only to the spirit of these occasions.

Of the Saturnalias and other turbulent celebrations for the magical creation of plenty, and from the drunken Dionysus processions, there remained in Christian Europe various sorts of carnivals presided over by the 'Pope of the Lunatics'. In these and other boisterous ceremonies offering relief from the dull, plodding daily round, the students played a principal role. According to the Paduan book of rituals, on such holidays the bishop had

213

to receive the 'bishop of the students' and this student could, and did, ask the bishop in jocular manner all sorts of awkward questions about his finances, policies and even his private life. Then they ordered wine and drank together. On these fiestas various parodies were played by the students; high-ups of Church and state were satirized; poets competed with their love lyrics.

Since the medieval middle schools taught music, writing poetry and singing, most schoolboys became accustomed to writing verse. The collections of medieval schoolboy poetry which have survived show that they wrote aggressive pamphlets in verse, ironic or descriptive poems; really school essays in metric form. All students wrote verse. When the age produced new passions and new ways of life, some young men turned into poets. Between the eleventh and the fourteenth centuries goliard poetry was flourishing in most of Europe.*

2

From the thirteenth century onwards new universities were being founded by kings, princes and bishops with politico-religious aims. These institutions were less independent than either of the two original models. At first many countries had no universities at all, and were quite content to send their students to the established ones abroad. The first German university was not founded until the middle of the fourteenth century,† while the first Scandinavian ones were founded in the fifteenth.

By the end of the fifteenth century there were already seventy-nine universities in Europe. Their proliferation had some questionable consequences. The original cosmopolitanism of the first

* The *Carmina Burana* collections of Latin and French, German or English medieval student poetry are well-known. See also K. Breul, *The Cambridge Songs, a goliard song-book of the 11th century* (Cambridge, 1915). The most famous goliard poets were Hugues d'Orléans (b. 1093), the English Walter Mopp (b. 1140), the German 'Archipoets' (b. 1130). The last and greatest goliard poet was, of course, François Villon.

† The first university in the German-Roman empire was that of Prague, soon to be followed by many others. The seventeen universities established before the reformation were:

1348	Prague	1409	Leipzig	1472	Ingolstadt
1365	Vienna	1419	Rostock	1477	Tübingen
1386	Heidelberg	1454	Treves	1477	Mainz
1388	Cologne	1456	Greifswald	1502	Wittenberg
1392	Erfurt	1456	Freiburg in Breisgan	1506	Frankfurt on the
1402	Wurzburg	1460	Basle		Oder

scholars and masters was gradually eroded. When the first score of universities was founded, they modelled themselves on Bologna, Paris or Oxford and hired masters from these or other older establishments. But with their number ever growing from the fourteenth to the eighteenth centuries, the universities gradually became tied to definite localities and were transformed into parts of the 'system of estates'. Professors claimed hereditary privileges, using their positions for gaining income from foes, bribes and even money-lending.

The loss of international mobility, the many ties to a city or a country, the fact that the majority of both students and masters tended to be subjects of the king or prince on whose territory they lived, eroded the independence of the university. As a consequence of the Reformation the migratory élite ceased to be united by a common religion; they became divided into sects. The rise of nationalism decreased further their cosmopolitan character, and even their common language was to decay. The universities lost much of their excellence and influence.

In their lazy, self-indulgent clericalism, the dons of the 18th century resembled the monks of the 15th, and were about as much use. Gibbon, a gentleman commoner who was admitted to the Fellows' table at Magdalen, Oxford, in 1752, thus described their habits: 'From the toil of reading and thinking or writing they had absolved their conscience.'[9]

During these centuries many universities were no longer centres for the disinterested pursuit of learning, nor were they fully independent corporations of students and masters, but they retained much of the medieval ritual, procedure and terminology. Rectors and vice-chancellors became similar to 'those licensed tyrants, the schoolmasters'. By the sixteenth century undergraduates were treated in many places just as cruelly as schoolboys were everywhere. One of the sanctions was flogging, previously unheard-of at universities.

The many revolts, mutinies, strikes and sit-ins at the universities from the sixteenth century onwards did not perplex their contemporaries, since apprentices or grammar-school and public-school pupils in England and those of the *lycées* in France were also in the habit of staging mutinies or occupying their schools.

The intellectual level of many universities deteriorated into petrified orthodoxy or mean pedantry. A great many masters were like the 1968 dons described by Professor Robert Nisbet: 'Sixty per cent of all academics in American universities have so profound a distaste for the classroom and for the pains of genuine scholarship or creative thought that they will seize upon anything . . . to exempt themselves respectively from each.'

Partly because of the retrograde educational system throughout Europe, schoolboys and students were brought up retaining some of the worst customs of past centuries. As we have seen, schoolboys and students were constantly armed. Emperor Maximilian gave the German students *Waffenrecht*, the right to carry weapons, in 1514. In France, even five-year-old schoolboys carried their *épée*, and these were by no means only ornaments or prestige symbols. L'Estoile describes an occasion in 1588 when the king sent judiciary and police officials, together with their sergeants, to the University of Paris to confiscate the weapons of the students. The *Ratio Studiorum* of the Jesuits in France prescribed that students' arms should be deposited when entering the college. In 1680, according to the regulations of the Collège de Bourgogne, 'on ne retiendra ni armes ni épées dans les chambres particulières et ceux qui en auront les mettrons dans mains du principal qui les conservera dans un lieu destiné à cet effet'.[10] ('Weapons and swords will not be kept in private rooms and those who possess any will hand them over to the principal who will keep them in a place expressly chosen for the purpose.')

The badly taught, unwisely disciplined, poor and often hungry students reacted with alternating waves of violence and lethargy. Student protest between the sixteenth and nineteenth centuries was often more violent than that, say, in the first part of 1970. The layman's image of the student was, however, influenced only by local or, at most, by national events. The townsmen of Uppsala could very well live out their life without ever having heard about contemporary student revolt in Germany or England. We do not know whether the first school occupation and sit-in occurred in the Talmudic academies of the Middle East between the fifth and eighth centuries or earlier, but from the sixteenth century onwards student revolts and university sit-ins became quite frequent.

A great many student mutinies were more dangerous and effective because of the fighting capacity of the armed students. These mutinies and the many student strikes and sit-ins* ceased

* '*La mutinerie n'allait pas toujours jusqu' à l'émeute à main armée: elle se traduisait parfois par une grève avec occupation. La cour en 1633 'avertie que les écoliers en Logique du*

216

in France only towards the end of the seventeenth century, in England only in the middle of the nineteenth century.

In England, the student mutinies became more violent and more frequent in the second part of the eighteenth century and the beginning of the nineteenth. The contemporary English image of the youth-of-today was the frequently flogged mutineer. It was not at all exceptional for apprentices or boys from public schools to stage more violent mutinies than the undergraduates. Being an apprentice or a pupil at, say, Eton, Rugby or Winchester meant inferior social status. Only boys of the lower classes, or the underprivileged younger sons of the middle and upper classes, or again, the 'hard cases' were sent to the dreaded and depised public schools. The first-born, the privileged, the good boys were taught in the safety of their homes.

For at least two centuries, parents saw private education as the only safeguard. In the family home, a boy or girl could be taught without exposure to contamination by a mob of boys or girls. Rousseau urged that fathers should educate their sons. Since Rousseau was a great advocate of the prolongation of adolescence, his advice to fathers was not difficult to follow; he wrote in *Emile*: 'Exercise his body, his limbs, his senses, but keep his mind idle as long as you can'. At that time schoolmasters had not yet earned the reputation for being more successful than the parents in impeding the development of the young towards maturity. Though often flogged, public schoolboys of those times were in many respects left to their own devices, and as toughened members of a society of angry young outsiders they caused a great deal of trouble.

Edgeworth wrote in 1789 that 'all desperate subjects are sent, as a last resource ... to a public school, as to a general infirmary for mental disease.'[12]

A contemporary poem, Cowper's *Tirocinium* (1785), gave this warning:

> Would you your son should be a sot or dunce,
> Lascivious, headstrong, or all these at once;
> Train him in public with a mob of boys,
> . . . .

collège de cette ville de Dijon ('équivalent des philosophes des nos lycées) se sont retirés sans la permission des recteurs et régens, et empêcheng leurs compagnons par violence at voyes de fait de retrer aud. collège', leur ordonne de retrer en classe, et au vicomte maieur de prêter mainforte aus préfets pour punir les révoltés.'[11]

There shall he learn, ere sixteen winters old
That authors are most useful pawned or sold;
That pedantry is all that schools impart
But taverns teach the knowledge of the heart.

King George III of England was simply guided by the popular image when he put the following stereotyped questions to some Etonians whom he encountered while walking on the outskirts of Windsor: 'Hm, boy, have you mutinied lately, eh, eh?' or 'Well, well my boy, when were you flogged last?' According to H. Cook,[13] brutal flogging of the boys was an integral part of the system, and since flogging was reserved for every Saturday it was called the 'bloody day'.

Not surprisingly, Eton, Marlborough, Rugby, Winchester and other public schools produced periodic revolts, student boycotts, strikes and large-scale mutinies that could be suppressed only by the army. In 1768 a revolt at Eton was led by the praeposters', the best students in the sixth form (or 'rhetoricians'), who seceded from the school. In 1783 during a violent revolt against the headmaster the students broke furniture and windows. In 1818 the mutiny at Winchester was suppressed by two companies of bayoneted soldiers. The last revolt at Eton was in 1832, when eighty boys were flogged. The last significant mutiny in the nineteeth century was at Marlborough in 1851.

This is some of the background to the reform of the English public schools in the eighteen-thirties, which turned them into well-disciplined aristocratic, or at least upper-class, institutions. The reformers, such as Thomas Arnold, headmaster of Rugby, and his colleagues strove to 'humanize' the public schools by breaking them up into large families ('houses') and at the same time to improve their reputation by excluding lower-class, mainly local boys. In the second part of the nineteenth century Eton, Rugby and the others established their high status by means of the conspicuous exclusion of all social inferiors.

The reforms carried out by Arnold and others were not aimed at raising the intellectual level of these schools or at decreasing their mindless sadism. Three decades after the Arnoldian reforms, Herbert Spencer wrote:

The discipline which boys meet with at Eton, Winchester and Harrow, etc., is much worse than that of adult life—much more unjust, cruel, brutal. Instead of being an aid to human progress, which all culture should be, the culture of our public schools, by accustoming boys to a despotic form of government, and an intercourse regulated by brute force, *tends to fit them for a lower state of society than that which exists.* And chiefly recruited as our legislature is from those who are brought up at these schools, *this barbarising influence* becomes a serious hindrance to national progress.[14]

3

Even the briefest sketch of the origins of universities would be incomplete without a mention of the authorities intended to manage the corporations of scholars and masters. The first administrators were the underlings of bishops, or officials of royal or ducal chancellories. The idea that masters and scholars could not manage their own affairs did not go down well at first. The creators of the first universities had their own conception of the role and function of students and professors. Even in the Paris type, which was a corporation of masters, the original students were not treated as schoolboys to be disciplined, but as independent individuals willing to pay for instruction. The Paris professors competed on the open market with each other, offering their services to students. It was only natural that the student, in his capacity as a potential buyer of the spiritual goods offered by the master, should have a say in what these spiritual goods should be.

But 'authority' strove for control and discipline. In Paris, in many German universities and elsewhere, the most conspicuous disciplinarians were the college janitors, the servants of the masters. They informed on the students, and one of them usually sat next to the magister on the pulpit during lectures. They carried a long cane for hitting not only the disorderly but also those who failed to give satisfactory answers. This was the practice in Paris for quite some time. These janitors were only one category of Frederic Barbarossa's 'most inferior persons', who manhandled students.

There were two university ideals or conceptions throughout the sixteenth century, as indeed for several centuries afterwards: the ideal university of the authorities and disciplinarians which produced obedient conformists, and that of the non-conformist students which produced generally cultivated, independent-minded creative men. Whatever the sixteenth century accomplished, it was attained against the violent opposition of the

219

authorities, and contrary to the conventional wisdom of the day. In fact the university dropouts (or rather 'ascends-up') and other dissidents and rebels accomplished far more in that century than did those dons and students who had the approval of their community.

The universities in Europe and in the Americas deteriorated after the Renaissance and the Reformation because of the pressure for conformity exerted by the authorities. From Paris to Uppsala, from Bologna to Mexico, from Oxford to Prague, there were sustained attacks against university instruction for ignoring new developments in science and scholarship. The university reforms that took place in the eighteenth and nineteenth century were carried out almost everywhere with great delays, most reluctantly, only under threat and acute danger. Academics desperately resisted efforts to widen the officially accepted corpus of knowledge. In some cases they maintained that all the change needed had been carried out by the last reform, two hundred years previously. In April 1850 Lord John Russell appointed a commission to inquire into and report on the state of the universities. At Oxford the Hebdomedal Board was extremely angry and declared that 'the Laudian reform of 1636 had done all that was needful'.

In the nineteenth century, thanks to the scientific revolution and to enormous outside pressures as well, many universities were reformed by incorporating science into their curricula. These leading universities began to regain some of the prestige that they had lost since the Renaissance.

The 'dark ages' at the universities followed the Middle Ages. During their dark ages the universities deteriorated on separate national lines. In France this utter decay lasted until 1896. The Revolution of 1789 abolished all of France's twenty-two universities, which sank to middle-school level. Prior to this, many professors had given up teaching altogether and were virtually selling degrees. These shadow universities were outside the eighteenth century world of science. Newton's *Principia* was lectured on in Paris sixty years after its publication. Napoleon replaced the provincial universities by a central bureaucracy. In the mid-nineteenth century, sixteen major French towns had various faculties, but very few housed all of them. Conservative governments distrusted even very meek school teachers. The Minister of Education from 1851 to 1856 warned the teachers against the dangers of knowledge. The teaching of the history of philosophy was banned from the Sorbonne curriculum as particularly dangerous. (For many years philosophy was blamed for student unrest, before this role was taken over by sociology.)

Victor Duruy reported to Napoleon III: 'All Paris has been rebuilt, the buildings for higher education have alone remained in a state of decay which contrasts painfully with the imposing grandeur of the edifices created for the other departments.'[15]

The provincial universities were officially re-established early in 1896, but French higher education had to wait many decades before the reforms that took place in nineteenth-century Germany and twentieth-century England were introduced in the land of Voltaire and Descartes. All that was new and vital in the sciences had a limited existence, not in the universities but in the *Grandes Écoles*, specialist institutes for producing specialists.

France did, however, play a role in clearing the way for the most important university reform of the nineteenth century; in fact, for a partial re-invention of the original university in the spirit of the age. This role was accomplished by Napoleon when he defeated Prussia. Rebellious intellectuals and radical reformers were free to act, even if in certain instances only for a few months.

After the battle of Jena in 1806, Hegel was quite successful in convincing his countrymen that 'education and intelligence had defeated crude efficiency'. Prussia was to profit from the lesson of history and concentrate on the flourishing of education and intelligence. Fichte in his famous *Addresses to the German Nation,* which after defeat needed not only explanation but also inspiration, spoke about 'education to the understanding of moral destiny'. He urged that 'the State, with all its compulsory measures, must regard itself as an educational institution for making compulsion unnecessary'.

Owing to the exceptional circumstances after the great defeat, Wilhelm von Humboldt, a bold spirit and a great philosopher of language, became Director of Ecclesiastical Affairs and Public Instruction in Prussia. In the short period from 1809-10 he managed to get royal consent to an educational restructuring, for which radical intellectuals had been striving for many decades. He established a new type of university that was a modernized version of the Bologna and Paris originals. Outside authorities, as in the originals, were again excluded. Being convinced that 'the state becomes a hindrance as soon as it tries to interfere', Humboldt prescribed that the state should secure and protect the spiritual and scientific freedom of the university to pursue science as such.

The King of Prussia signed the founding document of the new University of Berlin in 1809. There, and elsewhere in Germany, the conception of the university was enlarged by the incorporation of research and all other active pursuits of science in the broadest meaning of the word. The professors were to be scientific investigators, researchers and creative men in the arts. The student, according to the Humboldtian school, was to profit from his situation of 'loneliness and liberty'. Instead of becoming a narrow specialist, he was supposed to develop into a 'full human being in the service of science'. He was supposed to mature enough for 'study under his own guidance'. The university was again to be a free community of research, of teaching and of learning.

Humboldt and other radical intellectuals of those times were convinced that the universities could not be developed to the full potential offered by the age without a general educational reform. In Königsberg, Herbart established in 1810 a pedagogical seminary for improving the education of the *Gymnasium* teachers. Others were sent to Pestalozzi to be trained as 'educators of the educators'. The *Gymnasien,* middle schools of high standard, aimed at producing a good *allgemeine Bildung* or general culture. They taught languages and mathematics, and gave their students a good idea of the contemporary corpus of knowledge.

The German *Gymnasien,* the *Realschule* for the training of the commercial and technological middle classes, and the Humboldtian university became the models for the German-speaking countries and also for all parts of the Austro-Hungarian empire. The German rebels and radicals whom Napoleon liberated for a brief interlude from the stifling pressure of bureaucrats created the middle schools and universities that were to make a great contribution to the scientific revolution in the nineteenth and twentieth centuries.

In England (if not so much in Scotland) the faculties of theology, law and medicine decayed to almost the same extent as their counterparts in France. In Oxford and Cambridge the colleges limited themselves to something like the *studium generale* that in the Middle Ages had preceded professional studies, and that was almost surpassed by the two highest grades of the German *Gymnasien*. The faculties of arts were supposed to give some classical education coupled with some 'character training'. Even towards the end of the nineteenth century, the Oxford and Cambridge colleges were, according to Matthew Arnold: 'places where the youth of the upper class prolong to a very great age, and under some very admirable influences, their school education. . . . They are in fact still schools.' Oxford and Cambridge carried on in their traditional torpor, while the Victoria University of Manchester and the colleges of London University were already catching up with or overtaking the attainments of the reformed higher educational system in Germany.

The legal obligation of parents in Prussia to educate their children, with compulsory school attendance until fourteen, was regarded in Britain as one aspect of the 'despotic system of militarism'. Compulsory schooling existed in most German states, in some of them since the seventeenth century, in Prussia since 1769. Sarah Austin reprimanded her countrymen in 1834 for opposing the education of the people: '. . . we fear, that education will set them above their station, disgust them with labour, make them ambitious, envious, dissatisfied! We must reap as we sow.'[16]

Historians do not quite agree whether Britain was in the midst of a great or small Depression after 1870. However, it is beyond doubt that the rate of economic growth slowed down and that Britain's achievements in those industries where she had been dominant in the past were below those of Germany and America. This was partly caused by the fact that the prosperous owners of the previously successful older industries sent their sons to the public schools, where they were turned into upper-class gentlemen with prejudices against 'trade' and against change and innovation.*

The public schools and the sacred obsolescence of Victorian Oxford and Cambridge were responsible for the fact that Britain began losing her position as the leading industrializing nation after 1870.

The public schools facilitated the transmission of the culture of the landed gentry classes to the industrial classes, a culture which virtually ignored the economic life of the country; and by speeding up the transmission to a rate that would hitherto have been impos-

---

* According to the Public Schools Commission: 'Natural science . . . is practically excluded from the education of the higher classes in England. Education with us is, in this respect, narrower than it was three centuries ago, whilst science has prodigiously extended her empire . . . . This exclusion is, in our view, *a plain defect and a great practical evil*.'[17]

sible, *they produced a haemorrhage of talent, and perhaps of capital,* in the older industries which could not be made good.[18]

By the middle of the twentieth century, by means of a series of reforms that were, as usual, decades overdue, and compromises between various mutually contradictory solutions, Britain found a way of adopting the universities to the gigantic explosion of knowledge. The result in the nineteen-sixties was, in the words of Sir Eric Ashby:

We have virtually eliminated general education from our [university] system. . . . Britain did not respond to the growth of knowledge by lengthening courses of study . . . or by the creation of graduate schools; she kept the length of practically all first-degree courses down to three years and obliged every student to specialise. At the time of the Robbins Committee about seven out of ten university students in Britain were taking honours degree courses in one subject only.[19]

Harvard, Yale, Princeton, Dartmouth and all other colonial colleges set up in America before the Declaration of Independence were fashioned after seventeenth- or eighteenth-century Oxford or Cambridge, which were already in decay. The only difference was that the Puritan Fathers wanted the colleges to produce ministers and professional men for the intolerantly orthodox communities. Instead of a disinterested pursuit of learning, these colleges had to be orthodox instruments of the community and its faith.

The American colleges and universities were either clerical foundations to serve the Presbyterian, Reformed, Methodist or Catholic communites, or they were founded by the state. In both cases authority was exercised by outside laymen. Harvard's character, for instance, provided for a corporation of the president and the fellows, with a board of overseers. Soon, however, the lay overseers took over from the academics. The early American contribution to the changing of the concept of a university was that sovereignty resided not within but outside the university. The overseers, regents, or trustees were laymen who governed the university, employed the professors and the rest of the teaching staff, and appointed the administrators, who were their representatives in the day-to-day running of the college or university.

The other American contribution to the evolution of the university was the idea that it should be a vast, knowledge supermarket offering courses in an extremely varied range of subjects from how to drive cars, clown or dance, to how to embalm and bury the dead. In any subject for which the community needed 'know-how', the university had to offer courses. And since there must be people to teach the teachers of embalming or car-driving, there must be, and there are, doctors of philosophy in car-driving or embalming, who get their degrees from universities. (Ph.D. in Driver Education at Berkeley; degrees in embalming at Michigan, Minnesota and elsewhere; in Circus Arts and Clowning at Florida State University; for Drum Majorettes at the University of Oklahoma.)

The US knowledge supermarkets called 'multiversities' offer between 1,500 and 2,500 different courses in all possible and impossible subjects. Professor Clark Kerr wrote:

The University started as a single community—a community of masters and students. It may even be said to have had a soul in the sense of a central animating principle. Today, the large American university is, rather, a whole series of communities and activities held together by a common name, common governing board, and related purposes.[20]

It should be stressed that these series of communities of specialists mutually ignore one another. As an object of neglect, the undergraduate is second to none at the multiversities. Clark Kerr pointed out that 'there has always been an inherent conflict between undergraduate instruction and the other functions of the university'. In the multiversities this conflict has become even stronger.

The historian Henry Steel Commager said that 'the American University is the greatest success in the history of the world'. Future historians might call the American University of 1970 the greatest failure of its world.

The universities of the world (together with the military–industrial complex) were, in fact, sources of and participants in the explosion of science and technology in our age. But they are the greatest failures at the point of history when what mankind needs most is some degree of wisdom to save itself from itself and its successes. And wisdom is what our universities do not offer in any shape or form.

X

FROM THE BERKELEY EXPLOSION TO THE OHNESORG MURDER

'We have asked to be heard, you have refused. We have asked for justice. You have
called it anarchy. We have asked for freedom. You have called it licence. Rather
than face the fear and hopelessness you
have created, you have called us com-
munistic. You have accused us of failing to
use the legitimate channels. But you have
closed those channels to us. You, and not
us, have built a university based on distrust
and dishonesty.'

A University of California student in a
testimony to the Board of Regents

'The tighter you put the lid on, the bigger
the explosion is likely to be.'

John Gustad, Provost of New College,
Florida

1

The Berkeley explosion of 1964 is regarded by many Americans
on both sides of the barricades of hatred and ignorance as the
starting point of a new period of student revolt. At that time some
Berkeley students in their charming youth-centrism thought that
theirs was the first student revolt in history. A great many adults
managed to adopt a similar attitude. For them the Berkeley
Explosion in 1964 served and still serves as what I call the 'original
sin of the period'. It was seen as the first cause in a chain of
violence and lawlessness that brought about the lawlessness and
violence of the subsequent campaigns of punishment and
revenge.

Who put the lid on Berkeley? Everybody and nobody. Two

hundred years of American history. The slave ships that brought in the Negroes. The founders of the University of California, who never resolved the conflict between the students' constitutional rights as American citizens and their very limited freedom as California students. The explosion was prepared by the US Educational Policy Commission that defined the goal of American schools in 1951 as 'the pursuit of happiness' and in 1961 as 'the ability to think'. The explosion was prepared by the white people of Mississippi, Alabama, Arkansas and other Southern states who refused to stop the violence and lawlessness with which they had treated the Negroes for centuries.

In the deep South, a great many governors, mayors, judges, police chiefs, sheriffs and policemen were active participants in the horror regime crushing the Negroes. When Congress, the Supreme Court and the Federal Government decided at long last that Negroes, too, should have civil rights, the South answered by waves of lawlessness and violence against the advocates of these rights. In the nineteen-fifties, lynching Negroes and 'nigger-lovers' was no longer as safe a pastime as it used to be. Some murderers were exposed to all sorts of vexations. Though the lynchers were safe from the local police, at times the FBI would intervene and disturb the murderers by their pointless investigations. This was the case in Poplarville, Mississippi, where, on 25 April 1959, a mob of whites lynched a twenty-three-year-old Negro called M. C. Parker. Everyone in town knew the names of the eleven men who committed the act, the FBI cleared up the case, yet the Poplarville judge and grand jury dropped it. The judge said that the recent Supreme Court decision had been responsible for the lynching. One Mississippi official said: 'You couldn't convict the guilty parties if you had a sound film of the lynching.'[1] The Attorney General of the United States, William P. Rogers, termed the handling of the case 'a travesty of justice ... flagrant and calculated'.

Despite slight vexations, flagrant and calculated travesties of justice were committed in most of the Southern States in the 'sixties, too. The situation was still the same: 'you couldn't convict the guilty parties', though their deeds were frequently televised in great detail.

America and the world saw the beefy Southern 'law-enforcement officers' committing nauseating atrocities against non-violent civil rights workers. The extreme cowardice of these thugs can be examined in the film and TV archives of hundreds of companies all over the world. The typical, oft-repeated scenes involved two or three uniformed, fully armed men maltreating one person, in some cases a slender girl; two policemen holding a victim so that a third was able to kick him or her in the face or stomach, and so on.

Civil rights workers who waged a non-violent campaign for the enforcement of federal laws were persecuted with callous cruelty. The white and black civil rights workers of both sexes were beaten up and arrested on trumped-up charges. Their lawyers, the journalists covering their cases were beaten up by the police and/or by Southern whites, while the police looked on. Some of the civil rights workers were murdered in cold blood. In one case it became crystal clear that the Deputy Sheriff of Nashoba County, Mississippi, was one of the murderers of three young civil rights workers. Yet in 1964 there seemed to be no hope of the murderers being brought to justice.

White and black students kept going to the South to risk their lives in the very uneven struggle against the people and authorities of these states, to guard Negroes against lawlessness and violence. What these young men and women saw and experienced there determined the fate of an entire, politically engaged student generation. Karl E. Meyer, the American journalist, wrote that 'Mississippi is the emotional equivalent of the Spanish Civil War' for most of this generation. The Mississippi (and other Southern) experiences, however, proved to be far more explosive. The idealistic uncorrupted young saw how perfectly innocent people were unable to save themselves from corrupt and evil authorities.

One of the Northern civil rights workers was a Berkeley student called Mario Savio. The son of Italian immigrants, he was born in New York City in 1942. A gifted, hard-working boy, he graduated from his New York high school at the top of a class of 1,200. As a result of his high-school physics project he was granted a scholarship to Manhattan College. The next year he transferred to Queens College, also in New York, and instead of physics he majored in philosophy. His college achievements were well above the average. When his parents moved to California he entered the University at Berkeley. In the 1963 and 1964 summer vacations Savio worked as a member of the Student Non-Violent Coordinating Committee in the South. At the school for young civil rights volunteers he was trained in how to protect his face and various organs while being beaten up, since the volunteers pledged not to meet violence with violence. Savio worked in the notorious Holmes County, Mississippi. This took courage. It took even more courage when, later, he travelled south, to McComb. At that time McComb was considered to be one of the most dangerous spots in the United States for white civil rights workers. There was a Freedom School there, and Savio taught Negroes poetry, history, maths and genetics – 'a good subject to show how black and white people are the same'.

This young man and several hundred other white students of both sexes who spent their summer holidays braving the terror regime of the Mississippi police state began their journey back to their campuses in the autumn. Back at Berkeley in September 1964 Mario Savio found a change. What this change was and the role it played in sparking off the explosion should be described in the words of an official report commissioned by the omnipotent Regents (or governors) of the university. This report explained at length how the freedom of students to engage in political activity was curtailed at Berkeley, then went on:

The 'safety valve' was a small strip of sidewalk at the main entrance to the Berkeley campus where Telegraph Avenue met Bankcroft Way. It was the most heavily travelled place in the campus. It had been treated as 'off campus' by university authorities and it was freely available to anyone for political activity. There the civil rights activists side by side with other political advocates – conservative, liberal and radical – solicited money, volunteers and converts.

Legally, the strip of land is university property. Traditionally, it had been used by the students active in political and social movements to get up card tables for political advocacy, recruitment and fund raising. The university administration had winked at the enforcement of its own rules about the uses of its property and had permitted students to use the area as though it were off campus. The students assumed that it belonged to the city of Berkeley and took out permits for its use from the city.

A report by Jerome C. Byrne, a lawyer specializing in labour law who was brought in as an outside investigator by a committee set up by the Regents to look into the 'basic factors' behind the 1964 unrest, stated in 1965: 'A decision by the university administration – taken without consultation with the students – to enforce rules and regulations technically applicable on the 23x39 foot strip of land at the entrance to the Berkeley campus was *to unleash a crisis unprecedented in the history of the university.'** The main reason for this momentous decision was described by C. B. Cox, who was at that time visiting professor at Berkeley from the University of Hull:

The dispute goes back to the Republican National Convention in the Cow Palace, San Francisco, in June, during which Berkeley students took part in a demonstration in favour of Scranton. As a result, supporters of Goldwater put pressure on the university administration to enforce existing laws that prohibited political recruiting and fund raising on campus.[2]

Prior to the 1964 decision of the administration, the overwhelming majority of students and residents, including Berkeley city-officials, believed that the land belonged to the city. The returning civil rights workers were still affected by the impact of the murder of President Kennedy and of his alleged assassin; of the fate of Negro children who died in a dynamited Baptist church; and of the more recent murders of three members of the Student Non-Violent Coordinating Committee. They were convinced that it was more important and more urgent than ever to continue working on the campus for the cause of civil rights. They argued that only by this kind of work, everywhere, could America avoid murderous race riots. Instead they were told that from now on they could not set up a SNCC table. Like many other campus organizations the SNCC, too, defied the ban on political activities on that strip of land. When the police arrested a civil rights worker for this offence, three thousand students surrounded the police car and staged a spontaneous thirty-two-hour demonstration.

After the Free Speech movement was born in October, President Clark Kerr was quoted in newspapers as saying that 'forty-nine per cent of the hard-core [demonstrators] are followers of the Castro-Mao line'. Kerr claimed some months later that it was a misquote, but never retracted it in public. This accusation was a welcome pretext for the regents and administrators not to listen to these Castro-Mao liners. A professor of medicine called Mario Savio 'an imported New York trouble-maker', although there were also several thousand other students at Berkeley who were not born in California.

The students answered in passionate or low-keyed speeches, in

* Italics added.

230

resolutions, articles, memoranda. They answered with cartoons and jokes, and with impromptu songs, hymns, Christmas carols sung to Beatles tunes and Beethoven.

> Oski dolls, Pompom girls, UC all the way.
> Oh, what fun it is to have your mind reduced to clay.
> Civil rights, politics, just get in the way,
> Questioning authority when you should obey.

When the students in the Free Speech Movement were accused, or allegedly accused, by Kerr of being Castroite-Maoists, they sang an early carol:

> Joy to UC, the word is come :
> Clark Kerr has called us Red !
> If you are 49 per cent
> You can't work for the government :
> The knowledge-factory
> Turns out more GNP
> Without your subversion
> On its property.

'And sang it joyously. For what other sane response was possible, to a bankruptcy of heart whose dimensions were inexpressible in analytic prose? Certainly, we were seriousness personified; we have jail sentences to show for this. But faced with the absurd, in every sense, there is a dimension of response without which seriousness is meaningless.'[3]

During the weeks that followed the administration vacillated between concessions and crackdowns. The Free Speech Movement continued to demand 'freedom for students', which simply meant that students, too, should be subject to the rights and curbs of ordinary civil law. By the end of November 1964 the moderate majority on the academic Senate found a tentative compromise between the extreme anti-student-rights view of the administration, and the militant students. Then, according to the *Guardian*:

At this moment the administration announced that it was taking disciplinary action against the student leaders and liberal organisations for minor offences during the earlier demonstrations.

This sudden decision shocked the campus. Either the administrators were incredibly stupid, or they were deliberately trying to bring about a new conflict with the students. The situation moved inevitably towards tragedy.[4]

Over six thousand students showed by their actions that they believed that the administration wanted to provoke a large-scale conflict between masses of students and masses of police. This was also believed by many members of the academic staff, including members of the Academic Senate.

On 2 November 1964 the Free Speech Movement organized a protest meeting and planned a protest sit-in. Over six thousand students of both sexes assembled in front of the administration building, Sproul Hall. Some of the students brought with them sleeping bags, blankets, satchels full of books and food, thermos flasks.

Mario Savio, the philosophy student who, as we have seen, was described as 'an imported trouble-maker' because his parents had moved two years previously from New York to California, made a speech from the steps of the building. This speech and the mood of the entire meeting indicated that the six thousand students present were utterly convinced that the administration had gone out of its way to bring about a violent confrontation. The student girls and boys, on their side, did everything possible to stress that theirs was a non-violent protest. There were three sentences in Savio's speech that expressed the mood of an entire student-generation:

There is a time when the operations of the machine become so odious, make you so sick at heart, that you can't take part, you can't even tacitly take part. And you've got to put your bodies upon the gears and upon the wheels, upon the levers, upon all the apparatus, and you've got to make it stop. And you've got to indicate to the people who run it, to the people who own it, that unless you are free the machine will be prevented from working at all.

Next to Mario Savio stood the folk-singer Joan Baez. Barefoot, her long dark hair loose around her face, she asked the students to enter the hall not in anger but with love in their hearts. Then she began playing her guitar and singing 'We Shall Overcome'. The song finished, the students, with flags in hand, the Stars and Stripes waving above their heads, ascended the steps and began the occupation of the administration building. By the time the campus police had managed to lock and bar the entrance over a thousand students had succeeded in getting in. They immediately established for one night the Free University of California. Teaching assistants and older students lectured and led seminars.

Joan Baez and others sang. Groups of students wrote and pasted up wall newspapers. Some films were shown. In various parts of the building there were discussion groups. Although the Berkeley activists of those early days had a strong sense of humour, the 2-3 December sit-in was an earnest affair. Most of the seminars were on a high intellectual level.

The administration was astonished by the size of the protest meeting. Had the campus police not blocked the entrance later there would have been over three thousand students in the building the fact that since the police-car incident the number of activists had doubled from three to six thousand, was, indeed, significant. Over twenty per cent of Berkeley's 27,500 students were active supporters of the protest.

The Chancellor and the Regents requested the Governor of California to send in the state police. This was then an unprecedented act of giving up the extra-territorial status of the campus. Meanwhile students went to sleep in the offices and corridors. They were awakened at 3.15 in the morning by Chancellor Strong and the state police, who gave them an ultimatum to clear the building. About two hundred students were persuaded to leave. The others, over 800, declared themselves ready to go to jail. Fifteen minutes later the state police, ready to deal with these 'violent trouble-makers', invaded the building.

The students of both sexes offered non-violent resistance to the police violence. They went limp, lying on floors. The police dragged them by arms and feet and the long-haired girls by their hair out of the building, down the steps to the waiting police cars. Since it took two policemen to manhandle one limp student, boy or girl, the evacuation took a long time. Soon, several instalments of police reinforcements arrived to help in the evacuation.

By six o'clock in the morning there was already a crowd of students watching the police dragging away the demonstrators, listening to the thud-thud as the limp bodies were dragged down the steps. From an upstairs window, through a loudspeaker, students informed their colleagues of the events of the night and of police behaviour inside the building. The police tried to take the loudspeaker away, but student resistance was too strong, so they gave up. Some students rushed away and returned with cameras and film cameras. Others went to the back of the building and managed to climb in, so the police found that the more students they dragged out, the more there were inside. The prisons in Berkeley, Oakland and elsewhere in the San Francisco area were full of students, and there were still more to come. It was only by four o'clock in the afternoon of 3 December that the mass-arrest of students was completed.

The student organizations called a general strike. The teaching assistants, too, went on strike. The professors and other academic staff, to show their solidarity with the students, collected in a few hours nearly ten thousand dollars to bail out their students. In front of the prisons, where the demonstrators were held, there were queues of cars several miles long. Students, professors, parents of the imprisoned students were waiting to take them home.

After this episode the administration was again willing to permit political activity and fund-raising on the 'free strip' of the campus. The university authorities held out only for the right to add their own punishment to any that the courts might take against students for off-campus political demonstrations. According to this the students, graduate students included, were expected to have fewer rights than any American citizen of their age-group outside the universities, but at the same time, to be doubly punished for non-violent civil disobedience.

The Free Speech Movement naturally campaigned against this 'double jeopardy'. At this stage of the dispute, President Kerr assembled the members of the Berkeley campus in its huge open-air Greek Theatre to announce that the administration would stand firm, that the students must acquiesce when faced with the prospect of double punishment.

Suddenly Mario Savio's six-foot-two figure appeared from no-where and tried to take the microphone away from President Kerr. In front of over 13,000 spectators Savio was dealt with by the campus police. One policeman grabbed him round the throat while another twisted his arm in a hammer-lock. Then, when he was already lying on the ground, six policemen dragged him away by his hands, to arrest him. Minutes later he was freed. The students now yelled 'We want Mario! We want Mario!' So he was permitted to make the announcement he had originally in-tended to make. It was a brief and low-keyed announcement of a Free Speech Movement rally.

Next day the academic Senate, composed entirely of deans and professors sided with the students on the double jeopardy issue. By 824 votes to 114 they proposed that 'off-campus student politi-cal activity shall not be subject to university regulation'.

Later, a Berkeley municipal court judge, Rupert Crittenden, sentenced 754 of the arrested students to up to ninety days in jail. Nearly half of them informed Crittenden that they would not accept a probationary condition to refrain from any more illegal demonstrations for up to two years. The judge responded with tougher sentences, generally offering the option of paying higher fines or going to jail for longer terms. Among those who refused probation was Mario Savio, who told the court that he could not observe the ban because 'with American politics presently in the hands of the morally and intellectually bankrupt, rebellion is a positive duty'. Crittenden promptly gave Savio 120 days in jail.

Meanwhile, *Life* magazine published a photo of the people who had murdered three young civil rights workers in Nashoba County. They were shown eating, laughing and joking happily in the knowledge that they would not be punished.

2

The Berkeley Explosion in 1964 was sparked off by two decisions by the Regents, the first withdrawing traditional students' rights on the 'Hyde Park Corner' of the campus, the second calling on the police in November when a peaceful compromise solution was about to be reached. The twenty-four Regents of the University are vested according to the constitution with 'complete powers of organization and government'. In other words, they have virtually absolute power over the affairs of the university.[5] They are laymen. Their information concerning the affairs of the university comes from the administrators employed by them and from the newspapers they read. They are not in the habit of consulting the academic Senate consisting of all the deans and professors. The report of the Berkeley Academic Senate and other official reports made a special point of the fact that they had not been consulted before the two explosive decisions mentioned above:

It is intolerable that the Berkeley Senate has no formal channel for communication with the Regents regarding the acute problems that have arisen on this campus in the last few years.[6]

The crisis on the Berkeley campus at the end of the fall quarter brought the Regents into special session on December 6th. We find it appalling that no faculty committee was consulted. One source is not difficult to find. Many of the Regents still think of the faculty

235

essentially as employees, rather than as participants in the government of the university.*

As we have seen, the Regents are laymen influenced by what they have read in the papers. Their actions, prompted by prejudice, contribute to the escalation of bias. The first, entirely false, newspaper reports about the 'Berkeley explosion' provoked deliberately by 'imported trouble-makers', by 'non-students, like Mario Savio', became remembered facts in the minds of people everywhere in the world. These so-called facts contributed to the anti-student bias everywhere. They were still actively influencing events everywhere five years later.†

The Regents are successful and prosperous men, who see their task as acting as representatives of the conformist majority of citizens. In many cases it became obvious that the Regents were directly influenced in their decisions by what they had read in their local papers. Besides the assertions about Mario Savio and 'his like', the newspapers often reported that students who demonstrate are 'ignoramuses', neglecting their studies and 'wasting the tax-payers' money'. This, incidentally, is a consistent theme not only in America but everywhere else, too. Despite overwhelming evidence to the contrary, even people of the standing of George F. Bundy and George Kennan insist on talking about empty-headed student demonstrators who neglect their studies.

For obvious reasons the Free Speech Movement activists came under painstaking academic scrutiny. The list of activists was at hand. During the police-car incident described above 3,000 students demonstrated for thirty-two hours. The administration and the Berkeley police (not to mention other agencies) had a nearly complete list. There was also a list of the 765 students sentenced for their part in the sit-in of 3-4 December 1964.

Had these activists neglected their studies, had their results in the examinations been lower than the average, the Regents and their administrators would have been eager to publish this. They

* The Chairman of the University Senate Policy Committee in a report to the Berkeley Division. See also Senate Policy Committee: *State of the Campus Message*, minutes of 1965: 'Only with difficulty was the division's Emergency Executive Committee able to arrange a meeting during the free speech crisis, and then only with a Regental Committee and not the full Board.'

† Dealing with campus violence in 1969, Alistair Cooke wrote: 'It has been five years since a handful of students and imported non-student leaders raised havoc across the Bay, at Berkeley, with the first test of what are called" confrontation politics".'[7]

did not, because the facts, contrary to the opinion of Messrs Bundy, Kennan and Co. do not bear this out. The five main published studies about the 1964 Berkeley activists agree that the activists achieved significantly higher scores in their academic aptitudes and peformance than the non-activists.

Professor Joseph Katz, of the Institute for the Study of Human Problems at Stanford University, reported his results in *New Dimensions in Higher Education,* published by the US Office of Education in 1967. His findings, which are consistent with those of all other investigators, were:

(1) The activists' parents had higher incomes and occupational status and a better education than the parents of non-activists. They tended to be politically more liberal and had more affectionate relationships with their children than parents of non-activists.

(2) Activists achieved significantly higher scores than non-activists in verbal aptitude, in grade-point averages and on scales measuring theoretical orientation, liking for reflective thought, diversity of interests and aesthetic appreciation.

(3) Activist students, measured by a variety of test instruments, consistently achieved significantly higher scores in their degree of psychological autonomy, social maturity and lack of authoritarianism. This means that activists tended to be more flexible, tolerant and realistic.*[8]

The five studies of the Berkeley activists, and other studies of student activists in Chicago and at Pennsylvania State University, all conducted at roughly the same time, had, as has already been mentioned, similar results. The academic achievements of students cannot very well be held as controversial. But many other findings are controversial. Therefore it is significant that studies conducted by investigators from different social science disciplines, with different instruments and different research methods, broadly agree with Robert Sommers' remark that the student activists are 'a minority vital to the excellence of this university'.[10]

Writing about the American student activists of the period 1964-6, Professor Katz sums them up as:

. . . people who have a rich and complex inner life, a more pro-

* The only investigators who did not agress that FSM activists achieved significantly higher scores in grade-point average based their dissenting view on their sample of activists.[9]

nounced sensitivity, responsiveness to and a greater need of other people, and stronger humanitarian and idealistic tendencies than is average. . . .[They] are likely to smart under institutional conditions that restrict their opportunity for personal experience, sensitivity, and intense communication with other people.

These students are not nature's psychological noblemen. No human group is . . . . But in the light of often unfavourable descriptions of the activists in the press and in some educational circles, it is of major interest that they turn out to be people of some psychological attractiveness in the strength and richness of their intellectual, aesthetic, and emotional endowment.

Professor Katz and the other investigators emphasized that student activists should not be confused with the fully alienated students and non-students popularly known as hippies – a confusion often made by people who denounce 'weird, unwashed, pot-smoking, lazy student rebels'. Dr Keniston of Yale University found that: 'The higher the student's grade average, the more outstanding his academic achievements, the more likely it is that he will become involved in any given political demonstration.' Furthermore: 'Activists do not drop out of college as frequently as non-activists; they go on to graduate school in greater numbers.*

Several studies in various parts of the world showed that even when demonstrations and other disturbances occurred during the weeks or months preceding examinations, activists produced better exam results than non-activists. R. Cox and Dr E. Rudd examined the students who took a prominent part at Essex University's protests in the summer of 1968. Their report was submitted to the House of Commons Select Committee on Education. It turned out that the activists who took their finals had better results than the average students at the university. Although the disturbances occurred only about a month before the examinations, none of the militants gained anything less than a second-class honours degree.

Studies conducted in the recent past in North America, Western Europe and Japan, and documentary evidence from two East European countries, Hungary and Czechoslovakia, show that the top five to fifteen per cent of the students made up over ninety per cent of the activists.

* The over seven thousand Hungarian university students who escaped to the West after the 1956 revolution and who continued their studies abroad had less than half the drop-out rate than US students in the 1957-60 period.

The West-Berlin Senate Director, Harald Ingesand, who conducted an official investigation into student disturbances, stated in his June 1967 report to the Senate: 'It is not a question of the doings of a few lunatics; it is not a question of the usual youth radicalism. It is the best and most diligent students who are also the most active. It is a general and basic mood among young people that is being expressed now. . . .'

Dr Keniston pointed out, also, that 'student dissenters of all types arouse deep and ambivalent feelings in non-dissenting students and adults – envy, resentment, admiration, repulsion, nostalgia and guilt.'

3

'Speech may indeed best serve its high purposes when it induces a condition of unrest,
creates dissatisfaction with conditions as they
are, or even stirs people to anger.'

The Supreme Court of the United States
(Terminiello *v.* Chicago, 1949)

In 1949, there was no general outcry of protest when the Surpreme Court, in its doctrines on picketing and demonstrations, recognized that communication of ideas in non-violent but milit-ant demonstrative forms may be regarded as necessary in a free society. The Supreme Court, therefore, gave protection to speech that stirs people to anger. In the mid-nineteen-sixties, the majority of adult Americans did not want this kind of free speech. Biased against dissent in any shape or form, the American public com-plained more and more frequently of a handful of outside trouble-makers and of an untypical minority of students disturbing law and order at the universities. In 1963 nearly forty per cent of the eighteen-nineteen age-group was enrolled in college or univer-sity in the US. The proportion grew each year. In California it was already near seventy per cent in the mid-nineteen-sixties. In the overcrowded multiversities the undergraduates had a great many local and general reasons for protest. They did protest with growing frequency. Many of the protests were misreported. Many of the protests contributed to the growing anti-student bias.

Nineteen hundred and sixty-five was a year of violence in America. President Johnson sent planes to bomb North Vietnam and troops to invade the Dominican Republic. Throughout

America and the world there were teach-ins on Vietnam at colleges and universities. To some teach-ins, the US State Department sent representatives to defend Johnson's policy. The Students for Democratic Society movement sponsored a march of twenty-five thousand men on Washington, to protest against the war in Vietnam. Three Americans, Norman Morrison, Roger Laporte and Alice Herz, immolated themselves to force Americans 'to wake up and start to act to stop the war in Vietnam'.

Nineteen hundred and sixty-five was the year when Martin Luther King led thousands of Negroes and whites on a march from Selma to Montgomery, Alabama; the year of the Watts riots, of the Chicago demonstrations against segregation. In Berkeley, some students attempted to stop a troop train with their bodies, to dramatize their opposition to the Vietnam War.

Between 1 January 1964 and 1 January 1967 there were student disturbances in over 2,000 universities and other institutes of higher learning in more than thirty countries, not counting, of course, the anti-Vietnam War teach-ins that were held with the permission of the administrations. Each student disturbance and each teach-in contributed to the escalation of the cold war between the generations.

By now the anti-student bias was almost as virulent as the prejudice against long-haired unkempt young people. The appearance of the hippies, the *Provos* of Holland, the *Gammler* of West Germany and similar dissidents elsewhere helped to increase the hostility against youth and students. Ronald Reagan, the ageing star of second-class Westerns, was elected Governor of California partly because he exploited the anti-student hostility. One of his more popular promises was to deal firmly with 'sex, drugs and treason at Berkeley'.

Various surveys dealt with the rapidly growing trend of girls aged eighteen to twenty leaving the parental home because they could not coexist with their mothers.

In 1966, while a Munich *Gammler* complained of being treated as an outcast, 'as if I was wearing a yellow star', Brighton Town Council agreed to urge the Government to promote legislation so that Mods and Rockers, or others who caused disturbances, could be sentenced to periods of forced labour:

Alderman Gerald Fitzgerald said that since the notice of the motion had been published, he had received 108 letters, many of them from councillors in towns from Blackpool to St. Ives, agreeing with it. Only two letters opposed the idea.

The motion was passed by a two-thirds majority, the Labour Party abstaining from voting.[11]

That summer on the outskirts of certain towns in Britain police stopped groups of youngsters on motorcycles or scooters to 'avert unwelcome teenage invasion'. Beatniks and 'poorly dressed young people' were being expelled from France, Italy and Greece. In parts of the United States they were jailed as vagrants. The French anti-beatnik regulations stipulated that only those long-haired male tourists who had enough money with them were to be allowed to enter the country. But even ordinarily dressed young people of both sexes awoke the suspicion of many authorities whenever they moved or travelled in groups. Adult tourists were free to move in swarms, not so the young. There was also evidence from many young-looking adults that young people were being turned into an instantly suspected category.*

In 1966 the cold war between the generations and the mental gulf dividing people into mutually hostile camps were nowhere as great as in West Germany. It was ruled by the *Alte Herren* aged between sixty and eighty who wanted to defend their past-oriented Utopia. This was the dream of an earnest, Bismarckian *Spiessbürgertum* with all the old-fashioned private virtues, living in a traditionally authoritarian state system, while using all the comforts and money-making possibilities of the electronic age. In 1966 the ruling party announced a plan for a *Notstandgesetz* (Emergency Law) to give the state and the big employers exceptional power over any kind of dissidents. West German students protested against this plan and against the Vietnam War and demanded university reform. Most of the West German popular press was extremely biased against the students. Rudolf Walter Leonhard wrote in his *X-mal Deutschland* that the majority of German adults had closed minds:

If it were a question of industry, thoroughness, organizing talent, we would have nothing to fear. But I am afraid the world is going to ask of us just what we have the least of : the imagination to

* A tall and slim college professor from Massachussets (thirty-two year-old father of two children) found out during a summer trip that in many places on the Continent it was most disagreable to be young-looking, to have a beard and be casually dressed. Hotels turned him away, police stopped and questioned him, and, in some cases, he was refused service in cafés and restaurants.

understand somebody else's point of view and still preserve our own; the tough humility of the democrat.[12]

4

The Amsterdam Provos and the Chinese Red Guards contributed disturbing features to the layman's youth-of-today image in 1966 and 1967. Because of them – or rather because of the way their behaviour was reported almost everywhere – the cold war between the generations became more bitter and more intensive. Local youth, in many countries in the five continents, was somehow mistrusted or hated more because of the 'hooliganism of the Amsterdam Provos' or the 'murderous terrorism of the Chinese Red Guards'.

It would be difficult even to imagine two more different groups of people than the Provos and the Red Guards. They had only one thing in common: they were misreported, misunderstood and misdiagnosed by most of the world.

The Amsterdam Provos borrowed their name from a doctoral dissertation; their ceremonies from a jester-magician; their manifesto was written by a philosophy student with whom they disagreed; they were helped to fame by a few hundred policemen and by the acres of newsprint devoted everywhere to their doings, though their actual number rarely exceeded thirty.

'Provo', short for *provocateur,* first appeared in print in the doctoral dissertation 'Background to the Behaviour of Young Trouble-Makers', presented at Utrecht University in January 1965 by Wouter Buikhuisen. The author called a certain category of *nozems* (young troublemakers) 'Provos'. These were street *nozems* who, when bored, provoked for kicks. Dr Buikhuisen's work became known in intellectual circles, and soon a few graduate students, writers and artists felt like calling themselves Provos, to describe their general mood and attitudes. Some of them wanted to provoke as a matter of principle, others felt in a mood to *épater les bourgeois,* as Théophile Gautier and his friends did in nineteenth-century Paris.

An earnest Amsterdam philosophy student, Roel van Duyn, who also adopted the Provo label, experienced in May 1965 a 'happening' organized by a jester–magician called Grootveld. These happenings were staged round *Het Lieverdje* (the Little Rascal), the romanticized statue of an Amsterdam street urchin, donated by a cigarette manufacturer and placed on the Spui, a crossroads in the middle of Amsterdam. Grootveld regarded the Little Rascal as a monument to the 'addicted consumer of tomorrow' and every Saturday midnight held an anti-smoking, anti-consumer-society, anti-earnestness happening round the statue. Van Duyn and his Provos joined the magician's young adherents and gave the weekly happenings a political flavour. The Provos found that by adopting fantastic and absurd slogans and by behaving like carefree jesters their protests became more effective than the traditional forms of demonstrations. These Provos were influenced by Grootveld's poetic inventiveness and gentle non-violence.

The stencilled magazine *Provo* was first published in Amsterdam in July 1965. Because of its all-round irreverence and extremist content it was confiscated, and therefore became an instant success. Its manifesto was written by Roel van Duyn, who had a terrible vision of mankind's future. He felt that a nuclear holocaust was inevitable because the welfare state, having wrapped people in cotton-wool, was rocking them to sleep, making them unconscious accomplices of their own destruction:

We cannot convince the masses, we scarcely even want to. How anyone can place any trust in that bunch of apathetic, unenterprising, witless cockroaches, beetles and ladybirds is a mystery to me. . . . If only we could be revolutionaries. But we're more likely to see the sun rise in the west than a revolution in the Netherlands.

Van Duyn and his small circle were opposed to communism, social democracy and to all existing political parties. Despising the masses, they wrote that:

The Proletariat is the slave of the politicians. . . . . It has joined its old enemy the bourgeoisie, and now constitutes with the bourgeoisie a huge grey mass. . . . We live in a monolithic, sick society in which the creative individual is the exception. Big bosses, capitalists, communists impose on us, tell us what we should do, what we should consume. . . . But the Provotariat wants to be itself.

The first issues of the magazine *Provo,* despite its darkly pessimistic manifesto, attracted the attention of a number of creative individuals who did their best to transform the Provo phenomenon into an optimistic, artistically and politically positive happening. The Provos had no formal organization, no party platform, no agreed ideology. It was made clear again and again that each

Provo spoke for himself and about himself, never on behalf of Provos in general. What they had in common was their jester's spirit, their ambition to undermine complacency and conformism, their hostility to bureaucracy and routine, and their tendency to attract welcome and unwelcome followers and publicity. Bernhard de Vries, one of the leading Provos, wrote that the Provo artistic happenings were purely aesthetic mass manifestations:

'The police and the bourgeoisie were, of course, scandalized and countered with right-wing provocation, the conventional reaction of the philistine middle classes and their bogy-men-servants, the booted protectors of shocked mediocrity. The result: the artistic happening acquired a political tinge and became the Provo happening.'[13]

The tenth of March 1966 saw the wedding of Crown Princess Beatrix to the German Klaus von Amsberg who, in his youth, had been a soldier in Hitler's army. Many people in the Netherlands were against this marriage, and a great many Amsterdamers were against the wedding being held in their city. The place of the wedding was tactless and the authorities committed a number of lesser provocative acts, among them an attempt to use the Anne Frank House as a temporary police station during the wedding ceremonies. This incensed one part of the population. Eighteen Amsterdam councillors (out of forty-five), three chief rabbis and the Student Association refused the invitation to attend. The Provos, with a few hundred sympathizers, organized a protest demonstration. Because of the bad, rainy weather, most people were content to watch the festivities on television. On the nearly empty streets, the playful Provo 'protest happening', their earnest demonstration for a republic and, later, their smoke-bomb throwing was very conspicuous and made front-page news everywhere. Harry Mulisch, forty-two, the well-known novelist, described in his book *Bericht aan de rattenkoning* ('Report to the King Rat'), how he watched this event on television, how he was overcome with emotion when he grasped what had happened:

Other people, with more guts than me, had brought it off, were throwing smoke-bombs into living rooms throughout Europe, the Soviet Union, the United States, Japan, and were being pursued far along the canals and beaten up in doorways by policemen falling all over each other to get at them. Others were being shoved up against the bridge railings by mounted police, held tight by reins looped round their necks, and kicked senseless by spurred riding boots.

According to Dr Nuis:

Heavy-handed behaviour on the part of the police and—later —on the part of judges and magistrates became the order of the day during the next few weeks, primarily in response to humorous and non-violent demonstrations by Provos. As in the case of the Free Speech Movement at Berkeley, the police provided their opponents with the best propaganda. The disproportionate violence shocked the Amsterdamers, who (apart from the war years) had not seen such things for decades. Some, of course, cheered the police action, deducing the guilt of the law-breakers from the means taken to suppress them.[14]

'Heavy-handed behaviour' was, indeed, a mild expression. The twenty-four year old Provo writer Hans Tuyman was arrested and sentenced to three months' imprisonment for handing a policeman a pamphlet against police violence on April Fools' Day. Koosje Koster, a girl student in her twenties, was arrested for handing out raisins to passers-by in the street. For this grave offence she was also submitted to a humiliating physical search by a policewoman who, in the presence of policemen, examined her naked body.

By this time the Provo camp included Constant Nieuwhuys, forty-seven, a successful sculptor-architect; Simon Vinkenoog, thirty-seven, poet and novelist; Luud Schimmelpenninck, thirty, freelance technological consultant; Irene van de Weetering, twenty-seven, wife of Netherland's chess-champion and mother of two children; and Jef Last, the sixty-seven-year-old writer. ('Old people are welcome. After all, Socrates at sixty-five was a bigger Provo than when young.')

A group of Provos decided to make Amsterdam 'more liveable in'. They launched various 'White campaigns'. The white-bicycle plan was aimed at freeing the car-infested city centre from motor traffic by providing 50,000 white bicycles which anyone could use in the city, and then, after their journey, leave at the kerb for others to use. The 'white chimneys' plan aimed to solve the problem of air-pollution by forcing the authorities to make the whole of Amsterdam a smokeless zone. The 'white wives' campaign aimed at providing free family-planning and contraceptive advice centres, operated by volunteers (the 'white wives').

By this time, white had became the uniform of the Provos who, in order to back up their campaigns, wanted a seat on the forty-five man municipal council in Amsterdam. The leader of this campaign, Bernhard de Vries, wrote to the electors:

Provo happenings are collective manifestations of protest against an authoritarian system that has to assert itself at all costs, proving yet again by its perverse intransigence that authority and art are arch-enemies the minute art ceases to be mere embellishment and becomes the expression of independence, joy in life, criticism, and protest.

Provo is unique because it is the vanguard in a unique situation —that of a general state of welfare in which for the first time in history man has space to live his own life creatively. That the Provos are temporarily rewarded with sticks and stones for their insight only goes to prove that authorities always find the most obvious truths the hardest to grasp. The younger and youngest generations are marching right behind the vanguard, heading straight for the municipal council. TO THE HOMO LUDENS ! AGAINST THE ABUSE OF POWER ! PLAYFULLY ONWARDS TOWARDS A LIVEABLE–IN AMSTERDAM !

Although most of their young adherents were under voting age, the Provo list received over 13,000 votes in the Amsterdam municipal election on 1 July 1966, and the twenty-six-year-old Bernard de Vries became the city's first Provo councillor.

On 13 May 1967 there was a Provo gathering in the Vondel Park. Announced as a meeting to disband the movement (though it had never been formally launched), the event turned into an undecisive happening. A number of full-time Provos wanted to continue, others wanted to stop. The Provo-Anarchists issued a manifesto signed by sixteen members of the leading nucleus. Professor Thoenes, of the Institute of Social Studies in the Hague, had already used the past tense when writing about the Provos a month earlier :

In any event, Holland will never be quite the same again. . . . Although Provo has not been able, or even tried, to force us to change existing structures, it has left an indelible mark. . . . Provo has shown that one may use his imagination to envisage a different world. Why, after all, should the welfare state be the last phase of history before judgement day?[15]

For objective observers it was difficult to understand the amount of furious hatred the Provos brought upon themselves. Jan Hein Donner, chess Grand Master, was taking part in the chess championship in the Hague. During a break Donner went out for a stroll in front of the building. Being in his early thirties and wearing long hair, he was taken for a young enemy by a Hague policeman, who ran towards him with raised truncheon, shouting: 'You dirty Provo scum, get back to Amsterdam,' That night, after he had won the championship, Donner recounted this incident on television.

The anti-youth bias prompted people to seize any pretext to attack the Provos. Though most of the Provos were against colonialism and the Vietnam War, some foreign correspondents called them 'white racists' and 'colonialists' because of their white dress and 'white campaign'. These gentlemen evidently did not know that the Dutch language has two words for white – one for the colour of this paper (*wit*) and one for skin colour (*blanc*). As Aad Nuis commented: 'The contamination that the colour of innocence and fresh beginnings has suffered in the English-speaking world has not taken place in the Netherlands.'

To the world-wide youth-of-today image of 1966-7 ('one has only to read the papers to know what youth is like') the 'thousands of sex- and drug-crazed Provo hooligans' and their 'murderous disturbances' added some monstrous features. They were, naturally, endangering morality, since in the goodness of their hearts, some foreign correspondents described the 'white wives campaign' as a campaign for having wives in common.

The adult world was infected and went on infecting itself with irrational hatred for the young. The cold war atmosphere penetrated even such citadels of fair justice as the British law courts. In 1967, the pop singer Mick Jagger was sentenced to three month in prison for possessing a comparatively harmless drug that was used in Italy and elsewhere as a prophylactic against air-sickness. The *New Law Journal* commented in an editorial:

Since the sentence is indefensible in relation to the particular offence and the particular offender, and since it is not justifiable in terms of the social problem of drug-taking, then it can only be explained as marking disapproval of the general habits and way of life of a section of the community of whom the community apparently generally disapprove. On that it is enough to say, for the moment, that the section of the community in question was not on trial and that incurring public disapproval is not, happily, a criminal offence.[16]

Mass-media coverage created hundreds of Provo adherents or imitators in most cities, the same way as *Time* magazine's first cover story on the hippies created half a million instant pseudo-hippies.

Ever since the Middle Ages there have always been various 'Bohemias' in the larger cities consisting of small coteries of dropped-out, rebellious, carefree, absurd artists and intellectuals, *enfants terribles* of the arts and the sciences. These Bohemians were mostly young. Since the population had more than trebled or quadrupled in most cities, there were vast numbers of potential Bohemians. The generation conflict, the adult world's resistance to change and their hatred of the young produced large hippie communities. The adults drank alcohol, the Hippies smoked marijuana. After the Rolling Stones case an anonymous leaflet warned: 'THE LAWS WILL CHANGE   YOU WILL ALL DIE SOON, AND WE WILL WIN – YOU ARE DYING OFF ALL THE TIME, WE ARE BEING BORN ALL THE TIME – WHY NOT GET THINGS IN PERSPECTIVE ?'

5

The twenty-two million young people who in the 'summer of madness' of 1966 were to envelop the immensity of China in a horrible 'revolutionary hurricane' had no idea that spring that they were to be made into Mao's Red Guards. The 'Great Cultural Revolution' and the Red Guard movement were planned and prepared by Mao Tse-tung, the Defence Minister, Lin Piao, and their adherents in the greatest of conspiratorial secrecy. The day hundreds of thousands of young boys and girls were sworn in as storm troopers of the cultural revolution, they received their brand-new Red Guard uniforms and arm bands from various depots. The 'hurricane of the young' broke out because Mao Tse-tung planned that it should. He decided to use the great hostility between the generations to destroy the petrified party and state bureaucracy that he himself had built up.

In launching his cultural revolution, Mao had set out to 'remould the souls of the people'. The concrete expression of this was in the sixteen-point Decision of the CCP Central Committee of 8 August 1966, which noted that although, in the main, the bourgeoisie in China had been eradicated, the 'four olds' (old customs, old ideas, old culture and old habits) must be eradicated and replaced by the 'four news' (new customs, new ideas, new culture and new habits). The cultural revolution was an onslaught by the young on the established social order, represented and defended by the old. The Red Guard oath pledged 'to defend Chairman Mao all through life'. They also swore to 'destroy utterly the old world and create a new one in its place'.

In China, precisely because of the Mao-style terrorist dictatorship, the hatred the young felt for the adults was more virulent than anywhere else. In the vast party–state hierarchy there were hundreds of thousands of petty dictators who terrorized their subjects. These dictators were adults, often elderly men, while the subjects were young. (In 1966 over half the Chinese population was under twenty years of age.) Mao decided to select about twenty-two million young people from the ranks of 230 million young Chinese between fifteen and twenty-three and turn them into a vast army that would be ordered to carry out 'terror with fanfare'. His method was simple and most effective. He closed all schools and universities and recruited the most enthusiastic students, girls and boys, into the Red Guards. He sent them away from their families and from their home towns to distant cities and provinces, ordering them to attack the 'class-enemies', the corrupt power structure; to beat up adult officials; to end the domination of the old-fashioned professors; to destroy privilege; to humiliate the enemies of 'Mao Tse-tung Thought'. They were given special powers to kill, loot and burn, and were told all the time that the police and the army was on their side, that they were the shock troops of Chairman Mao's glorious cultural revolution.

They were forced to live as parasites on the population, to demand food and shelter from people with little food and living in terribly overcrowded homes. They were driven to mass hysteria and to brutal acts, by which they automatically became the hated enemies of the rest of the people. Each Red Guard unit was led by a 'more experienced comrade', that is, by a young officer of the *Kung An Pu* (KAP, Mao's Ministry of Public Security). Lastly, it was made crystal clear to every single Red Guard that not to do as all other Red Guards did meant instant arrest or even death.

For nearly two years these terrorized terrorists roamed all over China, beating up, arresting and killing those people whom their KAP leader designated as 'enemies of Chairman Mao'. They were ordered to commit outrages and were praised for them in solemn editorials and festive speeches. At first a great many of them believed in their war on the party despots and corrupt bureaucrats. After a few months, however, it was difficult not to realize that they were being ordered to attack and kill many innocent people.

The Red Guards could travel on the railways and river boats free of charge. But they were sent to many districts where there were no railways. They had to march, at times for weeks, through hostile terroritories. Tens of thousands froze to death, other tens of thousands starved.

Theirs was a revolution ordered from above. They caused much suffering, and they, themselves, suffered a great deal. Like the Provos of Amsterdam, they, too, were misreported. Since almost all information about the Chinese mainland goes through Hong Kong and Macao to the outside world, I stayed there some weeks in January-February 1967 to see how the anti-youth bias distorted information about the Red Guards. As it happened, I found a handful of Red Guards in these cities who had escaped or strayed over the border by chance. I quote a few typical or significant passages from the interviews they gave me.

Kuen Siu-mei, a former Red Guard, was seventeen and had old, worried eyes in her thin little face. She was still in hiding in Macao, hoping to get to Hong Kong, where she had an uncle she had never met, and where she had a chance of disappearing among the Chinese millions. The Western term 'defector' was quite meaningless in her case. She was a hunted human being, who had survived thousands of small and great dangers during a nightmarish half-year. That she was in Macao with some hope of survival was thanks only to thousands of chance and unforeseeable accidents.

A secondary-school student in a Hunanese small town south of Peking, she became a Red Guard ('Everyone volunteered; and I had to, my father is a worker') and was sent to the capital with the others.

'Did you leave behind many friends?'

A puzzled look on Kuen's face. 'Friend' seemed to be an exotic word for her.

'Did you like any of your teachers?'

'We like all teachers who have not chosen the capitalist road.' (This was a parrot-like answer. Kuen did not seem to be aware

250

of the fact that she, too, had chosen the 'capitalist road' by escaping.)

So this friendless creature who had had only a few warm, personal encounters in her whole life, was suddenly thrown into the tumult and shouting of Peking; into the hysteria of mass demonstrations with the cymbals and gongs crashings; into writing posters; into jeering at 'class enemies' with tall dunce's caps on their heads; into destroying the 'old things' – and endless readings from the little Red Book, *Quotations from Chairman Mao*.

Her face lit up for a second when she spoke about the mass meeting when she saw Chairman Mao. She gave the impression that she loved those hours of hysteria when she could abandon herself to adoration; when she had a chance to express 'warm feelings' and love, any kind of love.

While in Peking she often went hungry, was always tired and sleepy. She, with others, often slept in shacks, even under the open sky; at times in dormitories or crowded school buildings. Getting up early, roaming the streets late at night. . . .

'Did you take part in beating up people?'

'Yes, most Red Guards did.'

'Whose idea was it to beat up a certain person?'

'There were some more experienced comrades among us.'

'Those people whom you helped to beat up were strangers to you, weren't they?'

'Yes, but we were told about their bad deeds.'

These boys and girls, used to violent hunger pains in their bellies, always dead tired, had only one emotion: fear. Fear that the 'experienced comrade' among them should find them not sufficiently steeled and enthusiastic, should call them 'class enemies' who had 'wormed their way into the Guards'.

And these girls and boys had very few chances during the last six months of having a thorough wash, let alone a bath. This, of course, was much harder on the girls, at least for some days each month.

When winter came they were sent south from Peking. Waiting at times for two or three days at various railway stations, sleeping anywhere, marching at times thirty kilometres a day – the journey south was a hard one. At times they were chased away by angry peasants. Hostile city officials refused them food and shelter. In between there were demonstrations, poster painting, beatings-up and, of course, endless readings from the little Red Book.

251

How do I know that this girl is not a Macao Chinese and that she did not just invent her story, hoping to get some money for it? Quite apart from the fact that I checked up on her story in several ways, Kuen does have 'identity documents'. These are on her face, in her eyes; in the submissive way she took off her shoes when I asked to see her feet. They were full of half-healed wounds from the many, many marches.

I found Kuen and the other escaped Red Guards only thanks to some friends of my Chinese interpreters, who vouched for me; also thanks to my promise not to carry a camera, and to the few Hong Kong dollars I promised to give them. They needed the money to finance their escape from Macao.

Lam Pin-fong, a twenty-one-year-old student from Peitaho University, was the only one among the escapees who came from a somewhat articulate background and whose personality was comprehensible to people of the normal world, outside Red China. Lam was simply a normal adventurer. He joined the Red Guards only in October 1966, with the sole aim of escaping, ultimately, to Hong Kong.

'Didn't you think that you might get your father into trouble, by escaping?'

'No, not at all. Great numbers of Red Guards disappear. In and around Peking alone more than 20,000 died of cold or starvation. By the end of this Red Guard storm, there will probably be hundreds of thousands who have died or disappeared.'

'So you pretended to be a Maoist fanatic, though you are not.' (He nods assent.) 'You demonstrated and took part in beatings?'

'Yes. I had to appear loyal and trustworthy to be sent to the south and, of course, I also had to be lucky. It was pure luck that I got to Canton.'

'Did you find out who was the secret boss in your group?'

'I don't know. I always behaved on the principle that not a single Red Guard mate of mine could be trusted. So, I always pretended. For instance, during a rather long march, my feet were full of blisters that had burst open and I was walking on bleeding wounds. I was also very tired and faint with hunger. So, I simply sank down at the roadside. Then some others gathered around me and began to read me appropriate quotations from the Red Book. . . . What could I do? I shouted enthusiastically that the Thought of Chairman Mao had helped me, managed to smile and forced myself to get up and march on, though I was nearly fainting with pain. . . . This was another one of the "miraculous cures" of Mao Thought.'

One of the escaped Red Guards, a former minor official of the Young Communist League and still using the stilted Party language, explained why the young hated adult 'cadres':

Some cadres cruelly oppressed the masses, fined peasants at will and raped women and young girls at the point of a bayonet. Young people were sent by these cadres at a moment's notice to do physical labour in distant provinces. A student in Shanghai would be sent to Sinkiang, without any hope of seeing his native city again. Young married couples were separated senselessly and for ever. The distances are great and, without a travel permit, these families have no hope of being reunited.

Middle-aged and old cadres obtained the love of pretty young girls by threats. Party committees ordered young girls 'to cultivate love' towards an older official. This meant that the girl in question should not spend her free time with this or that young boy, or with her fiancé, but with the elderly cadre. Her lover would be sent to the other end of the country, and a similar fate awaited the girl if she did not 'cultivate love' well enough.

Of course, it is not only the young who hate these local despots. These lived on the masses like leeches. Most of us were happy when Chairman Mao at last turned against them. It was high time. The Chairman used this hatred to start this second revolution in China.

The remaining four ex-Red Guards we met were probably typical of at least ten million other unfortunates, those youngsters who conducted terror with fanfare in their own cities, towns or villages. These four all came from various parts of Kwantung Province, next door to the colony of Hong Kong. Their tragedy is that they took part in beating and humiliating older people in their own locality, in some cases relatives or close neighbours. Family ties, a respect for one's elders is still very strong among the masses of the people. These youngsters committed crimes against the very basis of the old Chinese way of life and morals. They have thousands of personal enemies at home. A possibility of escape being near, they got away.

But at least half of the twenty-two-million-strong Red Guard army took part in brutally treating the inhabitants of their towns or districts. God only knows what their fate was after the end of the Red Guard storm.

In Hong Kong, I organized interviews with nearly eight hundred witnesses of Red Guard disturbances. In normal times – and those were still normal times – about half a million Hong Kong and other Chinese expatriates visited their families on the mainland each year. In 1966, the number of travellers on the Hong Kong–Canton railway was slightly over a million. Between 11 and 25 February my three English-speaking Chinese assistants travelled twice daily on third-class carriages between Sheun Shui (the first station in the non-prohibited zone) and Kowloon terminal, to interview returning Chinese adults.

We prepared for our work by studying the events since 1 January 1967 in the press of the Chinese mainland, and the texts of the monitored broadcasts from the principal mainland stations. (Not speaking Chinese, I used the daily *Survey of Chinese Mainland Press* and *Current Background,* provided by the translation service of the US Consulate General.) The members of the interviewing team knew the street-plans of Canton and other nearby cities quite well. In using their short questionnaire they tried to pinpoint the exact locality of Red Guard disturbances. Each evening the resultant material was checked against information culled from the mainland press, from radio monitoring and other sources of information.

These interviews, besides filling in details of the general picture of the Red Guard turmoils, were also part of the raw materials for the study of Hong Kong as the main source of information about China and, in particular, about Chinese youth. Mainland passengers were met at Kowloon terminal by reporters from the local English and Chinese press. The Hong Kong papers published almost daily interviews with mainland arrivals. It was instructive to learn what sort of bias-screening and bias-amplifying was at work before the information given by the arrivals got into the local press and, in turn, through the agencies and foreign correspondents into the world press.

In most cases information about the sufferings of the Red Guards, though published in the local English press and often transmitted by agencies and correspondents, was not published in most of the leading Western newspapers. On 24 and 25 February, for instance, several people just back from Canton reported that many Red Guards were being detained in Canton mental hospitals after 'going mad from Mao Tse-tung Thought'. One of the returning travellers was at Canton station when Red

Guards were marched by soldiers to a train going to the North. Some of them screamed hysterically when they were dragged into the wagons. Some had to be taken to hospital. A Hong Kong woman of forty-five, one of whose relatives worked in a mental hospital, said that during the previous day about fifty Red Guards had been certified as insane. The interviewee could only guess at the reason for their insanity, but the information about the number of certified persons was later proved to be quite correct. This news, and a great deal of information about tens of thousands of Red Guards who died of starvation or were beaten to death by peasants, was not published in most of the world press. On the whole, atrocities committed by Red Guards were amply reported, but not the extreme hardships and misery these young people had to endure.

6

'Let's compare the group of demonstrators to a piece of liver-sausage. O.K. Then we have to stab it in the middle so that it squirts out at the two ends.'

Ex-Generaloberts Duensing, Police President of West Berlin, at a press conference on 5 June 1967

On 2 June 1967 a West Berlin student called Benno Ohnesorg was killed by a revolver shot fired at the back of his skull. For the first and last time in his life he had been an onlooker at a student demonstration. This murder and the utterly despicable behaviour of the West Berlin police force was at first denied, and for days the mayor and the police department made vigorous attempts to deceive the public. They gave out four completely untrue versions of the events, until an unprecedented public outcry and the intervention of the Attorney General forced them to admit some of the truth. But this took time, and many people abroad, and some even in West Germany, still believe the original police lies.

On 1 June, the day before the state visit of the Shah of Persia to West Berlin, a few thousand students of the Free University listened to two lectures about conditions in Persia. Dr Bahman Nirumand, the historian, and Dr Heldmann of Amnesty International gave them documentary reports about the arrest and torture of the Shah's political opponents. The students decided to protest against his visit. At noon next day about six hundred of them were in front of the city hall waiting for the Shah. Before his arrival, two buses drove into the area and about one hundred pro-Shah Persians got out to cheer their ruler and abuse his opponents. As soon as the Shah and his wife entered the city hall, these Persians attacked the students with sticks, steel pipes and knuckle-dusters. Some of the police looked on, others helped to club students. In the end, they arrested two students but none of the attackers, who were strong-arm men from the Persian secret police (SAVAC) and had been specially flown in.*

That evening, the Shah and his wife were invited to the Opera House for a performance of *The Magic Flute*. The Police President, Duensing, made a simple plan for ambushing and maltreating the students. The Opera House faces Bismarckstrasse. The demonstrators were permitted to stay on the pavement on the opposite side, hemmed in between a fortified barricade in front and six-foot-high wooden planks behind. This place began to fill up after seven. Besides student demonstrators there were many onlookers, among them young mothers with their children.

Facing the barricades stood rows of policemen with rubber truncheons in their hands. Some of the police began hitting the students before the arrival of the Shah. These beatings, witnessed by several hundred people, were still not enough to spark off violence from the students. Even when municipal buses arrived with men from the Persian secret service, who began to shout insults at the students, most of the students kept calm. A minority, however, began to throw smoke-bombs, eggs and tomatoes. All of these fell short of their target.

A few minutes before eight, the Shah arrived and the students shouted anti-Shah slogans as he and his retinue entered the Opera House. With this, as far as the students were concerned, the first part of their demonstration was over. Some of them tried to move in the direction of Krummestrasse. They all planned to return by ten, at the end of the performance. Some students noticed only now that the number of policemen was growing, instead of diminishing, once the Shah was safely inside the Opera House. Several rows of policemen faced the barricade, with rubber truncheons at

* This was also officially reported by the Committee of Inquiry of the West Berlin city council (Pol. Drucksache Nr. 161, 1967).

Besides the hundreds of students who were the victims of this unprovoked assault, there were available over fifty signed statements from witnesses of these scenes, in addition to many photos.

the ready. At a few minutes past eight, fourteen ambulance vans drove up to the middle of the street. The crowd was about to melt away; as yet no one panicked, because it seemed obvious that there would not be any trouble before the end of *The Magic Flute*.

This, however, was not ex-Generaloberst Duensing's plan. What happened in the next minute was described in *Die Zeit* a week later by Jürgen Zimmer, a journalist who was among the ambushed students:

> At 20.09 the massacre begins. Without any announcement through the police loudspeakers, without any warning from the policemen themselves, without any acute reason, the *'Stosstrupps'* begin to beat the demonstrators. . . . As the policemen beat over the barricades, a demonstrator shouts : 'let's sit', but the policemen beat those who are sitting, too. Girls beg : 'Please do not hit', but the policemen hit with full force, they hit people who have fainted, they hit students who want to help the wounded.[17]

Six witnesses from various parts of America stated that during the ten minutes after the Shah's arrival the crowd calmed down and some of the demonstrators started to leave:

> Then suddenly the police attacked the crowd with their night sticks. They gave no order to the crowd to leave, nor did they give any warning of their intention. They merely began hitting men and women, students and non-students, demonstrators and non-demon-strators alike. Within a few moments many injured persons were lying on the street. . . . Some persons, including some women, had received open and bleeding head and body wounds. . . . After this initial attack by the police, demonstrators and onlookers fled in panic into the side streets. . . . Groups of policemen began ganging up on single demonstrators and youthful looking bystanders, in some cases dragging them and then beating them and kicking them as they lay on the ground.
>
> A few months ago, a law was passed that the Berlin police officers must hand out identification cards on request. . . . . Members of the press and others who requested police identification cards on June 2 were refused, and many had their hands clubbed by police officers. Students who tried to help wounded companions were clubbed; bystanders who asked for the protection of the police, were also clubbed.*

* Signatories: Mr and Mrs John Flores (New Haven, Connecticut); Thomas Rose (University of Wisconsin); Jack Himmelstein (Philadelphia); Peter Taufest; Elsa Rassback (Denver, Colorado). Signed on 7 June 1967.

257

Since Police President Duensing was watching the scene, the majority of the police went quite wild. They singled out pretty girls whom they beat unconscious and then, when their victims were lying on the ground, they went on kicking. When ambulance nurses and doctors tried to attend to the victims they were beaten too. Elderly men who thought that their 'respectable' appearance would have some effect on the police tried to intervene, only to be clubbed down. Policemen were chasing people who in panic were trying to escape.

The German Union of Students has published a well-documented report[18] covering the demonstration and subsequent events. It contains detailed testimonies from many witnesses, among them Americans and Britons. Blows about the head with rubber truncheons; kicks against prostate bodies; the manhandling of one victim by three or four policemen resulted in over thirty hospital cases during the first ten minutes of the totally unprovoked assault.*

A few exceptional policemen were horrified by the sadistic fury of their colleagues. Jürgen Zimmer reported in *Die Zeit* that one policeman tried with outstretched arms to stop two of his brutal colleagues. Another excused himself to a heavily wounded student girl: 'For God's sake, please don't think that all of us are like this.'†

In accordance with Duensing's plan, the demonstrators and onlookers who tried to escape from the two ends of the 'liversausage' into the side streets fell into the hands of mixed units of uniformed and plain-clothes police. Members of the *Abteilung 1,* the political police, did not identify themselves as detectives. The students did not at first know who these civilians were who pounced on single students, in groups of two or three. These political detectives were instructed to find and arrest the 'chief troublemakers'. They chose bearded, long-haired, casually dressed young men, rushed forward and grabbed them, and took them to a few of the more secluded spots to give them an 'extra-good beating'.

---

* Two girl students, Ulrike Kruger and Dina Ter-Nedden, begged the police in vain not to maltreat them. Each of the girls was beaten with rubber truncheons all over the body, and when they fainted, they were kicked about. The hospital reports and medical testimonies showed how brutal these beatings were. Elfriede Rosenstrauch of Vienna was an onlooker who kneeled down, hoping that her passivity would avert police attack. Instead three policemen attacked her and clubbed her until she fainted.

† *'Um Gottes willen, glauben Sie bloss nicht, dass alle so sind.'*

One of the beating-up places that was frequently used was the large and empty parking area under a block of flats on stilts, Krummestrasse 66-7.

When students saw their friends being dragged away by aggressive civilians, they followed them to the parking area. There, other detectives and several uniformed police grabbed them and beat them to the ground. Among these was Benno Ohnesorg, twenty-six-year-old graduate continuing his studies in *Germanistik* and *Romanistik*. He was a pacifist and an active member of the Evangelical Student Community. He had got married a month before this event. This was the first time he had seen a demonstration. He told friends the previous day that he wanted to see with his own eyes whether the police really were as brutal as the activists claimed.

More uniformed police came running to the scene. Benno Ohnesorg got up and tried to run away. Detective Starke thought, however, that he had spotted in him one of the chief trouble-makers, because he was wearing a red shirt, cream-coloured trousers and sandals. He also had a moustache. Starke tried to grab him, but Ohnesorg got away, only to run into the arms of several uniformed policemen. They beat him with their truncheons until he lost consciousness.

It was a few seconds before half past eight. At about the same time the police began circulating rumours that a policeman was dying from a knife wound, while another one had been killed by the demonstrators. This was also announced by loudspeakers as an alleged fact. The American witnesses we have already quoted stated: 'Apparently this announcement was made in order to stimulate police brutality and terrorism, because all of the twenty policemen sent to hospital for first aid were released that evening.' Police President Duensing's explanation of the 'misunderstanding' was that a policeman who had been hit on the head by a stone was 'bleeding like a swine', blood was running down his neck, so it was thought that he had a knife wound. Herr Duensing did not explain why the false report about the dying policeman was announced over the loudspeakers a good ten minutes after the policeman had returned to the Opera House.

Was Herr Duensing expecting the death of some other policeman?

Beneath the block of flats at Krummestrasse 66–7, two policemen were holding up the limp body of Ohnesorg by his arms and were about to take him to a police-car when a plain-clothes man rushed to the scene. He was Karl-Heinz Kurras, a thirty-nine-year-old *Kriminalobermeister* in the political police. He had in his right hand his service revolver with the safety catch in the off position. Kurras raised the revolver when he was behind Ohnesorg and his captors and fired at them. The bullet entered Ohnesorg's skull over the right ear and destroyed part of his skull.*

Ohnesorg was taken to Moabit Hospital, where he died on the operating table. After a piece of skull measuring 6 x 7 centimetres had been taken out, the doctors closed the wound. According to the first police report, the cause of death was fracture of the skull.

A second after Kurras had shot Ohnesorg from behind, police-man Horst Geier turned back and screamed at Kurras: 'Are you mad, shooting here?'†

When the Mayor of West Berlin, Albertz, had received infor-mation about the events on the night of 2–3 June, he ordered a complete news black-out regarding all demonstrators now in hospital. The police kept an important piece of evidence, the piece of Ohnesorg's skull, which would reveal the trajectory of the police bullet. At that time, and for days afterwards, Duensing hoped to stop the world from learning the truth.) Albertz was so sure of his powers that that very night at 1 a.m. he made a pom-pous declaration, branding the victims of the unprovoked police assault as responsible for everything, including Ohnesorg's death. He forebade mourning ceremonies for Ohnesorg during the first few days after the murder. He said in his attack against the victims: 'I want to make it quite clear that I approve of the behaviour of the police . . . and I myself am convinced that the police showed restraint.'

This statement was the prologue for an orgy of untruths lasting several days. On 3 June, a Saturday, people in Berlin who had not been witnesses were given the information that Benno Ohnesorg was killed by the demonstrators. The newspaper *Bild's* giant headline was 'Bloody disturbances: 1 death' while the text said: 'A young man died yesterday in Berlin. He became the

---

* The service revolver was Modell PPK, No. 211319, of 7.65 mm. calibre. The witnesses disagree about the distance from which the shot was fired. A seventeen-year-old schoolboy, Frank-Rainer K., said that the shot was fired from ten to thirty centimetres. Two witnesses claimed that the distance was a little more, half a metre; others two or three metres. From two to three metres Kurras might have killed one of the two policemen holding Ohnesorg.

† *'Bist du denn wahnsinnig, hier zu schiessen?'*

260

victim of disturbances staged by political Teddies [Halb-starke]. ...' *BZ* reported that 'left-radical disturbers of the peace provoked a real street battle with the police' that involved death. According to *Telegraf,* demonstrators provoked a 'bloody battle' that had a fatal casualty. The *Berliner Morgenpost* called the students 'trained communist streetfighters', and went on to suggest that Benno Ohnesorg was not the martyr, but the victim of the Maoist students (*'Freie Universität Chinese'*).

That afternoon, *Abend* reported the police allegation that the students had provoked the policemen with a rain of stones and published the photo of a young woman with blood streaming down her face, calling her one of the victims of the demonstrators. This woman, after being released from hospital, declared that she was wounded by a truncheon-attack by policemen.[19]

By Sunday 5 June the rest of the West Berlin press had to publish the news that the victim was a student. *Welt am Sonntag* explained why a detective was forced to fire: 'He was dragged by demonstrators into a courtyard, there overpowered, kicked and threatened with knives.' It should be emphasized that this lie was given out by the police on Saturday. (Fifteen witnesses told the commission of enquiry that not a word of it was true.)

On Monday 6 June the principal Springer newspaper *Bild,* which up till then had consistently implied that the 'radikalinski students' had done the shooting, now suddenly changed its line. Its headline was 'Students threaten: we shall shoot back!' The editors who invented this did not stop to think that if the students were now threatening to shoot back who had done the shooting originally? Peter Behrendt, the *Bild* reporter who wrote the article, told the *Berliner Extradienst* later: 'I am ashamed of my paper. There was not a single word about "shooting back" in my article. That was added by the editors who wanted a sensational headline.'

More than two thousand witnesses of the unprovoked police attack, and the students of Berlin, did their best from the outset to inform the world and the people of Berlin about the truth. These efforts were branded by the *BZ* as anti-police agitation. *Bild* and the other Springer papers went on with their anti-student cam-paign. The professors and students of West Germany were resolved that the events of 2 June should be officially cleared up. Some newspapers criticized Mayor Albertz in no uncertain terms for his defence of police-state methods. A Munich paper wrote: 'What kind of a republican is one who doesn't know that demonstration is the duty of students everywhere in the world? . . . What kind of a "Berliner" must he be who agrees with police-state methods this side of the Wall, while he pretends to be against them beyond the Wall?"[20]

Professors such as Dr Karl-Dietrich Bracher of Bonn University stated that in West Berlin it was a question of 'conscious terror against non-conformists' (*Andersdenkende*). They denounced the oppression of minorities. Theodore W. Adorno, Golo Mann, Günter Grass, Martin Walser, Rudolf Augstein and others like them urged in an open letter that the facts of 2-3 June should be cleared up with the greatest possible objectivity, and that those responsible for offences should be sentenced by independent, conscientious judges.[21]

The liberal newspapers *Der Spiegel, Die Zeit* and *Frankfurter Rundschau* went out of their way to publish well-documented reports about the police assault and the murder of Ohnesorg. These papers sent to Berlin tens of thousands of special reprints containing the truth for students to hand out gratis to the public. The majority of West Berliners were too biased to pay attention to this material.

The Berlin authorities and the Berlin press still thought that they would be able to suppress the truth. Only when hundreds of thousands of students demonstrated all over the country, only when radio and TV gave the chance to students witnesses and journalists to give their version of the events, did the extremely biased West Berlin press change its tune.

As the days passed, some of the events of 2 June were cleared up. That Duensing planned an assault was proved when it turned out that at eight o'clock on the evening of 22 June the West Berlin ambulance centre learned from the official police radio that the '*Schlagstock frei gegeben werde*', i.e., the police will attack! They were just able to send fourteen ambulances to the scene before the police began their entirely unprovoked general attack.

It became perfectly clear that the Persian strong-arm men and the police had acted according to plan. Duensing at first denied that he gave orders that these Persians should be permitted to attack the demonstrators in front of the city hall and the Opera House. Four days later, when one of his police officials repeated this to his face, Duensing replied that, yes, he remembered this now, 'I forgot, because it was very warm on that day.'*

On 8 June 1967 Duensing was sent on an enforced vacation from which he was not to return. The resignation of Busch, the Senator for Internal Affairs, on 13 September was followed by that of Mayor Albertz. On 14 September he stated: 'I was weakest when I acted in the most severe manner during the night of 2 June, because that night I objectively acted incorrectly.'

The *Frankfurter Rundschau* gave an early summary of these events: 'The police actions on Friday night, characterized by unbelievable brutality, are the expression of hatred which has been escalated by the mass media, the political leadership and a sizeable section of the population, partly by design and partly due to ignorance.'

What followed was a travesty of justice. The authorities were intent not to leave a shadow of doubt that the principles of justice and general human rights do not apply to students and dissidents.

One of the many students who were arrested on 2 June was Fritz Teufel, member of a commune. The police decided to make him a scapegoat for the attack on students planned by Herr Duensing. The State Prosecutor kept Teufel under arrest from 2 June till 10 August. Teufel was accused of having thrown a stone at a policeman. Two policemen alleged this, many witnesses denied it. The court ascertained in December 1967 that the policemen in question lied.

Karl-Heinz Kurras, the policeman who killed Ohnesorg, was not arrested. The State Prosecution, which had refused to consider the defence evidence in the Teufel case, was quite extraordinarily reluctant to investigate the case against Kurras. The Prosecutor first heard the testimony of eighty-nine witnesses; he visited the place of the crime at the *Krummestrasse* several times; he considered a large amount of film, photo and sound tape material, before beginning proceedings against Kurras for the manslaughter (*Fahrlässiger Töltung*) of Ohnesorg.

Kurras was fine 400 marks in October 1967 for carrying a

<hr>

* *Mhm, ja, jetzt erinnere ich mich, die Anweisung gegeben zu haben. Wenn ich was anderes gesagt habe, so lag es daran, das as an diesem Tag sehr heiss war ....*

revolver without authorization. On 21 November he was found not guilty of the manslaughter of Ohnesorg with his unauthorized weapon.

The presiding judge announced: 'The sentence does not satisfy us fully. This deed was without doubt contrary to law.'* And, turning to Kurras, he said: 'The court is unanimous in the conviction that you acted objectively mistakenly.'†

Kurras committed a mistake, not a crime, although it was proved to the court beyond a shadow of doubt that Kurras did not act in self-defence; that nobody had threatened his life, least of all the unconscious Ohnesorg.

Karl-Heinz Kurras remained a member of the West Berlin police force.

Benno Ohnesorg's widow bore a son that winter.

---

* 'Das Urtail befriedigt uns nicht völlig. Die Tat war eindeutig rechtswidrig.'
† 'Das Gericht ist der einmutigen Überzeugung, dass Sie objektiv falsch gehandelt haben.'

IX

'TO EACH ACCORDING TO HIS IMAGINATION': PARIS–PRAGUE 1968

'Let us hope for a healthy conclusion – and prepare for it.'

Maurice Clavel, December 1966

'In fact there are no longer any *citizens* [in France]; there are only the masses which drift, at the mercy of events, between hope and fear.'

Le Monde, 1968

France was complacent, arrogant, resistant to change and proud of the extreme stability of the regime. Under the constitutional dictatorship of General de Gaulle the country turned into one of the most smoothly functioning neo-capitalist technocratic states of the Western world. Political life was at a standstill. The National Assembly was irrelevant. Troublemakers were summarily dealt with. The extreme brutality of the police and of the riot squads, the CRS (*Compagnie Républicaine de Sécurité*), did not abate at all during the General's majestic reign. The people were untroublesome. General de Gaulle said : '*Les français sont des veaux*' which roughly translated means that Frenchmen were sheep.

Maurice Clavel, who broke with De Gaulle after the Ben Barka affair, wrote about the France of his period: 'The country was anaesthetized. If a true Frenchman is a citizen who is conscious of his duty and his destiny, what is the funniest thing is that the Guallists managed to create a situation where there are no more Frenchmen. Only sheep.'

The restive students did not worry the ruler. His regime had dealt with the OAS, General Salan's highly trained secret army. Why should it not be able to deal with the students who, after all, are in De Gaulle's elegant phrase only 'bed-messers' (*chienlit* or *chie-en-lit*)?

Official France had a long tradition of neglecting the country's

265

youth. The inability of the rulers to mitigate the effects of swift technological transformation on human beings hit the students most. In the new age, when trained intelligence became the main productive force in society, the students (trainee intellectuals) were expected to develop critical intelligence in their studies and uncritical acceptance of a society created by previous generations. They were expected to turn themselves into a highly specialized and efficient intelligentsia who would do their work without questioning its purpose. Isolated in their student situation, physically isolated in vast residential campuses, they were placed outside both adult and non-adult French society.

They were denied all the important freedoms that the rest of youth was able to enjoy without adult hindrance. As far as their private life was concerned, they had fewer rights than sixteen-year-old apprentices and waitresses. While the rest of youth enjoyed *de facto* sexual freedom, students between eighteen and twenty-three were expected to live like monks and nuns. In the new residential campuses students were supposed to live according to regulations that applied to boarding-school children of the last century. The petty interference with their private lives went so far as to forbid them to decorate their rooms or affix anything to the walls. They were forbidden to receive guests of the opposite sex in their rooms.

Because successive governments ignored the tremendous increase in the number of children since 1945, the entire educational system was bursting at the seams. Worst hit were the nightmarishly overcrowded and under-staffed universities. The Minister of Education, Christian Fouchet, warned in 1966 that the absence of entrance examinations to the universities could only lead to disaster: 'The dam will break one day if we do nothing.' Nothing was done. Referring to this open-door university policy and the consequent fifty per cent drop-out of first-year students, another Minister of Education, Alain Peyrefitte, said in 1967: 'It is as if we were to organize a shipwreck in order to pick out the best swimmers.'

But in order to keep up the growth rate, France needed an even greater number of technocrats, specialists and all sorts of trained intellects. New universities were created at Amiens, Orleans, Rheims and Rouen. The Sorbonne overflow was housed in two vast wholesale markets (the *Halle aux cuirs* and the *Halle aux vins*). In the outer suburban belt of Paris two residential campuses were set up at Orsay and Nanterre. The first buildings were opened at Nanterre in 1964, with 2,300 students. By 1968 Nanterre had nearly 15,000 students, a few university buildings, segregated residential blocks for boys and girls, but no cultural amenities, no discothèques, no cafés, no cinemas and not even a library. In the industrial wasteland of this outer suburb, students enjoyed the sound of shunting freight trains and the sight of the university buildings that prompted one newspaper to ask: 'Architectural incompetence . . . or sadism?'

The revolt against the severe segregation of boys' and girls' hostels, for which Nanterre and D. Cohn-Bendit were so often blamed, first broke out in 1965 at Antony, the oldest and largest residential campus in France, some twenty minutes by train from Paris. Nearly 2,000 students physically prevented workmen from erecting a warden's lodge in front of the girls' hostel. The Rector called the police, who had to camp there until the building was completed. This was followed by three months of protests and demonstrations. Finally, in January 1966, a new director made a great concession: girls and boys over twenty-one could visit each other, those under twenty-one needed written parental permission to do so. (About ninety per cent of the minors did receive permission.) But this great concession was not introduced at other campuses.

The student movement demanding equal rights with the rest of the youth of the country grew in force in 1966 and 1967. In the autumn of 1966 some 'situationist' and anarchist students were elected to the student union at the University of Strasbourg. Using the funds of their union, they printed a pamphlet in 10,000 copies called 'On Student Poverty: considered in its economic, political, psychological, sexual and – particularly – intellectual aspects and a modest proposal for its remedy.'

The pamphlet was distributed at the official opening of the academic year and it gained wide publicity after its authors had been prosecuted for misappropriating student union funds for financing printing costs. Though they were elected officials of the union, they were found guilty. *Le Monde* wrote that the Strasbourg pamphlet 'with its high quality, must be considered as a systematic rejection of all social and political organizations as we know them in the West and the East, and of all the groups that are currently trying to transform them.'[1]

Since the Zengakuren mainstream turned against all political parties and all systems of East and West in 1960, the 'plague on all your houses' attitude was cropping up with greater frequency among rebellious students. Strasbourg was the first symptom that in France, too, many student militants were in a mood of total rejection. In France the Communist Party and the communist-run trade unions represent great and real powers; the revolutionary students therefore attacked the communists more often than students in other countries.* The official Communist Student Union, the UEC, lost so many members that by 1968 it had barely 1,500 left.

Students and schoolchildren backed the French version of the Vietnam Solidarity Campaign, the CVN, which would mobilize tens of thousands of boys and girls. In the prison-like, over-disciplined *lycées* the anti-Vietnam War movement spread like wildfire. Headmasters protested in vain. In 1967 the anti-Vietnam movement established a network of action groups, called *Comités d'actions lycéens* (CAL). The membership of these groups grew with great speed. The schoolboys, who were 'not supposed to speak when adult company was present', were in a revolutionary fervour ready to risk 'their life for the cause', as their predecessors had done during the Resistance.†

In 1967, exactly a year before the May Revolution, François Missoffe, Minister of Youth and Sport presented to the National Assembly a voluminous report on the youth of today. This was supposed to be 'the most thorough examination of the lives, difficulties and aspirations of French youth.' A month later, a short-ened version was published by *La Documentation Française* in 338 pages.[2] Though at the universities the predictable and predicted chaos set in, and though students and schoolchildren at the *lycées* came under the impact of a mounting revolutionary ferment, there was not a single allusion to the real mood of youth in the report. Authority, even when it went through the motions of 'listening to youth', was unable or unwilling to do so. There was

* The French Communist Party has had grave troubles with its student groups ever since the Hungarian Revolution 1956. To isolate the over-critical students from the rest of youth, the then existing communist youth organisation (UJRF) was split into four different organizations: for boys, girls, peasants and students. The new student organization (UEC) was carefully isolated from the rest. From 1960 onwards the UEC was purged several times. In 1966 some of the purged communist students founded their Trotskyist organization, JCR (*Jeunesse Communiste Révolutionnaire*).

† Hitler's Gestapo shot five schoolboys at the Lycée Buffon in Paris for their resistance work during the last war.

not the slightest hint of the degree and scope of dissatisfaction at the universities and in the *lycées*.

The ministry reported that only three per cent of young people wanted to go to a political meeting at least six times a year, or to do gymnastics, judo or yoga at least once a month. On the other hand, allegedly, 'thirteen per cent of French youth like to sit outside the front door of their homes and watch people go by, at least three times a week.' This report was the best documentary evidence that student protest during the nineteen-sixties was not violent and spectacular enough to shake the authorities from their complacent torpor.

In January 1968, M. Missoffe went to Nanterre to open a new swimming pool. After the ceremony was over Daniel Cohn-Bendit stepped out from the crowd of students and asked in a very loud voice: 'Mr Minister, you have drawn up a six-hundred-page-long report on French youth, but there isn't a word in it about our sexual problems. Why not?'

The Minister got angry: 'I am perfectly willing to discuss the matter with responsible people, but you are clearly not one of them. I, myself, prefer sport to sexual education. If you have sexual problems, I suggest you jump in the pool.'

'That's what the Hitler Youth used to say,' was the young man's reply.

Cohn-Bendit was born in France of German refugee parents, who took him back to Germany in his teens. He was in France now, with a German passport. A second-year sociology student, he took a leading part in the ten-day strike of Nanterre sociologists in November 1967. The strikers, instead of going on holiday, held a teach-in with their teachers about necessary reforms. Soon the entire faculty became involved with 10,000 students. The teach-in ended with the setting-up of a joint teacher–student committee, to draft reforms and send the proposals to the Ministry in Paris. The Ministry's attitude was, however, entirely negative. The students split into a moderate majority which still hoped for minor reforms, and a militant minority urging a 'total contestation' of existing society, together with its university. These militants called themselves *enragés,* after an extreme revolutionary group of 1793. Daniel Cohn-Bendit was one of the spokesmen of these *enragés.*

At the time of this encounter with Missoffe, Cohn-Bendit was already in trouble because of his part in the reformist sit-in. He was due to present himself soon to a special police committee that dealt with expulsion orders. The *enragés* meanwhile discovered that since the Minister's visit police agents had been busy on the campus, gathering material against the militants. They photographed policemen and suspected agents, and pasted blow-up photos of them on posters. With these in hand, about fifty of them marched up and down the hall of the Sociology building on 26 January 1968. Since political demonstrations were forbidden on the campus, Dean Grappin telephoned for police help. By noon, when great masses of students had left the lecture halls for their lunch-break, four van-loads of armed police drove up and began chasing the militants. The sight of the police attacking students on the campus transformed them all into momentary *enragés*. They attacked the police with stones, chair legs, benches, bottles. Heavily outnumbered, the police soon withdrew.

On 14 February 1968, St Valentine's day, there was a revolt against the monastic disciplinary regulations at nearly all residential campuses throughout France. Boys invaded girls' hostels. In Nantes, Nice and Montpellier the Deans called in the police. They, in turn, were chucked out from the hostels by the joint forces of boys and girls.

On 18 and 20 March anti-Vietnam War student commandos, using small explosives, blew up the plate-glass windows of the Paris offices of the Bank of America, the Chase-Manhattan Bank, TWA and the American Express. On 22 March the police arrested three students and three schoolboy activists of the *Comités d'Action Lycéens*. That evening the *enragés* called a meeting at Nanterre to protest against the arrests. At the end of this meeting it was decided by a majority of 142 (with two against and three abstentions) to occupy the administrative building. The '22 March Movement' was born.

By 2 April the movement had more than 1,200 adherents among the students, who on that day occupied the large lecture theatre of the faculty. This movement worried all the authorities, the French Communist Party included. On 25 April Pierre Juquin the communist *député* and Central Committee member, was prevented from speaking at the University in Nanterre. The *enragés* were so hostile that, at the end, he had to creep out through a back door. According to the Communist Party paper, those who had broken up the meeting were 'bourgeois pseudo-revolutionaries. . . . These false revolutionaries must be unmasked totally because, objectively, they serve the interests of the Gaullist authorities and the great capitalist monopolies.'[3]

Also on 25 April, there were clashes between left- and right-wing students on several campuses. At Toulouse a large police force separated the warring groups. Small commandos of extreme right-wing students had been making frequent attempts, since the end of the Algerian War, to intimidate the left. The para-military *Occident* (mostly followers of Maître Tixier-Vignancourt) and the federation of nationalist students now intensified their operations, while the 22 March Movement and other independent leftish groups were gaining so many new adherents.

All through March and April 1968 most French and foreign observers went on recording their firm conviction about the stability of De Gaulle's regime. It was, indeed, stable, as long as one ignored French youth. Even during the first days of May, several newspapers in various parts of the world alluded to De Gaulle's regime as one of the safest in the world. On 6 May, three days after the outbreak of the student revolt in Paris, *The Times* published a major article on its leader page with the title: 'France: stable, prosperous and infuriating.'

2

On Thursday 2 May a detachment of the extreme right *Occident* group attacked and set on fire the Sorbonne headquarters of the left-wing MAU (*Mouvement d'Action Universitaire*), led by graduate students and research workers. In the early afternoon, on Friday 3 May, about five hundred student militants held a protest meeting in the courtyard of the Sorbonne against the closure of the Nanterre campus. Spokesmen of the UNEF, the Nanterre *enragés* and other militant groups made speeches. University officials asked them to clear the courtyard; they went on, however, with a turbulent discussion of student politics and international affairs.

After a telephone consultation with Alain Peyrefitte, the Minister of Education, the Rector called in the police to clear the Sorbonne courtyard. The Prefect of Police, Maurice Grimau, told the Rector that he wanted the request for police intervention in writing. The request was signed.

The news that there were police detachments everywhere in

271

the vicinity of the Sorbonne drew further masses of students towards the Sorbonne. At about ten minutes to five the students outside saw the arrival of an army of police, ready for battle. They were helmeted, armed with large shields, rubber truncheons, gas grenades – everything. They marched into the courtyard through the rue des Ecoles entrance and pushed the students towards the chapel. There was hardly any resistance, since the students saw their leaders negotiating with Roger Grosperin, Assistant Director of the Paris Préfecture. This official told the leaders that the students would not be molested if they left quietly and at once. The leaders agreed and the crowd was about to disperse when another large police detachment, also heavily armed, invaded the courtyard, entering through the place de la Sorbonne entrance. Despite the pledge given a minute or so previously, the policemen surrounded the students and began to push them towards the entrance where, in groups of twenty to thirty, they were roughly thrown into Black Marias waiting close to the Sorbonne walls.

The next few minutes were like the culmination of a carefully set up laboratory experiment to examine the relevance of the 'tiny group of troublemakers' theory. With the arrest of more than 596 young men and women, the police captured all the student leaders of the Greater Paris campuses and their most militant followers.*

The students massed outside were now safely isolated from all the known 'troublemakers'. They knew only what they themselves saw. From adjacent streets they saw the police manhandling their comrades, throwing them into Black Marias. They saw the captured boys and girls through the wire mesh windows of the police vans. As the first of these nosed its way into the Place de la Sorbonne the crowd exploded in fury. Revolution, in the sense of the boiling-over of the masses, began.

The 'leaderless' students, the uncommitted students, the young men and women who usually thought only about their own future – they all were *enragés* now and roared in chorus: '*A Bas la Répression!*' They built barricades by lifting parked cars into the road; they formed human barricades round the Black Marias.

* Jacques Sauvageot, Vice-President of UNEF and some UNEF officials; Alain Krivine of the JCR; Cohn-Bendit and others from the Nanterre 22 March Movement; the activists of MAU; of FER; the extreme-left Trotskyist splinter; representatives of SNESUP, the university teachers' union; the UJC (M-L), the pro-Chinese Communist splinter-group, and others.

They threw stones; they wept and coughed as the police threw gas grenades; as the truncheons crashed on their heads; as truncheons broke legs. They wept and roared with anger.

The police went berserk. They clubbed students and old people, onlookers and demonstrators alike. Passers-by were beaten up and carted away in Black Marias. All through the afternoon, the evening and night, the battle went on. By midnight there had been over 600 arrests and nearly a thousand wounded.

The Rector closed the Sorbonne. UNEF called a protest strike of the 160,000 students of Greater Paris. SNESUP called a strike of university teachers. Grimau, the Prefect of Police, said that night that 'violence broke out spontaneously among the students gathered outside the university'. Premier Pompidou, in a later speech to the National Assembly, blamed the riots partly

. . . on determined individuals, supplied with considerable financial means, and with equipment suitable for street fighting, depending apparently on an international organization which, I think it would not be too adventurous to say, seeks not only to create subversion in Western countries, but trouble in Paris at the very moment when our capital has become the meeting place for peace in the Far East.

The 'determined individuals', that is, the student leaders and activists captured in the Sorbonne courtyard, were in police custody for twenty-four hours. The overwhelming majority of the activists, and the student leaders from Sauvageot to Cohn-Bendit, were not set free until the next evening. But that weekend four other students were sentenced to two months in prison. This act gave the students a new demand: *'Libérez nos camarades!'*

On Saturday and Sunday 4 and 5 May, the revolts of students and *lycéens* spread all over France. There were strikes and large-scale demonstrations at all provincial universities. For once, the right-wing *Figaro* and the communist *L'Humanité* agreed in their denunciation of the *groupuscules*, the tiny groups of trouble-makers, who were to be blamed for everything.

Jacques Sauvageot, vice-president of UNEF, the national student union, called a protest march for Monday morning (6 May). By nine o'clock there were already about five thousand students present. They marched round the Latin Quarter and, since the police did not attack them, they did not attack the police. In the afternoon, a large procession formed on the Quai Saint-Bernard, outside the new Science Faculty. The students of Greater

Paris were joined by many university teachers and about a thousand *lycéens*. As this large and orderly procession approached Notre Dame, they chanted with glee : *'Nous sommes un groupuscule.'* ('We are a tiny group.') As they headed towards the Sorbonne people on the balconies of their flats or on café terraces applauded the students. Teenagers from the *lycées,* girl and boy students, young and old professors, the whole procession was in a buoyant mood. They were already nearing the Sorbonne when, at about three in the afternoon, they were subjected to a totally unexpected – and unprovoked – attack by the police.

The shock of surprise was so benumbing that, at first, there was no resistance as the police waded deeply into the crowd with their flailing truncheons. But the shock was soon over and the students, the *lycéens* and the younger onlookers fought back. The small cobblestones, the *pavés,* were torn up and hurled at the police or were used to build barricades.

After their first attack had thrown the procession back towards the Boulevard Saint-Germain, the police began to bombard the students with gas grenades. There were sirens and screams and explosions, overturned cars started to burn, water canons hissed, fire engines roared and ten thousand young people fought on. There was no segregation of the sexes. Girls and boys were attacked with equal fury by the white and black police batons, and girls were just as tough, ingenious and brave fighters as the boys. The fight went on for nearly twelve hours. The Latin Quarter was enveloped in thick clouds of tear gas. The police handled brutally not only the student fighters, but also the wounded and those who were receiving first aid; they beat up Red Cross personnel, as well as elderly or middle-aged onlookers. They attacked everyone in sight.

On Tuesday 7 May some thirty thousand students and *lycéens* staged a five-hour protest march all over Paris, with the exception of the vicinity of the Sorbonne, which was in police hands. Thousands of students demonstrated in all the university towns of France.

Next day, five French Nobel prizewinners – Jacob, Kastler, Lwoff, Mauriac and Monod – sent a telegram to President De Gaulle: 'We ask you to make a personal gesture that will pacify the student revolt. Amnesty the students already penalized and reopen the faculty.' The French public opinion poll, IFOP, reported that four-fifths of Parisians were in favour of the students.

At that stage the general public was still shocked and angered by the indiscriminate police brutality. Only the cabinet seemed to be unimpressed by the previous days' demonstrations, at which over seventy thousand students and *lycéens* throughout France chanted : 'We are a tiny group.'

Education Minister Peyrefitte blamed 'specialists in agitation and elements foreign to the university' for the violence, conveniently forgetting that large-scale violence was triggered off on 3 May by the police invasion of the Sorbonne and the arrest of the participants at a student meeting. Both he and the Rector decided to call in the police not because violence had broken out, but because they, allegedly, feared that it might break out!

On Wednesday night about 20,000 students and *lycéens* marched in the Latin Quarter. They were joined by younger university teachers and research workers. Though the march lasted a long time, there was no violence. It was proved again that if the police did not attack the students, the students did not pick a fight with the police.

On Thursday 9 May the Rector and the Deans decided to reopen the Sorbonne. A few hours later Peyrefitte prohibited this. At that time there were still talks between government and students. These now broke down.

That night there was a mass meeting at the Salle de la Mutualité. Representatives of revolutionary students from Belgium, Holland, Italy, West Germany and Spain spoke to more than three thousand French students, mostly of the extreme left. Ernest Mandel, a Belgian, one of the three secretaries of the international Trotskyist movement, was feverishly applauded when he declared that the struggle of the students 'must lead to a general struggle of the working class for a socialist revolution'. It should be stressed here that this meeting (and many similar meetings) applauded no less enthusiastically other aggressively revolutionary declarations that were in strong conflict with Trotskyist strategy.

On Friday 10 May, the eve of the 'Night of the Barricades', the students' and university teachers' union (UNEF and SNESUP) called for the largest possible demonstrations against the government's refusal to release the arrested students and to reopen the Sorbonne. The demonstrators were to meet at 6.30 p.m. at the place Denfert-Rochereau, near Montparnasse. First to arrive were nearly nine thousand teenagers, mobilized by the *Comités d'action lycéens*. They were marching under black and red flags and periodically roaring *'Libérez nos camarades!'* Most of them looked like *lycéens;* neatly dressed, well-fed, with short back and sides, these revolutionaries aged between fifteen and seventeen were soon to prove with their consistency of spirit and their willingness to take pain that – unlike their parents – they had the courage of their convictions.

At the meeting place with the students and university teachers, there was a lot of 'schoolboy oratory' while the *lycéens* waited. They demanded freedom for political action in the *lycées* and pupil participation in the running of the schools. Police observers and agents of government intelligence no doubt reported the gist of the speeches. But the government was perfectly unaware that this impromptu meeting might prove to have been the first massive symptom of the shape of things to come during the seventies and eighties: the revolt of the fifteen- to eighteen-year-old trainee-intellectuals.

The vision of the Communist Party observers was distorted by 'communist racism': judging people by their class descent. And most of these boys and girls were of 'class-hostile' descent. That summer, when Italian students were maltreated by the police, Pier Paolo Pasolini expressed the typical anti-student bias of the communist 'oldies'. He wrote (in rough translation): 'Your faces are those of sons of good families, and I hate you as I hate your fathers. The good breeding comes through. ... Yesterday when you had your battle in the Valle Guilia with the police, my sympathies were with the police, because they are the sons of the poor.'

The smear campaign that *L'Humanité* and various Communist Party and trade union officials conducted against the student rebels aroused the curiosity of young workers. That afternoon and evening many hundreds of young workers came to the Latin Quarter. The consequence of what they saw (and did) during the Night of the Barricades led to unpleasant surprises for the French CP bureaucrats during the next few weeks.

There were already about 18,000 young people at the meeting place when the government sent an offer to the student leaders to reopen the Sorbonne and to withdraw the police from the Latin Quarter. The first and main student demand was not met: to release those arrested. When the proposal was put to them, the enormous crowd only roared: *'Libérez nos camarades!'* The procession first marched to the Santé Prison to demonstrate. They did not attack the police, but moved on. After a while, wherever they turned they came across black police phalanxes wearing helmets, goggles, long black raincoats, shields; their batons and gas grenade guns at the ready, the police blocked all the Seine bridges and most main approaches to the Quartier. Thirty thousand young Parisians, their numbers growing all the time, were encircled by thousands of well-protected and heavily armed riot-police; by CRS troops who soon earned the call 'CRS – SS'; by metropolitan police forces and *gendarmes mobiles*. The government mobilized an army against the young of the country. All over France there were similar confrontations.

The marchers moved down the Boulevard Saint-Germain. A further police blockade forced them up the Boul. Mich. towards the Sorbonne, now under massive police occupation. When the head of the vast column got to the Sorbonne, it became obvious that it could not move on.

Quite a few young men and women have equal right to claim that they were the first to shout: 'Let's throw out the *flics* from the Quartier!' 'The Quartier must be ours, whatever happens!'

The giant procession was halted. The wall-to-wall mass on the wide boulevard seemed to tremble for a while, then it began to throw out particles in every direction. *Groupuscules* rushed into side streets, emerged in squares and, wherever they encountered a police phalanx, built barricades. Between nine o'clock in the evening and midnight barricades mushroomed everywhere. Building sites were plundered for bricks and wood, streets and alleyways were denuded of their small cobble-stones; billboards, traffic signs and gratings were ripped up. Overturned cars, pavement-café tables and all sorts of debris were piled high. Despite Premier Pompidou's assertion that the 'uprising' was planned by a sinister conspiracy, some barricades were very amateurish affairs and none of them were built in accordance with some preconceived plan devised by an expert leader. There were no plans and no experts. The barricades were inspired by the revolutions of the past and the black police phalanxes of the present. Old ladies and all sorts of *citoyens* looked on, put their transitor radios in their windows, gave advice to the builders, dropped bars of chocolate and sandwiches.

The police did not attack the barricades. They were awaiting orders. After 10 p.m. the Rector, M. Roche, broadcast an invitation to the student leaders to open negotiations, in order to avoid a clash. As a mobile radio van had located Alain Geismar and other student leaders the negotiations were conducted by radio, with the whole of France listening in. Geismar declared that there could be no talks until the imprisoned students were freed and amnestied. The Rector urged the government to fulfil the students' demands and meanwhile asked Cohn-Bendit and other representatives to come to the Sorbonne for talks. While the talks went on the boys and girls continued building and perfecting their barricades. Thanks to mass-media reportage, all the young people living in and around the Quartier were on the streets. The curious young workers from the suburbs became participants, too.

The acting Premier, Joxe, and the Ministers of the Interior, the Army, Education and Information were in permanent consultation with President De Gaulle's advisers on security and intelligence. These men, contrary to the advice given by Roche, by the deans, by the Nobel prize-winners and contrary to common sense, ordered an all-out attack against the barricades.

The police got their orders for a synchronized all-out attack against all barricades at 2.15 a.m. The general offensive, without a declaration of war, began with a concentrated bombardment by gas grenades. They lobbed over the barricades tear gas grenades that caused violent weeping and choking, followed by CS grenades of the type used by the Americans in the Vietnam War and, lastly, offensive grenades, as used in the Algerian War, which have a considerable blast effect. Those students who protected their faces against tear gas with wet handkerchiefs soon found that the CS gas, when in contact with water, caused virulent skin-burns.*

Instead of retreating after the first concentrated gas grenade attack, the students, *lycéens* and young workers of both sexes defended their barricades with great courage. They bombarded the police with cobble-stones and anything else that could be thrown. Many policemen were immobilized when their own gas grenades were flung back at them. The fighting style of the two sides could not have differed more. The boys and girls, though enraged and outraged, though angry and in some cases moved by revolutionary fanaticism, never stooped to inhuman acts. The police did. The indescribable atrocities committed by the police during the Night of the Barricades have been filmed and photo-

* Professor Francis Kahn of the Lariboisire Hospital, declared in his report to the Russell Tribunal, that CS gas is toxic, basing his statement on evidence drawn from Vietnam, and on laboratory experiments on animals.

graphed by hundreds of professionals and private individuals. The thousands of eye-witness accounts of the horrors; of the wounded taken from stretchers and beaten up; of sadistic attacks against journalists, white-coated doctors and nurses, against old people sitting quietly in their homes; of the arrested being clubbed down – could fill and did fill volumes.

The inhabitants of the Latin Quarter were not only witnesses but also fellow victims of savage police terror. The police were not satisfied with breaking through barricades and forcing the young people to retreat. They did not rest until they could arrest and/or beat unconscious everyone they saw. Everywhere on all fronts they became infuriated when doctors and nurses tried to give first aid to the wounded. In wars, the Red Cross sign is respected. In the generation war, the police denied to young compatriots the sort of treatment that is usually accorded to an enemy.

In this cruel war *lycéens* and students of both sexes fought well. Many boys and girls displayed fantastic courage. As the students soon discovered, action did destroy faction. Political differences and ideological squabbles were forgotten. The communist bosses dreaded the idea of revolt and did their best to isolate the workers and the party faithful from the students. Nevertheless, only a few communist students stayed away from the struggle. The FER faction of the Trotskyists deserted their fellow-students on 'La Nuit des Barricades' after telling them to leave the revolution to the workers. The JCR faction of the Trotskyists, on the other hand, joined in the common fight. So did many young communist workers.

On Saturday 11 May, returning from a state visit to Afghanistan, Premier Pompidou took the initiative in placating the students by promising to release their arrested comrades and reopen the Sorbonne on Monday. But it was too late. Ten years of Gaullism had not anaesthetized the population sufficiently. Thousands of frantic parents were rushing to hospitals, jails and police stations in search of their missing children. Thousands of other parents were nursing their maltreated boys and girls at home. The sadistic mass assault of the police against French youth angered the people sufficiently to prompt them into action. The general mood of anger and distrust forced the trade-union bosses to declare a mass strike and mass demonstration for Monday. All the teachers of France, from primary schools to the universities, announced a protest strike against police brutality. Even the Com-

279

munist Party bosses came to realize that they had to join the band-waggon, at least in self-defence. So *L'Humanité,* with its usual overnight change of policy, began to pretend that Big Brother was always on the side of the students.

On Monday 13 May about one million students, workers and Parisians of all ages marched in the greatest protest demonstration of the decade. The student leaders were up front, the politicians, the trade-union leaders and the Communist Party bosses in the rear. Cohn-Bendit remarked: 'The Communist Party? Nothing gave me greater pleasure than to be at the head of a demonstration with all that Stalinist filth in the rear.'

Pompidou kept his promises. The police were withdrawn from the Sorbonne and the Quartier, the arrested students were released. Strasbourg University was already being held by students

That night, the students occupied the Sorbonne.

3

'It is not an accident that black flags now challenge the monopoly of red flags in street demonstrations. There is here the rebirth of an ideal of liberty. It is a timely reminder to some political and union leaders that a society without real democracy is a barracks.'

Albert Détraz of the *Confédération Française et Démocratique du Travail*

'In May 1968, in France, the industrial proletariat, far from being the revolutionary vanguard of society, was its dumb rearguard. . . . The most conservative, the most mystified stratum of society, the one most deeply ensnared in the trap of bureaucratic capitalism, was the working class, and more particularly that fraction of the working class which belongs to the Communist Party and the CGT.'

Jean-Marc Courday[4]

On Tuesday 14 May Premier Pompidou offered peace to the students. He also made a momentous admission when he declared in the National Assembly the most urgent task of those in authority:

'Everything must be rethought!'

But nothing really was. Bureaucratic authority was unable to think anew and act anew. The bureaucrats at the helm of the state apparatus, the directors of the Communist Party machine, the bosses of the communist-led trade-union federation CGT, were unable to grasp even the full implications of the spontaneous mass action and mass rethinking that was going on under their very noses. The rebellious actions of the *lycéens,* of students and of young workers were directed against all existing institutions, organizational patterns and methods. Acting spontaneously and independent of centralized bureaucracies, the young rebels evolved their own action committees, which proliferated everywhere in all professions and segments of French society. The committees had built-in defences against take-over by power groups. Every spokesman, every representative was permanently revocable. The committees were successful experiments in direct democracy and constant participation. These committees were about to take over old France and only an equally spontaneous alliance of Gaullists, communists, trade-union bureaucrats and right-wing generals could defeat them.

Radio Luxembourg, Europe Number One and the official France-Inter, which was less rigidly censored than TV, gave almost continuous front-line reports of the revolutionary turmoil. The whole of France learnt that the first General Assembly of students had declared the Sorbonne an autonomous popular university. It was run by a fifteen-man Occupation Committee, elected with a twenty-four-hour mandate. Members of this committee were not given a chance to be corrupted by power. They had to give an account of themselves each night to their electors and were not re-elected if they failed to satisfy them. This committee and the scores of sub-committees ran all the affairs of this republic. The Sorbonne became the capital of an independent republic of youth. Imagination took over power. The Sorbonne courtyard, the rooms and lecture halls became forums and platforms where, in an explosion of free speech, everything was critically re-examined. The old world was taken apart in endless debates, and thousands of young people struggled to dream up and invent a new world. What many wanted was the 'total re-organization of the game, as in 1793'; others wanted only radical reforms. In Edgar Morin's words, the students wanted 'to turn the courtyard of the Sorbonne into the launching pad of a revolutionary missile'.

Did they not succeed?

Students and workers, schoolboys and artists, lawyers and office employees made their new start: they went on strike, they formed action committees, they occupied schools, offices, factories. The occupation of the Sorbonne and of Strasbourg University was the first of thousands of occupations to follow. A few hours after De Gaulle arrived in Bucharest for a state visit to Roumania on 14 May the striking workers of the Sud Aviation plant at Nantes occupied their factory. This was the first factory occupation, to be followed by a great many others all over the country.

The generation war exploded everywhere in the factories. Since the Night of the Barricades, young workers had begun to turn against the majority of their mates: the TV-watchers, the docile CP members, the obedient followers of the trade-union bosses.

On 14 May men stopped working in a few workshops at the Renault plant in Cleon near Rouen. Next day about two hundred young strikers failed to persuade the night-shift to join them, so they barricaded themselves into the factory. On Thursday 16 May the factory was occupied. Coachloads of strikers went over to the Renault plant at Flis, which was also occupied.

To forestall a similar independent take-over of the vast central Renault works in the Paris suburb of Boulogne-Billancourt, the communist-led CGT sent their own occupation forces there. This move was intended to make the 25,000 workers of the Boulogne-Billancourt plant safe from infection by student revolutionaries. The workers' movement, which had immobilized French industry in a fortnight, gave a monolithic impression only to outsiders. A great many factories were originally occupied as a result of the spontaneous action of mainly young workers, others were counter-revolutionary occupations by commandos loyal to the CGT and the Communist Party.

The girls and boys working in the CALs, the action-committees of the *lycée* pupils, astonished teachers, parents and outside observers visiting their schools by their efficiency, maturity and earnestness. They, too, had their General Assembly, they, too, decided on a general strike and the occupation of their *lycées*. A great many *lycées* were actually occupied and boys and girls aged from fifteen to seventeen, breaking out from the prison of docile passivity, invited their teachers and parents to participate in their efforts to reform the French educational system. They were most businesslike in drafting their proposals for school reform. (Many of their proposals were, and still are, taken seriously.) In fact, the behaviour of the radical *lycéens* was far more earnest and dignified than that of the students on some campuses.

15 May: Revolutionary students occupy the Odéon theatre. The government fears that revolutionary youth may take over the radio and television buildings, the central post office and other vital focal points. The Communist Party and the CGT telephone their orders to their officials on the spot, instructing that students are to be stopped from entering factories and other buildings under their control. The left-wing social democratic, Catholic trade-union federation, the CFDT, declares its sympathy for the student movement.

16 May: The Communist Party hastens to the aid of the Gaullist regime. It issues a statement denouncing the proposed march on the radio station as a 'provocation'. About a thousand students march from Paris to the Renault plant at Boulogne-Billancourt. Among the banners they carry, one says: 'This flag of struggle will pass to the workers from our fragile hands.'

The workers, however, do not care for the flag of struggle. Approaching the factory gates, the students find a lorry parked across the road, barring the way. A CGT official informs them by loudspeaker that they cannot go in. The metal gates are bolted. The CGT man speaks about the dangers of provocation: 'If the students go too near the gates, this will give the management an excuse for calling in the police.' Sauvageot leader of the UNEF: 'When we arrived, I was much struck by the fact that only the young workers came to welcome us.' The students had more allies among the half a million unemployed workers, many among them aged between eighteen and twenty-six.

18 May: President De Gaulle returns post-haste from Roumania. Two million workers are on strike. The country is at a standstill: no air or rail traffic, no public transport in Paris and the other cities, no post.

22 May: Over ten million people on strike. The extra-parliamentary opposition, independent of all political parties, grows. Hundreds and hundreds of action committees are established by revolutionary adults in offices, city districts, rural areas. The revolutionaries are intent on toppling the regime. Their efforts are sabotaged by the workers' leaders, who choose this day to announce their readiness to negotiate with the management and the government over wage claims. Georges Séguy, CGT leader and member of the Communist Central Committee, attacks factory occupation and workers' control: 'Self-management is a hollow formula: what the workers want is the immediate satisfaction of their claims.'

24 May: The most dangerous day for the Gaullist state and for the regime which has continued without vital changes since the death of Napoleon Bonaparte. The regime is in retreat. The revolutionary mood of the young workers threatens to infect their mates. To strengthen the influence of the trade unions and to canalize the gigantic strike movement into 'normal' channels, the government announces round-table discusions with trade unions and employers about wage claims. President De Gaulle announces a referendum on his great plan for a new start based on 'participation'. If it is rejected, he will resign. The plans are vague but 'participation' is a magic word, a word taken from the vocabulary of the young rebels. There is an implied promise that participation will mean a greater say for people in their own affairs; less power for the big bosses in industry, and perhaps even some profit-sharing.

The communist-led CGT organizes well-disciplined demonstrations in two different parts of Paris in support of the strike. After the peaceful dispersal of these marches, young workers join the demonstration called by the UNEF, the 22 March Movement, SNESUP and others. The 22 March Movement wants this demonstration to be turned into an offensive to 'plant the banner of revolution' all over Paris. They want to occupy key buildings. The UNEF leaders, communist and Trotskyist student spokesmen are against this plan; nevertheless, they join the revolutionaries in their appeal for a massed assembly at the Gare de Lyon. There, about 20,000 young men and women listen to De Gaulle's referendum speech, which inflames most of them. During the speech, further demonstrators keep streaming into the area. By the time the main column and smaller columns of demonstrators start to march towards their objectives, and skirmishes begin with the police, their numbers are approaching 100,000.

Young workers carry banners proclaiming: 'Don't give in to Séguy!', 'Power is in the street!', 'Power for the workers!' They, and the students with their banners ('Adieu De Gaulle!'), are intent on smashing the regime by occupying key points. The columns, after failing to take the Town Hall, which was too heavily defended, capture the Stock-Exchange and set it on fire with shouts of: 'Burn down the temple of capitalism.'

Paris was a battlefield. Barricades were erected in several districts and in many provincial towns. It was the third 'bloody Friday' (after 3 and 10 May). Both sides fought with far greater vehemence than on the previous occasions. The gas grenades were fired by the police straight, and at times point-blank, at their young opponents. In the Latin Quarter a young man of twenty-six was killed by a shell fragment. In the savage battles in the provincial cities there were many seriously wounded. In Lyons, a police inspector was killed by an empty lorry sent rolling against a police barrier by the students.

The Gaullist regime and the 'old form of the game' existing since Napoleonic times had most helpful allies in the Communist Party, the CGT, and in the persons of many reformist student leaders. Those who believe that 24 May could have marked the end of the old order, maintain :

Paris was in the hands of the demonstrators, the Revolution had started in earnest ! The police could not possibly guard all the public buildings and all the strategic points : the Elysée, the Hôtel de Ville, the bridges, the ORTF [the French Broadcasting Service].... Everyone felt it and wanted to go on. *But then the political boys stepped in.* It was a leader of the far-left JCR [Revolutionary Communist Youth] who, in the place de l'Opéra, took charge and turned us back towards the Latin Quarter.... It was officers of the UNEF and PSU who stopped us taking the Ministry of Finance and the Ministry of Justice. . . . *As for us, we failed to realise how easy it would have been to sweep all these nobodies away.*

It is now clear that if, on 25 May, Paris had woken to find the most important Ministries occupied, Gaullism would have caved in at once—the more so as similar actions would have taken place all over the country.[5]

In fact similar actions did take place in various parts of France. Revolutionary peasants blocked roads, formed action committees and prepared for take-overs. The important city of Nantes was entirely taken over by the revolutionaries and was run from 26-31 May by the central strike committee of the students', workers' and peasants' unions. The Sud Aviation plant in Nantes was the first occupied factory in the country at which the revolutionary workers were immediately joined by students and *lycéens*. This movement culminated in the six days' rule of the Rebel Committee in complete independence from all state and local authorities.

There were signs in various other parts of the country, too, that the power of the Gaullist state had caved in as soon as it was seriously challenged by determined revolutionaries. But the trade unions were already negotiating about wages, the citizens had had enough of the disruption of normal life and politicians on the Left were ready to take over the leadership of the revolution from the people who had fought for it and in it.

On 27 May the CGT called for an end to the factory occupations and the strike and urged the acceptance of a substantial rise in wages. On 29 May De Gaulle disappeared to confer with his army chiefs about military intervention, if necessary. Next day he made the notorious speech to the nation that turned the tide. He spoke against communist subversion, against the threat of communist dictatorship. In this speech the communists, who were President De Gaulle's most loyal opposition, who were the most consistent enemies of all revolutionary *lycéens,* students and young workers now served the General in their other, vital role, as His Excellency's Most Important Villains. The President offered France, in effect, a choice between a Stalinist regime of terror and his enlightened rule.

There were tanks on the outskirts of Paris. The right-wing generals were ready to defend France against the evils of communism; the workers were ready to accept wage rises; and the *citoyens* were ready to vote for law and order.

And so Gaullism was saved. And so the power of the French communist bureaucrats was saved, too; and so France again had a stable regime.

For how long?

4

In the name of huge and distant truths lies
were spread through the lives of the people.'
Prague student, March 1968

The most courageous and extremely prudent attempt in Czechoslovakia to transform the totalitarian system forced on them by Moscow into 'communism with a human face' was not the outcome of a youth revolt nor of an exclusively 'youth do'. But students certainly gave an impetus to the political reform movement, and without the moral stand, courage and self-discipline of Czechoslovak youth the Czechoslovak people could not have inflicted such an immense moral defeat on the bureaucratic despotism of the USSR in 1968.

Owing to most exceptional circumstances, from January to May 1968, it almost seemed likely that the peaceful democratization and normalization of communism was possible within the Soviet bloc. This would have been the peaceful victory of the Third Revolution that began in Kronstadt in 1921 and has flared up periodically over the decades.

By 1967 Czechoslovakia had reached a critical situation. The ills which two decades of terrorist dictatorship had brought were recognized, but the nature of the regime made the application of remedies impossible. If somebody came up with an idea that differed from the view of a top official his initiative was doomed from the outset. Czechoslovakia, a developed country, was gradually turned into an undeveloped one by mindless monopoly bureaucracy. The looming economic crisis was coupled with a near-total moral bankruptcy. Although statues of Stalin had been removed and streets called after him renamed, the victims of the show trials were not rehabilitated as elsewhere, and the party boss and President Antony Novotny did not permit the replacement of any of the compulsory lies even with new half-truths. The civil liberties guaranteed by the constitution were annulled by the existing criminal code. Censorship was far more severe than a hundred years earlier under the Hapsburg empire. The writers were in open revolt against censorship.

Like the writers, students and other young people had also caused great concern to the party bureaucrats by their independence of mind and their refusal to accept compulsory lies or ready-made opinions. The party's hypocritical lip-service to 'de-Stalinization' only angered young people. Students used every opportunity for verbal and written protest against this situation. One student, for instance, wrote: 'Despite all the assurances given by many people, rarely has a young generation had to live through so many disappointments as we have. . . . Young people keep asking: "What principles have changed in this structure and what guarantees are there that the past will never be repeated?" '

President Novotny and many of the then party-state leaders were deeply implicated in the crimes of the country's long Stalinist era. The workers, like everyone else in the country, had no means of self-defence against arbitrary, oppressive rule and against severe exploitation by the new ruling class. The great lie that made their lives miserable was the pretence that the means of production were owned by the working class. In fact there was bureaucratic ownership of the means of production and the defenceless working class could not exercise the least little bit of economic, social or political power.

Like the students, the workers, too, strove for 'bourgeois-democratic freedoms'. They wanted to have an organized system of self-defence against the ruling bureaucracy by having trade unions completely independent of the state and with the right to organize economic and political strikes.

Although university students continually demanded to have their own organizations, they had to belong to the national organization of all young people. This way the students were thrown together with restive young workers.

As in Hungary in 1956, the long years of dull despotism and pointless misery created a vast negative unity in the people as a whole.

The event that sparked off the fateful Czechoslovak Third Revolution occurred on a cold and dark October evening in 1967. In the Strahov district of Prague there was a power failure. That year people had got used to almost nightly power failures. This time students whose hostels were in the district emerged from their rooms carrying candles and slowly formed a procession, about a thousand strong, shouting 'We want light! We want to study! We want light!' As they marched, here and there police cars barred their way. Finally, when the police commandant felt that he had large enough forces, he gave orders to disperse the students. By this time the crowd was so dense that the students in the front rows had no chance of retreating and tried to hold back the oncoming police cars with their hands. The police started to use their clubs. Some policemen, as they beat the students, shouted 'There's your light.' As the crowd began to retreat the police attacked them with tear gas bombs. All these scenes were filmed by newsreel and TV cameras.*

* In March 1968 Prague cinemas had on their programmes a newsreel which gave the true story of these events, with eyewitness accounts, interviews with professors and with hospital staff who had attended the students beaten by the police. About the same time an official police declaration admitted that the students' complaints were justified, and that during the last period of the Novotny regime lies had been broadcast and printed about the event.

Next day the press gave a horribly distorted account of these incidents. The students were described as unruly hooligans and stooges of capitalism and were accused of having attacked innocent policemen, who were quietly minding their own business. These lies angered the students even more than the unprovoked police violence. Incensed by this latest demonstration of the existence of organized public falsehood, the students circulated their own roneoed version of the night of police brutality. Students, young intellectuals and young workers began to condemn quite openly the 'lack of freedom and humanism' in the country. Their spontaneous but very widespread campaign gave an impetus to the process of democratization. The majority of the Central Committee wanted change, too. On 5 January 1968 Alexander Dubcek replaced Novotny as First Secretary of the CP. Under his leadership the Communist Party, which 'at the beginning of January had reached the edge of its deepest moral and political crisis [had] won unbelievably high moral credit within half a year through its will and determination for reform.'[7]

Dubcek wanted, as he put it, the ruling Communist Party to rely on 'free and fully informed public opinion instead of discredited bureaucratic police methods'. A freedom of expression unknown for twenty years prevailed; the abolition of censorship was demanded by the censors themselves. On 9 April 1968 the Czechoslovak Communist Party's Action Programme was outlined. Its objects were to provide a basis for genuine popular support for the CP by carrying out democratic reforms – freedom of speech and the press and judicial reforms, including the complete rehabilitation of all victims of injustice in the fifties. Politically, Czechoslovakia was to remain firmly within the socialist camp. There was no question of secession from the Warsaw Military Pact or of pursuing a policy of neutrality, as Imre Nagy and the Hungarian Revolution had done on 1 November 1956.

From January 1968 onwards the great negative unity of the people was replaced by a curious positive unity. A people who passionately wanted truth and freedom of speech after twenty years under the yoke of nauseating lies, big and small, was prepared to moderate its passion with prudence. Young and old did their best, within reason, not to provoke the Kremlin rulers. But this was not enough. The emergence of free public opinion in Czechoslovakia angered and frightened the USSR leaders. This, and the other aspects of democratization, endangered, according to them, the bureaucratic dictatorship of the central apparatus. They were afraid that the Czech example would be infectious. They were determined to ignore the vital difference between Czechoslovak communism with freedom of speech, and the multi-party system which had sprung up during the Hungarian Revolution. They associated civil liberties with imperialist capitalism.

As a sad symptom of the times, Czech students were reminded of the fact that the Kremlin rulers and the young Western revolutionaries who opposed them had one thing in common: both were captives of their respective ideologies.

In April 1968, a week before he was shot in Berlin by a right-wing fanatic, Rudi Dutschke, one of the best-known spokesmen of the revolutionary students' movement in West Germany, visited Prague to discuss democratization in Czechoslovakia with students at Charles University. This meeting revealed that there was an immense gap between the thinking of the anti-authoritarian Western SDS students and that of the Prague students. Dutschke, like his SDS comrades, regarded everything from an intense ideological viewpoint. On many basic questions Dutschke's was a closed mind. The Czech students regarded an open-minded approach about anything and everything as the basis of a free and humane society. They fought, and meant to continue to fight, for the right to remain open-minded. They distrusted lofty abstractions if these were part of a closed system of thought. It was a total ideology that had brought the Czechoslovak people slavery coupled with moral and economic bankruptcy.

Dutschke was worried lest the Czechoslovak attempt to attain 'communism with a human face' should lead to the 'weakening of the anti-imperialist camp'. There was a time when Dutschke was sick and tired of Marxist-Leninist phrase-mongering. He had escaped from East Germany in 1961, two days before the Berlin Wall was built. Since that time he had been an outspoken critic of the rule of bureaucracy and the 'alienation between the party and the masses' in the USSR. In time, however, he and his friends began working out their own ideology, cleansing Marxism from what they called Stalinist distortions. This neo-Marxism became a fighting ideology during the struggles against the West German regime, and it blinded its adherents to the realities within the Soviet bloc.

As for the Prague students, as one of them put it: 'It's embarrassing really, to sit down with Western students, and find *them* quoting Marxist phrases at *you!* Just when we are reaching out for a new, pragmatic approach ... we're enveloped once again in this tear-gas of German metaphysics. ... No, thank you! We need advice neither from Herr Ulbricht, nor from Herr Dutschke's friends.'

It was a long meeting. Dutschke answered questions and comments for six hours. 'Following the discussion, a blonde Czech girl, who had argued with Dutschke at length, apologized to him for scoffing at his ideas. He laughed and said it was good for him to learn something about *another historical situation.*'[8]

The standpoint of the Prague students was summarized later by one of their spokesman, Jan Kavan:

For us, the classic civil liberties assume the utmost importance. In a socialist society, freedom of speech, freedom of the press, freedom of assembly and freedom of association are essential if the people are to exercise any control at all. ... I have often been told by my friends in Western Europe that we are only fighting for bourgeois-democratic freedoms. But somehow I cannot seem to distinguish between capitalist freedoms and socialist freedoms. What I recognise are basic human freedoms.[9]

Prague students and, indeed, the whole of Czechoslovakia were guided in their actions by the historical situation within the Soviet world. They were determined to avoid steps like those which provoked the Soviet occupation of Hungary in 1956. They were also determined that their democratization should not be undone during the years to come, as happened to the Poles after their bloodless revolution in 1956.

In the spring of 1968, in Warsaw and other university towns in Poland, the police led one brutal offensive after another against students demonstrating for civil liberties. The Prague students were busy studying a famous open letter that two young Warsaw university lecturers, Jacek Kuron and Karol Modzelewski, had written to the party leadership in 1964. They were imprisoned for it – for three and three and a half years respectively – but the text of their letter had been circulating again in many countries, including Czechoslovakia. To Kuron and Modzelewski, the Polish 'October' of 1956 was the 'first anti-bureaucratic revolution' and they discussed the reasons why it had proved to be a fiasco. The revolution had petered out because the more liberal elements of the party leadership had succeeded in bringing in measures that conciliated the masses. Eventually, however, press censorship was reimposed and internal party discussion was halted. 'In this way, all the achievements of October which exceeded the framework of an internal reform of the system were repudiated and the October Left was finally crushed.'

The behaviour of young Czechoslovaks before and after the Soviet occupation was exemplary in its sanity and courage. They stepped through the boundaries of their self-imposed prudence only if and when they were provoked in the extreme. Countless numbers of young men and women risked their lives in order to show the world that the Czechoslovak people unanimously backed their leaders. Together with the workers and everyone else in the country, young people fought against the re-imposition of bureaucratic despotism and the great lie, for as long as this was humanly possible.

In November 1968, there was a total university strike. The worker-student committees that were so difficult to set up in France were a great success in Prague and elsewhere. In the big factories workers elected workers' councils and mobilized people in the defence of popular interests and classic civil liberties. The co-operation between students and workers was smooth and efficient.

When, by 1969, it became obvious that 'communism with a human face' was about to be strangled by the Kremlin rulers, youth gave a last warning. On 16 January 1969, Jan Palach, a twenty-one-year-old philosophy student, burned himself to death in Prague's Wenceslas Square in support of demands for the abolition of censorship, a ban on *Zpravy* (the publication of the Soviet occupation troops), and the resignation of Soviet Quislings.

Palach handed a letter to a friend the day before his death. After enumerating their demands, the letter concluded:

Should these demands not be met within five days, and should the people not call a general strike on their behalf, new torches will flare up.

Realize that it might well be your sons and daughters or your brothers and sisters and loved ones who may be destined to become flaming torches, and that their deaths may be caused by your attitude; their lives are in your hands. You can become saviours or murderers.

I would like to warn the staff and workers of the CKD in Prague that your children are among those involved. With greetings.

The Torch

P.S. But I am convinced that our people will not require a further light to guide it.

XII

'A MAN LOOKETH UPON HIS SON AS AN ENEMY'

'The land spins around like a potter's wheel. . . . Nay, but great and small say: "I wish I were dead". . . . A man looketh upon his son as an enemy.'

Leiden Papyrus I: Ipuwer to the King at the time of the break-up of the Old Kingdom, about 2500 BC.[1]

'A society that hates its young people has no future.'

Frederick Dutton[2]

1

When in 1855 two hundred thousand Londoners gathered in Hyde Park to protest against the licensing laws, an eyewitness called Karl Marx exclaimed: 'The English Revolution has begun.'

What would have been his reaction had he witnessed such a tremendous spectacle as the '1968 Show' that we, of the global village, have seen on our television screens? What would have been his exclamation had he seen all the horror and all the glory that was Paris and Prague in 1968 and the rest of the 'show' in which unarmed young people in more than a thousand cities of the world were attacked by gas-masked police, planes, helicopters, tanks and armoured cars? What would he have said about the millions of students who risked pain, prison and even death in order to act as the critical conscience of their society?

The year 1968 clearly marked the beginning of a new phase in the civil war between the generations. The equipment of common sense and the weapon of logic began to be replaced by the logic of weapons.

Significantly, hatred of youth became most violent in a country in which tens of thousands of students demonstrated their tolerance, their prudence and many other civic virtues: in the United States of America.

One of the surprises of 1968 was the great, and totally unexpected success of the 'youth crusade' for Senator Eugene McCarthy's presidential candidacy. At the beginning of Senator McCarthy's bid for the Democratic nomination, it was described as an entirely hopeless gesture, a mere symbolic act, by all American political experts. The Senator had no campaign organization, no financial backing and no power bases in the Democratic political machine. Yet the student activists and their youth crusade for McCarthy helped the Senator to a series of victories, each of which surprised the political pundits.

One of the starting points of this youth crusade was the University of Wisconsin. In 1967 it seemed most unlikely that this university would become a centre of large-scale student activism. In October 1967 there were only about 300 activists demonstrating against the Vietnam War. Their sit-in and demonstration led to an encounter with the police, and police brutality led in its turn to a great increase in the number of student activists.

After these events, a girl student at the University of Wisconsin told newspapermen: 'I've never marched, I've never demonstrated. But when I came out of my class and saw these policemen bashing in heads and throwing tear-gas grenades, that did it. I shall be up there demonstrating next time.'

The small groups of Wisconsin and other militants of 1967 produced some of the 1968 pro-McCarthy student campaigners whose good sense and political maturity were admired by many thoughtful Americans. The 'Students for McCarthy' movement was launched after the Senator made his lone stand against President Johnson and the Vietnam War. Soon thousands upon thousands of students of both sexes showed that they were willing and able to take on gigantic tasks in a good cause. It was a minor, but telling point that they were also willing to cut their long hair, shave off their beards and, instead of their ultra-casual gear, wear clothes that conservative American adults would approve of. Their work was most effective. Many Americans agreed at the time with the assessment of Anthony Howard, Washington correspondent of the *Observer,* who wrote:

Senator Gene McCarthy's student army is as extraordinary a weapon as has ever been forged in the whole history of American politics. . . . No one knows exactly how it all started—least of all the cigar-smoking 'old pros' of American politics who still betray the bewildered, bemused expression of men not knowing quite what hit them.[3]

In the end the political machine won against the young Democrats. But in the spring of 1968 many newspapers throughout the world carried headlines like these: STUDENT CRUSADERS ROCK LBJ. . . . YOUTH ENDANGERS JOHNSON'S POSITION.

Much of President Johnson's boundless unpopularity was of his own creation. His political opponents and young critics simply had to quote in proper sequence from his speeches on the Dominican Republic or on Vietnam in order to expose what was almost too politely called Johnson's 'credibility gap'. For years tens of thousands of young voices had shouted: 'Hey, hey LBJ – How many kids did you kill today?' During 1967 and early 1968 LBJ was shown again and again that the young opponents of the Vietnam War had made it virtually impossible for him to appear in any large or small political gathering.

During the ferociously stubborn Johnson-Rusk leadership, the bombing of South Vietnam reached the level of nearly 130,000 tons a month: two Hiroshimas a week. The napalming of suspect South Vietnamese villages, the defoliation crusades in South and North Vietnam, unwilling young Americans sent to their deaths – all this created an equally ferocious stubbornness in the anti-war camp of youth. In the end their opposition played a major role in President Johnson's decision not to run again for the presidency.

The prudence and effectiveness of McCarthy's student army and the realization that the young peaceniks represented a real threat to the 'bomb-and-napalm generation' only increased the hatred felt against the young. Student power and youth power were no longer empty slogans but a sign that 'the game may be changing'.

The history of the past few years and the present realization of the potential power of the young led directly to an escalation of the civil war between the generations. The outbreaks became more frequent and more violent during 1968 than in previous years. Student protests became more numerous and far more bitter. The adult authorities began to realize that student dissent and revolt knew no national or ideological frontiers; yet for this very reason, they were determined brutally to suppress local outbreaks. If student protest gave the impression of a world-wide epidemic, so did the over-reaction of the police and the military.

The police went berserk in many countries in the five continents when faced with demonstrating youth, and committed far graver offences against law and order than the demonstrators themselves. The horribly growing prejudice against youth and the hatred of students had the greatest effect on policemen, particularly in countries like the United States where they are 'underpaid and under-educated'.[4]

According to the President's National Advisory Commission on Civil Disorders, it became evident during the 1967 race riots that 'the racial hate that is splitting US society affected to a pathological degree the police and the trigger-happy National Guard'. These two used 'excessive and unjustified force, killed innocent bystanders and carried out senseless reprisals just when the disorders had begun to die down by shooting up shops run by Negroes'. Of the twenty-six people killed between 12 and 17 July 'at last eleven homicides were matters of grave concern and should be exhaustively and quickly investigated'.

Among the ten members of the commission there were two former governors, a bishop, several lawyers and two company chairmen. The commission's meticulously documented 1,489-page report angered much of American public opinion by its objectivity.

During the second part of 1967 it had already become evident that the racial hatred that was splitting American society was matched, if not surpassed, by the hatred that the no-longer-young felt for the young. Hippies, dissenters and war-resisters were regarded by many law-and-order-abiding adults as not deserving any legal rights – they should be instantly punished for what they were. One of the Deans of New York City College, Eugene Avalon said about them in November 1967: 'The first thing I'd do with those kids is pour a bottle of castor oil down their throats, just like Mussolini did, to clean out their insides. Then I'd throw each of them into a vat of lye and get their outsides clean. Then I'd give each of them a haircut and a shave and then I might talk to them.'

Also in November 1967, Captain Eddie Rickenbacker, seventy-seven, the First World War flying ace, told the National Press Club in Washington: 'If I had my way, I'd give draft-card burners a good lashing and a good haircut; I would give beatniks the same, and get a good old-fashioned horse-curry brush and give them a good bang. I'd put these odds and ends out in front in

Vietnam to fight with the enemy in front and bayonets in the back.'

The college dean who was eager to imitate Mussolini and the hundreds of after-dinner speakers who suggested forced labour and worse for long-haired young men were rarely reminded by the press that in their eagerness they were following in the footsteps of Hitler, with the difference that their Jews were the young.

Some government officials resorted to lies in order to smear the students. On 13 January 1968 the Pennsylvania Commissioner for the Blind announced that six students had gone blind after staring at the sun while under the influence of LSD. Newspapers all over the world carried the tragic story of how 'six students went to a wood next to their college in Western Pennsylvania, took LSD, stretched out on the grass and stared into the sun. Because of LSD they did not realize that they were looking into the sun. Some other students found them in the evening, blind and helpless.' When the Pennsylvania Attorney General began to investigate, the Commissioner for the Blind confessed that the story was invented and that he himself had told a secretary to include it in a report to the Department of Health in Washington. The report of this confession, however, did not hit the front pages of newspapers.

Similarly, the lie that student demonstrators daubed themselves with tomato ketchup, red ink or red paint to appear injured was stated in newspaper reports or in captions under photos in many countries. Several London newspapers for instance, carried a picture after the anti-Vietnam War demonstration on 27 October 1968 of a student being led away by policemen with his face covered in what the police said was red paint. A few days later Scotland Yard admitted that after investigation it turned out to have been blood. The picture with the untrue caption was prominently featured, while the truth received but a few lines.

During this period Dr S. I. Hayakawa, President of the San Francisco State College, defended the right of the riot police to attack peaceful students trying to go to their classes. He declared: 'There are no innocent bystanders in this situation. A bystander, even of innocent intent, serves to shield with his body the activities of trouble makers.'[5] And since in police practice troublemakers have to be instantly punished without any judicial process, innocent bystanders have to take the same punishment.

This climate of hatred led in 1968 to a series of major and minor police riots in the USA. Many US policemen seemed to regard children, too, as enemies. For instance, in Waterbury, Connecticut, on 3 April 1968, a peaceful group of children was gassed on the flimsiest of pretexts. About 150 boys and girls between nine and fifteen gathered to watch two girls who began to fight on their way home. Policemen rushing to the scene used the chemical spray Mace to disperse them. The police superintendent hastened to explain that 'the officers were only doing their duty'.

2

One typical major police riot was that in Chicago in August 1968, during the Democratic Convention. Before this convention many US and foreign quality newspapers reported that the majority of the members of the Democratic Party would (if it had been in their power) have elected Senator Eugene McCarthy as their presidential candidate. The party machinery, however, gives no chance for a one-man-one-vote decision within the party. The young protesters had at least some rational basis for using their democratic rights by demonstrating their dissent. They also protested in a provocative manner against the war in Vietnam and against 'fat, dieting leaders in Washington ordering the destruction of the rice fields of a poor, hungry people'.[6]

The outrages committed by the Chicago police against law and order were typical of what became known as 'police riots', encouraged and prompted by higher authorities. In this case the prompter was Mayor Daley, who following rioting earlier that year had ordered the police to 'shoot to kill arsonists and shoot to maim looters'. This was a proclamation to the effect that in the Chicago police state the judicial system of the United States was not applicable. Policemen were ordered to act as instant judges and instant executioners. After such prompting, the Chicago police riot during the Democratic Convention surprised nobody. The television viewers of America and the world saw scenes that might have been part of a horror film about guerrilla war in a city. The only difference was that in a guerrilla war both sides are armed. In Chicago, as in officially encouraged police riots elsewhere, the police were protected by shields, steel helmets, gas masks; the police were heavily armed and the young demonstrators were

According to the authoritative Walker report on these events, unprotected and unarmed.

299

released by Dr Milton Eisenhower, chairman of the Commission on Violence:

The vast majority of the demonstrators were intent on expressing by peaceful means their dissent, either from society generally or from the Administration's policies in Vietnam.

... The nature of the response was unrestrained and indiscriminate police violence on many, many occasions, particularly at night. ... The police had been conditioned to expect that violence against the demonstrators would be condoned by city officials.

... The weight of violence was overwhelmingly on the side of the police. ... Their violence was often inflicted upon persons who had broken no law, disobeyed no order, made no threat.

The report found that during the clashes on 25 and 26 August the attacks by the Chicago police on peaceful demonstrators, innocent bystanders and reporters were often 'ferocious, malicious, mindless and amounted to ... what can only be called a police riot'.

It was also typical of many other occasions in that a large proportion of the American public was not angered by the unspeakable police brutality in Chicago, but by the television and radio networks and the quality newspapers for exposing it. A fairly large proportion of American adults of both sexes hated the dissident youths with greater intensity than any enemies against which US armies had fought in the past. When newspapers reported that policemen treated and arrested young as the Gestapo treated their victims, many American grown-ups made it obvious that they thought that against peaceniks any sort of violence is justified.

The world-wide epidemic of officially encouraged police riots had spread quite well by this time. The proverbially staid and sober Swiss authorities were also infected by it. In fact the Zurich police staged their riot a good two months before that of their Chicago counterparts. On 29 and 30 June 1968 10,000 young people demonstrated in Zurich for an autonomous youth centre and against police brutality. The police attacked with water cannons and with baton charges. More than 200 young people were hospitalized and about 250 were arrested. The Zurich police went really berserk when they had the arrested young at their mercy. After the young people were finally released, eighteen well-known intellectuals led by the writer Max Frisch published the *Zurich Manifesto*, in which they stated that there was 'a pogrom against youth'. The *Zürcher Manifest* group later published its *Dokumentation I,* ninety-six closely typed pages of eyewitness accounts of police brutality. According to this, the arrested demonstrators were beaten up and tortured by the police; many were stripped naked before the beatings; girls were beaten on their genitals, boys until they became unconscious. *Sie und Er,* the Swiss illustrated magazine, also published a large exposé. And, as in Chicago, the Zurich police received hundreds of presents, flowers and offers of support from the numerous youth-haters after these revelations.

In Zurich and Chicago and in hundreds of other cities of the world, the police, contrary to the principles of law and order, punished dissent, legal or illegal demonstration with ferocious brutality. The fact that this type of police rioting broke out with increasing frequency during 1968 and 1969 demonstrated that adult societies do not insist on law and order whenever the victims of law-breaking are young people.

The over-reaction to revolutionary movements was even greater. In these two years riot squads, the regular army and paratroops helped the police to fight against high-school and university students in more than thirty countries. In the era in which the two super-powers based their safety on their capacity to 'over-kill' potential opponents, the murderous war against young rebels had the approval of the majority of public opinion.

In 1967 there were only a few Ohnesorgs, in 1968 there were already hundreds. In Brazil, in Rio de Janeiro, four students were killed by police bullets during disturbances in April and June. In the Argentine on 31 May twenty people were killed during demonstrations protesting against the earlier killing of three students. In Mexico the revolutionary movement of high-school and university students led to several massacres of youth. The 1968 *Manifesto to World Youth* issued by this movement stated:

We students must become the critical conscience of our countries. . . . [In Mexico] we have broken the thirty years of demagoguery and official lies and . . . demand the democratization of our country, the unrestricted application of the constitution, an end to government and trade-union corruption, chronic unemployment and to the misery which marks the Mexican countryside.

The Mexican regime that during the 1956-58 rural unrest ordered the bombing and strafing of several – predominantly Indio – villages, one of which was only thirty-odd miles from

Acapulco, used no less drastic measures against the restive inhabitants of the cities. The wave of political strikes in 1956-8 staged by industrial and intellectual workers, from railway men to doctors of medicine, was brutally suppressed. Doctors whose only crime was striking were summarily deported. Thousands of strikers were arrested and many of them were still in detention after ten years or more, without any charges being brought against them. These and other illegally held political prisoners numbered about three thousand in 1968.

Like the political prisoners, the Indios, the original inhabitants of Mexico, also waited in vain for the 'unrestricted application of the constitution'. During one of the demonstrations in Mexico City an Indio student carried a poster with the statement: 'I have been an Indio for 428 years and I am fed up.'

The student demonstrations in the summer of 1968 were caused by the fact that the Mexican regime was moving not towards democratization, but towards full military dictatorship. The student movement represented a grave danger to the repressive regime because Mexico happened to be one of the youngest countries in the world. More than sixty per cent of its forty-eight million people were under twenty years of age. Feeling heavily outnumbered by the young, not only the police and the army, but also the entire government seemed to go mad. The adult state staged a riot against the protesting young. Demonstrating students were attacked by machine-gun units, by armoured cars, tanks, armed helicopters and planes.

In July, August and September 1968 at least two hundred Mexican university and secondary-school students were killed by the police and the army. This was, however, not enough for certain quarters. On 2 October, at a time when student unrest had clearly calmed down, the government ordered a surprise attack on a student rally in the Plaza de las Tres Culturas in Mexico City. It was almost like an ambush. As the student rally was about to end peacefully, army helicopters fired green flares as a sign for the plain-clothes men of the police and of the *Guardias Presidenciales* to seize student leaders addressing the meeting and to begin firing on the public. After the provocative shootings, the army, in a well-synchronized operation, moved in, firing indiscriminately.

These events were witnessed by hundreds of foreign journalists from all over the world who had came to cover the Olympic

Games. In the Plaza de las Tres Culturas alone over a hundred young people were killed. Among the thousands of wounded were several journalists. Oriana Fallaci, for instance, was wounded three times while she watched the scene from the 'Orator's Balcony'. Later she was dragged down the stairs by her hair and was placed under arrest in hospital. In that hospital, according to newspaper reports, the scores of wounded lying on the floor, many with smashed faces, reduced doctors to tears.

The plain-clothes agents of the police and of the presidential guards, who mingled with the crowd to start the shooting, were easily distinguishable because they all wore a white glove on one hand. Journalists were maltreated mainly because they evidently recognized the clumsy *agents provocateurs*.

The student council's statement accused the police of having provoked the shooting, which was 'one of the most bloody political crimes in our history'. A team of *Sunday Times* reporters described the event as a 'massacre' and wrote that 'violence so far appears to have been something which government forces have initiated'. Maryvonne Fear, writing in the *Guardian*, commented: 'The killings this week have been nothing new. In the last week of July alone, thirty-two students were killed. So many have disappeared since, that it is impossible to estimate how many died in August and September.' In 1968, the killings of this or that week 'were nothing new', if the victims were young. It was a war between the generations and, as in wars, the men who killed the enemy were regarded as brave men doing their duty. None of the policemen or troopers were tried for killing the young of their own country. It was a year of escalation both in the Vietnam War and in the generation war. Two American scientists who made a study of the devastated areas in Vietnam calculated that in 1968 no fewer than 2,600,000 craters up to 30ft deep and 45ft wide were left after B52 bombing. The moonscaping of Vietnam continued in 1969, and so did the generation war.

By 1969, American society was entirely split in two by the hatred the majority of adults felt for the young. How far adult America was blinded by youth hatred was demonstrated in May 1969 in Berkeley, California, when the alleged offences of illegally establishing a 'People's Park' and planting trees and flowers was suppressed by bayonets, by firing at people and killing them, and by attacking the encircled enemy (young and not-young

303

Americans) from the air by means of helicopters spraying the same nerve gas that is used against the Vietcong.

On a large vacant lot owned by the university, students and the local residents began to set up a People's Park on 20 April. Local merchants contributed money and supplies. Over the next three and a half weeks the park blossomed and grew. A thousand people used the park every weekday, and on weekends nearly 5,000 a day came to plant flowers and to cultivate the turf. Meanwhile, the university authorities were uncertain whether to start proceedings. At a mass meeting of 15,000 students, eighty-five per cent supported the People's Park. On 14 May a meeting of local residents and students voted to protect the park against invaders and to initiate negotiations with the university. The chairman of the university's committee on housing and environment, Professor Sym, issued a statement which read in part: 'I think the People's Park was a great idea ... but the University [meaning the Chancellor] didn't seem to be very interested in negotiations.'

The Chancellor of Berkeley was within his legal rights; the university owned the land on which the People's Park was illegally established. The fact that many Berkeley residents, the majority of students and a sizeable minority of the faculty approved of the People's Park did not diminish the Chancellor's legal right to ask the police to evict the squatters, and to remove the freshly planted trees and flowers. On the morning of 15 May, an 8ft steel link fence was put up around the site on the order of the Chancellor. At midday about three thousand people marched to the park and were attacked by the police with a barrage of tear-gas before they could reclaim the site. The police waded into the crowd and began to beat people with clubs. They fought back with the only weapons they could find – bottles, stones and other street debris. The police then opened fire. More than a hundred people were shot with birdshot, buckshot and rocksalt from shotguns. One man, twenty-five-year-old James Rector, was watching the scene from the roof of a nearby bookstore when a policeman began firing at him. He died later in hospital from buckshot in the heart. Another young spectator, Alan Bruchard, co-manager of a theatre, was permanently blinded by gunfire on a nearby rooftop. Most of the scores of wounded were hit in the back by gunshot wounds as they fled.

The police claim that they shot only in self-defence was refuted by scores of witnesses, and also by a photograph printed in the

San Francisco Chronicle on 19 May showing an Alameda County sheriff's deputy taking careful aim at the back of a running man two car-lengths away from him. The photographer reported that having gunned the man down, the policeman made no attempt to arrest him, but simply walked away. He, and a great many other policemen, regarded their function as meting out instant punishment by shooting, rather than bringing to justice.

The Governor of California that night ordered 2,750 men of the National Guard to Berkeley, together with tanks and helicopters. From 16-19 May there were several demonstrations, punished by tear gas attacks and by bayonet charges. Some National Guardsmen bayoneted people in the back. In the evening of 19 May James Rector died. Next day, Berkeley became the first city in the United States to come under military attack from the air. An army helicopter swooped low over the university campus, spraying CS gas developed for use against the Vietcong. At the same time gas-masked soldiers blocked all but one exit from the plaza, making the dispersal of the terrified crowd almost impossible. The gas drifted all over the campus and the surrounding area. According to the *Sunday Times* the attack 'was an unmitigated military disaster. It gassed faculty wives with small children two miles away from the park. A local hospital was forced to stop operations, move patients and place one man in a respirator.'[7]

Atrocities committed by the police and by the National Guard were reported in detail in the *San Francisco Chronicle* and in the 2 June edition of *Newsweek*. An Episcopal bishop, C. Kilmer Myers, described California's Governor Ronald Reagan as 'the one who has unleashed the dogs of war in Berkeley ...':

It is no longer sufficient to say that the police and the military have 'over-reacted'. The change of violation of the law, both civil and moral, must be laid at their feet rather than at the feet of the helpless. We remember that this is the same Governor who advocated paving over Vietnam. He is a warmonger in Southeast Asia and he is a warmonger in California. The system of violence which spawns persons like the Governor of California is all of one piece.[8]

In a letter to *The Times* on 5 June 1969 a Berkeley professor, Richard Dawkins, wrote that Governor Reagan's action was not a tactical error but a 'grave crime against humanity which it seems to us here.... It may not be too surprising that the police and military should tend to favour Gestapo tactics for dealing with student rebels. What is really disturbing is that the Governor of the State can markedly improve his chances of re-election by allowing and encouraging such methods.'

I.F. Stone's Weekly placed the affair in perspective on 16 June 1969: 'That helicopter spraying 50 pounds of CS gas indiscriminately over campus demonstrators, nearby elementary schools and hospital facilities in the Berkeley People's Park clash may be a preview of what can be expected elsewhere.'

3

> 'The entire machine of State and police breaks down when they attempt to deal with us because they are only geared to deal with subversion which is directed from abroad. They are not prepared or trained to deal with a democratic mass opposition based on responsible individuals.'
>
> Wolfgang Lefèvre, member of the SDS Political Committee[9]

> 'We do not advocate the throwing of stones but we will not permit the police to smash us without defending ourselves. . . . The political question is this: Why has academic youth been forced to resort to violence in self-defence despite the fact that it has good arguments and knows how to use them in discussion?'
>
> Karl Dietrich Wolff and Frank Wolff (President and Vice-President of SDS)[10]

The attacks by military planes against the young in Mexico City and in Berkeley were, indeed, previews of things to come. Total war between the young and the adults, however, has not yet broken out; Berkeley and Mexico City, Prague, Paris, Tokyo and the other clashes were only minor or major 'frontier incidents' that might or might not lead to war. But the war parties in the camps of the young and within the adult establishments are already infatuated with violence. For these 'hawks', the justice of their cause is beyond the realm of reason. And as the number and the ferocity of the conflicts increases, it no longer matters for most people who began it, who is or was right. As in the decades-long vendettas in the Sicily of the past, since the fifties both sides have, or believe they have, things to revenge.

Demonstration replaced discussion as a means of communication between the camps. The ever-larger age-groups of children who pass into high schools, *lycées* or *Gymnasien* are being taught by the daily TV news the realities of the generation conflict. Adult governments, state attorneys and police forces are still trying to find their stereotyped 'handful of troublemakers', at a time when the number of young people between twelve and twenty-five will soon reach one thousand million; and most of them, for innumerable reasons, want to change society and to become a different kind of human being from their parents and grandparents.

Unfortunately, the events of 1968 and 1969 closed not only many old minds but also many young ones that had previously been open to alteration. In the 1964-7 period students activists tended to be intellectually more flexible, more realistic and more tolerant than the average non-activist and the majority of adults. This was no longer true in 1969. The events of the previous year increased not only the proportion of militants but also that of fanatics and captive minds among the young. Even open-minded students who tried to guard the independence of their critical intelligence betrayed in adrenalin-influenced situations a surprising amount of hatred for everybody who was not on their side in their 'struggle for human survival'.

In the previous period the protest movements of the young were led by ever-changing, rather amorphous vanguards without intense ideological viewpoints. Writing about these vanguards, Jack Newfield emphasized the American New Left's indifference to ideology, discipline, economics and conventional political forms:

What is explicitly new about the New Left is its ecumenical mixture of political traditions that were once murderous rivals in Russia, Spain, France and the United States. It contains within it, and often within individuals, elements of anarchism, socialism, pacifism, existentialism, humanism, transcendentalism, bohemianism, populism, mysticism, and black nationalism.[11]

Barely a year later, the indifference to ideology was disappearing in most groups. The emotional basis of the young white radicals' revolutionary consciousness remained a vaguely defined 'existentialist disgust', but the New Left began splitting into intensely ideological factions. The majority of the groups seemed to be addicted to various forms of 'latter-day Marxism'. By 1969 the very widespread factional fights among young radicals worried most of the factions. A typical spokesman of one of the vaguely Marxist groups, the Anglo-Pakistani journalist Tariq Ali, wrote:

> Those of us who form the hard core of today's new revolutionaries are still Marxists but we abhor Stalinism; we believe in Leninism, but prefer the emphasis upon 'democracy' rather than 'centralism'; we are Guevaraist, but can appreciate and analyse the mistakes made by Ché. We are puzzled by *the tendency among many Left factions in the developed countries to devote as much time and energy to attacking each other* as to attacking capitalism. The new revolutionaries will fight against sectarian tendencies.[12]

Many orthodox and non-orthodox Marxist groups denied that confused militants of Tariq Ali's type formed the hard core of today's new revolutionaries. It is, of course, easy to show that one cannot abhor Stalinism if one is a Leninist; and that the emphasis on 'centralism' is the very essence of Leninism. The fact remains, however, that thousands of young militants became captivated by precisely this paradox. In the volume edited by Tariq Ali, Ernest Mandel wrote: 'As much as we are on the side of the Soviet Union and the "socialist camp" in any confrontation with imperialism or the bourgeoisie, we support also ... the workers and students of Warsaw and Poland in their fight against bureaucracy and for real Soviet democracy based on workers', students', and poor peasants' councils *as Lenin taught us*.'

He was answered by Dzierszinski Daszinski: 'But it was Lenin, not imperialism, who destroyed the workers' councils and founded the modern Soviet state, with all its tyranny and which Mandel is prepared to support!'[13]

While in Prague, Warsaw and Moscow students and intellectuals struggled against the stranglehold of obsolete Marxist dogmas on their lives, hundreds of variations on these dogmas infected young Western minds with intolerance. The helicopter spraying nerve gas on Berkeley demonstrators offer a preview of what can be expected from fanatical adult authorities elsewhere. The sectarian fights among student groups give a preview of what can be expected from the young if the infatuation with various dogmas and with violence goes on spreading.

The most persistent warnings about the deterioration of critical intelligence in the youth camp came from Japan. In 1968 there were violent disturbances at 131 of the country's 845 universities. In Tokyo and in the other large cities student militants fought pitched battles against the police and against each other. The militant student groups turned themselves into warring sects. The helmets of the militant students were painted in bright colours and bore on the front the insignia, the name of the faction to which the wearer owed allegiance. A glance at this insignia showed whether one faced friend or foe. The warring sects attacked each other with pieces of wood five feet long, bamboo spears or lengths of piping. Battles were fought, casualties suffered and prisoners-of-war taken. The captors in most cases tried to convert their prisoners-of-war. In cases of success, the converted captives were released after public 'self-criticism'; the others were beaten up. Heretical rivals were treated with the utmost brutality, one student in Tokyo was blinded in one eye, another was left with a broken collar-bone, two broken ribs and two broken legs. There were several cases of torture of captives.

In 1968-9 the numerous sects were at war with each other and with the adult world. Only during the desperate battles against thousands of armed police were the wars between the sects interrupted. The detailed chronology of this great war and the wars within the great war would fill volumes. A brief description of one of the longer campaigns gives an idea of the general war in Japan.

In June 1968 revolutionary student organizations captured the campus and the complex of buildings of Tokyo University. They successfully defended it against police siege for more than six months. Not until January 1969 did a concentrated attack by 8,000 gas-masked police, protected with metal shields and with police helicopter support, succeed in retaking the university. During the first onslaught the police took nineteen of the buildings. In the barricaded stronghold of the main administration building, with its nine storeys; the students beat back a six-hour combined attack. From the roof they poured rocks, flaming petrol bottles, acid bombs and smoke sticks on police trying to break through the main door of the Yashida Auditorium. The police attacked with powerful water cannons, firing a mixture of water and tear gas. Police helicopters hovered over the building dropping hundreds of tear gas grenades on the defenders.

The battle, or rather battles, of Tokyo University ended in considerable concessions being offered by the university authorities. But the mutually hostile student factions were not prepared to make concessions to one another. The fragmentation of the militant student movement in Japan reached a new stage in the nineteen-sixties when the Mainstream Zengakuren (itself only a larger part of the All-Japan Federation of Student Self-governing Associations) split into the Japan Marxist Students' League (Marugakudo), the Socialist Students' League (Shagakudo) and the Japan Socialist Youth League Liberation Front (Shasheido Kaihoha).

Soon the Marxist Students' League was subdivided into the CORE faction (Chukakuha) and the Revolutionary Marxist Faction (Kakumaruha), which formed its own Zengakuren. There is also an 'Anti-Yoyogi' and a 'Pro-Yoyogi' Zengakuren. The Communist Party HQ in Tokyo is at Yoyogi. In December 1966 three factions split off from the Mainstream Zengakuren and formed their own Sanpa (Three-Factions) Zengakuren. In July 1968 this three-factions union split into two new Zengakuren. The pro-communist and the anti-communist factions were subdivided into seven further splinter groups. Was this a preview of things to come?

In 1969, there seemed to be little hope that the process of infecting some students with fanaticism would be stopped in the foreseeable future. Those entering university were and are made susceptible to this kind of infection by their entire environment. The violent clashes between rival sects and the pitched battles with the riot police led to a general brutalization of the atmosphere at the universities. Even at times when the strikes or siege lasting weeks or months did not stop teaching altogether, many professors were effectively silenced by the students. If members of one or more sects disagreed with the views of a certain professor, they disrupted his class by shouting: 'Nonsense! Nonsense!' whenever he tried to speak. Since it was almost impossible to find a school of thought which was not regarded as despicable by one or other of the sects, teaching was almost impossible in the sect-infected universities. In the conflicts with the Japanese university authorities elderly officials were held prisoner for several days at a time, subjected to constant abuse and occasional violence.

The Japanese youth camp, however, was by no means the only one to be infected with blind fanaticism. In the war psychosis of the generation conflict, dissenting student factions in many other countries, too, began to deny the right of dissent to other groups. In the bitter struggle to gain self-determination for all men, the original aim got lost and they demanded instead uniformity of views and convictions, claiming immunity for their school of thought from examination by critical intelligence.

Most of the fanatics seemed to be struggling for the victory of various obsolete revolutions of the past, that is for revolutions which do not destroy centralized power but just place it into other hands – theirs. The aim of their revolutionary movements was to replace a set of ruling dogmas with their dogma, a repressive rule with their repression, a dictatorship with their dictatorship.

The mindless violence of these types of young fanatics was exploited in this period by conformists, so as to urge repressive measures against students whose demonstrations were prompted by rational-altruistic motives. Every disturbance of their 'academic peace' was regarded by some observers as evil or obscene or both, while the university was idealized out of all recognition. In his essay 'Obsolete Youth' Dr Bruno Bettelheim of Chicago University, for instance, felt it relevant to emphasize that: 'The contrast between an institution devoted to the highest achievements of reason, and the obscene and violent happenings perpetrated there, makes it all the more fascinating. On this fascination, student militants try to build their success.'[14]

Some 'violent happenings' are morally and intellectually justifiable. It is clear, for instance, that a university department devoted to the highest achievements of bacteriological warfare is far more obscene than the student demonstration against it, however violent. And by now it is a truism that many universities from Japan to America have become branch plants of the military industrial complex. In hundreds of university departments knowledge has been reduced to information, bits of which can be programmed into student automatons. In America, as James Ridgeway has shown, many universities have become 'closed corporations', service stations for vested interests and/or for the Pentagon:

MIT and Johns Hopkins run centers which design missiles; half of MIT's budget and three-quarters of Johns Hopkins' budget come from running defence labs. Cornell designs more effective bombs for Vietnam; Princeton breaks codes and runs conventions for CIA; Michigan is first in photo reconnaissance and helps out with counter-insurgency. Pennsylvania and fifty other universities have recently been involved in chemical, germ and biological warfare research. . . . Princeton and the Davis campus of the University of California are working on new ways to get leaves to fall off trees, thus helping to defoliate more of Vietnam. [The Pentagon's] Project Thesis intends to bring in some of the smaller colleges which heretofore had been excluded from Defense work.[15]

Students do not demonstrate against universities because these are 'devoted to the highest achievements of reason' but because they serve unreason. They question the professors' right to work for the Pentagon, the CIA and the industrial monopolies.

Many of the student demonstrators were described or denounced as disciples of Herbert Marcuse and as having been influenced by his famous essay 'Repressive Tolerance'. In fact, Professor Marcuse in this essay, and in his *A Critique of Pure Tolerance* analysed the ideas of tolerance in advanced industrial societies, and doing so found some of the objective causes of the present world-wide student revolt:

What is proclaimed and practised as tolerance today is in many of its most effective manifestations serving the cause of oppression.

Violence and suppression are promulgated, practised and defended today by democratic and authoritarian governments alike as necessary deterrents against nuclear war ... or as police action against subversion. The people subjected to these governments are educated to tolerate policies, conditions and modes of behaviour which should not be tolerated because they are impeding, if not destroying, the chances of creating an existence without fear and misery.

... Tolerance toward that which is radically evil now appears as good because it serves the cohesion of the whole on the road to affluence or more affluence. ... The tolerance which enlarged the range and content of freedom was always partisan – intolerant toward the protagonists of the repressive status quo. ... If democratic tolerance had been withdrawn when the future [Nazi] leaders started their campaign, mankind would have had the a chance of avoiding Auschwitz and a World War.

... When tolerance mainly serves the protection and preservation of a repressive society, when it serves to neutralise opposition and to render men immune against other and better forms of life, then tolerance has been perverted.[16]

It is because of the prevailing repressive tolerance that the weight of real opposition is quite insignificant in a system of mass communication. Student opposition is forced by objective conditions to replace dialogue with demonstration. One of the spokesmen of the Radical Student Alliance in Britain, David Adelstein, defined student power as 'the ability of the students' block to inflict, if necessary, sanctions of sufficient economic, social or political magnitude to force its opinion to be heeded.'

Since the precondition of repressive tolerance is centralized power, many student movements aim at a society in which centralized power itself is made redundant. This seems to be the essence of the present revolution of revolution. This is expressed in a great many different forms. According to Dutschke the West German extra-parliamentary opposition aimed at a 'long march through existing institutions and this includes political parties, parliament and other institutions' to arrive at a 'counter-society ... with the aim of softening-up and destroying the established order'. In the France of May 1968, Alain Geismar said that for him 'socialism can be defined negatively, with respect of existing structures, by a rejection of all bureaucracy, of all centralized direction ... the central authority only to have a co-ordinating role, not a repressive one'.

For the anarchists:

... the ultimate tactical question must be, *not the seizure of power, but its dissolution*! We must destroy all structures based on the authority of hierarchical power. Not to impose a new ideology on reality, to create another monolithic (USA, USSR, China) style culture, but to allow men to follow the logic of their personal development, to implement the technology which will free men from labour, to liberate the unconscious from its repression, to reintroduce man and society into an ecological harmony with nature and to re-establish community as the arena in which the lost content of real human relations can once again flourish.[17]

Many groups preach the present urgency of negation:

Negation is the real message of transcendence, the hope of liberation. Today the social systems, East and West ... have sunk back from this truth. They offer to close the world of genuine change in the name of the 'positive'.... The positive means the Status Quo — potentially it may mean NAPALM, NUCLEAR WAR, EXTERMINATION ... so revolutionaries start their abc learning to say No to illusory freedom, No to pseudo needs, to bureaucratic regulation, to racialism.[18]

Who the hell wants to 'make it' in America any more? The American economy no longer needs young whites and blacks. We are waste material. *We fulfil our destiny in life by rejecting a system which rejects us.*[19]

It's not necessarily the responsibility of the critic to produce a solution to the problem he sees. We feel that the existing society is repressive (tolerant tho' this repression may seem). We seek to end this repression. This is ample work for the present. Would you ask the prisoner escaping from a concentration camp to produce a 'better alternative'? (Better what? A better concentration camp?)[20]

The revolution of revolution affected in different ways and to different degrees the affluent societies of the West and the countries of the Soviet orbit. It was Fidel Castro who said that within the world communist movements the Roman Catholic Church had become in certain places a revolutionary force, while the Communist Parties had become impotent churches.

From Hungary and Poland to Czechoslovakia the Communist Reformation strove for socialism with a human face. Dubcek and his millions of followers were convinced that this could be achieved only after the restoration of intellectual freedom and of all basic human rights; after the monopolistic power of the party bureaucracy has been destroyed and replaced by a democratically restructured system of government. But intellectual freedom, workers' councils and popular participation is anathema to the Kremlin-type communists. Therefore the attempt at rejuvenation was countered with moronic brute force. Yet on 21 August 1968, when Czechoslovakia was invaded in the name of communism by the grave-diggers of communism, the striving for rejuvenation through freedom and participation was not crushed. Neither was it crushed a year later, when the anniversary demonstrations were suppressed by tanks and troops. In the Soviet Union, prisons and camps are once again being filled with political prisoners. Protesting students and intellectuals are being exiled or sent to lunatic asylums, yet the ferment and the protest continue.

Kremlin propagandists fight on two fronts against student rebels. They try to save the Communist Parties of the West from being corrupted by 'anarchist and ultra-left ideas', hence the violent attacks on Herbert Marcuse in Moscow Radio's foreign language broadcasts for 'flattering the students that they formed the only true revolutionary force'. For home consumption in 1970, from papers *Pravda* to *Voprosy Filozofii* and *Literaturnaya Gazeta* warned their readers against 'nonsensical theories about the special role of young people' and 'the revolutionary exclusiveness of youth'. The Chinese have had no hesitation in asserting that the Soviet leaders fear student discontent within their own camp. One reason why the Soviets had reacted with hostility to the American students' struggle and described their demands as irrational, a *People's Daily* commentary said, was because Moscow was scared of it – fearing that it might spark off 'the awakening of the Soviet proletariat and working people'.[21]

In Germany and elsewhere in the West the 'Anabaptists of the Affluent Society' share, according to Erwin Scheuch,[22] one essential characteristic with the extreme left of the Reformation in believing that revolution is a state of mind. The revolutionaries of the Reformation attained a state of grace and this way the Reformation was accomplished in their minds and hearts. The Anabaptists of the nineteen-sixties believed that once you achieved revolutionary consciousness, the modern counterpart of a state of grace, then you could not help turning into a revolutionary. By acquiring hundreds and thousands of converts to revolutionary consciousness, the revolution broke out even though there were no barricades and bloody clashes.

The West German 'Anabaptists' of the nineteen-sixties were mostly 'Latter-day-Marxists', opposed by and to all established Communist Parties throughout the world. They earned the wrath of the CP leaders by their adherence to various versions of socialism with a human face, and for having been influenced by gurus as diverse as Herbert Marcuse and Karl Mannheim on the one hand, and by Ché Guevara on the other. From Marcuse they learnt intolerance 'towards all forms of repression, towards hypocrisy and violent, complacent imperialism'. Like Marcuse himself, they too appear to be partly guided by Mannheim's sociology of knowledge. This emphasized the vital importance of a class of free intellectuals, independent of the momentarily existing social order.

The hippie movement, though non-political, is acting ideally as the yeast of the permanent revolutionary ferment in manners and morals: the striving towards an entirely new humanity with a new way of life. The hippies have affinities with the New Anabaptists. They attain a state of grace not by revolutionary consciousness but by their act of conversion: by 'turning-on'. The turned-on person, by his or her commitment to universal love and to a permanent willingness to share all possessions with anyone who might need them, and by 'dropping out of corrupt society', became a new kind of human being.

All this, of course, is their ideal. But the present Christian or communist morality ideal is attained by far fewer individuals. According to this ideal, by denying his selfish impulses the individual demonstrates his state of grace; in this state, the 'universal principles of morality', in other words, the Kantian categorical imperative guides him to rational self-restraint. The hippies deny this, their revolutionary message is: 'Do your own thing, otherwise you'll be dominated, suborned and dehumanized.' They believe in the unique value of the individual, in the importance of sincerity and spontaneity. The credo of 'doing your thing' is limited only by universal love, which keeps you from hurting others.

The ever-changing number of various types of hippie in the cities, the number of the hippie tribes and communes in their rural exile, is not known. But this quasi-revolutionary, quasi-religious movement with its great many sects seems to affect the political revolutionaries. The hippie movement itself is opposed, of course, to all rigid social orders whether despotic or democratic, whether meritocratic or oligarchic. Some observers claim that, ultimately, the hippie movement and related movements might become more effective than political revolutions in changing Man.

The ultimate in leftish extremism was represented in the nineteen-sixties by the Resurgence Youth Movement, a 'new anarchist movement based on the world revolution of youth and the birth of a new psychedelic Afrasian-American soul'. Founded in the summer of 1964, the movements' magazine declared in a programmatic article: 'Resurgence' has not yet defined any limits. We may be three billion persons, we may be a negative universe, reaching out across the void. . . . Revolution is the total destruction and creation of society. . . . All science and art is crap. We will not submit and we will not coexist.'

The magazine envisaged a planet on the brink of the apocalypse and offered asinine new slogans: 'Logic and metaphysic to the torch!' . . . 'Turn our culture upside down and cut its head off!' . . . 'Go wild! Go naked!'

4

The adherents of the Autocratic Society did their best in 1969 to persuade themselves and others that 'the great wave of student confrontation is passing', and that brutal suppression of all forms of dissent will intimidate and finally silence the majority.

Sociology Professor, Robert Nisbet, of Berkeley stated in a September 1969 article that 'the student revolution is dead'. A few months later he wrote an article called: 'Who Killed the Student Revolution?' (*Encounter*, February, 1970).

Meanwhile, there were mass-protests and anti-war demonstrations all over the world. With the exception of vacation-periods, there was no week in 1969-70 without university unrest somewhere in the world.

In 1969, more than six hundred thousand people between the ages of sixteen and thirty migrated to Woodstock, New York, for a giant rock-festival, which seemed to indicate the arrival of a new generation. In the US, the Moratorium and the Mobilization involved millions of people in nation-wide anti-war demonstrations, while the small 'Weathermen' faction of the SDS turned to urban terrorism.

Half a million young people were at the November 1969 Peace Mobilization in Washington. The White House sent up a military helicopter to take pictures of the Peace Mobilization rally, and then put teams of 'photo-interpreters' to work counting the dots of greatly enlarged prints of the scene, in order to prove that not five hundred thousand but only four hundred and fifty-three thousand people were protesting against the Vietnam war.

Similar attempts were made to minimize the significance of the Peace Mobilization rallies elsewhere in America. The White House refrained, however, from publishing the revised sum total of 'peacenik' activists, because they represented too large a proportion of American youth.

By the onset of the 1970s, the cold war between generations often turned into hot wars between students and right-wing conformists. In Holland, students and hippies were physically assailed by young sailors, in New York by building workers (the hard hats), in Britain by young proletarian 'skinheads'. The educationally underprivileged (among them some of the police) were incited in many countries against the students by Agnew-type propaganda.

In March 1970 in Nanterre, the Paris police rioted out of control of their own officers. Crying 'death to the students', they went completely berserk. In the end, the authorities felt compelled to send special mobile-guard forces to protect the students. The mobile-guard units had to use a considerable degree of force before they were able to quieten down the police.

The prophets of the end of the student revolution did not think of the possibility that the conduct of the American, Soviet and other governments might shock and anger further year-groups of students. The year 1970 furnished these shocks, and these prompted some student groups to adopt the politics of rage, others the politics of outrage. As Norman Cousins observed, the extremist fringes of the student masses began to imitate the brutal and irrational conduct of the state: 'Even those who seek to resist the violence and the irrationality of the state tend to speak the language of the state and adopt its irrationality. . . . The government of the United States was conceived by men who believed it possible for a nation to become a moral instrument. They rejected the notion of a double standard under which the state can itself be immoral, mendacious, brutal or irrational while demanding that its citizens adhere to a code of responsibility and reason.'

In America, university administrations, egged on by governors like Reagan of California, or his erstwhile mentor, Rhodes of Ohio, increased the conformity pressure on the young. Students were to conform and join the pro-Nixon silent majority, or be sternly punished. At Kent State University of Ohio, the University Administration began its campaign of repression in April 1969 which reached its crescendo a year later with the killing of four students.

By 1970, there were strong trends in several countries of the world to make dissent a crime. In America, the Chicago Conspiracy Trial was a symptom of this trend. After nearly five months of verbal battles between the defendants and the judge, the jury threw out entirely the government's intricately woven theory of conspiracy between seven accused – that they had crossed state lines to incite riots in Chicago during the 1968 Democratic National Convention. But then the panel went on to convict five of the defendants of individually crossing state lines to foment riots.

The trial was the first test of the 'Rap Brown law', which makes it a crime simply to cross a state line 'with riotous intent'. The trial 'made a mockery of the judical process', charged New York Mayor John Lindsay, and he went on to say: 'When a trial becomes fundamentally an examination of political acts and beliefs, then guilt or innocence becomes almost irrelevant. . . . The blunt hard fact is that we in this nation appear headed for a new period of repression – more dangerous than at any time in years.'

In 1970 the French Parliament passed a law which gives the police powers to arrest anyone, at any time, anywhere within hailing distance of a forbidden demonstration – and the tendency was to forbid almost all demonstrations. 'Arrest' – as a *Sunday Times* report put it – 'in this context is virtually synonymous with a serious beating up.'

In April, for the third time in six months, American youth staged nationwide demonstrations against the continuation of the Vietnam war. On hundreds of campuses the moderates had the upper hand, on others the extremists took over. The demonstrations were the most violent on the Harvard campus and on the Berkeley and Isla Vista campuses of the University of California. Governor Reagan of California declared that the student revolution will be overcome only after a 'bloodbath'.

In May, the US invaded Cambodia. Strikes followed at more than fifteen hundred American universities, colleges and schools. High School unrest alarmed American educators. Vice-President Agnew stepped up his propaganda campaign against the 'weirdoo peaceniks'. President Nixon enlightened a circle of Pentagon officials in a widely reported impromptu speech about 'campus bums':

'You know, you see these bums, you know, blowing-up the campuses. Listen, the boys on the college campuses today are the luckiest people in the world – going to the greatest universities – and here they are burning up the books. I mean, storming around about this issue, I mean, you name it, get rid of the war, there'll be another one. And then, out there, we've got kids who are just doing their duty. And I've seen them and they stand tall and they're proud.'

The lucky students of Kent State University in Ohio also protested against the invasion of Cambodia. The moderates protested peacefully, the radicals threw bottles at police cars and burned down a rickety hut on the campus. Governor Rhodes promptly declared martial law and ordered men from the 107th Armored Cavalry Regiment and the 145th Infantry Battalion to Kent. Attributing the violence against police cars and the ROTC hut to students 'worse than the brown shirts and the Communists ... the worst type of people that we harbour in

319

judged irrelevant that the 'Greek Week' gave moral support to the Greek colonels' torture regime, but it was not held irrelevant what radical political views one of the defendants had expressed in an article.

In the end, the judge sentenced six students to terms of imprisonment ranging from nine to eighteen months, while two others were sent to Borstal. Seven students were acquitted. Eight of the defendants were charged with 'riot' and nothing else. In other words, they were not alleged to have committed any single act of violence or to have incited or abetted any such acts. One was said to have suggested in vain that those around him should charge the police dogs. Six were said simply to have been present (alongside with some four hundred others who had not been charged), shouting slogans. Another was said to have been seen 'pushing' and on one occasion he was 'in front of the crowd, shouting, facing the police.' For this offence he was sentenced to nine months in prison.

The judge emphasized that the sentences would have been heavier had he not been satisfied that the students had been 'exposed to the evil influences of some senior members of their university.' Whether or not this evil influence consisted in implanting in their students too strong a belief in democracy and human rights, and a detestation of murderous dictatorships, the judge did not say.

The *Law Guardian,* the only legal journal circulated to all judges, barristers and solicitors, commented in its July 1970 issue:

'It is monstrous and fatuous, that a demonstration against the violence and lawlessness of the present Greek government should itself have taken a lawless and violent form. But the judicial behaviour of Melford Stevenson J. was just not good enough ... Altogether the opportunity seems to have been missed to impress upon the public gallery, which was largely filled with students, the impartiality of English justice ...

'A question mark also hangs over the part played by the university proctors ... The peculiar, nanny-ish processes of discipline in Oxford and Cambridge universities were evolved at a time when students went up as boys in their early teens. In 1970 most students are adult citizens, under our new law.

'By all means let the university make such dispositions as it sees fit, medieval or otherwise, for the conduct of students while they are invitees upon university premises, but when they are at large in the City of Cambridge or Oxford, they should have the same rights and duties of any other resident in those cities, no less and no more.'

Two days after the trial, about fifty Cambridge students staged a protest vigil against the sentences. They carried placards and handed out leaflets outside the city's Guildhall. Their protest was scrupulously peaceful. Soon, however, a middle-aged man arrived with eggs, tomatoes, rotten fruit and a sack of flour. He handed them to young people among the spectators, urging them to pelt the students. The bombardment began at once. About thirty 'skinheads' joined in and increased the vehemence of the bombardment. Some market stallholders were handing out free supplies of fruit and vegetables to the anti-student forces. One woman who appealed for an end to the entirely unprovoked assault, had an egg smashed on her head.

Finally, a few policemen arrived on the scene, detained two persons for a short while but in the end no charges were brought. The man inciting to violence was middle-aged, while the harm done to property was to students' clothes, and the violent attackers were non-students. This incident indicated that in Cambridge and in many other places in Britain, there is one kind of justice and law-enforcement for students, and another kind for non-students.

In the autumn, the Court of Appeal had substantially given its blessing to the results of the Cambridge riot trial, thereby giving British students a national issue of the type which has fuelled many student uprisings abroad. One Cambridge lecturer said : 'The trial has created an interest in politics that was never there before. We are now getting a political ferment in Cambridge which has not been experienced since the 1930s.'

By the end of 1970, dissent by young people was treated virtually as a crime in the majority of countries in the United Nation Organization.

XIII

THE CHAMPIONS OF
THE IMPOSSIBLE

'The limits of the possible constantly shift...
It is from the champions of the impossible
rather than the slaves of the possible that
evolution draws its creative force.'

Barbara Wootton[1]

1

The student revolt was regarded by many observers as a global
epidemic. The spread of fanaticism and an addiction to the
'pornography of violence' gave the impression of an epidemic
within the epidemic. Dr G. T. Stewart of the Department of
Epidemiology, School of Medicine, Tulane University, suggested
the application of a mathematical model to be used for a
'sociometric analysis of the student riots in order to arrive at a
rational basis for prevention and control'. Discussing the common
aim of the student revolt, he asked:

Is it purposeful, or is it just anarchic? Is it a multicentric declaration of no confidence in established authority in all its political
disguises; a subconscious thalamic reaction engendered by loss of
faith in reason; or a conscious rejection of reason as being a redundant faculty in an absurd world? ...
Is it a reaction to too much authority or too little; a deficiency
syndrome—lack of satisfying exertion, lack of inhibitions, lack of
faith in society; anger at depersonalisation in the multiversity? Or is
it the traditional revolt of powerless humanity, whose only strength
is in numbers? Whatever the cause, or causes, in its intellectual contagion, this movement is spreading like an epidemic, not without
mortality, not without widespread injury to people and places.[2]

The answer is that it is all this and much else. Almost every
hypothesis used to explain student revolt in one country or city
can be disproved in some other country or city. Whatever its

causes, revolt is a political phenomenon and there is no sense in trying to reduce politics to pure pathology. This was attempted in the notorious Project Camelot (described in Chapter III), by treating all revolutionary movements as 'social pathology'. The programme of this kind of 'counter-insurgency prophylaxis' or the Soviet practice of keeping sane dissenters in lunatic asylums differs, of course, in motivation from Dr. Stewart's suggestion. But to regard student revolt as an epidemic – as he and numerous others suggest – still implies the assumption that the societes and institutions which they rebel against are healthy.

The gist of the case against this assumption was indicated by another epidemiologist:

The students, disruptive as they are, have not yet reached the destructive level attained by their elders. They have loosed no bombs, they have laid waste no cities, they have dropped no napalm. On the contrary, they have spoken, pleaded, demonstrated,, finally rioted against such actions. Before we embark on prevention and control, let us consider who are the parthogens and who the victims.[3]

Dissent and rebellion are manifestations of political life. Even the most cursory glance at the process of human evolution reminds one that what we now call dissidence played a principal role in the evolution of civilized man. The conformism of unthinking majorities has always clashed with the critical conscience of thinking minorities. Turning against the majority always required reasoning, imagination, and the courage to act as a moral agent.

Man became the *sapiens*, the thinking species of the genus *Homo*, because he used a minute part of his mental capacities for more rational conduct than his rivals for survival.

The brain of lion, rhinoceros, and other powerful animals lack the mechanism of imagination, or we should not be here to discuss the matter. They cannot envisage changes in their environment, so they have never sought to alter it in all their efforts to retain lordship of their habitat. .... Very early in the human story the brain must have acquired the mechanism of what we recognise in action as imagination, calculation, prediction. Later came the process of abstract reason and the control of what we call violence.[4]

Ever since Neanderthal and Cromagnon times, the evolution of *Homo sapiens* was marked by a slight increase in the use of reasoning and imagination, accompanied by more and more 'ethical' conduct. Tribes survived as tribes because not all of their members were all the time governed by their immediate urges. There was an untypical tiny minority with proto-human behaviour. The Neolithic Revolution and all other steps on the way towards true *Homo sapiens* were the outcome of conflicts between primitive egotist-conformist majorities and equally primitive dissidents and 'imaginers', who already had traces of rational–altruistic attitudes in their make-up.

All through human history the majority of people have almost always been incapable of rational–altruistic behaviour, even when unselfish-reasonable conduct did not entail any dangers or hardships. Each innovation, each invention was resisted by desperate struggles, some lasting for many generations. There was a magical fear and hatred of change.

Most of humanity did not want to become human.

What most majorities lacked during five thousand years of recorded history was not so much intellectual capacity as moral character. In the age of H bombs and other colossal man-made dangers the need for a minimum standard of moral conduct should be obvious to everyone, save some political leaders and the criminally insane.

Throughout the evolution of the species, the dissidents, the non-conformists, the champions of the impossible played an enormous role. They were opposed by the conformists who resisted change, as something that is against eternal and unchangeable human nature. This, of course, slanders *Homo sapiens*. Only animals are chained to the behaviour pattern of their species. Dissent, non-conformism and individual adjustment are unknown and impossible in the totalitarian societies of the ants. The ants are slaves of their biological programming. Humans are not.

There has been no essential change in human nature—if we mean by that the neurological equipment of man—in the last thirty or fifty thousand years. In this same period we have passed from the cave to the modern urban industrial civilisation, from stone culture to the later Paleolithic to the empire of machines. ... Human nature is no rigid biological entity presenting sharply limited responses, but a highly flexible thing, capable of a wide variation of reactions according to the diversity of stimulation applied.[5]

Mankind's destiny is not eternally determined by the biological and psychological make-up of millions of human beings. Man is a social animal in historical development, who shapes his destiny as a member of society. The social animal – that is, civilized man – literally thought himself out of a 'state of nature', prompted by moral attitudes. Important among these is altruism, a concern for the good of the group, the community, and for the future of all mankind. The basic principle of human society is that one must consider other people.

Great religions and great schools of philosophy have preached and taught ethical conduct for thousands of years, yet very little scientific research has been devoted to the study of moral character. The best systematic theory of moral development in our century is given in *The Psychology of Character Development* by Robert F. Peck, with Robert J. Havinghurst and Ruth Cooper, Jesse Lilienthal and Douglas More. The five principal authors and several other scientists have cooperated since 1940 in studying moral character by means of a wide variety of psychological methods ranging from interviews and formal objective tests to sociometric and projective tests.*[8]

The authors postulate five main types of character for the 'successive stages of the psychosocial development of the individual':

Character Type		Developmental Period
amoral	=	infancy
expedient	=	early childhood
conforming	}=	later childhood
irrational–conscientious		
rational–altruistic	=	adolecence and adulthood

According to Peck, Havinghurst and their associates, the amoral type is infantile in having no moral principles at all. This type of person is 'contradictory, inconsistent, antagonistic, and often openly hostile in his or her behaviour'.

The expedient type is one who has come to terms with society in a way: but this is the way of the young child, who conforms in order to avoid adult punishment or disapproval.

Like a child, he is shortsighted, does not look ahead to foresee the long-range consequences of his behaviour, even though this may

---

* Their typology is partly based on the formulations of Jean Piaget: *The Moral Judgement of the Child* 1948. Their study combined projective test methods TAT and Roschach test with more objective methods of testing and observation. The tests were used to get at underlying elements in the personality which give regularity and stability to moral behaviour.

thwart the very purposes of self-gratification he has in mind. . . . He does not always succeed in maintaining consistent adaptation even in his surface behaviour, since at times his negativistic, basically hostile feeling to society breaks through his rather weak self-control.

The authors found that 'a sizeable minority of adults are heavily amoral or expedient in character. They treat their children this way and their children strongly tend to turn out just about like their parents.'

The conforming type 'is like a child who has come to accept the dictates of his family and society in a placid, uncritical way. . . . He is not capable of very complicated rational thought, or at least has never learned to exercise it. . . .'

The irrational–conscientious type is 'just as much like a child in his own way. He is not emotionally capable of questioning his conscience or asking if it always serves a genuinely moral purpose. He does not have the freedom to perceive life whole, nor to act on rational assessment of particular situations, even if he wanted to.'[7]

A large segment of the adult population in the United States, 'perhaps over fifty per cent, are largely conforming or irrational–conscientious in their character dynamics. These people, often with a sense of high moral righteousness, treat their children in such a way that their children turn out to be either passively compliant sheep in search of a shepherd, or self-entrapped slaves to unalterable dogma.' Needless to say this applies to most countries of the world from the USSR to Japan and China.

The rational-altruistic type is 'a continuously maturing person. He has not reached a level and stopped there for life. . . . He is in as full, rational control of himself as it is possible for a human to be. There is no particular age level which he represents, except that he is what is hoped for in the genuinely mature adult. . . . His conscience is an integral part of all the principles which he incorporates or develops; and he tests them out in action to make sure that they achieve that well-being of self and others which he actively desires.'[8]

The Peck–Havinghurst group found that the proportion of American adults who were rational-altruistic, that is truly mature in type, was no greater than in their sample of sixteen year-olds. Summarising their twenty-year study of the psychology of character development, the authors state: 'The unthinking conformer, who often does not want to think for himself, probably

328

makes up the largest single group of Americans, and perhaps of humanity everywhere.'*[9]

The authors point out that the rational–altruistic type is the equivalent of David Riesman's 'autonomous character', Fromm's person with 'productive orientation', Erikson's individual 'with a firm identity', or Freud's 'genital type'. I prefer the Peck-Havinghurst terminology because of its simplicity and its relevance to both past and present. If it is applied to the past, it is immediately obvious that all through recorded history the overwhelming majority of people had no chance and not even any theoretical right to be anything else but unthinking conformers in all religious and public affairs. And whenever the majority had a chance to act as majority, they usually behaved as masses of conformists and irrational–conscientious persons.

The spread of literacy and the very slow and very gradual growth of the educated minority did not change the situation. Whether educated or uneducated, each generation and each establishment or system strove to perpetuate, if possible, its prevailing character types quite unchanged. The invention of printing and the spread of literacy became strong factors in preserving the conventional wisdom of the previous generations.

Most schools and universities pay lip service to the desirability of producing rational–altruistic people, but in fact, like most of the organized religions, political parties and ideological camps, they are extremely hostile to truly mature individuals.

What the university authorities, political systems, organized religions, together with most of the adult world, really want is at best conformist or irrational–conscientious character-types.

In Chapter V we discussed in detail the terror-induced political maturity of the population in the Soviet orbit. In open societies the overwhelming majority of the population is not politically mature. In these societies the majority is usually passive, neutral, uncommitted as far as public affairs are concerned. The man in the street wants to be left alone to mind his own business, nothing but his own business. This attitude, so prevalent in so-called democracies, is essentially immature and undemocratic.

When democracy was born in Greece people were forbidden to be uninterested or neutral in the affairs of the city-state. The law-givers of Athens were well-acquainted with the general

* Riesman, Remmers, Whyte and many others, both in America and in Europe reported similar findings.

tendency of 'prudent adults' to contract out of public affairs. Athenian law did not permit one to remain neutral and punished with loss of citizenship those who did not want to take sides in political debates or even in factional strife. The citizen was obliged to be concerned with public affairs and was forbidden to reduce himself to being a purely private person. In this context it is well to remember that the word 'idiot' comes from the Greek *idiotes,* meaning 'private persons'!

When open societies are being turned into dictatorships, the insistence of millions of private persons in sticking to their own business greatly helps the establishment and consolidation of totalitarian rule. It seems to be one of the lessons of contemporary history that only very grave and immediate dangers can force the majority of adult populations to think and act as rational-mature individuals. Then the majority of adults is forced to become, for a short period, politically attentive, committed and even active. But as soon as the imminent danger is over people revert to their normal behaviour as selfish private persons. The student situation, on the other hand, offers the most favourable environment for the unfolding of rational–altruistic inclinations.

Most of the Peck–Havinghurst and similar studies were made before the great millennial change. The adolescents they studied were born before the year of the gigantic generation-divide – 1940. In their past and in their world (they had completed the MS of their book early in 1960) it was still true that 'children – and the next generations – do as we do, *not* as we say'.

With those who were five or six years old or less in 1948 the age-old chain of conformity-transmission began to be broken. A large and growing minority of these children, and of this generation, contracted out. They do not do as we do or say.

Dr Margaret Mead told the London conference of the World Federation of Mental Health in August 1968 that for the first time in human history we were living in a world where the young knew more than the old:

In this world the adults were the immigrants, children the natives. Change had come so fast in the last 25 years that adults were not able to assimilate it. . . . Children were growing up in a world that was strange to their parents. Children now were brought up by television. They were members of no pattern, religious, national or ethnic known to their parents—they belonged to the whole world.

It is quite obvious that mental and moral maturity is quite specifically related to particular situations and environments. The global-village situation that has existed since 1948 is the new environment, in which the adult conformists are the confused, ignorant immigrants and the young are at home.

Freud takes seven as the age when the Child's direct contact with his society—socialisation without primary parental mediation—begins to become decisive. Seven in 1948 means 26 now. . . . 'Don't trust anyone over 30' really means : *that no one not raised in post-1948 America can see the world with our eyes. The Gap cannot be crossed.*

(A malicious footnote for those who rub their hands and chuckle in anticipation : 'He-he, sonny, soon you'll be 30 yourself.' No, we'll be under 30 forever, in this sense : *1948 won't change: the Gap can't be crossed the other way either.*)*

This generation moulded by the global-village situation of the electronic age seems to produce a far greater proportion of rational–altruistic types than any other previous generation, including that of the Golden Age of Athens under Pericles.

Although I agree with Margaret Mead that only a few of the school and university buildings should survive from the present educational system, even this obsolete system endangers the rule of *Homo Sapiens*. Despite the earnest striving of many authorities to prevent this, the universities of the world have produced a larger proportion of rational–altruistic adults since about 1962, than that minimum which makes the rule of *Homo Nonsapiens* entirely safe.

All through history the proportion of rational–altruistic individuals has been exceedingly small. The result of the great qualitative change that is occurring in our age is that we have more potential *Homines Sapientes* among us than any previous generation.

The world-wide youth revolution that is now unfolding is ultimately caused by the fact that today the proportion of rational–altruistic individuals in the age-group sixteen to twenty-six is far greater than in the entire 'adult' population aged over twenty-six. This statement is not based on complex sociometric and psycho-

* Michael Rossman, 'The Generation Gap: A Speculation', an essay prepared for the seminar on youth at the Centre for the Study of Democratic Institutions, Santa Barbara, California, in October 1967. Michael Rossman is a graduate of Berkeley and was one of the leaders of the Free Speech Movement in 1964-7.

logical research but on the behaviour of youth on the one hand, and of the adult world on the other. The adult world has behaved in home and international affairs in a way that has prompted some young people to exclaim that 'history is a nightmare from which we have awakened'.

The adult world went on and goes on with the nightmare.

A few minutes of thought should suffice for the realization that most governments, those of the two super-powers very much included, behave in an amoral–infantile way, or, at best, like human beings in their early or middle childhood. To paraphrase Peck and Havinghurst: '. . . like children, those governments are short-sighted, they do not look ahead to foresee the long-range or middle-range consequences of their policies, even though this may thwart the very purpose of party-political or national success they have in mind.'

2

> 'We study history to discern the alternatives within which human reason and human free-dom can now make history. . . . Freedom is – first of all, the chance to formulate the available choices, to argue over them – and then, the opportunity to choose. This is why freedom cannot exist without an enlarged role of reason in human affairs.'
>
> C. Wright Mills[10]

> 'What the world needs most, the university, and only the university could supply, and that is intellectual leadership. The university could fashion the mind of the age. Now it is the other way round. The demands of the age are fashioning the mind, if one may use the expression, of the university.'
>
> Robert M. Hutchins[11]

The student revolt and the violent clashes everywhere between conformism and critical intelligence do not constitute a global epidemic that will be over as soon as some effective 'anti-toxins' have been found. Whatever its forms, this revolution and this generation war is a fight to ensure that human reason and human freedom make history. This revolution is concerned with intellectual and moral leadership and with the university which could supply it.

The *Bulletin of Atomic Scientists* has a doomsday clock on its cover. From 1953 until 1968 the hands stood at twelve minutes to midnight, the hour which symbolizes the outbreak of nuclear war. In 1968 the hands were moved to five minutes to midnight, because the last fifteen years 'have brought mankind further down the road to nuclear disaster'. During those fifteen years several student generations fought for hundreds of different causes, but the overwhelming majority violently opposed nuclear armament and preparations for chemical and biological warfare; they opposed the mindless rush towards 'super-achievements' that threaten to make urban existence unbearable and the countryside uninhabitable.

Was this the 'common aim' of the adult world?

Conformist adults feel that there is no justification for this question, because the adult world does not rebel, does not want changes, it only wants to carry on with its 'normal everyday activities'. Only rebels are expected to have clearly defined and, if possible, common long-term aims. The statement that it is precisely these normal everyday activities of the adult world that permit or lead to colossal destruction of life and values in the present and threaten to bring about human extinction is regarded as pointless, because 'what can a private person do?' The answer is simple: the private person is powerless in the present situation only if he sticks to the illusion of bringing about basic change by rational argument and the 'orderly democratic process' of the present. This process has proved to be impotent. Only by demonstrating, rioting and rebelling can he expect to achieve anything.

Mass societies cannot be influenced by rational argument and moral persuasion in the same way as the ancient Greek city-states were influenced by debates in the *agora* or as nineteenth-century liberal towns were by discussion at the town meeting. In the *agora* or the town meeting the participants shared common principles, were more or less equally informed and their vote represented some degree of direct power. In mass societies nearly all rationality and morality is replaced by dominant group interests, and by clashes between impersonal economic and technological forces. In the *agora* or at the town meeting a change of policy was achieved by convincing a sufficient number of individuals of the necessity of change. In present-day mass societies the policies of governments, the actions of the military–industrial complex and of other dominant groups can be changed only by the pressure of mass opposition, and ultimately, by subjecting their hitherto uncontrolled, arbitrary power to effective control by new versions of *agora* and the town hall.

Until and unless this stage of participatory democracy is reached, there is not much point in striving to convince communities of 'mature, rational individuals' that they should stop drifting towards various major and minor catastrophes. Such communities do not exist, and if, exceptionally, they do, they are entirely powerless.

C. S. Lewis, the Catholic poet, then aged seventy, raised the question in 1968 'whether the great evil of our civil life is not the fact that there seems now no medium between hopeless submission and full-dress revolution?'

This situation prompted the already quoted question: 'Why has academic youth been forced to resort to violence in self-defence despite the fact that it has good arguments and knows how to use them in discussion?' The powers-that-be are not interested in good arguments and oppose discussion that leads to radical change. The students, and many others, were forced by reality to lose faith in rational argument.

Reason has been made a redundant faculty in and by the absurd world of Western and Eastern mass societies, in which the impotence of the many is ensured by the power of the few. This power is growing in all directions, not least towards an ever greater degree of irresponsibility. Centralized bureaucratic power can and does manipulate opinion, shape news and turn rational 'publics' into apathetic, mindless 'masses'. The impotence of reason and morality is enforced by the same centres of monopolistic power.

Mass societies are drifting in clearly discernible catastrophic directions because governments, dominant groups and conformist majorities refuse to consider the ultimate consequences of their actions and behaviour.

The universities of the world became the principal battlefields in the world war between the generations precisely because their original task of establishing truth and providing wisdom had been abolished. Hundreds of thousands of students fought in effect for the restoration of truth and wisdom. The universities declined to the level of technological centres of specialists and their apprentices. At best, these centres of learning became 'institutes specializing in specialization. . . . If wisdom is needed, why not take direct aim at it? Why merely hope for it as a by-product of other efforts?'[12]

The futility of this hope and the entire situation have prompted hundreds of thousands of students to revolt against the *status quo* at their universities. They want to transform, rejuvenate, recreate or reinvent the university, and recreate or reinvent society (or democracy) with it.

The decline of university education as regards fundamental disciplines and ultimate goals did not and does not stop many young people from becoming rational–altruistic adults during their student phase. The proportion of those who strive to become a *Homo sapiens* is still higher among university students than in any other comparable age-group. Since the proportion of students in the total population is still rising steeply everywhere, the much smaller but vital proportion of rational–altruistic adults is also growing. Therein lies the hope of the future.

Ultimately the revolt is about wisdom and goals. It is about government. To paraphrase Karl Mannheim, 'governments carry out entire series of functionally rational actions accurately without having any idea as to the ultimate end of these actions'. Their behaviour is determined by a limited rationality that has abdicated even from the idea that foresight and wisdom is necessary. These governments and the mass societies of adults they rule feel no responsibility to the young and to future generations for the kind of society they leave behind.

The original meaning of the word 'governor' was that of helmsman or steersman (derived from the Greek *kybernetes*). And though statesman still like to talk about the 'ship of state', by governing they mean ruling the ship of state and its passengers, without carrying out the functions of the helmsman. The young feel as if they are trapped by their elders in a rudderless ship, or in a vast lorry without a chauffeur at the steering wheel. Those in power regulate the lives of the passengers and carry out all sorts of rational actions, but prefer aimless drifting to steering the lorry in a definite direction. The young do not want to be sentenced by their elders to further drifting towards catastrophes.

The overwhelming majority of the revolutionary student groups were convinced that their fight for the destruction of the present obsolete university system and the creation of a new one was the precondition of creating a wise and good social order that would imply less frustration, less waste, less pain and less violence.

In 1969 there was little hope of their succeeding. Instead of autonomous-thinking communities fashioning the mind of the age, the flight from sanity went on. Various vicious circles were in effective operation. All through 1970 legislative bodies in the Western world were considering several hundred proposals for drastic repressive measures against student rebels. Scores have been passed already. Drastic repression inevitably increased the number of fanatics, whose brutal acts led to new proposals for even more draconian repression. The fanatics of repression and of revolutionary destruction were products of the war psychosis and were also a cause for its further intensification.

3

Writing a few years ago about 'The University in Transitition', James A. Perkins, then President of Cornell University, referred to the well-known Brontosaurus Projection, which shows what happens if and when growth gets out of hand. With a Brontosauric body-growth curve far exceeding the growth of the mind, the university is doomed to perish because of its tremendous bulk, like the prehistoric monsters. Since that time the multiversities and megaversities in America, Japan or elsewhere have nearly doubled their size, and numerous university presidents, vice-chancellors, professors and thousands of students have asserted that the university has lost (or is losing) its soul or mind or identity. Others have argued that the Brontosaurus Projection does not apply to the modern university. There is no danger that the university's body-growth curve will enormously exceed the mind-growth curve, because the university does not have a central governing 'mind' which could lag behind its physical expansion. For this reason, the university cannot with its present system act as society's brain or central nervous system.

But if the university is not the brain of society, what is?

If the university is not expected to act as humanity's reservoir of critical intelligence for guiding and controlling humanity's destiny, how should we provide for the wise management of what has been optimistically called 'our common human household'? Through the existing pluralistic solution of governments, pressure groups, military–industrial complexes, public opinion and the

336

mass media consulting a plethora of expert advice and opinion? The specialists and experts make their conflicting proposals in their isolated fields and the sum total of all this is supposed to lead, somehow, to wise general decisions. This, of course, is only an extension of the *laissez-faire* illusion in economics, according to which the selfishness of all individuals is the best guarantee of the prosperity of the country, or, in other words, 'the best good of all is served by everyone looking out for himself'.

Applied to *Homo sapiens,* as master of his own future destiny, this is the illusion that the mindless shortsightedness of groups and individuals will, somehow, add up to the general wisdom of the community.

When the revolutionary students agitated for the reinvention of society, most of them insisted that democracy was still a future goal. They contended that real democracy cannot be created without the invention of a new university for the new society. These revolutionary young people were not alone in their views. E. H. Carr expressed the considered view of several generations of scholars when he wrote, some years ago, about the need for creating democracy:

> To speak today of the defence of democracy as if we were defending something which we knew and had possessed for many decades or many centuries is self-deception and sham. Mass democracy is a new phenomenon—a creation of the last century.... We should be nearer to the mark, and should have a far more convincing slogan, if we spoke of the need, not to defend democracy, but to create it.[18]

After being improvised in the last century, mass democracy has degenerated rapidly since the middle of this century under the impact of the population and the mass-media explosion. The advent of the alienated mass-man and of rationality-without-wisdom was accompanied by the devaluation of religious and ideological convictions. The idea that some intellectual and moral values are universally valid in a given situation, and therefore above factional or ideological controversy went out of fashion. All truth, all history, all morality became relative and therefore controversial.

Max Born warned that since science is playing an ever more dominant role in human society, since science is morally neutral, since the complexities of the technology it has created are such that there is no longer any understandable connection between action and effect, man has ceased to be a moral agent.[14] The precondition of the creation of a democratic society is the restoration of man as a moral agent. The minimum premise of a moral attitude is the willingness to act as rational–altruistic individuals in order to ensure the survival of mankind. In a manifesto circulated in Moscow and elsewhere in Russia shortly before the invasion of Czechoslovakia, Soviet Academician A. D. Sakharov wrote:

Today the key to a progressive restructuring of the system of government in the interest of mankind lies in intellectual freedom. This has been understood, in particular, by the Czechoslovaks, and there can be no doubt that we should support their bold initiative which is so valuable for the future of socialism and all mankind.

Professor Sakharov's memorandum is a forbidden document in the USSR, the government of which is extremely hostile to intellectual freedom. Elsewhere, the non-dictatorial regimes do not oppose intellectual freedom as long as it does not lead to any radical restructuring of the system.

Faced with the dilemmas (or rather 'multilemmas') on the solution of which mankind's survival depends, societies need institutions that act as the brain of the community. Only the reinvented and recreated universities could be such institutions. They could be the establishers of non-controversial general truths that are valid whatever the regime or whatever the religion of the people. They could fashion the mind of the age and function as the central nervous systems of participatory democracies, in which millions of educated individuals are committed to act as moral agents.

Champions of conformism encouraged their camp throughout 1969 with the assertion that the student revolution in the United States was dead, that the backbone of the German or French youth revolt had been broken, that the Polish universities would no longer be able to launch offensives against the ruling bureaucratic depotism. In an obituary of the US student revolt written in 1970, Professor Nisbet of Berkeley wrote of:

... the widening popular acceptance of ... power in its most brutal manifestations.... A substantial majority of the American people approved of the Chicago police actions they saw on television and read about in the newspapers in the summer of 1968. If they could approve the ugly and vicious buffooneries that generally passed for police action in Chicago, it is not difficult to assume their approval of the far more sophisticated techniques of police power that exist today is most cities of the world. And these are techniques of power that have thoroughly permeated the American campus.[15]

Many conformists do believe, or hope, that the over-reaction of the majorities and the police power that permeates the world's campuses will stop coming generations of students from rebelling against increasing repression. Conformists believe or hope that it will be easier to turn the youth of the coming decades into passively compliant sheep than the youth of the fifties and sixties.

There are, in fact, very few grounds for this belief and hope.

By 1970, there were nearly 800,000,000 individuals aged between twelve and twenty-six. Their number will have increased by another 200,000,000 by 1980. The increase in the size and the number of universities is being accelerated. The proportion of students and university graduates is growing all the time and many graduates refuse to revert to the conduct of the conformist majorities.

Since 1950 intellectual power has gradually become recognized as one of the great forces of the future, besides economic and military power. 'The highly educated man has become the central resource of today's society, the supply of such men the true measure of its economic, military and even political potential.'[16] Intellectual power is growing, together with the significant increase of critical intelligence in all age groups. Former student rebels of the fifties and the sixties are or soon will be in influential positions throughout society. When the Brezhnevs and Agnews speak with contempt of students, academics and 'other intellectual slobs', they pretend to be unaware of the strength of their enemies. In the USSR, just as in the USA, the camp of students, teachers, academics and other intellectuals is well over ten million. This camp, like the entire youth camp, is growing much faster than the general population.

Youth has no political power today. Its numerical majority can be ignored; its educational needs can be neglected; it can be excluded from the election registers; its rights can be denied; its opinions, protests and demands can be left out of political considerations – but the results will be a series of explosions.

The champions of repression mean to push the generation war to the bitter end. In their determination to stop the transformation of society they are willing to risk all-out guerrilla wars in the cities between old and young. They, like some fanatics of the left, want to forget that the conformity–nonconformity clash is eternally necessary. If total conformity had prevailed in the societies of early man, mankind could not have made even the first steps on the long road towards the still distant goal of *Homo sapiens.* Total nonconformity, however, would have had precisely the same effect.

All through history, majorities have believed that contingent human arrangements and roles are parts of the structure of the immutable universe. The endemic conformity of the majorities has always helped to consolidate improvisations and innovations, later to conserve them, and still later to petrify them into sacred customs and institutions.

The dissident minorities that have fought for innovations or created new institutions have always been aware of possible alternatives. The majorities were not. After long struggles, the choice of the minorities has been turned by later majorities into 'destiny', which has prevailed until the next choice of the non-conformist minorities becomes the next destiny.

In our age the actions and behaviour of past generations has led to a situation in which only revolutionary change can avert total catastrophe. In this situation almost nothing that has been handed down is still valid. At no time in history has critical intelligence and critical conscience been as important for the bare survival of the human species as in the present completely inter-dependent world, in an era of colossally rapid change. The con-formist majorities are coming face to face not only with the revolt of youth but also with the rebellion of facts. The war between the generations is likely to assume proportions that have not been previously imagined.

Five thousand years ago a man looked upon his son as an enemy because he could not bear the idea of revolutionary change. Today and tomorrow, sons become enemies for the same reason.

SOURCE NOTES

CHAPTER I

1 *A Canticle for Leibowitz* (New York, 1967).

CHAPTER II

1 *International Encyclopedia of the Social Sciences*, Vol. 1 (New York, 1968).

2 Philippe Aries, *Centuries of Childhood: A Social History of Family Life* (New York, 1962).

3 *ibid.*, p. 26.

4 F. Musgrove, *Youth and Social Order*, The International Library of Sociology and Social Reconstruction (London, 1964).

5 Bruno Bettelheim, 'The problem of generations', in *Daedalus, Journal of the American Academy of Arts and Sciences*, issue devoted to 'Youth: Change and Challange', winter 1962.

6 Kenneth Walker and Peter Fletcher, *Sex and Society* (London, 1958), pp. 81-2.

7 F. Musgrove, *op. cit.*

8 Dr J. M. Tanner, Professor of Child Health and Growth in the University of London, 'Earlier Maturation in Man', in *Scientific American*, (January 1968), pp. 21-7.

9 See the review of surveys into the onset of menstruation by Leone Zacharias and Richard J. Wurtman of the Massachusetts General Hospital in *New England Journal of Medicine*, 17 April 1969.

10 V. G. Vlastovsky, 'The secular trend in the growth and development of children and young persons in the Soviet Union', in *Human Biology*, Vol. xxxviii, no. 3, September 1966, pp. 219-30; H. Milicer, 'The secular trend in growth and maturation as revealed in Polish data', in *Tiidischrift voor Sociale Geneeskunde*, Vol. xl, (Amsterdam), 1966, pp. 562-8; V. M. Oppers, 'The secular trend in growth and maturation in the Netherlands', in *Tiidischrift voor Sociale Geneeskunde*, Vol. xliv, (Boston, Mass.), 1966, pp. 539-48.

11 *Newsweek* (New York, 29 July 1968).

12 F. Musgrove, *op. cit.*

13 J. and M. Rowntree, 'Youth as a class', in *International Socialist Journal*, no. xxv (February 1968).

14 R. Touraine, 'Naissance d'un mouvement étudiant', in *Le Monde* (Paris, 7-13 March, 1968).

CHAPTER III

1 MEGA (*Marx–Engels Gesamtausgabe*), Vol. v, p. 138 (Berlin, 1928).

2 V. I. Lenin, 'Left-wing communism: and infantile disorder', in *Selected Works* (London, 1938), Vol. x, pp. 57-8.

3 V. I. Lenin, *Selected Works* (London, 1937), Vol. v, pp. 347-8; italics added.

4 *ibid.*, pp. 355-6 and 398.

5 *Iskra* (March 1904).

6 First published in *Iskra* and *Neue Zeit* in 1904; English text quoted from R. Luxemburg, *The Russian Revolution* (Michigan, 1968), p. 102.

7 V. I. Lenin, *Works*, fourth Russian ed., Vol. xxx (Moscow 1953), p. 444; italics in original.

8 V. I. Lenin, *Selected Works*, Vol. ix, p. 170; italics added.

9 Rosa Luxemburg, *Organization of the Social Democratic Party in Russia*, manuscript, 1918 (Michigan, 1968).

10 *Kronstadt Izvestiya* (8 March 1921).

11 Joseph Revai, 'Das Problem der Taktik', in *Kommunismus*, the journal of the Communist Internationale, Vol. ii, 1920; italics added.

12 Rosa Luxemburg, *op. cit.*, pp. 71-2; italics added.

13 E. Petrov-Skitaletz, *The Kronstadt Thesis* (New York, 1964); and Ida Mett, *The Kronstadt Commune* (solidarity pamphlet no. 27, London, November 1967).

14 Speech in the US Senate.

15 *The US and Revolution*, an Occasional Paper on the Free Society, published by the Centre for the Study of Democratic Institutions (Santa Barbara, California, 1961).

16 Hannah Arendt, *On Revolution* (London, 1963), p. 219.

17 Document released on 4 December 1964 via the Office of the Director of the Special Operations Research Office (SORO) of the American University in Washington, DC.

18 SORO 'working paper', known as *Project Camelot*, Quoted Irving Louis Horowitz (ed.), *The Rise and Fall of Project Camelot*, studies in the relationship between social science and practical politics (Massachusetts Institute of Technology, 1967).

19 *Project Camelot*, pp. 77-8.

20 *ibid.*, p. 17.

21 André Maurois, *Open Letter to a Young Man,* (New York, 1967); italics added.

22 V. I. Lenin, *Collected Works,* fourth Russian ed., Vol. xxvi (Moscow, 1964); italics added.

23 *The US and Revolution, op. cit.,* p. 21.

24 F. R. Corwell, *The Revolutions of Ancient Rome* (London, 1962), p. 13.

CHAPTER IV

1 E. J. Dingwall, *The American Woman* (New York, 1958), pp. 247-8.

2 Gerhard Sanden, 'Die Zwanzig bis Dreissigjährigen tarnen sich', in *Handelsblatt* (Hamburg, 12 March 1954).

3 Margareta Berger-Hamerschlag, *Journey into a Fog* (London, 1955), p. 59.

4 Curt Bondy, Jan Braden, Rudolf Cohen, Klaus Eyferth, *Jugendliche stören die Ordnung* (Munich, 1967).

5 H. Schelsky, *Die Skeptische Generation* (Düsseldorf-Cologne, 1963), p. 387.

6 *Juvenile Delinquency in Post-War Europe,* Council of Europe (Strasbourg, 1960).

7 *ibid.,* p. 16-17.

8 Dr Josephine Macalister Brew, *Youth and Youth Groups* (London, 1957); italics added.

9 *Newsweek* (New York, 14 September 1959).

10 *Reporter* (New York, 20 August 1959); italics added.

11 Harrison Salisbury, *The Shook-Up Generation* (London, 1959).

CHAPTER V

1 Alexis de Toqueville, *L'Ancien Régime et la Révolution* (Paris, 1856); italics added.

2 George Fletcher, 'Against the Stream', in *Ten Years After* (London, 1966); this book was published to commemorate the tenth anniversary of the Hungarian Revolution.

3 Professor A. S. Trace, Jr, *What Ivan knows that Johnny doesn't* (New York, 1961); Professor Trace is from the Russian Study Centre at the John Carrol University in Cleveland. See also Charles C. Walcutt (ed.), *Tomorrow's Illiterates* (Boston, 1961).

4 *Nowa Kultura* (Warsaw, 15 April 1956).

5 *Trybuna Ludu* (Warsaw, 22 March 1956).

6 *Po Prostu* (Warsaw, 25 March 1956).

7 Konrad Syrop, *Spring in October: The Story of the Polish Revolution of 1956* (New York, 1957), p. 52.

8 Soviet Centcom resolution of 30 June 1956.

9 Konrad Syrop, *op. cit.*, pp. 73-7.

CHAPTER VI

1 Paul Kecskemeti, *The Unexpected Revolution—Social Forces in the Hungarian Uprising* (Stanford, 1961), p. 115.

CHAPTER VII

1 E. P. Thompson, article in *New Reasoner* (summer 1959).

2 Jack Kerouac, article in *Encounter* (August 1959).

3 F. Musgrove, *Youth and the Social Order* (London, 1964); italics added.

4 Jack Kerouac, lecture to students of New York University, quoted in *Encounter* (August 1959), p. 59.

5 *ibid.*, p. 60.

6 V. S. Pritchett, article in *New Statesman* (6 September 1958).

7 Study made at Trafalgar Square, April 1958.

8 Christopher Driver, *The Disarmers: A Study in Project* (London, 1964), pp. 58 and 59.

9 *New Statesman* (15 December 1961), p. 916.

10 Victor Zorza, article in *Guardian* (12 July 1962).

11 J. B. Priestley, 'Fifty Years of the English', in *New Statesman* (19 April 1963), p. 566.

12 *New Scientist* (London, 19 December 1963), p. 739.

13 Kingsley Martin, article in *New Statesman* (London, 27 March 1964), p. 482.

14 Colin Fletcher, 'Beat and Games on the Merseyside', in *New Society* (London, 20 February 1964).

15 Claude Anet, *Notes sur l'Amour* (Paris, 1908).

16 Simone de Beauvoir, *Le Deuxième Sexe* (Paris, 1949), Part iv, Chapter i; italics added.

17 Grace and Fred M. Hechinger, *Teenage Tyranny* (New York, 1962), pp. x-xi.

18 R. C. Lucas, letter to *The Times* (22 May 1964).

19 *The Times* (22 May 1964).

20 Letter from a seventeen-year-old female Mod to the *Evening Standard* (London, 20 May 1964).

CHAPTER VIII

1 R. D. Tomasek (ed.), *Latin American Politics, twenty-four studies of the contemporary scene* (New York, 1966), p. 116.

2 Tad Szulc, *The Winds of Revolution* (London, 1964), p. 96; italics added.

3 *Time* (New York, 9 May 1960), pp. 20-1.

4 George Paloczi-Horvath, *Jugend, Schicksal der Welt. Ein Dokumentabericht aus 4 Erdteilen* (Zurich, 1965), p. 211.

5 F. Musgrove, *op cit.*, pp. 4-5; italics added. Such evidence was found by R. Lynn in his 'Two Personality Characteristics related to Academic Achievement', in *British Journal of Educational Psychology* (London, 1959).

5 F. Musgrove, *op. cit.*, pp. 4-5; italics added.

6 R. Lynn, *op. cit.* (London, 1959).

7 Ferdynand Zweig, *The Student in the Age of Anxiety* (London, 1965), p. xiv.

8 Loomis and Green, 'Patterns of Mental Conflict in a Typical State University', in *Journal of Abnormal Social Psychology* (Chicago, 1947); Webster, and others, 'Personality Changes in College Students', in Nevitt Sanford (ed.), *The American College* (1962); the Tokyo Institute for Student Problems (*Gakusei Mondai Kenkyusho*) in its publications offers numerous indications of the existence of similiar phenomena, plus studies on entrance anxiety and related topics; see also 'Education for Frustration', in the *Indian Thought* (Calcutta, 22 and 29 October 1966).

9 Webster and W. D. Furneaux, 'The Psychologist and the University', in *Universities Quarterly* (London, 1962).

10 D. E. Broadbent, *Perception and Communication* (London, 1958), p. 153.

CHAPTER IX

1 In one of his *Authentica,* quoted in Werner Klose, *Freiheit schreibt auf eure Fahnen – 800 Jahre Deutsche Studenten* (Hamburg, 1967), p. 11.

2 F. Musgrove, *Youth and Social Order* (London, 1964).

3 *Abaelard* (Leiden, 1934). See also Charles Homer Haskins, *The Renaissance of the Twelfth Century* (London, 1927).

4 G. M. Trevelyan, *op. cit.*, p. 67.

5 Hastings Rashdall, *The Universities in Europe in the Middle Ages,* revised ed. in three vols (Oxford, 1936).

6 G. M. Trevelyan, *op. cit.*, pp. 67-8.

7 *International Encyclopedia of the Social Sciences,* Vol. xvi: (New York, 1968), p. 192.

8 Robert M. Hutchings, *The University of Utopia* (Chicago, 1953), pp. 76-7; italics added.

9 G. M. Trevelyan, *op. cit.*, p. 381.

10 Philippe Aries, *op. cit.*, pp. 352-3.

11 *ibid.*, p. 355.

12 M. and R. Edgeworth, *Practical Education* (London, 1789), Vol. 2, p. 150.

13 H. Cook, *Winchester College* (London, 1917).

14 Herbert Spencer, *Education* (London, 1861), p. 170; italics added.

15 Quoted by Theodore Zeldin in his article on French higher education in *Journal of Contemporary History,* Vol. 2, no. 3 (London, 1967), p. 56.

16 V. Cousin, *Report on the State of Public Instruction in Prussia,* trans. Sarah Austin (London, 1834), p. xvii.

17 *Clarendon Report of the Public Schools Commission* (London, 1864), pp. 28-33; italics added.

18 David Ward, 'The Public Schools and Industry in Britain after 1870', in *Journal of Contemporary History,* Vol. 2, no. 3 (London, 1967), p. 52; italics added.

19 Sir Eric Ashby, *The University in America,* an occasional paper published by the Centre for the Study of Democratic Institutions (Santa Barbara, California, 1967), pp. 28-33.

20 *The Uses of University* (Harvard, 1963).

CHAPTER X

1 Claude Sitton, reporting in the *New York Times* (4 January 1960).

2 'Berkeley's Angry Young Man', in *Guardian* (1 December 1964).

3 Michael Rossman, 'Barefoot in a Marshmallow World', in *Ramparts* (New York, January 1966).

4 C. B. Cox, article in *Guardian* (12 December 1964).

5 *Byrne Report* (Berkeley, 1965).

6 *Report of the Study Commission of University Governance* (University of California, Berkeley, 15 January 1968), p. 17.

7 *Guardian* (10 June 1969).

8 Joseph Katz, *New Dimensions in Higher Education,* published by US Office of Education, 1967. See also, by the same author, 'Personality Characteristics of Students arrested during the Berkeley Sit-in of 1964', in *Growth and Restraint in College Students* (Stanford Cols., 1967).

9 William A. Watts and David N. E. Whitaker, 'Free Speech Advocates at Berkeley', in *Journal of Applied Behavioral Sciences,* Vol. 2 (New York, 1966), pp. 41-62.

10 Robert H. Sommers, 'The Mainspring of the Rebellion: A Survey of Berkeley Students in November, 1964', in S. M. Lipset and S. S. Wolin (eds.), *The Berkeley Student Revolt,* pp. 530-7. The other studies referred to concerning this period are: Jeanne H. Block, Norma Haan and M. Brewster Smith, 'Activism and Apathy in Contemporary Adolescence' in J. F. Adams (ed.), *Contributions to the understanding of*

Adolescence (Boston, 1967); Richard Flacks, 'The Liberated Generation: An Exploration of the Roots of Student Protest', in *Journal of Social Issues* (Boston, 1967); Paul Heist, *Intellect and Commitment: the Faces of Discontent at Berkeley*, mimeographed paper sponsored by the Centre for the Study of Higher Education (University of California, 1965); Kenneth Keniston, 'The Sources of Student Dissent', in *Journal of Social Issues* (Harvard, 1967); Seymour Martin Lipset and Philip G. Altbach, 'Student Politics and Higher Education in the United States', in *Comparative Education Review,* Vol. 10 (Washington, 1966), pp. 320-49; Glen Lyonns, 'The Police Car Demonstration: A Survey of Participants', in Lipset and Wolin (eds.), *op. cit.,* pp. 519-30; D. Westby and R. Braungart, 'Class and Politics in the Family Background of Student Political Activists', in *American Sociological Review,* Vol. xxxi, 1966, pp. 690-2.

11 *The Times* (London, 23 June 1966).

12 R. W. Leonhard, *X-mal Deutschland* (Berlin, 1960).

13 Bernhard de Vries, 'Provo Inside Out', in *delta: a review of arts and thought in the Netherlands* (Amsterdam, autumn 1967), pp. 78-9.

14 Aad Nuis, *Wat is gebeurd in Amsterdam?* (Amsterdam, 1966).

15 Piet Thoenes, article in the *Nation* (The Hague, 17 April 1967).

16 *New Law Journal* (London, 6 July 1967).

17 *Die Zeit* (Hamburg, 9 June 1967).

18 Knut Neverman (ed.), *Der 2. Juni 1967: Dokumente zu den Ereignissen anlassich des Schah-Besuchs* ('Documents relating to the events on the occasion of the Shah's visit'), (Cologne, 1967).

19 *Der Spiegel* (Berlin, Hamburg, Munich, no 26, 1967), p. 62.

20 *Abendzeitung* (Munich, 7 June 1967).

21 *Die Zeit* (Hamburg, 9 June 1967).

CHAPTER XI

1 *Le Monde* (Paris, 9 December 1966).

2 *Jeunes d'Aujourd'hui–d'après le rapport d'enquête du Ministère de la Jeunesse et des Sports* (Paris, June 1967).

3 *L'Humanité* (Paris, 3 May 1968).

4 *Mai 1968: La Breche, premières refléxions sur les évenements* (Paris, 1968), by Edgar Morin, Claude Lefort, and Jean-Marc Coudray.

5 D. Cohn-Bendit *Obsolete Communizm – The Left-Wing Alternative* (London, 1968), trans. by Arnold Pomerans, pp. 70-1; italics added.

6 *Kulturny Zivot* (Prague, 13 May 1966).

7 Ota Sik, article in *Rude Pravo* (Prague, 27 July 1968).

8 *Guardian* (London, 19 April 1968); italics added.

9 Jan Kavan, *Ramparts* (New York, September 1968).

CHAPTER XII

1 Quoted in J. H. Breasted, *History of Egypt* (London ed., 1946), p. 205.

2 *Washington Post* (Washington, 2 June 1969).

3 *Observer* (London, 24 March 1968).

4 Jerome Skolnick (ed.), *The Politics of Protest*, report published for the National Commission on the Causes and Prevention of Violence (Washington, 1969).

5 *Guardian* (London, 5 December 1968).

6 Elizabeth Hardwick, article in the *Sunday Times Colour Supplement* (London, 29 December 1968); the author is advisory editor of the *New York Review of Books*.

7 *Sunday Times* (London, 25 May 1969).

8 *San Francisco Chronicle* (26 May 1969).

9 *Berliner Extra Dienst* (Berlin, 4 May 1968).

10 *Der Spiegel* (Berlin, Hamburg, Munich, 22 April 1968).

11 *A Prophetic Minority* (New York, 1968).

12 Tariq Ali (ed.), *New Revolutionaries: Left Opposition* (London, 1969); italics added.

13 *International Times* (London, 14-27 February 1969).

14 Bruno Bettelheim, 'Obsolete Youth – Towards a Psychograph of Adolescent Rebellion', in *Encounter* (London, September 1969).

15 James Ridgeway, *The Closed Corporation: American Universities in Crisis* (New York, 1968).

16 Herbert Marcuse, *Repressive Tolerance* (essay in *A Critique of Pure Tolerance*, Boston, 1965).

17 'Totalist' – article in *Anarchos,* no. 2 (New York, 1968); italics added.

18 Bob Wistrich, article in *International Times,* no. 29 (London, 12 December 1968).

19 Jerry Rubin, 'An Emergency Letter to my Brothers and Sisters in the Movement', in the *New York Review of Books* (13 February 1968); the author was a Yippie (Youth International Party) organizer.

20 From a leaflet produced by student militants at Columbia University, New York, in December 1968.

21 *People's Daily* (Peking, 22 May 1969).

22 Erwin Scheuch (ed.), *Die Wiedertaufer der Wohlstandgesellschaft* (Cologne, 1969); the editor of this collection of essays is a sociologist who directs a research institute in Cologne.

CHAPTER XIII

1 *Social Sciences and Social Pathology* (London, 1959).

2 Dr G. T. Stewart, 'Epidemiological Aspects of Student Riot', in *The Lancet* (London, 22 March 1969).

3 Dr Zena Stein, article in *The Lancet* (London 10 May 1969); the author is a doctor working in the Division of Epidemiology in the Faculty of Medicine in Columbia University.

4 Dr W. Grey Walter, *The Living Brain* (London, 1965), p. 26.

5 Harry Elmer Barnes, 'Education versus Enlightment', in Calverton and Schmalhausen, *The New Generation* (London, 1930).

6 *The Psychology of Character Development*, second 'Science Edition' (New York, 1967).

7 *ibid.*, pp. 98-9.

8 *ibid.*, pp. 100 and 196-9.

9 *ibid.*, p. 196.

10 *The Sociological Imagination* (O.U.P. 1959), p. 174.

11 *The University in America* (Santa Barbara Occasional Paper, 1967), p. 7.

12 W. H. Ferry, article in *The University of America,* an Occasional Paper issued by the Center for the Study of Democratic Institutions at Santa Barbara, California, 1967.

13 E. H. Carr, *New Society* (London, 1963), pp. 75-6.

14 *Bulletin of Atomic Scientists* (December 1965).

15 Robert Nisbet, 'Who killed the Student Revolution?', in *Encounter* (London, February 1970), p. 18.

16 P. F. Drucker, *The Landmarks of Tomorrow* (London, 1959), p. 87.

DATE DUE

AP 25'88	APR 18 '88		
GAYLORD			PRINTED IN U.S.A.